Trauma,
Recovery,
and Growth

Trauma, Recovery, and Growth

Positive Psychological Perspectives on Posttraumatic Stress

Edited by

Stephen Joseph

P. Alex Linley

WILEY

John Wiley & Sons, Inc.

Contents

Preface

Positive psychology is a rapidly developing area of psychological research with exciting potential for applications in psychology, counseling, psychotherapy, and social work. In this book, we focus on what positive psychology has to offer in our work with survivors of stressful and traumatic events. Exposure to stressful and traumatic events can have severe and chronic psychological consequences. In adopting the positive psychology perspective, there is no denial of the suffering often caused by trauma. However, there is also a growing body of evidence testifying to the positive psychological changes that can result from people's struggle with stressful and traumatic experiences. These two sets of literatures have evolved somewhat independently, so that one group of researchers is largely concerned with posttraumatic stress and another is concerned with posttraumatic growth; and little work is going on that explicitly connects these two areas of research. Our aims have been to develop a synthesis between them and to explore the relevance of positive psychology to trauma practice. This book presents the efforts of researchers and practitioners to explore how positive psychology can inform our understanding of posttraumatic stress and posttraumatic growth, and especially to develop a more integrative understanding of the interplay between these outcomes following traumatic events. It is our firm belief that by conceptualizing traumatic reactions more holistically, we will be better qualified and informed in our efforts to help survivors of trauma facilitate their resilience, recovery, and growth. This book is our attempt to catalyze that process.

Stephen Joseph
P. Alex Linley

March 2007

Contributors

David Albert, PhD
School of Medicine
University of Connecticut
Farmington, Connecticut

Michael H. Antoni, PhD
University of Miami and
UM Sylvester Comprehensive
    Cancer Center
Miami, Florida

Roni Berger, PhD, LCSW
School of Social Work
Adelphi University
Garden City, New York

Margit I. Berman, PhD
Department of Psychology
University of Maryland
College Park, Maryland

Lisa D. Butler, PhD
Department of Psychiatry and
    Behavioral Sciences
Stanford University School
    of Medicine
Stanford, California

Lawrence G. Calhoun, PhD
Department of Psychology
University of North Carolina—
    Charlotte
Charlotte, North Carolina

Joanna Collicutt McGrath, PhD
Heythrop College
University of London,
    United Kingdom

Matthew J. Cordova, PhD
Pacific Graduate School of
    Psychology
VA Northern California Health
    Care System
Martinez, California

Julian D. Ford, PhD
School of Medicine
University of Connecticut
Farmington, Connecticut

Patricia A. Frazier, PhD
Department of Psychology
University of Minnesota
Minneapolis, Minnesota

John H. Harvey, PhD
Department of Psychology
University of Iowa
Iowa City, Iowa

Gonzalo Hervás, PhD
School of Psychology
Complutense University
Madrid, Spain

Stephen Joseph, PhD
School of Sociology and
    Social Policy
University of Nottingham
Nottingham, United Kingdom

Elizabeth J. Krumrei, MA
Department of Psychology
Bowling Green
    State University
Bowling Green, Ohio

Debra Larsen, PhD
Institute of Rural Health
Idaho State University
Pocatello, Idaho

Suzanne C. Lechner, PhD
University of Miami
    Miller School of Medicine
    and
UM Sylvester Comprehensive
    Cancer Center
Miami, Florida

Gregory A. Leskin, PhD
National Center for PTSD,
    Education Division
VA Palo Alto Healthcare
    System
Palo Alto, California

Rachel Lev-Wiesel, PhD
School of Social Work
University of Haifa
Haifa, Israel

P. Alex Linley, PhD
Centre for Applied Positive
    Psychology
Coventry, United Kingdom

Judith A. Lyons, PhD
VA Trauma Recovery Program/
    South Central MIRECC and
University of Mississippi
    Medical Center
G. V. Montgomery VA Medical Center
Jackson, Mississippi

Annette Mahoney, PhD
Department of Psychology
Bowling Green State University
Bowling Green, Ohio

Leslie A. Morland, PsyD
National Center for PTSD, Pacific
    Island Division
VA Pacific Island Healthcare
    System
Honolulu, Hawaii

Kenneth I. Pargament, PhD
Department of Psychology
Bowling Green State University
Bowling Green, Ohio

Pau Pérez-Sales MD, PhD
Grupo de Acción Comunitaria
    and
La Paz University Hospital
Madrid, Spain

Beth Hudnall Stamm, PhD
Institute of Rural Health
Idaho State University
Pocatello, Idaho

Brenda L. Stoelb, PhD
Department of Rehabilitation
    and Medicine
University of Washington
Seattle, Washington

Richard G. Tedeschi, PhD
Department of Psychology
University of North Carolina—
  Charlotte
Charlotte, North Carolina

Howard Tennen, PhD
School of Medicine
University of Connecticut
Farmington, Connecticut

Carmelo Vázquez, PhD
School of Psychology
Complutense University
Madrid, Spain

Tzipi Weiss, DSW, LCSW
Social Work Department
Long Island University
Brookville, New York

PART I

TOWARD AN INTEGRATIVE POSITIVE PSYCHOLOGY OF POSTTRAUMATIC EXPERIENCE

CHAPTER 1

Positive Psychological Perspectives on Posttraumatic Stress: An Integrative Psychosocial Framework

STEPHEN JOSEPH and P. ALEX LINLEY

IT IS WELL known that exposure to stressful and traumatic events can have severe and chronic psychological consequences. In adopting the positive psychology perspective, it must be made clear at the outset that there is no denial of the suffering often caused by trauma. There is, however, a growing body of evidence testifying to the positive psychological changes that can result from people's struggle with stressful and traumatic experiences. These two sets of literatures have evolved independently, with some researchers interested in posttraumatic stress, others in posttraumatic growth. In this chapter, we introduce the positive psychological perspective and begin developing a synthesis between these two areas of research and practice. Our goal is to show that posttraumatic stress and posttraumatic growth can be understood within an integrative psychosocial framework.

POSITIVE PSYCHOLOGY

The study of positive changes following stressful and traumatic events is part of the wider positive psychology agenda pursued by psychologists in recent years (e.g., Linley & Joseph, 2004b; Seligman & Csikszentmihalyi, 2000; Snyder & Lopez, 2002). Positive psychology, as we know it, was launched by Martin E. P. Seligman's Presidential Address to the American Psychological Association's Annual Convention on August 21, 1999. Seligman argued that since World War II, psychology had largely neglected its mission to make the lives of all people more productive and fulfilling, and to understand and nurture high talent (Seligman, 1999). Instead, psychology had largely become a medically oriented discipline interested in identifying and alleviating the increasing number of psychopathologies that came to be included in the *Diagnostic and Statistical Manual of Mental Disorders* (*DSM-IV*; American Psychiatric Association, 1994). In relation to posttraumatic stress disorder, this focus is hardly surprising. The establishment of the U.S. Veterans Administration (VA) in 1946 created many roles and funding streams for psychologists who wanted (and were needed) to work with people who had been in combat. Following the Vietnam War and the establishment of the diagnosis of posttraumatic stress disorder (PTSD) in the diagnostic nomenclature, this work expanded substantially to relieve the suffering and psychological problems experienced by Vietnam veterans. The myriad career paths and opportunities open to clinicians enabled them to help a great many people with psychological distress.

These events, combined with the longer history of clinical psychology being broadly under the umbrella of psychiatrists in psychiatric hospitals (Albee, 2000; Maddux, Snyder, & Lopez, 2004), created an illness ideology that pervaded the science and practice of clinical psychology (of which the diagnosis and treatment of posttraumatic stress disorder was very much a part). Why was this? First, clinical psychology practitioner training typically occurred in psychiatric hospitals and clinics, where clinical psychologists worked primarily as psycho-diagnosticians under the direction of psychiatrists trained in medicine and psychoanalysis. Clinical psychologists tended to adopt, uncritically, the methods and assumptions of their psychiatrist counterparts, who were trained specifically in the medical model and the illness ideology. This might be entirely appropriate for physical disorders, but not, we would argue, for all psychological problems, including those of posttraumatic stress.

Second, as noted, the U.S. Veterans Administration, established shortly after World War II, developed training centers and standards for clinical psychologists primarily within psychiatric settings that were steeped in biological and psychoanalytic models. To reject the medical model and its attendant illness ideology would have been anathema to many clinical psychologists of this period, leading to a further acceptance and implicit osmosis of the illness ideology into the science and practice of clinical psychology.

Third, the U. S. National Institute of Mental Health (NIMH), founded in 1947, focused—despite its name—all its millions of research and practice dollars on treating mental illness, which irrevocably shaped the direction and practice of clinical psychologists. Again, rejecting the medical model and the illness ideology would have meant rejecting the opportunity offered by this research and practice funding—a stiff test of theoretical values against pragmatic career choices.

Fourth, the assumptions of clinical psychology, grounded in the illness ideology, were enshrined in the standards for clinical psychology training at the American Psychological Association conference in Boulder, Colorado, in 1950. This led to "the uncritical acceptance of the medical model, the organic explanation of psychological problems, with psychiatric hegemony, medical concepts, and language," and became the "fatal flaw" of the scientist-practitioner model that "has distorted and damaged the development of clinical psychology ever since" (Albee, 2000, p. 247).

Grounded in this medico-psychiatric historical context, the illness ideology has permeated the language of clinical psychology, leading it to become the language of medicine and psychopathology. Characterized thus, clinical psychology narrows our focus to what is weak and deficient rather than to what is strong and healthy. It emphasizes abnormality over normality, poor adjustment over healthy adjustment, and sickness over health. Inherently, therefore, it has emphasized posttraumatic *stress disorder* rather than posttraumatic *growth* as the outcome following traumatic events, despite consistent evidence that most people are at least resilient in the face of trauma and many report positive changes (Linley & Joseph, 2004a).

Further, this illness ideology prescribes a certain way of thinking about psychological problems that tells us what aspects of human behavior should receive our attention. Maddux et al. (2004) identified three primary ways in which the uncritical adoption of the illness ideology has determined the remit and scope of clinical psychology. First, it promotes dichotomies between normal and abnormal behaviors, between clinical and nonclinical problems, and between clinical populations and nonclinical populations. Second, it locates human maladjustment inside people, rather than in their interactions with the environment and their encounters with sociocultural values and social institutions. Third, it portrays people who seek help as victims of intrapsychic and biological forces beyond their control, and thus leaves them as passive recipients of an expert's care.

The medical model and illness ideology of clinical psychology can be seen to be founded on four basic assumptions (Maddux et al., 2004):

1. Clinical psychology is concerned with *psychopathology*—deviant, abnormal, and maladaptive behavioral and emotional conditions. Thus the focus is not on facilitating mental health but on alleviating mental illness. This excludes the millions of people who might experience problems in everyday living for the benefit of the much smaller number of people experiencing severe conditions. Hence, the focus on posttraumatic stress

disorder and the medicalization of the condition have made it into something that is enduring and distinct from normal reactions of cognitive-emotional processing following trauma.

2. Psychopathology, clinical problems, and clinical populations differ in *kind*, not just in degree, from normal problems in living, nonclinical problems, and nonclinical populations: They are considered to be independent and distinct entities. This *categorical model* presents the remit of clinical psychology as being categorically different from normal problems, thus requiring different theories. With this implicit categorization, posttraumatic stress has been considered to be fundamentally different in kind from posttraumatic growth, leading to the evolution of disparate research groups and foci instead of a more appropriate integrative approach to understanding. We have started to develop this approach elsewhere (Joseph & Linley, 2005), and it is a primary focus of this book.

3. Psychological problems are analogous to biological or medical diseases in that they reflect conditions inside the individual (the illness analogy), rather than in the person's interactions with his or her environment. From this premise, it is easy to understand the search for biological markers of posttraumatic stress in isolation from wider social and psychological factors. Posttraumatic growth research has tended to focus on the social psychology of the growth experience; posttraumatic stress disorder research has often focused on the biology, physiology, and neurochemistry of disease.

4. Following from this illness analogy, the role of the clinical psychologist is to identify (diagnose) the so-called disorder inside the person (patient) and to prescribe an intervention (treatment) for eliminating (curing) the internal disorder (disease). These interventions are referred to as *treatment* unlike often equally successful attempts on the part of friends, family, teachers, and ministers. This approach persists even though many people following a traumatic event neither seek nor require a professional intervention. For many, the support of existing social networks are sufficient.

In sharp contrast, positive psychological approaches to clinical psychology reject these implicit assumptions, and instead present four assumptions of a positive clinical psychology (Maddux et al., 2004):

1. Positive clinical psychology is concerned with everyday problems in living to the same extent as it is with the more extreme variants of everyday functioning that we might refer to as *psychopathology*. Positive clinical psychology is also as much concerned with understanding and enhancing subjective and psychological well-being and effective functioning as it is with alleviating subjective distress and maladaptive functioning.

2. Psychopathology, clinical problems, and clinical populations, differ *only in degree*, not in kind, from normal problems in living, nonclinical problems,

and nonclinical populations: They are considered to be related entities falling somewhere on a *continuum* of human functioning. This *dimensional model* suggests a focus on health and fulfillment as much as on illness and distress, since they are related constructs that can be defined by the same psychological theories. Within this dimensional model, normality and abnormality, wellness and illness, and effective and ineffective psychological functioning lie along a *continuum* of human functioning. They are not separate and distinct entities, but are considered to be extreme variants of normal psychological phenomena.

3. Psychological disorders are *not* analogous to biological or medical diseases. Instead, they reflect problems in the person's interactions with his or her environment, and not only and simply of problems within the person. Further, these problems in living are not construed as being located within an individual, but rather as being located within the interactions between an individual, other people, and the larger culture. This demands a closer inspection of the much more complex interplay of psychological, social, and cultural factors that bear on an individual's psychological health.

4. Following from these three former assumptions, the role of the positive clinical psychologist is to identify human strengths and promote mental health. The people who seek this assistance are clients or students, not patients, and the professionals providing these approaches may be teachers, counselors, consultants, coaches, or even social activists, and not just clinicians or doctors. They use educational, relational, social, and political strategies and techniques, not medical interventions. Further, the facilities providing this assistance may be centers, schools, or resorts, not clinics or hospitals.

Hence, in the context of adaptation following trauma, the new approaches emerging from the positive psychology perspective contrast greatly with the traditional emphasis by psychologists on illness and psychopathology. At first glance, the new field of positive psychology might seem to offer little to those who study and work in the field of traumatic stress. But, as we have shown with the preceding assumptions, we can start to reconfigure our understanding of the evolution of clinical psychology and the forces that shaped it. We can also learn how this pervasive illness ideology has separated the study of posttraumatic stress from that of posttraumatic growth, instead of developing an integrative perspective for understanding these experiences in the same framework of human experience.

Many literatures and philosophies throughout human history have conveyed the idea that personal gain is to be found in suffering (see Linley, 2003), and this idea is central to the existential-humanistic tradition of psychology (Jaffe, 1985; Yalom & Lieberman, 1991). The motif of the value that can be found through suffering permeates many religions of both the East

(Buddhism) and West (Christianity); it is a recurrent theme in great European literature (Dante Alighieri's description of his search for his lost love Beatrice, taking him through Hell and Purgatory to reach Paradise in *The Divine Comedy*; Fyodor Dostoevsky's redemption of the murderer Raskolnikov when he embraces the suffering of the prison camps to atone for his actions in *Crime and Punishment*), and also in the continental existential philosophy tradition (e.g., Kierkegaard and Nietzsche), and the creativity and growth that followed World War II (Simonton, 1994; see Linley, 2003, for a fuller review).

It is only in the past decade that the topic of growth following adversity has become a focus for much empirical and theoretical work, attracting researchers from a variety of perspectives and clinical contexts (e.g., Affleck & Tennen, 1996; Aldwin & Levenson, 2004; Frazier, Conlon, & Glaser, 2001; Harvey, Barnett, & Overstreet, 2004; Linley, 2000; McMillen, Smith, & Fisher, 1997; Siegel & Schrimshaw, 2000; Tedeschi & Calhoun, 2004). In this book, we have brought together a collection of international authors and experts in the field of trauma and growth to write about their work and its implications for practice.

THEORETICAL INTEGRATION: THE PSYCHOSOCIAL FRAMEWORK

The study of growth following adversity has largely developed separately from the study of posttraumatic stress for the reasons previously explored. Although there have been early attempts to integrate the two, with at least an acknowledgment of the gains that may follow from trauma and how these relate to posttraumatic stress (Lyons, 1991; van der Kolk, 1996), our aim in this book is to begin developing a synthesis between these two largely distinct literatures. It is not possible to fully understand recovery from posttraumatic stress without awareness that for some people this involves positive changes beyond their previous levels of functioning and well-being; and vice versa, it is not possible to fully understand growth following adversity without knowledge of the traumatic distress that serves as the trigger for such change.

At a broad level, we propose that posttraumatic stress and posttraumatic growth can be integrated within a single framework. Joseph, Williams, and Yule (1995, 1997) presented a multifactorial psychosocial framework of posttraumatic adjustment that integrated social and cognitive perspectives (see Joseph & Williams, 2005 for a recent overview). The main components of the psychosocial framework are presented in Figure 1.1. The description starts with the occurrence of a traumatic event and continues in a clockwise direction through event cognitions, appraisals, emotional states, cop-

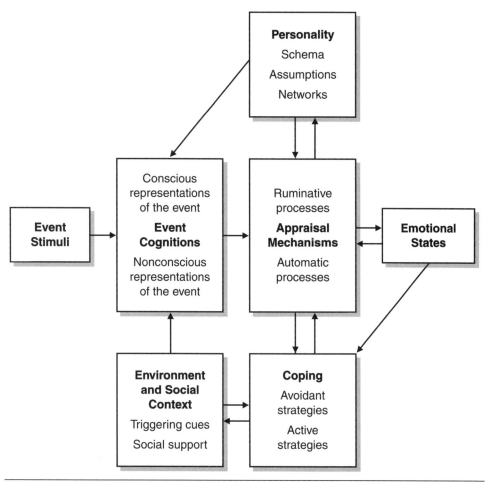

Figure 1.1 Psychosocial Framework of Postraumatic Stress Reactions. *Source: Post-Traumatic Stress: Psychosocial Perspectives on PTSD and Treatment,* by S. Joseph, R. Williams, and W. Yule, Chichester, England: Wiley, 1997. Copyright John Wiley & Sons Limited. Reprinted with permission.

ing, appraisals with cognitions being influenced by both personality and memory representations and the social environment, culminating in either a circular flow through this cycle or in changes within the representational state that constitutes resolution.

In brief, event stimuli provide the basis for event cognitions, the conscious and nonconscious representations of the traumatic experience. Event cognitions, in turn provide the basis for appraisal processes. Appraisal can take the form of consciously controlled cognitive processes or automatic processes, indicative of an ongoing need for cognitive-emotional processing. The occurrence of cognitive appraisals and reappraisals may be associated with distressing emotional states, such as fear, anger, guilt, and shame (or positive emotional states such as hope, joy, humor, gratitude, as discussed in Chapter 17). The occurrence of these cognitive and emotional states leads to various states of coping, as individuals try to manage their emotional states and make sense of their experience. These individual processes occur in a social context that influences event cognitions and coping. Because the level of affect involved in trauma is high, individuals may need the support of others, either professionals or those close to them, in allowing themselves to remember and talk about a trauma. Input from others can interact through appraisal processes to influence the individual's meaning attributions, emotional states, memory structures, and coping in a helpful or harmful manner. The significance of each set of factors may differ between individuals and explain individual variation as well as group similarities.

POSTTRAUMATIC STRESS

Thus, the psychosocial framework describes how the interaction between psychological and social factors operates to impede or promote cognitive-emotional processing. It is a psychosocial framework because although cognitive-emotional processing is an internal psychological experience, the speed and depth of cognitive-emotional processing are affected by personality and social psychological factors. Importantly, the psychosocial framework is not grounded in medical ideology and so does not explicitly refer to posttraumatic stress as a separate outcome but views posttraumatic stress as the process inherent in the interaction of these factors. Phenomena characteristic of posttraumatic stress—reexperiencing, avoidance, and arousal (American Psychiatric Association, 1994)—are understood within the psychosocial framework as experiences of event cognitions/appraisal, coping, and emotional states, respectively. Within the psychosocial framework, reexperiencing, avoidance, and arousal are viewed, not as pathology indicative of disorder, but as indicative of the need for cognitive-emotional processing of the new trauma-related information (see Joseph & Williams, 2005). Furthermore in the psychosocial framework, reexperiencing, avoidance, and arousal are viewed as continuous variables rather than as dichotomous states that are either present or absent.

POSTTRAUMATIC GROWTH

Relevant to this discussion is that the psychosocial framework recognizes that changes in personality/assumptive worlds can occur as part of the process of adjustment in relation to new appraisals. When these changes involve a positive reconfiguration of schema, this is what is referred to as posttraumatic growth. Whereas much of the previous literature on the effects of traumatic events has focused on the relationship between appraisal mechanisms and distressing emotional states, understanding positive growth processes involves a shift of focus to the relation between appraisal mechanisms and personality/assumptive world (Joseph & Williams, 2005). Unlike the subjective psychological experiences of re-experiencing, avoidance, and hyperarousal following trauma (which are states indicative of the need for cognitive-emotional processing of the traumatic information), the experience of posttraumatic growth is more concerned with fundamental positive changes in personality schema and people's assumptive worlds.

Understood in this way, growth following adversity is not about emotional states and subjective well-being (SWB), it is about psychological well-being (PWB). The distress that arises from the subjective states of re-experiencing, avoidance, and hyperarousal can be understood as reflections of the person's subjective well-being. In contrast, psychological well-being is about engagement with the existential challenges of life. It comprises dimensions of self-acceptance, environmental mastery, personal growth, autonomy, positive relations with others, and having a purpose in life (Ryff, 1989; Ryff & Singer, 1996). These dimensions can be readily associated with the three broad dimensions of posttraumatic growth: changes in life philosophy (PWB: purpose in life, autonomy); changes in perceptions of self (PWB: environmental mastery, personal growth, self-acceptance); and changes in relationships with others (PWB: positive relations with others). Understood in relation to posttraumatic adaptation, it becomes clear that the positive shifts in personality schema and assumptive worlds that are characteristic of posttraumatic growth can be understood as reflections of one's psychological well-being. On a broad level, subjective well-being is about the hedonic perspective, whereas psychological well-being is about the eudemonistic perspective (Ryan & Deci, 2001), a distinction that we have drawn out elsewhere in mapping an integrative understanding of adaptation following traumatic events (Joseph & Linley, 2005).

Growth is not about changes in subjective well-being; it is about personality development—how people develop psychological well-being (understanding of one's place and significance in the world; engagement with the existential challenges of life, of which trauma is certainly one). In this way, the psychosocial framework provides a broad understanding of the relation between posttraumatic stress and posttraumatic growth: how personality influences the cycle of appraisal, emotional states, and coping (that constitute the posttraumatic stress reactions), which in turn influences personality (that constitutes posttraumatic growth).

ORGANISMIC VALUING THEORY

Moving to a more specific theoretical level, Joseph and Linley (2005) have begun to integrate the preceding ideas more explicitly into a positive psychology model, the organismic valuing theory of adaptation to threatening events. This new theory is (a) consistent with the psychosocial framework, (b) grounded in the person-centered meta-theoretical position that people are intrinsically motivated toward growth, and (c) builds on the new positive psychology literature to provide a more detailed theoretical account of the relationship between appraisal processes and personality/assumptive worlds. In particular, it specifies the different directions in which cognitive-emotional processing can proceed as the person moves through the cycles of appraisal, emotional states, and coping. Figure 1.2 shows a schematic representation of the organismic valuing theory of growth through adversity.

ASSIMILATION VERSUS ACCOMMODATION

It is proposed that as the person moves through the cycle of appraisals, emotional states, coping, and further appraisals, new trauma-related information can only be processed in one of two ways. Either the new trauma-related information must be *assimilated* within existing models of the world, or existing models of the world must *accommodate* the new trauma-related information.

To illustrate the idea of assimilation, victimizing events may have a shattering effect on just world beliefs, as discussed by Janoff-Bulman (1992). To assimilate experience so that just world beliefs are maintained requires complex cognitive strategies. Self-blame is one such strategy. If people are to blame for their own misfortune, then the world remains a just one in which they get what they deserve. In contrast, victims who accommodate their experience, by appraising and accepting that the new trauma-related information is incongruent with preexisting beliefs, must modify their perceptions of the world. These individuals no longer perceive the world as just, but as random or unjust, and they modify their existing models of the world to accommodate this new information. Accommodation requires people to change their worldviews, whether that change is in a positive or a negative direction.

POSITIVE VERSUS NEGATIVE ACCOMMODATION

By definition, cognitive accommodation processes can be in either a negative or a positive value direction. At the experiential level, a person can accommodate new trauma-related information (e.g., that random events happen in the world and that bad things can happen at any time), in one of two ways.

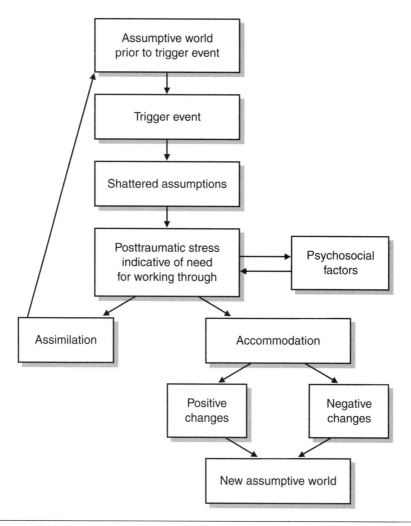

Figure 1.2   Organismic Valuing Theory of Growth through Adversity, Schematically Represented

Accommodation may be made in a negative direction (e.g., a depressogenic reaction of hopelessness and helplessness), or in a positive direction (e.g., that life is to be lived to the full in the here and now). Thus, cognitive accommodation can lead to negative changes in worldview and resultant psychopathology, or to positive changes in worldview and growth.

THREE COGNITIVE OUTCOMES

In the organismic valuing theory, three cognitive outcomes to the psychological resolution of trauma-related difficulties are posited. First, experiences are assimilated, leading to a return to the pretrauma baseline, but also leaving the person vulnerable to future retraumatization. People who assimilate their experience maintain their pre-event assumptions despite the evidence to the contrary and would be expected to develop more rigid defenses, which in turn leave them at increased vulnerability for future development of posttraumatic stress. Second, experiences are accommodated in a negative direction, leading to psychopathology such as borderline personality problems, depression, and helplessness. Third, experiences are accommodated in a positive direction, leading to growth (e.g., living in the moment, valuing relationships, and appreciating life).

SOCIAL SUPPORT PROCESSES

Assimilation or accommodation is influenced by the extent to which people have a supportive social environment and a malleable personality schema that is open to revision. A rigid personality schema that does not permit any information contrary to that already held by the person would lead to assimilation, with the person fitting the new trauma information to the preexisting schema. This then leaves the person with increased vulnerability for future posttraumatic stress. Accommodating the new trauma information involves changes in personality schema, which will manifest either as some form of psychopathology or as posttraumatic growth, depending on whether the information is negatively accommodated or positively accommodated, respectively.

PROCESS VERSUS OUTCOME

Although we have referred to these as three cognitive outcomes, it is also appropriate to think of these as three broad directions of processing. Certainly, in research, we may employ measures to assess change as an outcome, but the processes described here are developmental and continuous across the life span, so that a person cannot be said to reach an endpoint at which processing of new event-related information ceases.

MULTIFACTORIAL SELF-STRUCTURE

Furthermore, although these three directions of processing provide a useful conceptual framework, the self-structure is multifaceted. Thus, it might broadly be the case that a person emotionally processes experiences in one of these directions, but we would propose that different facets of the self-structure can be accommodated, some positively and some negatively, whereas other facets may be assimilated. Thus, we do not propose the three directions of processing as mutually exclusive categories. In the previous illustration, self-blame maintains that facet of self-structure concerned with the perception of the world as just. The person has assimilated trauma-related information in such a way as to maintain just-world beliefs. But the very process of self-blame has implications for other facets of self-structure that must now accommodate the new information about the self that arises as a result of this appraisal process. To fully understand the processes of assimilation and accommodation, we need to conceptualize the self-structure as multifaceted.

GROWTH AS A UNIVERSAL HUMAN TENDENCY

The organismic valuing theory posits that people are intrinsically motivated toward positive accommodation, but circumstances and environments may restrict, impede, or distort this intrinsic motivation. A person's social environment may not be supportive of their newly developed worldviews, or well-intentioned others may intervene in a way that distorts the natural directions of the person's recovery. But irrespective of the predispositional personality and social environment that shapes these possible outcomes, it is a fundamental premise of the organismic valuing theory that people are motivated to pursue positive accommodation following trauma, just as they are throughout life in general. In this way, the organismic valuing process is not seen as specific to posttraumatic adaptation, but rather as a universal human tendency. It may become especially noticed in the aftermath of trauma, but it is always present to a greater or lesser extent.

CLINICAL AND RESEARCH CONSIDERATIONS

The possibility of the three cognitive outcomes helps resolve the question of why it is that previously traumatized people often appear to be more vulnerable instead of more resistant to the effects of future stressful and traumatic events. This is what we would predict when people assimilate their experiences rather than accommodate them. However, we also would predict that people who accommodate their experiences would be more resilient to future similar traumatic experiences because their assumptive world has been revised to be more congruent with the trauma-related information.

The main clinical implication is the assertion that what we know about the alleviation of posttraumatic stress does not necessarily apply to facilitating growth, as hypothetically, the reduction of PTSD should occur through either assimilation or accommodation, but only positive accommodation can be considered to support growth. It is possible that existing therapies for trauma may sometimes thwart growth-related processes.

There is a need to understand how these three directions of processing are influenced by psychosocial factors. The psychosocial framework emphasizes the role of the social context, social support, and social capital in influencing how the person moves through the cycle of appraisals, emotional states, and coping. The organismic valuing theory of growth through adversity develops the social perspective further through its grounding in the person-centered psychology of Carl Rogers (Rogers, 1959) who emphasizes the importance of nonjudgmental, empathic, and genuine relationships. Nondirective relationship-based therapeutic approaches may be beneficial to the facilitation of growth (Joseph & Linley, 2006); and some more directive approaches, however well-intentioned, may actually distort clients from the pathways and directions that are right for them in their recovery and growth following trauma.

Our endeavor has been to develop an understanding of posttraumatic adjustment processes that can synthesize the literature in posttraumatic stress and posttraumatic growth. The psychosocial framework provides an understanding of the cycle of appraisal, emotional states, coping, followed by further appraisal, influenced by personality and social context. Organismic valuing theory adds to this an understanding of the three broad directions that this cognitive-emotional processing can take. Further theoretical and research work is needed to address the issues that arise out of the preceding framework. However, as a first step toward an integrative positive psychological theory, it offers several new research questions and a useful perspective for those working clinically.

AIM OF THIS BOOK

In editing this book, our aim has been to provide coverage of this new field of research, review theoretical models of growth, and to open discussion on the implications of growth for clinical practice. Much has been written about treatments for posttraumatic stress, but we cannot simply assume that what we know about the treatment of posttraumatic stress will generalize to the facilitation of posttraumatic growth. It is possible that some current treatments for posttraumatic stress may actually thwart people's growth following trauma.

SYNTHESIS OF THE POSITIVE AND THE NEGATIVE

The facilitation of posttraumatic growth includes the wider ambitions of the positive psychology movement toward developing ways of thinking and working that integrate the negative and positive aspects of human experience (Linley, Joseph, Harrington, & Wood, 2006). As therapies aimed at facilitating growth following adversity are developed, we need to research not only whether they help people move toward growth, but also whether they help alleviate the experiences of posttraumatic stress. For this book, we have invited leading researchers and practitioners in the field of growth following adversity to discuss how their new way of thinking can alleviate psychological distress and facilitate the psychological well-being of survivors of stressful and traumatic situations.

Case Studies in Trauma and Growth

We have encouraged contributors to include case material, where appropriate, to illustrate their points. We hope that this book proves particularly valuable for practitioners, who want not just a summary of the field, but an overview of current applications of the growth paradigm in different clinical contexts, as well as a real-world look at putting positive psychology into practice.

Contents and Contexts

Part I of the book. "Toward an Integrative Positive Psychology of Posttraumatic Experience," includes this introductory chapter as well as a review chapter on the state of the art of psychometric assessment of growth following adversity (Stephen Joseph and P. Alex Linley).

Part II, "Growth and Distress in Social, Community, and Interpersonal Contexts," first provides two chapters that examine a salient theme for modern times: the impact of terrorism. Leslie A. Morland, Lisa D. Butler, and Gregory A. Leskin examine social trends in the United States following the September 11, 2001, terrorist attacks, and show how resilience and thriving are outcomes equally meritorious of our attention as the traditional focus on distress and psychopathology. Carmelo Vázquez, Pau Pérez-Sales, and Gonzalo Hervás then explore an individual and social perspective on terrorism that is informed by wider community psychology perspectives, as well as their experiences in the aftermath of the March 11, 2004, Madrid train bombings and their wider impact on Spanish society. Next, Tzipi Weiss and Roni Berger explore posttraumatic growth in the context of immigration, noting the multiplicity of potential stressors in immigration, and hence the complex dynamics of adaptation, both positive and negative. Moving toward a more individual focus, Annette Mahoney, Elizabeth J. Krumrei, and Kenneth I. Pargament review how divorce can be interpreted as a spiritual trauma with attendant positive and negative outcomes. John H. Harvey extends this theme by considering growth through loss and adversity in close relationships, while Rachel Lev-Wiesel considers how childhood sexual abuse can ultimately be transformed toward a growth experience in adulthood. Patricia A. Frazier and Margit I. Berman conclude Part II with their chapter examining the relationship between positive and negative life changes in women following sexual assault.

Part III, "Clinical Approaches and Therapeutic Experiences of Managing Distress and Facilitating Growth," looks at the question of positive and negative changes following trauma through the lens of different clinical contexts. Matthew J. Cordova opens the discussion with his work on the facilitation of posttraumatic growth following cancer. This theme is extended to group-based therapies for benefit finding in cancer from Suzanne C. Lechner, Brenda L. Stoelb, and Michael H. Antoni. Judith A. Lyons uses her substantial experience of working with veterans to present a life span developmental model of growth and recovery that integrates developmental tasks and milestones across the life span into different recovery and growth trajectories following trauma. Joanna Collicutt McGrath extends the focus of the facilitation of growth in clinical settings into positive rehabilitation practice for people dealing with brain injury, arguing that a shift is needed from focusing only on what has been lost to addressing also what has been retained or what could be developed to enhance recovery and rehabilitation. Concluding Part III, Debra Larsen and Beth Hudnall Stamm explore the implications of working with trauma for practicing clinicians, reviewing both the negative and positive outcomes that may be experienced.

Part IV, "Beyond the Stress–Growth Distinction: Issues at the Cutting Edge of Theory and Practice," views wider perspectives about appropriate methodologies for researching and assessing growth, reflections on clinical experience, and considerations of what a future integrative psychology of both positive and negative posttraumatic adaptation might look like. Julian D. Ford, Howard Tennen, and David Albert take a contrarian view to growth following adversity and unpack many methodological hurdles facing the field. Lawrence G. Calhoun and Richard G. Tedeschi share their perspectives from decades of working in the field as both researchers and clinicians. In the final chapter, we draw together the key themes explored throughout the book and offer our reflections on theory and practice in posttraumatic stress, showing how a more integrative approach, informed by the new perspective of positive psychology, can advance both research and applications that are aimed at improving the lives of all people following the inevitable negative, stressful, and traumatic events that we all encounter at some point in our lives.

We have asked our contributors to be particularly mindful about how work on growth following adversity can speak to the practical needs of people suffering from posttraumatic stress, and to write with practitioner psychologists and other professionals in mind. We hope this book will inspire the research and practice of graduate students and others in psychology and related disciplines such as social work, counseling and psychotherapy, nursing, and psychiatry, as well as academics and practitioners in the field of trauma. It is only through our united and sustained efforts that we can enhance and improve the lives of the thousands of people who grapple with trauma and its aftermath on a daily basis, whether those efforts are focused on alleviating distress, facilitating growth, or simply enabling all people everywhere to lead more fulfilling lives. The struggle with adversity is one way that we may discover new strengths within ourselves, revitalize our relationships, and enhance our life's meaning.

REFERENCES

Affleck, G., & Tennen, H. (1996). Construing benefits from adversity: Adaptational significance and dispositional underpinnings. *Journal of Personality, 64,* 899–922.

Albee, G. W. (2000). The Boulder model's fatal flaw. *American Psychologist, 55,* 247–248.

Aldwin, C. M., & Levenson, M. R. (2004). Posttraumatic growth: A developmental perspective. *Psychological Inquiry, 15,* 19–22.

American Psychiatric Association. (1994). *Diagnostic and statistical manual of mental disorders* (4th ed.). Washington, DC: Author.

Frazier, P., Conlon, A., & Glaser, T. (2001). Positive and negative life changes following sexual assault. *Journal of Consulting and Clinical Psychology, 69,* 1048–1055.

Harvey, J. H., Barnett, K., & Overstreet, A. (2004). Trauma growth and other outcomes attendant to loss. *Psychological Inquiry, 15,* 26–29.

Jaffe, D. T. (1985). Self-renewal: Personal transformation following extreme trauma. *Journal of Humanistic Psychology, 25,* 99–124.

Janoff-Bulman, R. (1992). *Shattered assumptions: Toward a new psychology of trauma.* New York: Free Press.

Joseph, S., & Linley, P. A. (2005). Positive adjustment to threatening events: An organismic valuing theory of growth through adversity. *Review of General Psychology, 9,* 262–280.

Joseph, S., & Linley, P. A. (2006). Growth following adversity: Theoretical perspectives and implications for clinical practice. *Clinical Psychology Review, 26,* 1041–1053.

Joseph, S., & Williams, R. (2005). Understanding posttraumatic stress: Theory, reflections, context, and future. *Behavioral and Cognitive Psychotherapy, 33,* 423–441.

Joseph, S., Williams, R., & Yule, W. (1995). Psychosocial perspectives on post-traumatic stress. *Clinical Psychology Review, 15,* 515–544.

Joseph, S., Williams, R., & Yule, W. (1997). *Post-traumatic stress: Psychosocial perspectives on PTSD and treatment.* Chichester, West Sussex, England: Wiley.

Linley, P. A. (2000). Transforming psychology: The example of trauma. *Psychologist, 13,* 353–355.

Linley, P. A. (2003). Positive adaptation to trauma: Wisdom as both process and outcome. *Journal of Traumatic Stress, 16,* 601–610.

Linley, P. A., & Joseph, S. (2004a). Positive change following trauma and adversity: A review. *Journal of Traumatic Stress, 17,* 11–21.

Linley, P. A., & Joseph, S. (Eds.). (2004a). *Positive psychology in practice.* Hoboken, NJ: Wiley.

Linley, P. A., & Joseph, S. (2004b). Positive change following trauma and adversity: A review. *Journal of Traumatic Stress, 17*, 11–21.

Linley, P. A., Joseph, S., Harrington, S., & Wood, A. M. (2006). Positive psychology: Past, present, and (possible) future. *Journal of Positive Psychology, 1*, 3–16.

Lyons, J. A. (1991). Strategies for assessing the potential for positive adjustment following trauma. *Journal of Traumatic Stress, 4*, 93–111.

Maddux, J. E., Snyder, C. R., & Lopez, S. J. (2004). Toward a positive clinical psychology: Deconstructing the illness ideology and constructing an ideology of human strengths and potential. In P. A. Linley & S. Joseph (Eds.), *Positive psychology in practice* (pp. 320–334). Hoboken, NJ: Wiley.

McMillen, J. C., Smith, E. M., & Fisher, R. H. (1997). Perceived benefit and mental health after three types of disaster. *Journal of Consulting and Clinical Psychology, 65*, 733–739.

Rogers, C. R. (1959). A theory of therapy, personality, and interpersonal relationships, as developed in the client-centered framework. In S. Koch (Ed.), *Psychology: A study of a science: Vol. 3. Formulations of the person and the social context* (pp. 184–256). New York: McGraw-Hill.

Ryan, R. M., & Deci, E. L. (2001). On happiness and human potentials: A review of research on hedonic and eudaimonic well-being. *Annual Review of Psychology, 52*, 141–166.

Ryff, C. D. (1989). Happiness is everything, or is it? Explorations on the meaning of psychological well-being. *Journal of Personality and Social Psychology, 57*, 1069–1081.

Ryff, C. D., & Singer, B. H. (1996). Psychological well-being: Meaning, measurement, and implications for psychotherapy research. *Psychotherapy and Psychosomatics, 65*, 14–23.

Seligman, M. E. P. (1999). The president's address. *American Psychologist, 54*, 559–562.

Seligman, M. E. P., & Csikszentmihalyi, M. (2000). Positive psychology: An introduction. *American Psychologist, 55*, 5–14.

Siegel, K., & Schrimshaw, E. W. (2000). Perceiving benefits in adversity: Stress related growth in women living with HIV/AIDS. *Social Science and Medicine, 51*, 1543–1554.

Simonton, D. K. (1994). *Greatness: Who makes history and why.* New York: Guilford.

Snyder, C. R., & Lopez, S. J. (Eds.). (2002). *Handbook of positive psychology.* New York: Oxford University Press.

Tedeschi, R. G., & Calhoun, L. G. (2004). A clinical approach to posttraumatic growth. In P. A. Linley & S. Joseph (Eds.), *Positive psychology in practice* (pp. 405–419). Hoboken, NJ: Wiley.

van der Kolk, B. A. (1996). The complexity of adaptation to trauma: Self-regulation, stimulus discrimination, and characterological development. In B. A. van der Kolk, A. C. McFarlane, & L. Weisaeth (Eds.), *Traumatic stress: The effects of overwhelming stress on mind, body and society* (pp. 182–213). New York: Guilford Press.

Yalom, I. D., & Lieberman, M. A. (1991). Bereavement and heightened existential awareness. *Psychiatry, 54*, 334–345.

CHAPTER 2

Psychological Assessment of Growth Following Adversity: A Review

STEPHEN JOSEPH and P. ALEX LINLEY

G ROWING INTEREST IN positive change following trauma and adversity has prompted the development of new psychometric instruments. In this chapter, we provide a brief introduction to the measurement literature. First, we describe existing measures. Second, we review what is known about the structure of growth following adversity as well as the question of the relation between positive and negative changes, and how this informs considerations for choosing appropriate measures. Third, research directions and clinical implications are discussed, with recommendations for the future of psychometric assessment in this area.

Positive change following trauma and other adversity has been referred to by a variety of terms: perceived benefits (McMillen & Fisher, 1998), positive changes (Joseph, Williams, & Yule, 1993), posttraumatic growth (Tedeschi & Calhoun, 1996), stress-related growth (Park, Cohen, & Murch, 1996), and thriving (Abraido-Lanza, Guier, & Colon, 1998). Researchers have often used qualitative methods to ask about positive changes following adversity (see Park & Lechner, 2006); the focus of this review, however, is on published self-report psychometric instruments. These include the Changes in Outlook Questionnaire (CiOQ: Joseph et al., 1993), Perceived Benefit Scales (PBS: McMillen & Fisher, 1998), Posttraumatic Growth Inventory (PTGI: Tedeschi & Calhoun, 1996), Stress-Related Growth Scale (SRGS: Park et al., 1996), and the Thriving Scale (TS: Abraido-Lanza et al., 1998). These published self-report scales, which are described in detail later in this chapter, have been developed by authors from different academic and professional backgrounds in social psychology, clinical psychology, and social work; and despite the different terminology, all seem to be describing a similar construct. Although our review focuses on these established measures of growth following adversity, a wider pool of measures is available for assessing the potential for positive outcomes of negative events that are often more specifically tied to a particular stressor, such as illness (Silver Lining Questionnaire, Sodergren & Hyland, 2000; Sodergren, Hyland, Singh, & Sewell, 2002), breast cancer (Benefit Finding Scale; Cruess et al., 2000), heart attack (Affleck, Tennen, Croog, & Levine, 1987), rheumatoid arthritis (Tennen, Affleck, Urrows, Higgins, & Mendola, 1992), sexual assault (Frazier, Conlon, & Glaser, 2001), and multiple sclerosis (Illness Cognition Questionnaire—Perceived Benefits Subscale, Evers et al., 2001; Benefit Finding in Multiple Sclerosis Scale, Pakenham, in press), and combat (Waysman, Schwarzwald, & Solomon, 2001), among others (see Park & Lechner, 2006).

In relation to the growth following adversity literature, whereas measures of posttraumatic stress have been developed to reflect the American Psychiatric Association's *Diagnostic and Statistical Manual of Mental Disorders* (*DSM-IV*) definition of posttraumatic stress disorder (PTSD; American Psychiatric Association, 1994), there is no commonly agreed-on definition of what constitutes growth following adversity. Thus, although we can test for the construct validity of measures of posttraumatic stress, this is not possible with growth measures. Each has been developed on its own theoretical base, and although there would seem to be substantial overlap between measures, we cannot be certain that each of the measures is assessing exactly the same construct. Also, PTSD refers to reactions in response to a defined extreme traumatic stressor, but it is recognized that growth can arise following a wide range of stressful and traumatic events that may not always be within the definition of a traumatic event as described by the *DSM* definition of PTSD.

Growth following adversity is not the absence of posttraumatic stress reactions, but the presence of positive states. Furthermore, growth following adversity does not refer to subjective well-being (SWB), rather the construct of growth is concerned with psychological well-being (PWB; see Joseph & Linley, Chapter 1, this volume). Whereas SWB refers to affective states, PWB being refers to engagement with existential challenges in life and issues of meaning.

MEASURES

CHANGES IN OUTLOOK QUESTIONNAIRE

The CiOQ (Joseph et al., 1993) is a 26-item measure consisting of 11 items measuring positive changes (CiOP: e.g., "I value my relationships much more now"), and a 15-item scale assessing negative changes (CiON: e.g., "I don't look forward to the future anymore"). Each item is rated on a 6-point scale ranging from strongly disagree (1) to strongly agree (6) so that there is a potential range of scores of 11 to 66 for CiOP, and 15 to 90 for CiON, with higher scores indicating greater positive and negative changes, respectively. Joseph et al. (1993) report satisfactory properties of internal consistency reliability for the positive and negative change scales, .83 and .90, respectively, and that the positive and negative change scales were uncorrelated, at $r = -.12$, ns. Higher scores on the negative change scale were associated with higher scores on the Impact of Event Scale (IES) at $r = .40$, $p < .025$, and the General Health Questionnaire (GHQ) at $r = .53$, $p < .001$. Positive changes were not related to scores on the IES or the GHQ. Subsequent psychometric work has confirmed the psychometric properties of the CiOQ (Joseph, Linley, Andrews, et al., 2005). A short 10-item form of the CiOQ has also been developed (Joseph, Linley, Shevlin, Goodfellow, & Butler, 2006).

Perceived Benefit Scale

The PBS (McMillen & Fisher, 1998) consists of 30 positive-change items and 8 negative change items. Each item (e.g., "This event taught me I can handle anything," "As a result, of this event, I am more sensitive to the needs of others," "Because of this event, I learned how good people can be") is rated on a 5-point scale ranging from 0 (*not at all like my experience*) to 4 (*very much like my experience*). Thus scores on the total positive scale have a potential range of 0 to 120, with higher scores indicating greater levels of growth. Scores on the total negative scale have a potential range of 0 to 32, with higher scores indicating greater negative change. The positive items can also be scored as eight positive subscale scores of Enhanced Self-Efficacy (6 items), Increased Community (4 items), Increased Spirituality (3 items), Increased Compassion (4 items), Increased Faith in People (4 items), Lifestyle Changes (4 items), Enhanced Family Closeness (3 items), and Material Gain (2 items). McMillen and Fisher (1998) report Cronbach's alpha reliability coefficients for the PBS positive subscales range from .73 to .93, and test-retest correlation coefficients reported over 2 weeks range from .66 to .97. Information for the PBS negative scale was not reported. Strong correlations between the PBS and the PTGI were reported. Correlations are reported with well-being, with all subscales except for material gain being related to greater well-being. Higher scores on the IES Intrusion subscale were associated with greater Compassion, Lifestyle Changes, and Family Closeness. Higher scores on the IES Avoidance subscale was associated with lower Faith in People and greater Lifestyle Changes.

Posttraumatic Growth Inventory

The PTGI (Tedeschi & Calhoun, 1996) is a 21-item measure. Each item (e.g., "My priorities about what is important in life," "An appreciation for the value of my own life," "I developed new interests") is rated on a 6-point scale ranging from 0 (*I did not experience this change as a result of my crisis*) to 5 (*I experienced this change to a very great degree as a result of my crisis*) so that scores on the total scale have a potential range of 0 to 105, with higher scores indicating greater levels of growth. The PTGI can be used to yield a total score and five subscale scores of Relating to Others (7 items), New Possibilities (5 items), Personal Strength (4 items), Spiritual Change (2 items), and Appreciation of Life (3 items). Tedeschi and Calhoun (1996) report a Cronbach's alpha reliability coefficient for the PTGI of .90, and a test-retest correlation coefficient of .71 over 2 months. Cronbach's alpha for the five subscales were .85 for Relating to Others, .84 for New Possibilities, .72 for Personal Strength, .85 for Spiritual Change, and .67 for Appreciation of Life, and test-retest correlations over 2 months for the five subscales ranged from .37 to .74. Some association was reported for social desirability, with higher scores on Appreciation of Life being related to lower scores on the Marlowe-Crowne Social Desirability Scale at $r = -.15$, $p < .01$. Correlations were reported between scores on the PTGI and personality variables, with higher PTGI scores associated with greater optimism, intrinsic religiosity, extraversion, openness to experience, agreeableness, and conscientiousness. A short clinician version is available (PTGI-S) although psychometric information is not reported (Calhoun & Tedeschi, 1999).

Stress Related Growth Scale

The SRGS (Park et al., 1996) is a 50-item measure. Each item (e.g., "I learned to be nicer to others," "I feel freer to make my own decisions," "I learned that I have something of value to teach others about life") is rated on a 4-point scale ranging from 0 (*not at all*) to 3 (*a great deal*) so that the scale has a potential range of 0 to 150, with higher scores indicating greater levels of growth. In the original study, Cronbach's alpha for the 50-item measure was .94; test-retest correlation over 2 weeks was .81 (Park et al., 1996). Higher scores on the SRGS were associated with higher scores on the IES at $r = .31$, $p < .001$. No association was found with social desirability at $r = .00$, ns. Detailed examination of the association between the SRGS and other measures was also reported, showing that the higher scores on the SRGS were related to increases in optimism, positive affectivity, satisfaction with social support, and number of social support sources. Scores on the SRGS were also validated through corroborative ratings from significant others, at $r = .21$, $p < .05$. The original SRGS was reported with a unidimensional structure that was supported in subsequent research (Cohen, Hettler, & Pane, 1998). A revised version (with substantial rewriting of items and a change in the scoring format) reported an 8-factor structure (Armeli, Gunthert, & Cohen, 2001). There is also a 15-item short form of the SRGS, for which Pargament, Koenig, and Perez (2000) report a Cronbach's alpha reliability coefficient of .90.

THRIVING SCALE

The TS (Abraido-Lanza et al., 1998) is a 20-item measure that was developed by adapting items from the Stress-Related Growth Scale (15 items; Park et al., 1996) and the Posttraumatic Growth Inventory (3 items; Tedeschi & Calhoun, 1996), together with adding two new items developed by the authors. Each item (e.g., "I learned to look at things in a more positive way," "I learned that I am stronger than I thought I was," "I learned to be a more optimistic person") is rated on a five-point scale ranging from 0 (*not at all*) to 4 (*a great deal*) so that scores on the total scale have a potential range of 0 to 80, with higher scores indicating greater levels of growth. The TS can also be used to yield a total score and eight subscale scores of Appreciation of Family (3 items), Appreciation of Life (2-items), Appreciation of Friends (1 item), Gained Positive Attitude (2 items), Personal Strength (4 items), Enhanced Spirituality (2 items), Empathy (2 items), and Patience (4 items). Abraido-Lanza et al. (1998) report a Cronbach's alpha reliability coefficient for the TS of .92. No test-retest information is reported.

Each of the preceding measures has been found to possess adequate psychometric properties of reliability and validity. However, the extant research evidence on growth following adversity is limited with few studies to date using multiple measures. Thus, although each measure appears to be assessing a broadly similar construct, empirical evidence on the comparability of the measures is sparse. Reviews of the literature have generally treated the measures as interchangeable because of the scarcity of literature to enable more fine-grained analysis, but we have cautioned that this may lead to misleading conclusions (Linley & Joseph, 2004). More recent work suggests that although correlated, the measures may not be so highly correlated as to be considered identical. In their investigation of the convergent validity of the CiOQ, Joseph, Linley, Andrews, et al. (2005) found associations ranging from $r = .42$, $p < .001$ to $r = .66$, $p < .001$ between the CiOP and the PTGI, PBS, SRGS, and TS. Thus, the measures do not appear to be identical and it is likely that research findings will be influenced by the particular choice of measure used. In our own research, we have tended to employ at least two measures simultaneously, usually the CiOQ and the PTGI. What is interesting is that we have found differential associations with other measures. In one study of vicarious growth in trauma therapists, we found that, although the CIOP and the PTGI were associated at $r = .52$, $p < .001$, the CiOP was associated with scores on the Sense of Coherence Scale (SOC) at $r = .27$, $p < .001$, but the PTGI was not at $r = -.10$ (Linley, Joseph, & Loumidis, 2005). Other studies have shown similar anomaly between the two measures (Linley & Joseph, 2005, 2006; Linley, Joseph, Cooper, Harris, & Meyer, 2003). It was suggested that although substantially related, the two measures may be tapping different aspects of the growth experience, with the CiOQ perhaps assessing more existential changes. A facet of growth experience unique to the CiOQ is attitude toward death. Although not originally developed to assess attitude toward death, the CiOQ includes two items ("I don't worry about death at all anymore," "I fear death very much now"). Factor analytic data shows that these two items can be summated and scored separately (see Joseph, Linley, Andrews, et al., 2005).

For the preceding reasons, we would strongly recommend that researchers and clinicians do not rely on one measure but rather employ a battery of measures. Although this is likely to be less of a problem for researchers, it may pose problems for clinicians. As noted, several short forms of the various measures have also been developed that are suitable for clinical use. In choosing which measures to use, one must be guided by the research questions. First, are specific facets of growth to be assessed? Second, is there a need to assess negative changes as well as positive? If it is necessary to assess specific facets of growth, then the PBS, PTGI, and TS are to be recommended because of their multidimensional structure. If positive and negative changes are to be assessed, then the CiOQ and the PBS are to be recommended.

The preceding questions are important in choosing which measure to use, but they are also empirical questions for investigation. First, is growth unidimensional or multidimensional? As is evident from the description of measures, there is no single agreed structure. Some of the measures are unifactorial, others multifactorial, and the number of proposed factors ranges from five to eight.

Second, two of the measures contain subscales to assess positive and negative changes, recognizing that schematic reconfiguration in the aftermath of adversity can be in both positive and negative directions (Joseph & Linley, 2005; Joseph & Linley, Chapter 1, this volume). The relationship between positive and negative schematic changes is uncertain, and the question is whether these are indeed separate dimensions or opposite poles of a single construct. In the following sections, we address each of the previous questions and review psychometric research in these areas.

POSITIVE CHANGES: UNIDIMENSIONAL OR MULTIDIMENSIONAL?

The conceptualization of growth following adversity varies across measures, with some adopting a unidimensional approach, others a multifactorial approach (Cohen, Cimbolic, Armeli, & Hettler, 1998; Nolen-Hoeksema & Davis, 2004; Park & Lechner, 2006). But it is not yet established whether growth is multidimensional or unidimensional. The development of subscales has been on the basis of varying psychometric procedures, and the case for multidimensionality has not been well established. The PTGI has been the most widely used multidimensional measure and several factor analytic investigations of its structure are now available. These are briefly reviewed here.

The original PTGI was developed on a sample of 604 college students. Principal components analysis revealed five factors that were labeled as Relating to others, New possibilities, Personal strength, Spiritual change, and Appreciation of life. Using a German translation of the PTGI with a combined sample of 141 adult university students and medical patients of a clinic for internal medicine, Maercker and Langner (2001) reported a five-factor structure using exploratory principal components analysis. Their five-factor structure was broadly consistent with Tedeschi and Calhoun (1996), except that six items (including all four items on the Personal Strength factor) loaded on different factors, and there were five items with substantial cross-loadings on other factors. Second, with 219 Australian students, Morris, Shakespeare-Finch, Rieck, and Newbury (2005) reported a five-factor structure using exploratory principal components analysis. Their five-factor structure closely replicated Tedeschi and Calhoun (1996), except for a few cross-loading items, and the fact that the PTGI was slightly modified to expand the pool of items related to religion and spirituality. One study has questioned the five-factor model. Using a Bosnian translation of 20 of the 21 items from the PTGI with 136 refugees of the war in the former Yugoslavia, Powell, Rosner, Butollo, Tedeschi, and Calhoun (2003) reported a three-factor structure using exploratory principal components analysis. The three factors were labeled as changes in self/Positive life attitude; Philosophy of life; and Relating to others. Eight of these 20 items had substantial cross-loadings. The reliability of this study is limited due to its relatively small sample size for factor analytic work. Nonetheless, it provides an alternative conceptualization to the five-factor model.

With a sample of 372 participants who had experienced a range of adverse life events, Linley, Andrews, and Joseph (2007) used confirmatory factor analysis to test the relative fit of the correlated three-factor model as reported by Powell et al. (2003) and the correlated five-factor model originally reported by Tedeschi and Calhoun (1996). CFA results support the original five-factor structure, as well as indicating that a single higher-order construct, with five first-order latent variables, provides an acceptable fit. Thus, the PTGI appears to be multidimensional, although the factors are highly correlated and load together as a higher order factor.

These four studies provide evidence for the multidimensionality of PTGI, but there are issues that need to be considered. First, samples have tended to be with undergraduates, and whether the five-factor structure is replicable in people who have experienced more intense traumatic events is uncertain. Second, the PTGI was designed to assess these factors and several similar items were developed to assess each component, leading to the possibility that results reflect bloated specific effects. Third, although the results are informative about the psychometric properties of the PTGI, we must be cautious not to assume that these results apply more widely to understanding the construct of growth following adversity.

There is a need to develop a common definition of growth following adversity to inform future measurement development. One way to establish this would be to look across existing measures to establish their commonalities. Joseph, Linley, and Harris (2005) conducted principal components analysis of measures of growth completed by 176 adults who had experienced some stressful or traumatic event. Included were the three multifactorial measures, that is, the five subscales of the PTGI, and the seven positive subscales (excluding material gain) of the PBS, and the eight subscales of the TS. Together, the PBS, PTGI, and TS contain 20 positive change subscales.

The 20 subscale scores were entered into a principal components analysis with varimax rotation. Three components had eigenvalues greater than 1.00 (10.35, 1.99, and 1.76, respectively) and accounted for 71% of the variance. Inspection of the subscales loading highly on each component provided evidence for three broad dimensions of growth: (1) changes in perception of self, (2) changes in relationships with others, and (3) changes in philosophy of life.

The eigenvalues-greater-than-one criterion has the potential to inflate the number of factors to be extracted, because it is sensitive to the number of variables in the analysis (Cattell, 1966; Zwick & Velicer, 1986). Inspection of the scree plot showed only one component above a marked elbow, and thus a forced one-component solution was also conducted that showed all subscales loaded greater than 0.54 on the component, proving that growth may be best assessed as a unidimensional phenomenon, although it may also comprise three second-order components.

The fact that the eigenvalues-greater-than-one criterion potentially inflates the number of factors to be extracted is an important statistical consideration, and scale developers may not have taken this into account sufficiently. McMillen and Fisher (1998) reported five factors with eigenvalues greater than one in the development of the PBS, but inspection of their scree plot shows one factor above a marked elbow point suggesting that a more appropriate solution may have been one factor rather than eight. Tedeschi and Calhoun (1996) reported six factors with eigenvalues greater than one although they don't report their exact values or produce the scree plot. Thus, it is possible that the case for multidimensionality has been overstated.

What is needed most is evidence whether the subscales enable researchers and clinicians to better understand people's reactions to trauma, compared with using total scores alone to establish that these various factors show discriminant or incremental validity in predicting key outcome variables such as quality of life, self-esteem, psychopathology, or physical health.

RELATIONSHIP BETWEEN POSITIVE AND NEGATIVE SCHEMATIC CHANGES

The preceding factor analytic research has been concerned with the structure of growth using measures that focus on positive changes. But an additional aspect of this question is the dimensionality of positive and negative schematic changes. Do positive changes shade into negative schematic changes, or are these separate dimensions of experience? Although the PBS and the CiOQ conceptualize positive and negative schematic changes as independent dimensions, positive and negative schematic changes may represent opposite poles of a single construct.

Thus, Joseph, Linley, Andrews, et al. (2005) investigated the component structure of the CiOQ using confirmatory factor analysis to test whether a one- or two-factor model was the best fit. Confirmatory factor analysis supported the two subscale structure, indicating that the positive change items cohered as a single construct, and the negative change items cohered as a single, but separate, construct.

Results showed that changes following trauma can be usefully grouped into two factors of positive and negative changes, as opposed to viewing changes as statistically bipolar. This is consistent with theoretical work on accommodation processes, in which it is recognized that people can accommodate new trauma-related information in either positive or negative directions, and that some aspects of schematic change may be positive, whereas others are negative (Joseph & Linley, 2005; Joseph & Linley, Chapter 1, this volume).

Furthermore, Joseph, Linley, Andrews, et al. (2005) discuss how the association between positive and negative changes may vary at different points in time subsequent to the traumatic event. They hypothesize that the initial reaction to adversity consists of a breakdown and disorganization of schematic structures, and it is only over time as people emotionally process their experience that changes in outlook become organized in a meaningful way. Thus, positive and negative schematic changes are likely to be positively correlated in the immediate aftermath, but then become increasingly disassociated, eventually becoming negatively associated as people cognitively accommodate their experience in either a largely positive or negative direction.

DISCUSSION

Several self-report measures of growth following adversity have been developed. Psychometric properties of all measures appear adequate. A concern is that although all the measures have been developed to assess growth following adversity, it would be premature to conclude that all measures are interchangeable. It is likely that, despite substantial conceptual and empirical overlap, there are important differences in what each of the measures is tapping. For this reason, we recommend that researchers and clinicians employ a battery of measures wherever possible.

The facilitation of growth is fast becoming of interest to those in the trauma field (see Tedeschi & Calhoun, 2004). Several short versions of the scales have also been developed that will be useful to clinicians and researchers. We urge clinicians working in trauma to adopt the growth framework and to include these new measures alongside the more traditional measures of posttraumatic stress and psychological distress. As emphasized elsewhere (Joseph & Linley, 2006), the alleviation of trauma symptoms is not synonymous with the facilitation of growth. It may be that the alleviation of trauma symptoms often results in growth, but it is also possible that this is not the case, and sometimes treatments for trauma may inadvertently impede growth-related processes. Thus, we recommend that clinicians attend to both posttraumatic stress and growth in their evaluations. There is a need for clinical case studies and single-case experimental investigations to understand growth-related processes in therapeutic encounters.

The measures reviewed here promise to be useful both for clinical practice and for research. We have found that using growth measures in clinical practice is a way of introducing clients to positive change. We include the measures as a part of an overall assessment battery, while being careful not to imply to clients that they ought to have experienced growth. What we often see is that the very completion of the measures will fuel discussion directed by the client into talking about their own changes.

We hold that the promotion of growth is a valuable clinical outcome in itself. However, for those concerned with more traditional psychiatric outcome measures, growth would seem to be an important predictor variable. In a 6-month naturalistic longitudinal study of trauma survivors who reported a prior traumatic event, but who were still experiencing psychological distress, we found that people who reported positive changes at the first time point reported lower levels of depression, anxiety, and posttraumatic stress symptoms at the 6-month follow-up (Linley, Joseph, & Goodfellow, 2007). Similarly, Frazier et al. (2001) found that self-reported positive changes in the initial weeks following a sexual assault predicted lower subsequent levels of distress when the initial positive changes were maintained, but not when the initial positive changes were lost. These early studies indicate that positive changes may have an impact on the subsequent experience of psychological distress. There is a need for further prospective research to establish the predictive utility of growth-related measures.

We would also emphasize the need for further factor analytic work to better understand the structure of growth following adversity. Exploratory research supports a single higher-order factor of general growth, with three factors as first-order factors: First, people often report that their relationships are enhanced in some way (e.g., they now value their friends and family more and feel an increased compassion and altruism toward others). Second, people may change their views of themselves in some way (e.g., they may have a greater sense of personal resiliency, wisdom, and strength, perhaps coupled with a greater acceptance of their vulnerabilities and limitations). Third, there are often reports of changes in life philosophy (e.g., people may report finding a fresh appreciation for each new day and renegotiating what really matters). There is a need for confirmatory factor analysis to test the relative fit of the three-factor hierarchical model.

There may be circumstances under which clinicians and researchers find it useful to consider these distinct domains of growth. This may be so if distinct domains of growth presented different clinical or predictive utilities, a subject that remains a focus for future investigation. It is not yet clear how different events may affect growth outcomes, or if the dimensionality of growth may differ by factors such as time since the event, sociodemographic variables, or personality variables (Linley & Joseph, 2004).

Future research should address these questions, as well as whether there are differential associations between proposed domains of growth and indicators of distress and adjustment. An understanding of the structure of growth is the foundation for developing further knowledge.

It is important to emphasize that here we are concerned with changes in schema and the assumptive world, and not with psychological distress and posttraumatic stress. How positive and negative schematic changes relate to posttraumatic stress and psychological distress is a separate question. The relation of schematic change to posttraumatic stress and psychological distress is mixed (see Linley & Joseph, 2004), which generally reflects the limitations of the cross-sectional methodologies that have often been used. What is called for is longitudinal and experimental research to investigate schematic changes and their relation to subsequent posttraumatic stress, psychological distress, and other health-related functioning.

Although growth-related measures are potentially useful, they have been subject to criticism (see Smith & Cook, 2004). One criticism is that they rely on respondents' retrospective account of their changes. The measures previously described all require respondents to rate how they perceive themselves to have changed in relation to a previous event. The use of retrospective reports is problematic in trauma research (e.g., Krinsley, Gallagher, Weathers, Kutter, & Kaloupek, 2003; and see Ford et al., Chapter 15, this volume), and this is a serious issue in the validity of growth-related measures (Park & Lechner, 2006). An interesting example of when retrospective measures such as the PTGI are problematic is when people rate themselves as not having changed in relation to a life experience because they perceived themselves to already be high on growth prior to the event. Thus, whereas one person might indicate having experienced considerable growth following an event, and another person indicates having changed only minimally as a result of the event, the second person actually may be higher on personal growth. Measures of growth like the ones described here are limited because of their retrospective nature and we would caution that what they measure is the person's perception of the amount of change they have experienced since an event; they do not provide an individual difference measure of personal growth per se.

SUMMARY

Growth following adversity is not a new phenomenon, it is simply a way of describing an increase in PWB that arises as a result of exposure to a stressful life event. Thus, although there will often be circumstances in clinical and research work when it is necessary to assess growth retrospectively, there will be other circumstances when the assessment of growth need not be retrospectively reported. When conducting longitudinal research, we do not need to rely on retrospective accounts and can simply track changes in growth using other well-established measures such as the measure of PWB developed by Ryff (1989; Ryff & Singer, 1996). We recommend that researchers work toward developing a greater integration with the wider positive psychology literature where possible. Ryff proposes six dimensions of PWB—environmental mastery, personal growth, purpose in life, autonomy, self-acceptance, and positive relations with others. In looking for a common language to integrate the growth literature, it may be useful for researchers in growth to integrate this wider and more established literature on PWB.

Summary Points

- Growth following adversity refers to psychological well-being rather than subjective well-being. The concept of growth is concerned with issues of meaning, personality schemas, and relationships, all aspects of psychological well-being, rather than with positive and negative affect, or life satisfaction, which make up subjective well-being.
- Five measures of growth following adversity have been developed: *Changes in Outlook Questionnaire, Stress Related Growth Scale, Posttraumatic Growth Inventory, Perceived Benefit Scale,* and *Thriving Scale.*
- The preceding measures are intercorrelated, but not so strongly as to suggest that they are interchangeable. Furthermore, differential association has been found with other measures.
- Factor analytic studies of the PTGI items have shown that the five-factor structure reported by Tedeschi and Calhoun (1996) is replicable, but that growth as assessed by the PTGI can also be understood as a single higher order construct. It should be recognized that work of this nature only confirms the factor structure of a particular measure of growth, not the nature of growth.
- Factor analytic research using multiple measures of growth suggests that growth may be represented as a higher order construct with three second order components. The three second order components are (1) enhancement of relationships, (2) new self-perceptions, and (3) changes in life philosophy.
- Confirmatory factor analytic work is needed to confirm the structure of growth following adversity.
- Evidence suggests that positive and negative changes represent separate dimensions of experience rather than opposite ends of a single continuum. As such, they have a range of possible associations, and the assessment of both positive and negative change following trauma

is recommended, such that their interrelationships over time can be better understood.

REFERENCES

Abraido-Lanza, A. F., Guier, C., & Colon, R. M. (1998). Psychological thriving among Latinas with chronic illness. *Journal of Social Issues, 54,* 405–424.

Affleck, G., Tennen, H., Croog, S., & Levine, S. (1987). Causal attributions, perceived benefits, and morbidity after a heart attack: An 8 year study. *Journal of Consulting and Clinical Psychology, 55,* 29–35.

American Psychiatric Association. (1994). *Diagnostic and statistical manual of mental disorders* (4th ed.). Washington, DC: Author.

Armeli, S., Gunthert, K. C., & Cohen, L. H. (2001). Stressor appraisals, coping, and post-event outcomes: The dimensionality and antecedents of stress-related growth. *Journal of Social and Clinical Psychology, 20,* 366–395.

Calhoun, L. G., & Tedeschi, R. G. (1999). *Facilitating posttraumatic growth: A clinician's guide.* Mahwah, NJ: Erlbaum.

Cattell, R. B. (1966). The scree test for the number of factors. *Multivariate Behavioral Research, 1,* 140–161.

Cohen, L. H., Cimbolic, K., Armeli, S. R., & Hettler, T. R. (1998). Quantitative assessment of thriving. *Journal of Social Issues, 54,* 323–335.

Cohen, L. H., Hettler, T. R., & Pane, N. (1998). Assessment of posttraumatic growth. In R. G. Tedeschi, C. L. Park., & L. G. Calhoun (Eds.), *Posttraumatic growth: Positive changes in the aftermath of crisis* (pp. 23–42). Mahwah, NJ: Erlbaum.

Cruess, D. G., Antoni, M. H., McGregor, B. A., Kilbourn, K. M., Boyers, A. E., Alferi, S. M., et al. (2000). Cognitive-behavioral stress management reduces serum cortisol by enhancing benefit among women being treated for early stage breast cancer. *Psychosomatic Medicine, 62,* 304–308.

Evers, A. W. M., Kraaimaat, F. W., van Lankveld, W., Jongen, P. J. H., Jacobs, J. W. G., & Bijlsma, J. W. J. (2001). Beyond unfavorable thinking: The Illness Cognition Questionnaire for chronic diseases. *Journal of Consulting and Clinical Psychology, 69,* 1026–1036.

Frazier, P., Conlon, A., & Glaser, T. (2001). Positive and negative life changes following sexual assault. *Journal of Consulting and Clinical Psychology, 69,* 1048–1055.

Joseph, S., & Linley, P. A. (2005). Positive adjustment to threatening events: An organismic valuing theory of growth through adversity. *Review of General Psychology, 9,* 262–280.

Joseph, S., & Linley, P. A. (2006). Growth following adversity: Theoretical perspectives and implications for clinical practice. *Clinical Psychology Review, 26,* 1041–1053.

Joseph, S., Linley, P. A., Andrews, L., Harris, G., Howle, B., Woodward, C., et al. (2005). Assessing positive and negative changes in the aftermath of adversity: Psychometric evaluation of the Changes in Outlook Questionnaire. *Psychological Assessment, 17,* 70–80.

Joseph, S., Linley, P. A., & Harris, G. (2005). Understanding positive change following trauma and adversity: Structural clarification. *Journal of Loss and Trauma, 10,* 83–96.

Joseph, S., Linley, P. A., Shevlin, M., Goodfellow, B., & Butler, L. (2006). Assessing positive and negative changes in the aftermath of adversity: A short form of the Changes in Outlook Questionnaire. *Journal of Loss and Trauma, 11,* 85–89.

Joseph, S., Williams, R., & Yule, W. (1993). Changes in outlook following disaster: Preliminary development of a measure to assess positive and negative responses. *Journal of Traumatic Stress, 6,* 271–279.

Krinsley, K. E., Gallagher, J. G., Weathers, F. W., Kutter, C. J., & Kaloupek, D. G. (2003). Consistency of retrospective reporting about exposure to traumatic events. *Journal of Traumatic Stress, 16,* 399–409.

Linley, P. A., Andrews, L., & Joseph, S. (2007). Confirmatory factor analysis of the posttraumatic growth inventory. *Journal of Loss and Trauma, 12,* 321–332.

Linley, P. A., & Joseph, S. (2004). Positive change following trauma and adversity: A review. *Journal of Traumatic Stress, 17,* 11–21.

Linley, P. A., & Joseph, S. (2005). Positive and negative changes following occupational death exposure. *Journal of Traumatic Stress, 18,* 751–758.

Linley, P. A., & Joseph, S. (2006). Positive and negative aspects of disaster work. *Journal of Loss and Trauma, 11,* 229–245.

Linley, P. A., Joseph, S., Cooper, R., Harris, S., & Meyer, C. (2003). Positive and negative changes following vicarious exposure to the September 11 terrorist attacks. *Journal of Traumatic Stress, 16,* 481–486.

Linley, P. A., Joseph, S., & Goodfellow, B. (2007). *Positive changes in outlook following trauma and their relation to subsequent posttraumatic stress, depression, and anxiety.* Manuscript submitted for publication.

Linley, P. A., Joseph, S., & Loumidis, K. (2005). Trauma work, sense of coherence, and positive and negative changes in therapists. *Psychotherapy and Psychosomatics, 74,* 185–188.

Maercker, A., & Langner, R. (2001). Persoenliche reifung durch belastungen und traumata: Validierung zweier deutchsprachigerf Fragebogen versionen [Posttraumatic personal growth: Validations of German versions of two questionnaires]. *Diagnostica, 47,* 153–162.

McMillen, J. C., & Fisher, R. H. (1998). The Perceived Benefits Scales: Measuring perceived positive life changes after negative events. *Social Work Research, 22,* 173–187.

Morris, B. A., Shakespeare-Finch, J., Rieck, M., & Newbury, J. (2005). Multidimensional nature of posttraumatic growth in an Australian population. *Journal of Traumatic Stress, 18,* 575–585.

Nolen-Hoeksema, S., & Davis, C. C. (2004). Theoretical and methodological issues in the assessment and interpretation of posttraumatic growth. *Psychological Inquiry, 15,* 60–64.

Pakenham, K. I. (in press). The nature of benefit finding in multiple sclerosis. *Psychology, Health and Medicine.*

Pargament, K. I., Koenig, H. G., & Perez, L. (2000). The many methods of religious coping: Initial development and validation of the RCOPE. *Journal of Clinical Psychology, 56,* 193–207.

Park, C. L., Cohen, L. H., & Murch, R. L. (1996). Assessment and prediction of stress-related growth. *Journal of Personality, 64,* 71–105.

Park, C. L., & Lechner, S. C. (2006). Measurement issues in assessing growth following stressful life experiences. In L. G. Calhoun & R. G. Tedeschi (Eds.), *Handbook of posttraumatic growth: Research and practice* (pp. 47–67). Mahwah, NJ: Erlbaum.

Powell, S., Rosner, R., Butollo, W., Tedeschi, R. G., & Calhoun, L. G. (2003). Posttraumatic growth after war: A study with former refugees and displaced people in Sarajevo. *Journal of Clinical Psychology, 59,* 71–83.

Ryff, C. D. (1989). Happiness is everything, or is it? Explorations on the meaning of psychological well-being. *Journal of Personality and Social Psychology, 57,* 1069–1081.

Ryff, C. D., & Singer, B. H. (1996). Psychological well-being: Meaning, measurement, and implications for psychotherapy research. *Psychotherapy and Psychosomatics, 65,* 14–23.

Smith, S. G., & Cook, S. L. (2004). Are reports of posttraumatic growth positively biased? *Journal of Traumatic Stress, 17,* 353–358.

Sodergren, S. C., & Hyland, M. E. (2000). What are the positive consequences of illness? *Psychology and Health, 15,* 85–97.

Sodergren, S. C., Hyland, M. E., Singh, S. J., & Sewell, L. (2002). The effect of rehabilitation on positive interpretations of illness. *Psychology and Health, 17,* 753–760.

Tedeschi, R. G., & Calhoun, L. G. (1996). Posttraumatic Growth Inventory: Measuring the positive legacy of trauma. *Journal of Traumatic Stress, 9,* 455–471.

Tedeschi, R. G., & Calhoun, L. G. (2004). A clinical approach to posttraumatic growth. In P. A. Linley & S. Joseph (Eds.), *Positive psychology in practice* (pp. 405–419). Hoboken, NJ: Wiley.

Tennen, H., Affleck, G., Urrows, S., Higgins, P., & Mendola, R. (1992). Perceiving control, construing benefits and daily processes in rheumatoid arthritis. *Canadian Journal of Behavioral Science, 24,* 186–203.

Waysman, M., Schwarzwald, J., & Solomon, Z. (2001). Hardiness: An examination of its relationship with positive and negative long term changes following trauma. *Journal of Traumatic Stress, 14,* 531–548.

Zwick, W. R., & Velicer, W. F. (1986). Comparison of five rules for determining the number of components to retain. *Psychological Bulletin, 99,* 432–442.

PART II

GROWTH AND DISTRESS IN SOCIAL, COMMUNITY, AND INTERPERSONAL CONTEXTS

CHAPTER 3

Resilience and Thriving
in a Time of Terrorism

LESLIE A. MORLAND, LISA D. BUTLER, and GREGORY A. LESKIN

THIS NEW CENTURY opened with deeply disturbing instantiations of terrorism and combat around the world. The heinous nature of terrorism and the psychological aftermath of fear and horror have forced experts to examine the impact of such events on the individual, the community, and society as a whole, including the effects on fundamental beliefs about safety and well-being. Although changes following such traumatic experiences are often inevitable, the nature, process, and course of these changes can range dramatically at the individual level.

OUTCOMES FOLLOWING TRAUMA

It is a truism that traumatic experiences can change a person's life. Extensive clinical research has documented the deleterious effects of such experiences on subsequent adaptation in the short and longer term (e.g., Kessler, Sonnega, Bromet, Hughes, & Nelson, 1995), and clinical interventions have been developed to reduce symptoms and facilitate recovery (Foa, 2006; Foa, Keane, & Friedman, 2004). The outcomes of traumatic event exposure are not all necessarily negative. Although Seligman and Csikszentmihalyi (2000) have stated, "Psychology has, since World War II, become a science largely about healing" (p. 5), the discipline of late has been widening its focus to examine a more complete range of possible outcomes (e.g., Carver, 1998; Joseph & Linley, 2005; O'Leary & Ickovics, 1995; Tedeschi & Calhoun, 1995, 2004), some of which may not in fact require "healing." In particular, there has been increasing interest in identifying factors that confer protection to individuals or aid their recovery and those that contribute to positive trauma-related developments or transformations in the postevent period. In short, the study of posttraumatic adjustment now includes resilience and thriving.

To understand the ingredients of adaptation to traumatic events, it is necessary to examine the *process* of that adaptation, not just a final cross-sectional presentation. A process view investigates trajectories of functioning over time from pretrauma levels to the present (for more detailed discussions, see Butler, Morland, & Leskin, 2007; Carver, 1998; O'Leary & Ickovics, 1995). At the most general level are the ways in which a person may maintain, return to, or exceed pretrauma levels of functioning (positive trajectories), in addition to those presentations that involve disturbance, decline, and permanent disability (negative trajectories). Understanding the present in terms of the past—both before and after the event—contextualizes the functioning and delineates any changes.

With respect to negative trajectories, if the individual never fully recovers (e.g., remains symptomatic or impaired in daily functioning), then the trajectory may be described as *survival with impairment.* Although the individual has lived through the event, it has left a psychic scar that has impaired or diminished functioning over the long term. This is the common province of therapeutic intervention; with respect to traumatic events in general, more than a third of individuals with posttraumatic stress may fail to fully recover (even with treatment) in over a decade (Kessler et al., 1995). For others, the decline may continue and they may not survive their traumatic experience. This has been termed *succumbing* (Butler et al., 2007; O'Leary & Ickovics, 1995). The condition is evident when traumatized individuals take actions that result in their death by suicide or through physical injury secondary to maladaptive behaviors (e.g., substance abuse or recklessness), or when psychological events result in serious physical disturbances or exacerbations of preexisting conditions that lead to death (Kloner, 2006).

Many people can tolerate a great deal, or they bounce back and return to their baseline level of functioning after the initial postevent readjustment period. Indeed, findings from the traumatic stress literature suggest that the majority of those who face life-threatening experiences or loss events during their lives will fare relatively well, bearing few long-term impairments (Kessler et al., 1995; Norris et al., 2002). Until recently, though, this group has been comparatively less studied because those with positive postevent trajectories of resilience and growth—those who report few negative effects, or an uncomplicated recovery, or even enhancements to their adjustment following trauma—are not typically seen by clinicians, nor studied by clinical researchers.

RESILIENCE

Foa and colleagues (2005) have proposed:

> [R]esilience can be thought of as one end of a continuum of vulnerability to
> emotional dysfunction and psychopathology when exposed to a stressful ex-
> perience. Thus, an individual at the extremely vulnerable end of the contin-
> uum may experience great distress, dysfunction, and even significant
> psychopathology in response to even relatively minor stressors that most
> people would cope with readily, while a person at the resilient end would
> require a great deal of stress to cause significant impairment in functioning.
> (p. 1808)

This view emphasizes the meaning of resilience as a marker of a higher
threshold for the onset of distress. Instantiations of resilience may be somewhat more nuanced than that; elements of resilience may be seen both in
psychological *outcomes* following challenge and in the *process* of adaptation
or trajectory of response to the stressor. In this way, resilience can be noted
in the initial reaction to a traumatic event, in features of the recovery path
associated with achieving a return to baseline functioning, and in the final
product of the adaptation (Butler et al., 2007).

Other factors contribute to the course adaptation takes and its final
product, including the specific features of the experience (e.g., degree of
exposure, injury, or loss, and peritraumatic reactions), features of the individual's personality and history (e.g., premorbid functioning, trauma history, and personality factors such as hardiness and positive attitude),
emotion regulation strategies and other styles of coping (e.g., active problem-focused engagement versus avoidance), cognitive representations of
the experience (whether meaning and benefits can be identified), and environmental factors (such as the quality and quantity of available social support), which we have reviewed elsewhere (Butler et al., 2007; Garlan, Butler,
& Spiegel, 2005).

Lepore and Revenson (2006) have highlighted different aspects of resilience by delineating the ideas of recovery, resistance, and reconfiguration. In *recovery*, the elasticity of response is emphasized; people bend but
do not break in the grip of the stressor and ultimately return to their original state. This is probably the most commonplace understanding and usage
of the term resilience. With respect to earlier functioning, the individual is
challenged and possibly temporarily impaired, but ultimately returns to
baseline. This can be seen in findings following the terrorist attacks of September 11, 2001, where high and almost universal distress was reported initially (Schuster et al., 2001), though few Americans experienced long-term
impairments (Schlenger et al., 2002; Silver, Holman, McIntosh, Poulin, &
Gil-Rivas, 2002).

In the case of *resistance,* the person's functioning is not appreciably affected by the stressor or, if it is, the effect is relatively minor and short-lived (see also stress resistance; Garmezy, 1985), such as has been found in a large proportion of those experiencing typical bereavement (reviewed in Bonanno, 2004). It is unclear whether the experience of typical bereavement—which is a normal part of life—would be directly applicable to predictions about responses to exposure to traumatic events, such as the violent loss of a loved one.

Clinical skepticism also may be aroused by claims of unscathed outcomes following significant trauma (Wortman & Silver, 1989). Clinical assessment and judgment may be necessary to distinguish between remarkable resilience and defensive denial or repression, particularly in the case of combat veterans who place high value on self-discipline, personal control, and psychological toughness (Elder & Clipp, 1989). Nonetheless, the idea of resistance highlights one end of the range of possible outcomes and is perhaps a more common one than previously understood (Bonanno, 2004).

Finally, the term *reconfiguration* conveys the idea of permanent adaptation to or alteration as a consequence of the trauma—changes that accommodate the demands of the traumatic situation and may also alter the ways in which the individual reacts to future events (see also Carver, 1998). This latter type of resilient functioning shares much with adversarial or posttraumatic growth (Joseph & Linley, 2005; Tedeschi & Calhoun, 1995, 2004), particularly its consequences for future adaptation. It calls to mind the idea of *positive accommodation* as described by Joseph and Linley (2005) in their model of adversarial growth.

GROWTH

Over a decade ago, researchers began to document the benefits and positive changes that some individuals reported following adversity (e.g., Joseph, Williams, & Yule, 1993; Tedeschi & Calhoun, 1995). There are observations that positive changes in outlook can accompany negative changes following disasters (Joseph et al., 1993) and terrorism (Butler et al., 2005; Linley, Joseph, Cooper, Harris, & Meyer, 2003), and that benefits and growth can be construed in the context of a wide range of challenges (Affleck & Tennen, 1996), including combat (Elder & Clipp, 1989; Fontana & Rosenheck, 1998), POW experiences (Erbes et al., 2005), terrorism (Butler et al., 2005), and grieving (Nerken, 1993). In these studies of combat, reported benefits included solidarity, comradeship, enhanced coping skills, self-discipline, and appreciation of life. Indeed, as Tedeschi and Calhoun (2004) have noted, "[R]eports of growth experiences in the aftermath of traumatic events far outnumber reports of psychiatric disorders" (p. 2). Around the same time, there was also a gathering impetus across a range of disciplines to move beyond a model of adaptation limited to vulnerability or deficit to one that encompassed successful adaptation (Garmezy, 1985; Masten, 2001; O'Leary & Ickovics, 1995), including psychological growth (Tedeschi & Calhoun, 1995).

The idea of positive adaptation—labeled as posttraumatic growth (Tedeschi & Calhoun, 1995, 1996), adversarial growth (Joseph & Linley, 2005), and thriving (O'Leary & Ickovics, 1995), among other appellations—signifies postevent adaptation that *exceeds* pre-event levels of functioning. The readjustment experience is transformative (O'Leary & Ickovics, 1995), or as Tedeschi and Calhoun (2004) have noted, "the general paradox of this field: that out of loss there is a gain" (p. 6). These gains are generally reported in the areas of heightened appreciation of life, more meaningful personal relationships, awareness of increased personal strength, changes in life priorities and recognition of new possibilities, and a deepening of engagement with spiritual or existential concerns and the enhancement of faith.

Tedeschi and Calhoun (1995, 1996, 2004; Calhoun & Tedeschi, 1998) have written extensively about the factors that impel such growth and the elements of its process. They have argued that traumatic experiences severely disrupt, and sometimes shatter, the individual's usual modes of belief about self and the world, overwhelm adaptive resources and typical means of coping, and in many cases negate previously valued goals and strivings. The psychological upheaval that ensues is marked by significant distress, at times incredulousness or conscious denial, and the struggle to come to terms with the new reality of the individual's posttraumatic existence and the world. The struggle is evidenced in cognitive efforts, in the form of unbidden ruminations, to adapt to the experience and its aftermath. By disclosing and examining the experience (through talking, writing, praying), accepting what cannot be changed, disengaging from previous goals and beliefs where necessary, and eliciting the emotional scaffolding and means of disclosure provided by social contact, clients may alter schemas and develop a new narrative understanding of the experience and its meaning.

According to Joseph and Linley's (2005) *Positive Adjustment to Threatening Events,* it is not enough for individuals to *assimilate* the experience into existing cognitive models (find a way to graft the information into their present worldview so that it is consistent within it); growth requires schematic reconfiguration or, as they term it, *positive accommodation,* wherein what people have learned from the traumatic experience fundamentally changes their worldview in a manner consistent with their inherent tendencies toward positive growth, authenticity, and actualization. (If, instead, the schema is reconstituted as a defeatist, nihilistic, or self-destructive worldview, this is described as *negative accommodation,* and it signals a lasting psychological wound and ongoing impairment.)

FINDING MEANING

A critical aspect of growth is the search for meaning in the experience, which is generally viewed as central to posttraumatic adaptation (Janoff-Bulman, 1992; Taylor, 1983), and the perception or construal of positive aspects or benefits to the experience (Affleck & Tennen, 1996; Joseph et al., 1993; McMillen & Fisher, 1998). (In many reports, the term *benefit finding* actually refers to the growth observed across areas of personal life; Affleck & Tennen, 1996.) In a study of posttraumatic growth following the September 11, 2001, terrorist attacks in the United States (Butler et al., 2005), the single greatest predictor of posttraumatic growth across all domains, both in the short term and 6 to 9 months after the attacks, was the level of positive changes in existential outlook initially reported.

Additionally, Joseph and Linley (2005) have noted that with respect to growth, an important distinction needs to be made between meaning as comprehensibility and meaning as significance (Janoff-Bulman & Frantz, 1997), or between making sense of experience versus finding positive aspects to it (Davis, Nolen-Hoeksema, & Larson, 1998). The significance of the distinction is that although survivors may grapple initially with the challenges of making the experience comprehensible, for growth to occur, the significance of the event in the person's life must come to the fore. This important distinction maps onto the two domains in which the work of postevent adaptation may be done (Janoff-Bulman & Frantz, 1997): (1) managing or ameliorating distress and other symptoms—which requires, in part, making sense of the event; and (2) transforming the personal meaning of the experience and its impact on one's life—which can involve identifying benefits that flowed from living through the experience and new life- and meaning-affirming ways of living now.

APPLICATION TO DIFFERENT POPULATIONS

The psychosocial impact of traumatic events such as terrorist attacks or combat can pervade virtually every dimension of life across a nation, affecting individuals, families, communities, and society as a whole. The range of survivors include those directly experiencing the event, grieving loved ones, first responders, rescue and recovery teams, and medical personnel, in addition to those who may not have experienced the events directly, but are left with disturbing feelings of helplessness and anxiety about the future. In the case of September 11, 2001, and in the years following, many Americans experienced the impact of terrorism, continuing dread of additional attacks, and—because immediately following the attacks of September 11, the U.S. government initiated the Global War on Terrorism—for some, the anxiety, losses, and other difficult consequences of combat suffered by this new generation of war veterans, their families, and American society.

ILLUSTRATIONS OF POSTTRAUMATIC IMPAIRMENT, RESILIENCE, AND GROWTH

The following three case examples illustrate aspects of the different posttraumatic trajectories and outcomes and some salient elements of the process involved in adaptation to a major stressor. The first example illustrates ongoing distress and impairment following a soldier's deployment to Afghanistan and the difficult struggle to make sense of the traumatic events he experienced there. The second example illustrates the coexistence of distress and growth following many years of active duty military experience, including deployment to Iraq. The third example illustrates positive accommodation; in this case, a woman who had been living in New York City at the time of the terrorist attacks was deeply changed by that experience in a manner consistent with her inherent tendencies toward positive growth, authenticity, and actualization.

Case Study 1

Mr. A entered the Army right out of high school "as an opportunity to get out." He had been raised in a small farm town in the Midwest, was close to his family, had a strong religious faith, and had not experienced any previous traumatic events. Before joining the Army, he had never been on an airplane or traveled out of the Midwest. Immediately following his enlistment and basic training, he was deployed to Afghanistan. He served in the infantry, and his battalion was the first to enter Afghanistan with the task of "taking control" of the airport. That task took approximately 30 days. Mr. A reports that during that time he "never slept" and felt "on guard" at all times. He says that he "saw a few gruesome things, but the worst part wasn't what we saw or what actually happened, it was that feeling, that tension. At every moment of every day, I was tense. We always felt like something terrible could jump out at us. In a way, our fears screwed with our heads worse than the reality." Mr. A describes fears of being attacked by biological or chemical weapons, being tortured at the hands of terrorists, and of being hit by friendly fire. "I felt like I had just joined the Army, I was sleep deprived and didn't know what I was doing. I wondered if the kid next to me was in just as bad shape." The worst event was a bombing where his friend died in a fire in front of him. Mr. A recalled feeling overwhelmed with helplessness, anger, and grief. After 3 years of active duty service, Mr. A was discharged.

Mr. A recalls that immediately on his return to the United States, he started drinking heavily. The following 6 months were a "quick slide down a slippery slope. At first it was at night just to sleep, and then it was during the day to calm my nerves. I just couldn't relax. I still felt all keyed up all the time." His drinking led to discipline problems as well as poor work performance. He received a medical discharge from the Army due to an orthopedic injury, "but the real reason was that I was so messed up in the head. They didn't want to make me look bad, but they must have known what was going on."

Not having anywhere else to go, Mr. A went to visit his family in the Midwest. "That didn't last long. After about a week, they drove me crazy. They just kept asking questions about Afghanistan and I didn't want to talk about it. They kept harassing me about my drinking. Looking back, I can see that they were just worried about me, but at the time, I was totally pissed off that they wanted to tell me what to do after what I had gone through."

He bought a one-way ticket to a big city in another state. "I'm not sure why I thought things would be better there. I guess I thought that I could be anonymous, that people would just leave me alone. I kept thinking that I could pull myself together if I just had some time." Mr. A continued to drink excessively and became involved in drugs. His nightmares and sleep difficulties worsened and he further isolated himself. He reported feeling irritable and angry most of the time. He reported continually going over in his head the events that had occurred in attempt to make some sense. Looking back, he believes that his drug and alcohol use was "self-medicating [his] PTSD." He had no social support and felt "disconnected" from other people. "With my military experience, it was easy to get jobs as a security guard. It was the perfect job, I could be alone, awake all night. But I just couldn't handle it." He reports that he was fired from multiple jobs due to excessive absences or odd behavior such as "checking the perimeter intensely." "It took me a long time to admit that it was my fault, it seemed normal to be paranoid about being attacked."

Mr. A eventually went to the Vet Center to inquire about the financial benefits he might be entitled to. He states, "Right away, the counselor knew that I was using, that I was messed up. He tried to get me to go to counseling but I didn't want any part of it. He convinced me to go to a support group and I agreed. I wanted to talk to other guys who knew what I had been through." Mr. A credits the other members of the support group for getting him into counseling. "I didn't believe it until I heard it from them. Some of them had seen shrinks and they said it helped. I figured I had nothing to lose so I gave it a try."

Mr. A's course of treatment was unstable. His attendance in therapy was at first sporadic due to avoidance, continued substance abuse, and distrust in the therapist. The initial stages of therapy focused on building trust with the therapist and establishing a sense of safety. Much of his therapy focused on his anger and guilt around a particular event that had occurred in Afghanistan. After approximately 6 months of therapy, Mr. A had improved enough to get a job at the Vet Center. "It's nothing glamorous, but it feels good to do something productive and it feels safe being around other vets."

Mr. A has held that job for the past year, but he continues to report substantial PTSD symptoms and struggles to find meaning in his deployment. He feels angry and betrayed by the military (because he believes certain events could have been prevented), and he is still estranged from his family and friends. In short, Mr. A has not fully recovered; he continues to experience great distress and significant impairment. He continues to drink but has cut back substantially. He notes that much of this distress occurred early in his deployment and has persisted since his return, despite some improvements during therapy.

Case Study 2

Mr. B was raised on an Army base in the Midwest, the son of a combat veteran who served four tours in Vietnam. Mr. B enlisted in the Marine Corps shortly after graduating from high school. After 3 years of active duty service, he was discharged. He attended college and then reentered the Marine Reserves following his college graduation. He stayed in the Marine Reserves until 2001 and then 6 months later joined the Navy Reserves, 12 days prior to the September 11 terrorist attacks. Mr. B was mobilized by the Reserves in late 2002. In early 2003, at the age of 37, Mr. B deployed for Iraq leaving behind his wife, a new son, and a burgeoning career in broadcasting.

Mr. B served as a gunnery sergeant, and he was one of the first Religion Program Specialists to attain that position. He was in Iraq for approximately 9 months and describes his entire deployment experience as "very stressful." He recalls the "day-to-day pressure to perform and be on top of your game and deal with all this death and dying and then deal with the troops who are dealing with the death and dying." Mr. B described several incidents during his deployment that were particularly traumatic for him. "The experience never leaves me. We got fired at, attacked, ambushed. But that is war . . . and you can't put your gun down for a second."

Mr. B was demobilized in August 2003 and returned to live with his family. As soon as he returned home, he noticed that "something was not right." He reports that he could not tolerate being in crowds, had a "really short fuse" with his family and at work, and frequently experienced PTSD symptoms including nightmares, difficulty sleeping, hypervigilance, anger, and irritability. After about 14 months of these difficulties, both he and his wife realized that he had a significant problem.

In early 2004, Mr. B started individual therapy through the local Vet Center. During this time, he also faced another serious setback when one of the men in his battalion commit suicide while Mr. B was on the phone with him. Through the course of therapy, Mr. B processed much of his trauma, worked to decrease his PTSD symptoms, and tried to find meaning in his current life. Through the process, during which he suffered tremendous distress, Mr. B continued therapy and managed to thrive in his job, reconnect with his family, and find meaning in his combat experiences. Mr. B believes his experience changed two important aspects of his core values. "[I] realize that I do not want to waste another minute of my life. There is a process now. In everything, I see a process that I need to go through refining my character." He also vows to never again deprive his family of his time.

Almost 2 years after his deployment, Mr. B continues to struggle with PTSD symptoms but feels a heightened sense of appreciation for his life. He reports, "I do not give my time to inane things anymore. . . . I am not chasing a ring anymore; I have a different set of priorities." Mr. B also feels a responsibility to "give back to the Navy so people do not have to go through what I went through" on returning home.

Mr. B's story shows how distress and growth can coexist. Like Mr. B, many individuals can fare well in some areas and even experience growth while still struggling with distress and impairment following adversity. In his case, therapy played an instrumental role in the process of benefit finding and growth while simultaneously addressing a reduction in symptoms of distress.

Case Study 3

In some situations, the process of readjustment following adversity results in both a positive adaptation and a positive transformation. For Ms. C, who experienced tremendous distress and psychological upheaval during and immediately following the September 11, 2001, terrorist attacks on the World Trade Center, her process of coming to terms with these experiences resulted in a deepened sense of personal authenticity and a greater appreciation for living a meaningful life.

Ms. C was raised in New York City until the age of 11. Her family moved away, and she returned to New York City in 1996 for graduate school. She was working and living less than 1 mile from the World Trade Center at the time of the attacks. She recalls that on the morning of September 11, she was in her apartment on the phone when she heard a plane overhead that was "really loud, flying really low and in the wrong direction. I made note of it, but continued the conversation." Minutes later, she turned on her television to see the weather report and saw images that she assumed were from a movie. She turned the sound up and realized that there actually was "a big hole and fire coming out of one of the World Trade Center towers." She got dressed and was running down the stairs when she heard "lots of sirens, more sirens than [she] had ever heard at one time." For the next few minutes, dozens of her neighbors congregated on the sidewalk discussing what had occurred. She remembers being in a state of disbelief saying over and over "I don't think you're right, I think you're wrong, that can't be true." She recalls that within a few minutes "all the buildings had emptied onto the street, the streets were crowded with pedestrians, and it was a state of chaos." And then a few minutes later, "we started to see the zombies." Ms. C recalls seeing, "a huge mass of people, like a marathon running up 6th Avenue. People who had escaped the towers somehow, ran out of the building and just kept running." Ms. C recounts conversations with people who were hysterical, some of whom had only escaped by luck and were horrified by the knowledge that all of their coworkers must have been killed. "Over the course of an hour, the nature of it changed and there were more people who were cut and torn and bleeding and covered with soot. There was this huge black cloud of dust and the people were coming out just covered with soot."

Following her initial disbelief, Ms. C's immediate reaction was to problem-solve. "I felt like I needed to *do* something. I felt unbelievably helpless just standing there watching the disaster." Ms. C describes what followed as feeling "more and more apocalyptic." "There was no way to help, we just stood around and then different risks that I hadn't thought about started to occur to me. It was just more frightening when it was dark. I was afraid to drink my tap water. The air didn't feel very safe; the water didn't feel very safe. It was so scary; no one knew what would happen next."

Over the days and weeks following September 11, Ms. C exhibited many of the symptoms of acute stress disorder such as nightmares, difficulty sleeping, mild derealization, and hyperarousal. These symptoms eventually subsided. "The turning point for me was getting back to work at the nonprofit, knowing that I was doing something to help. Also, Mayor Giuliani's campaign to get people out to restaurants and plays really helped. It gave us permission to have fun and we felt like we were helping to rebuild the city."

Ms. C reports that many of her friends and colleagues left New York after the attacks. "Some people left out of fear, but most left because they wanted a higher quality of life. It made me start questioning my commitment to that lifestyle. For the first time, I started to wonder if the stress and pressure of the City was worth it. Was that what I really wanted out of life?" Ms. C stayed in New York for another 2 years and then moved to "a warmer, more laid-back city" on the West Coast. "Now I get to do outdoor activities every weekend that I only used to do on vacation. I actually get to spend time with my friends. I may not have the same career opportunities or go to great nightclubs all the time, but overall my life feels more meaningful."

Ms. C reports no current posttraumatic stress symptoms. She does, however, continue to react to the incessant media coverage of the attacks and the war on terrorism, particularly around the anniversary of 9/11. Consequently, she has chosen to limit her exposure to radio, Internet, and television coverage. She also reports that her survivor guilt has not dissipated with the passage of time.

The preceding clinical examples illustrate different ways in which three individuals responded to traumatic events (in these cases, combat or terrorism). These stories demonstrate how each individual struggled with the meaning of the event, adopted coping strategies that were either adaptive or maladaptive, and found—or failed to find—benefits and meaning in their experience.

DISTRESS AND GROWTH CAN COEXIST

According to Elder and Clipp (1989), many World War II and Korean conflict veterans see their combat experience from a "dual perspective": It is "remembered for its destructiveness and trauma, and also for the comradeship, exhilaration, and lessons for living" (p. 332). This dual perspective is a striking feature of two of the present vignettes, wherein there is the evidence of growth alongside distress. Mr. B remains symptomatic yet has increased in his appreciation of life, made conscious positive changes in his life priorities, and now seeks to use his difficult experiences to help others. Ms. C has recovered from her experiences and made significant changes in her lifestyle that are in accord with her values, even though she continues to feel guilt about her survival (and possibly her growth), and she is still reactive when faced with reminders of the event.

Although perhaps surprising, distress and growth can, and often do, coexist (Joseph & Linley, 2005; Tedeschi & Calhoun, 1995, 2004)—an assertion that has been confirmed in terrorism (Butler et al., 2005) and combat (Elder & Clipp, 1989) samples. People can fare relatively well in some areas, and even grow in others, while still experiencing distress. As Elder and Clipp (1989) have noted, "[T]raumatic events can produce both pathology and health or resilience, even within the same individual" (p. 318). This observation suggests that assessing a single global outcome may obscure the true faceted nature of the person's condition; it also implies that the challenge may reveal a range of vulnerabilities and strengths.

The seeming paradox of the coexistence of distress and growth is less problematic when one considers that the experience of a highly stressful or traumatic event is a necessary precondition for growth, which may account for the positive association between distress and growth noted in some, though not all, studies (reviewed in Linley & Joseph, 2004; Tedeschi & Calhoun, 2004). Additionally, some distress, such as experiencing intrusion and avoidance symptoms, may be understood as efforts at cognitive processing of the event, a necessary element to successful adaptation and growth (Garlan et al., 2005; Janoff-Bulman, 1992; Linley & Joseph, 2004; Tedeschi & Calhoun, 2004).

The relationship between distress and growth may not be straightforward. In the study of growth following September 11 (Butler et al., 2005), the relationship between PTSD symptoms and posttraumatic growth was actually curvilinear, with growth increasing as symptoms increased up to a point; after that point, however, increasing symptoms were associated with a decline in reported growth. The point at which growth started to decline corresponded to symptom levels indicating a probable PTSD diagnosis. This suggests that, although catastrophic events may be necessary conditions for growth, there is a limited range of distress that can accompany, or perhaps facilitate, it. Outside those bounds, levels of distress may be insufficient to spur growth or, conversely, they may overwhelm natural tendencies to find or identify meaning and benefits.

Other researchers have reported related findings. In one study, soldier reports of psychological benefits in war were highest for those with intermediate levels of exposure (Fontana & Rosenheck, 1998), though Elder and Clipp (1989) found that "men who served in heavy combat (in World War II or Korea) became far more assertive and resilient up to mid-life, when compared with veterans with light or no combat" (p. 330). In another study, posttraumatic growth among cancer patients was highest for those with Stage II disease when compared with those with Stages I, III, or IV (Lechner et al., 2003; staging refers to severity of illness, and indicates degree of life threat).

These findings underscore that it may be necessary to address the primary symptom complaints and avoidant coping strategies of patients before they can be reasonably expected to find and report benefits in their experience. This issue is perhaps the limiting factor in Mr. A's present level of adaptation; he remains highly symptomatic and engaged in maladaptive coping, in this case alcohol use. Mr. A. also appears to lack (perhaps even reject) the social resources that might nurture and support positive changes (Butler et al., 2007; Garlan et al., 2005). In contrast, Mr. B, though highly symptomatic, addressed many of his complaints in therapy, retained and reaffirmed the value of his support network, and transformed his experience into positive lessons for his life. Ms. C's circumstances differed from the other two cases in that she had limited direct personal exposure to threat, which perhaps circumscribed her traumatic reaction to an acute period. Her experience was sufficient to spur her to reconsider her priorities, but at the same time, it left her with the requisite resources to make significant life-affirming changes.

CENTRAL ROLE OF MEANING-MAKING TO POSTEVENT ADAPTATION

Another important feature common to these accounts is the impetus to find meaning both in the traumatic event and in life following the event. Janoff-Bulman and Frantz (1997) have described these two constructions of meaning as the difference between meaning as comprehensibility (about the event, and life and the world in general) and meaning as significance (with respect to one's own life); we can find this distinction in the present cases. Mr. A's postevent condition is marked by an ongoing struggle to find meaning in his deployment, suggesting that until that is achieved it may be difficult for him to turn to the task of finding significance in his present life. In contrast, Mr. B notes that through therapy he found meaning both in his combat experiences and in his present life, which resulted in positive changes in his values, priorities, and work. Ms. C reports that her turning point was going back to work in a context in which she could help others and in her reevaluation of her lifestyle, which she came to realize was lacking a depth of significance she now needed.

According to Janoff-Bulman and Frantz (1997; see also Janoff-Bulman, 1992), because trauma confronts its victims with issues of fundamental survival, initial efforts at meaning tend to be existential in theme. Survivors experience the extent of their true vulnerability and fragility, and they grapple with "the horror of a meaningless universe and shattered assumptions" that creates in them "a state of disequilibrium, dread, and hyperarousal" (p. 95). Seeing the news accounts of the planes hitting the World Trade Center and witnessing the "zombies" and the injured survivors violated Ms. C's core assumptions of safety and security, leaving her with an overwhelming sense of helplessness, uncertainty, and dread, and plagued by distressing thoughts and fears, and deeply threatening feelings that the experience was "apocalyptic."

A critical aspect to ultimate adaptation is the survivor's ability to manage the distress. The coping strategies one engages in following traumatic

experience appear to be critical in determining the trajectory of adjustment, with disengagement and avoidance strategies being associated with
poorer outcomes (Silver et al., 2002; reviewed in Butler et al., 2007). Mr. A
turned to alcohol to numb his anxiety and distress and to address his
sleeplessness and nightmares. This, coupled with his self-imposed social
isolation, enabled him to avoid confronting his condition, which in turn
contributed to his ongoing impairment. The impulse to control emotions
during the acute phase is common and "may even be adaptive when it allows the individual to manage the challenges that the crisis presents"
(Garlan et al., 2005, p. 156), as may be the case in the midst of combat
(Elder & Clipp, 1989). To come to terms with the meaning of their experience, patients need to learn to manage and modulate the strong emotions
that attend it. Consequently, a central feature of the early stages of therapy is stress management (Janoff-Bulman & Frantz, 1997), which can help
reestablish the patient's feeling of safety and provide the needed stability
to undertake the task of processing the event.

It is not uncommon for early efforts to involve a search for comprehensibility and causation, including one's own possible contribution to the traumatic event, as a way to wrest some control of what happened. According to
Janoff-Bulman and Frantz (1997), this attempt to assign blame should be
understood as an attempt to cope that typically gives way to other more
adaptive impulses to make meaning in other ways. An example of this is
found in survivors' desires to make choices and take actions in the world
(such as the interpersonal and altruistic activities that both Mr. B and Ms.
C mention) that can help them "perceive a contingency between actions
and outcomes, evidence that the world is not wholly random" (p. 101) and
highlight life activities of personal value.

Following this, survivors turn to other issues of meaning and value.
Initially patients may seek to find benefits in the traumatic experience—
the positive elements that the crisis showed or taught them, such as recognizing the personal strengths they showed in the ordeal and the value and
sustenance that their social relationships provided (such as Mr. B reports). Many individuals also observe a deepening of their faith, or come
to seek deeper meaning in their lives (as did Ms. C) or to focus on what
gives their life value (as did Mr. B). "Meaning-making occurs through a
process of recognizing or creating significance and worth in one's daily
existence" (Janoff-Bulman & Frantz, 1997, p. 98). Thus, meaning-making
following trauma comes to focus on the present and the future.

The preceding case examples represent different instantiations of adaptation following traumatic experience. These examples illustrate the range
of trajectories following adversity and the importance of contextualizing
one's functioning to delineate these changes and areas of adaptation.

CLINICAL APPLICATIONS FROM A
GROWTH PERSPECTIVE

Several authors have examined the potential to directly incorporate facilitation of posttraumatic growth within the context of psychotherapy (Calhoun & Tedeschi, 1998; Saakvitne, Tennen, & Affleck, 1998; Zoellner & Maercker, 2006). Zoellner and Maercker point out that growth following trauma is a "new perspective" not a new treatment type. This new approach represents an important shift from a singular view of traumatic response as a constellation of symptoms and deficits to one that incorporates the struggle to find meaning or benefits, ruminative thought processes, or even distress as the antecedent signs of potential growth.

The overwhelming majority of scientific literature addressing clinical interventions for combat stress reactions or exposure to terrorist attacks focuses on the reduction of emotionally or physically painful symptoms. However, an increasing number of psychotherapeutic models now also encourage individuals toward the development of positive strivings or growth through adversity (Joseph & Linley, 2005); among these have been applications to disaster workers (Paton & Stephens, 1996), law enforcement (Gersons & Carlier, 2000), civilian survivors of the Bosnian war (Rosner & Powell, 2006), and Holocaust survivors (Lev-Wiesel & Amir, 2006). The clinical applications of the posttraumatic growth perspective incorporate both empirically validated assessment tools and therapeutic techniques.

Several quantitative questionnaires are available for clinicians and researchers to use to measure an individual's growth following a traumatic or stressful life event, including the Stress-Related Growth Scale (SRGS; Park, Cohen, & Murch, 1996), Posttraumatic Growth Inventory (PTGI; Tedeschi & Calhoun, 1996), and Changes in Outlook Questionnaire (CiOQ; Joseph et al., 2005). The CiOQ provides two scales including an 11-item scale for assessing positive changes (e.g., "I feel more experienced about life now") and a 15-item scale assessing negative changes (e.g., "My life has no meaning anymore"). Use of validated questionnaires such as the CiOQ in clinical practice has been recommended (Joseph, 2004), based on findings that positive changes experienced in the days and weeks after a traumatic event predict less distress and more posttraumatic growth at 6-month (Butler et al., 2005) and 1-year follow-up (Frazier, Conlon, & Glaser, 2001).

IMPLICATIONS FOR PSYCHOTHERAPY WITH TRAUMA SURVIVORS

Calhoun and Tedeschi (1998, 1999) have provided a set of guidelines for incorporating posttraumatic growth into clinical settings. Accordingly, clinicians can facilitate growth by "listening carefully to how the trauma survivor's descriptions of events include ways they showed strength and capability before, during, and after the traumatic event" (Calhoun & Tedeschi, 2006, p. 295). A primary objective of many therapeutic treatment models for PTSD is the advancement of cognitive processing of the trauma by creating a cohesive narrative of the event (telling the story) and making meaning of the experience (Hembree & Foa, 2000). According to the posttraumatic growth perspective (Calhoun & Tedeschi, 1998), therapists can assist the facilitation of growth through both the creation of the narrative and the making of meaning by (a) supporting and encouraging positive changes that are described by the patient, (b) simultaneously acknowledging the patient's struggle and pain as well as positive changes or benefits experienced as part of the traumatic event, and (c) avoiding superficial statements such as "look at the bright side" or "let's focus on the positives" because such statements may actually encourage denial or cognitive avoidance.

Finally, it is entirely possible that some individuals who have experienced the worst types of traumatic experiences are unable or unprepared psychologically to identify benefits or growth. Aldwin (1994) identified potential barriers that prevent perceptions of positive benefits following trauma, including a predominant focus on emotional distress and an inability to gain long-term perspective or future orientation. For individuals unable to identify benefits or growth, psychotherapeutic treatment should primarily be aimed at reducing emotional distress through active coping and at identifying and challenging distorted thought process by means of cognitive behavioral therapy (e.g., Foa, 2006).

WAYS TO BUILD RESILIENCE

Additional tools exist for clinicians to assist adult survivors of terrorism and combat, as well as first responders, military families, and others in fostering resilience to cope with the stress of such events. The American Psychological Association's Task Force on Resilience in Response to Terrorism developed a series of recommendations for clinicians (e.g., Butler, Hobfoll, & Keane, 2003; Carlson, James, Hobfoll, & Leskin, 2003; Leskin et al., 2003). These recommendations include:

- Seeing stress as a challenge to solve, rather than a threat to avoid.
- Being flexible. Accepting change as a natural part of life.
- Teaching active coping strategies to manage stress.
- Learning to have a positive view of one's self and others.
- Maintaining and practicing self-care throughout the recovery process.

- Developing a positive, future orientation. Fostering hope.
- Staying connected and developing a positive supportive social network.

Finally, clinicians should be vigilant for "red flag" behaviors that may indicate the individual has become overwhelmed by the traumatic event. These include substance abuse, extreme avoidance or withdrawal, anger or rage behaviors, and engaging in high-risk activities.

SUMMARY

Terrorist attacks can spread fear and anxiety throughout a nation or geographic area well beyond the area of the specific physical threat; indeed, that is the objective of such acts. There are ways people can adapt in the face of terrorism. Clinical research has broadened its focus to take account of postevent trajectories that include the means by which a person may maintain, return to, or exceed pretrauma levels of functioning (positive trajectories), in addition to those presentations that involve disturbance, decline, and permanent disability (negative trajectories). To understand the nature and course of adaptation following a traumatic experience, it is necessary to examine the *process* of that adaptation over time, rather than just a final cross-sectional presentation. In an attempt to understand this course of development, research has highlighted factors that contribute to the adaptation *process* including specific features of the traumatic experience, the individual's personality and history, trauma history, personality factors, emotional regulation and coping, cognitive representations of the experience, and environmental factors (Butler et al., 2007; Garlan et al., 2005). A critical aspect to ultimate adaptation is the survivors' ability to *manage* their distress, underscoring the role of coping strategies in ongoing adaptation to trauma (reviewed in Butler et al., 2007).

Factors known to influence positive adaptation following adversity can also be optimized in the process of psychotherapy. The early stages of therapy may focus on teaching active coping and helping the client develop a positive social support network and a positive future orientation, in addition to establishing safety and stability. These efforts may help metabolize the trauma to the extent that the client can then move on to the task of finding significance. Finding meaning may shift sequentially from finding meaning in the event or in the world to finding personal meaning or personal significance in the event. In some cases, distress and growth can coexist. Distress, such as experiencing intrusion and avoidance symptoms, may be understood as efforts at cognitive processing of the event, which may be a necessary element to successful adaptation and growth. In some cases, distress may be a necessary antecedent or impetus to the process of growth.

Finally, resilience can be viewed as a buffer that can be fostered at any stage of the recovery process and as a collection of resources that can be drawn on in the promotion of growth in the therapeutic process. Although additional research is needed to fully delineate the protective processes and mechanisms that enable resilience and positive adaptation in the face of adversity, therapy can be an important venue to optimize an individual's resilience and thriving in these times of terrorism.

Summary Points

- Not all changes due to traumatic experience are negative. A range of outcomes following trauma are possible, including positive trauma-related developments such as resilience and thriving.
- When considering possible adaptations following trauma, it is important to look at the process of adaptation, not just the final outcome. A process view investigates trajectories of functioning over time from pretrauma levels to the present.
- Several factors, including the following, contribute to the course adaptation takes and to its final product: specific features of the traumatic experience, the individual's personality and history, personality factors, emotion regulation strategies and other styles of coping, cognitive representations of the experience, and environmental factors (Butler et al., 2007; Garlan et al., 2005).
- Resilience can be identified in the initial reaction to a traumatic event, in features of the recovery path associated with achieving a return to baseline functioning, and in the final product of the adaptation (Butler et al., 2007).
- Growth is signified by postevent adaptation that exceeds pre-event levels of functioning.
- Finding meaning—both in comprehending the event and in identifying its personal significance—is common to positive adaptation (Janoff-Bulman & Frantz, 1997).
- Distress and growth can coexist, suggesting that people can fare relatively well in some areas, and even grow in others, while still experiencing distress. Thus, a single global outcome measure may not truly capture the presentation.
- There has been an important shift in the clinical view of traumatic responses, from one concerned with symptoms and deficits to one that also encompasses the struggle to find meaning or benefits or even the experience of distress as antecedents of potential growth.

- Psychotherapy can facilitate positive adaptation following trauma. Clinicians can facilitate growth by attending to how survivors showed strength and ability throughout the course of their lives and their traumatic experience (Calhoun & Tedeschi, 2006).
- Clinicians can also support the growth that the client achieves by means of the creation of the trauma narrative and endeavors to make meaning of the event by (a) supporting and encouraging positive changes in therapy, (b) acknowledging both their patients' struggle and pain and the positive changes or benefits they have experienced, and (c) avoiding superficial statements that may instead encourage denial or cognitive avoidance (Calhoun & Tedeschi, 1998).
- Many tools are available to clinicians to assist survivors of terrorism and combat, as well as first responders and military families, in fostering resilience during recovery (e.g., Butler et al., 2003; Garlan et al., 2005; Carlson et al., 2003; Leskin et al., 2003).

REFERENCES

Affleck, G., & Tennen, H. (1996). Construing benefits from adversity: Adaptational significance and dispositional underpinnings. *Journal of Personality, 64,* 899–922.

Aldwin, C. M. (1994). *Stress, coping, and development: An integrative perspective.* New York: Guilford Press.

Bonanno, G. A. (2004). Loss, trauma, and human resilience—Have we underestimated the human capacity to thrive after extremely aversive events? *American Psychologist, 59,* 20–28.

Butler, L. D., Blasey, C. M., Garlan, R. W., McCaslin, S. E., Azarow, J., Chen, X., et al. (2005). Posttraumatic growth following the terrorist attacks of September 11, 2001: Cognitive, coping and trauma symptom predictors in an internet convenience sample. *Traumatology, 11*(4), 247–267.

Butler, L. D., Hobfoll, S. E., & Keane, T. M. (2003). *Fostering resilience in response to terrorism: A fact sheet for psychologists working with adults.* Washington, DC: American Psychological Association.

Butler, L. D., Morland, L. A., & Leskin, G. A. (2007). Psychological resilience in the face of terrorism. In B. Bongar, L. M. Brown, L. E. Beutler, J. N. Breckenridge, & P. G. Zimbardo (Eds.), *Psychology of terrorism* (pp. 400–417). New York: Oxford University Press.

Calhoun, L. G., & Tedeschi, R. G. (1998). Posttraumatic growth: Future directions. In R. G. Tedeschi, C. L. Park, & L. G. Calhoun (Eds.), *Posttraumatic growth: Positive change in the aftermath of crisis* (pp. 215–238). Mahwah, NJ: Erlbaum.

Calhoun, L. G., & Tedeschi, R. G. (1999). *Facilitating posttraumatic growth: A clinician's guide.* Mahwah, NJ: Erlbaum.

Calhoun, L. G., & Tedeschi, R. G. (2006). *Handbook of posttraumatic growth research and practice.* Mahwah, NJ: Erlbaum.

Carlson, L., James, L., Hobfoll, S. E., & Leskin, G. A. (2003). *Fostering resilience in response to terrorism: For psychologists working with military families* (Fact Sheet). Washington, DC: American Psychological Association.

Carver, C. S. (1998). Resilience and thriving: Issues, models, and linkages. *Journal of Social Issues, 54,* 245–266.

Davis, C. J., Nolen-Hoeksema, S., & Larson, J. (1998). Making sense of loss and benefiting from the experience: Two construals of meaning. *Journal of Personality and Social Psychology, 75,* 561–574.

Elder, G. H., & Clipp, E. C. (1989). Combat experience and emotional health: Impairment and resilience in later life. *Journal of Personality, 57*(2), 311–341.

Erbes, C., Eberly, R., Dikel, T., Johnsen, E., Harris, I., & Engdahl, B. (2005). Posttraumatic growth among American former prisoners of war. *Traumatology, 11*(4), 285–295.

Foa, E. B. (2006). Psychosocial therapy for posttraumatic stress disorder. *Journal of Clinical Psychiatry, 6,* 740–745.

Foa, E. B., Cahill, S. P., Boscarino, J. A., Hobfoll, S. E., Lahad, M., McNally, R. J., et al. (2005). Social, psychological, and psychiatric interventions following terrorist attacks: Recommendations for practice and research. *Neuropsychopharmacology, 30,* 1806–1817.

Foa, E. B., Keane, T. M., & Friedman, M. (2004). *Effective treatments for PTSD: Practice guidelines from the international society for traumatic stress studies.* New York: Guilford Press.

Fontana, A., & Rosenheck, R. (1998). Psychological benefits and liability of traumatic exposure in the war zone. *Journal of Traumatic Stress, 11,* 485–503.

Frazier, P., Conlon, A., & Glaser, T. (2001). Positive and negative life changes following sexual assault. *Journal of Consulting and Clinical Psychology, 69*(6), 1048–1055.

Garlan, R. W., Butler, L. D., & Spiegel, D. (2005). Psychosocial resilience and terrorism. *Directions in Psychiatry, 25,* 151–163.

Garmezy, N. (1985). Stress-resistant children: The search for protective factors. In J. E. Stevenson (Ed.), *Recent research in developmental psychopathology* (pp. 213–233). Oxford: Pergamon Press.

Gersons, B. P. R., & Carlier, I. (2000, March 16–19). *Helping police in coping with trauma: A public health approach.* Paper presented to the third world conference for the International Society for Traumatic Stress Studies, Melbourne, Australia.

Hembree, E. A., & Foa, E. B. (2000). Posttraumatic stress disorder: Psychological factors and psychosocial interventions. *Journal of Clinical Psychiatry, 61,* 33–39.

Janoff-Bulman, R. (1992). *Shattered assumptions: Towards a new psychology of trauma.* New York: Free Press.

Janoff-Bulman, R., & Frantz, C. M. (1997). The impact of trauma on meaning: From meaningless world to meaningful life. In M. Power & C. Brewin (Eds.), *Transformation of meaning in psychological therapies: Integrating theory and practice* (pp. 91–106). Chichester, West Sussex, England: Wiley.

Joseph, S. (2004). Client centered psychotherapy, posttraumatic stress and posttraumatic growth: Theoretical perspectives and practical implications. *Psychology and Psychotherapy: Theory, Research, and Practice, 77,* 101–120.

Joseph, S., & Linley, P. A. (2005). Positive adjustment to threatening events: An organismic valuing theory of growth through adversity. *Review of General Psychology, 9*(3), 262–280.

Joseph, S., Linley, P. A., Andrews, L., Harris, G., Howle, B., Woodward, C., et al. (2005). Assessing positive and negative changes in the aftermath of adversity: Psychometric evaluation of the Changes in Outlook Questionnaire. *Psychological Assessment, 17,* 70–80.

Joseph, S., Williams, R., & Yule, W. (1993). Changes in outlook following disaster: The preliminary development of a measure to assess positive and negative responses. *Journal of Traumatic Stress, 6,* 271–279.

Kessler, R. C., Sonnega, A., Bromet, E., Hughes, M., & Nelson, C. B. (1995). Posttraumatic stress disorder in the National Comorbidity Survey. *Archives of General Psychiatry, 52,* 1048–1060.

Kloner, R. (2006). Natural and unnatural triggers of myocardial infarction. *Progress in Cardiovascular Diseases, 48*(4), 285–300.

Lechner, S. C., Zakowski, S. G., Antoni, M. H., Greenhawt, M., Block, K., & Block, P. (2003). Do sociodemographic and disease-related variables influence benefit-finding in cancer patients? *Psycho-Oncology, 12,* 491–499.

Lepore, S., & Revenson, T. (2006). Relationships between posttraumatic growth and resilience: Recovery, resistance, and reconfiguration. In L. G. Calhoun & R. G. Tedeschi (Eds.), *Handbook of posttraumatic growth* (pp. 24–46). Mahwah, NJ: Erlbaum.

Leskin, G. A., Morland, L. A., Whealin, J., Everly, G., Litz, B., & Keane, T. (2003). *Fostering resilience in response to terrorism: For psychologists working with first responders* (Fact Sheet). Washington, DC: American Psychological Association.

Lev-Wiesel, R., & Amir, M. (2006). Growing out of ashes: Posttraumatic growth among holocaust child survivors. In L. G. Calhoun & R. G. Tedeschi (Eds.), *Handbook of posttraumatic growth: Research and practice* (pp. 248–263). Mahwah, NJ: Erlbaum.

Linley, P. A., & Joseph, S. (2004). Positive change following trauma and adversity: A review. *Journal of Traumatic Stress, 17,* 11–21.

Linley, P. A., Joseph, J., Cooper, R., Harris, S., & Meyer, C. (2003). Positive and negative changes following vicarious exposure to the September 11 terrorist attacks. *Journal of Traumatic Stress, 16*(5), 481–485.

Masten, A. S. (2001). Ordinary magic—Resilience processes in development. *American Psychologist, 56,* 227–238.

McMillen, J. C., & Fisher, R. H. (1998). The Perceived Benefits Scales: Measuring perceived positive life changes after negative events. *Social Work Research, 22*(3), 173–187.

Nerken, I. R. (1993). Grief and the reflective self: Toward a clearer model of loss resolution and growth. *Death Studies, 17,* 1–26.

Norris, F. H., Friedman, M. J., Watson, P. J., Byrne, C. M., Diaz, E., & Kaniasty, K. (2002). 60,000 disaster victims speak: Pt. I. An empirical review of the empirical literature, 1981–2001. *Psychiatry, 65,* 207–239.

O'Leary, V. E., & Ickovics, J. R. (1995). Resilience and thriving in response to challenge: An opportunity for a paradigm shift in women's health. *Women's Health: Research on Gender, Behavior, and Policy, 1,* 121–142.

Park, C. L., Cohen, L. H., & Murch, R. L. (1996). Assessment and prediction of stress-related growth. *Journal of Personality, 64,* 71–105.

Paton, D., & Stephens, C. (1996). Training and support for emergency responders. In D. Paton & J. Violanti (Eds.), *Traumatic stress in critical occupations: Recognition, consequences, and treatment.* Springfield, IL: Charles C Thomas.

Rosner, R., & Powell, S. (2006). Posttraumatic growth after war. In L. G. Calhoun & R. G. Tedeschi (Eds.), *Handbook of posttraumatic growth: Research and practice* (pp. 197–213). Mahwah, NJ: Erlbaum.

Saakvitne, K. W., Tennen, H., & Affleck, G. (1998). Exploring thriving in the context of clinical trauma theory: Constructivist self development theory. *Journal of Social Issues, 54,* 279–299.

Schlenger, W. E., Caddell, J. M., Ebert, L., Jordan, K., Rourke, K. M., Wilson, D., et al. (2002). Psychological reactions to terrorist attacks: Findings from the National Study of Americans' Reactions to September 11. *Journal of the American Medical Association, 288,* 581–588.

Schuster, M. A., Stein, B. D., Jaycox, L. H., Collins, R. L., Marshall, G. N., Elliott, M. N., et al. (2001). A national survey of stress reactions after the September 11, 2001, terrorist attacks. *New England Journal of Medicine, 345*(20), 1507–1512.

Seligman, M. E. P., & Csikszentmihalyi, M. (2000). Positive psychology: An introduction. *American Psychologist, 55,* 5–14.

Silver, R. C., Holman, E. A., McIntosh, D. N., Poulin, M., & Gil-Rivas, V. (2002). Nationwide longitudinal study of psychological responses to September 11. *Journal of the American Medical Association, 288,* 1235–1244.

Taylor, S. E. (1983). Adjustment to threatening events: A theory of cognitive adaptation. *American Psychologist, 38,* 1161–1173.

Tedeschi, R. G., & Calhoun, L. G. (1995). *Trauma and transformation: Growing in the aftermath of suffering.* Thousand Oaks, CA: Sage.

Tedeschi, R. G., & Calhoun, L. G. (1996). The Posttraumatic Growth Inventory: Measuring the positive legacy of trauma. *Journal of Traumatic Stress, 9*(3), 455–472.

Tedeschi, R. G., & Calhoun, L. G. (2004). Posttraumatic growth: Conceptual foundations and empirical evidence. *Psychological Inquiry, 15*(1), 1–18.

Wortman, C. B., & Silver, R. C. (1989). The myths of coping with loss. *Journal of Consulting and Clinical Psychology, 57*(3), 349–357.

Zoellner, T., & Maercker, A. (2006). Posttraumatic growth in clinical psychology— A critical review and introduction of a two component model. *Clinical Psychology Review, 26*(5), 626–653.

CHAPTER 4

Positive Effects of Terrorism and Posttraumatic Growth: An Individual and Community Perspective

CARMELO VÁZQUEZ, PAU PÉREZ-SALES, and GONZALO HERVÁS

T HE NEGATIVE IMPACT of terrorism on people and communities is well known (Danieli, Brom, & Sills, 2005). But there is also increasing evidence of positive elements and, eventually, of possible posttraumatic growth associated with the individual and community impact of terrorist acts. In this chapter, we review those elements. Social and community aspects are difficult to assess, but it is essential to study the community impact of terrorism because the goal of terrorist acts is to intimidate society as a whole. Therefore, social researchers and mental health professionals should look at the effects, both negative and positive, that terrorism may have on society in addition to its direct impact on individuals.

Can collective traumas promote positive social changes? Is contemporary European society better off after the two devastating wars in the twentieth century? Did the nuclear bombs dropped by the United States on Hiroshima and Nagasaki, or the testimonies about the European *Shoah* promote a more profound and human social view? These issues are related to the debate about whether extreme situations can be historical opportunities for positive collective actions (Lifton, 1993) and whether it makes any sense to talk about progress in the history of humanity (Nisbet, 1980).

Extreme adverse situations, such as collective violence, can also be an element of improvement of the social fabric (Martín Beristain, 2006;

We wish to thank Nansook Park and Virginia Navascues for their help in translating this chapter and Maitane Arnoso for her invaluable help with the data search.

Tedeschi, 1999). Studies based on field investigations, polls, and surveys, or even studies about negative psychological reactions, allow us to address this issue. In the following pages, we present a review of the literature about the impact of terrorism on diverse positive domains of personal and group functioning: (a) development of new strengths and skills, (b) altruism, (c) sharing emotions, (d) changes in cognitive schemas, and (e) positive emotions.

THE IDIOSYNCRASY OF TERRORIST VIOLENCE

According to the World Health Organization (WHO), terrorism can be defined as collective violence that is inflicted by "larger groups such as states, organized political groups, militia groups and terrorist organizations" (WHO, 2002, p. 31). The type of violence inflicted is specified in the United Nations definition of terrorism:

> Any act intended to cause death or serious bodily injury to a civilian, or to any other person not taking an active part in the hostilities in a situation of armed conflict, when the purpose of such acts, by their very nature or context, is to intimidate a population, or to compel a government or an international organization to do or to abstain from doing any act. (Article 2(b) of the International Convention for the Suppression of the Financing of Terrorism, United Nations, 1999)

Almost all definitions consider two large categories of terrorism: (1) State terrorism seeks the control of society and its citizens through the real or psychological use of intimidation and terror; it probably is and has been the most usual type of terror; (2) terrorism as *asymmetric warfare*, is defined as a form of conflict in which "an organized group—lacking conventional military strength and economic power—seeks to attack the weak points inherent in relatively affluent and open societies. The attacks take place with unconventional weapons and tactics and with no regard to military or political codes of conduct" (WHO, 2002, p. 241). In both kinds of terrorism, the aim of the terrorist actions is to achieve political goals by frightening and provoking panic in the civil population (Chomsky, 2004). As of the 1980s, there are data about the effects of state terrorism on the civil population, mostly based on the individual and community works of groups of psychologists and psychiatrists in countries under military governments, especially in Latin America (e.g., Agger & Buus Jensen, 1996; Lira, 1989; Martin Baró, 1990). Much less literature has been published on terrorism as a sort of irregular war (Corrado & Tompkins, 1989).

Terrorist violence may be potentially more devastating than other disasters and types of violence (Baum & Dougall, 2002; Curran, 1988; Torabi & Seo, 2004) for the following reasons:

- It involves deliberate intention of harm.
- It can target populous areas rather than specific targets.
- It often lacks a clear end point as the threats are usually permanent.
- In terrorism, nobody can be sure whether the worst is over or is yet to come.

The kind of terrorism observed in the 9/11 attacks and similar acts (the bomb explosions in Madrid, March 11, 2004, or in London, July 7, 2006) represent a specific modality of terrorist attack: a single episode, unrepeated, and coming from external enemies (in these attacks, the author was probably al-Qaeda). Terrorism can have even more devastating personal and collective effects when it is the consequence of civil conflicts or is carried out by terrorists from the one's own social group. The attacks on the United States by al-Qaeda resulted in an upsurge of patriotism, a greater feeling of social cohesion, and stronger faith in any decision that the government might take, whereas in Sri Lanka (Somasundaram, 2004), Northern Ireland (Campbell, Cairns, & Mallett, 2004), or the Basque Country in Spain (Tejerina, 2000), internal terrorist violence, carried out by members of the same community or country, has probably had negative effects on the population by creating a climate of collective suspicion, mistrust, and destruction of the moral system of the country.

Because "the purpose of most terrorists is to change the behavior of others by frightening or terrifying them" (Fullerton, Ursano, Norwood, & Holloway, 2003, p. 2), studies of the effects of terrorism in the general population, which is typically the ultimate target of terrorist activity, is particularly relevant. Most of these studies have been carried out with direct victims or with persons who were close to the victims, rather than in the general population (Danieli et al., 2005; Norris et al., 2002), and generally were done months or years after the events (North & Pfefferbaum, 2002). The 9/11 attacks on American soil led to an important change in this tendency. First, researchers responded rapidly to assess the psychological impact of the attacks. The earlier studies were conducted 2 to 3 days after the massacre (Schuster et al., 2001) and 1 to 2 months later (Galea et al., 2002; Schlenger et al., 2002; Silver, Holman, McIntosh, Poulin, & Gil-Rivas, 2002). Second, the populations under scrutiny were not only those directly affected who lived in the New York City metropolitan area or in Washington, DC (Galea et al., 2002; Schlenger et al., 2002) but also citizens from distant areas of the country whose exposure to the events was mainly indirect, through the intensive media coverage provided by TV, radio, and newspapers (Schlenger et al., 2002; Whalen, Henker, King, Jamner, & Levine, 2004). This double strategy (rapid studies focused on general population) has also been set up in subsequent terrorist attacks in Madrid (Miguel-Tobal et al., 2006; Vázquez, Hervás, & Pérez-Sales, 2006) and London (Rubin, Brewin,

Greenberg, Simpson, & Wessely, 2006). Therefore, a large part of the data that we present here mentions studies of 9/11 and afterward, while acknowledging a rich tradition of previous studies of previous conflicts, many of a qualitative nature (e.g., Lira, 1989; Martin-Baró, 1990; Martín Beristain, 1989).

A third relevant aspect that has characterized research after 9/11 is that it generated an extensive series of studies, not only in the well-known area of psychopathological reactions to stress (see reviews in Miller & Heldring, 2004; Vázquez, Pérez-Sales, & Matt, 2006) but also about citizens' attitudes, beliefs, values, and behaviors, some of which could be considered positive. This broader view, to some extent, overcomes the typical limitations of studies on the impact of trauma that have focused almost exclusively on the analysis of symptoms and reactions to stress in the direct victims of the traumatic events (Mehl & Pennebaker, 2003).

THE EFFECTS OF TERRORISM IN THE GENERAL POPULATION: PSYCHOPATHOLOGY, RESILIENCE, OR POSITIVE CHANGES?

Violence has harmful effects on human beings of any culture, geographic area, or social class (WHO, 2002). There is abundant literature on the effects of traumatic events and disasters on human beings (Norris et al., 2002). As expected, terrorist attacks have important psychological effects on the direct victims (e.g., DiMaggio & Galea, 2006), which, moreover, seem long-lasting (Baca, Baca-García, Pérez-Rodriguez, & Cabanas, 2005; Desivilya, Gal, & Ayalon, 1996).

But what about the general population, which is the end target of terrorist attacks? The existing data offer a very different panorama from that of direct victims. Despite the frequently alarmist discourse of the political and academic authorities (see Pérez-Sales & Vázquez, in press), the data show that the impact is usually much more limited than would be expected (Silver et al., 2005; Vázquez, 2005). Despite numerous initial reactions of moderate or high stress in the general population (Galea et al., 2002; Miguel-Tobal et al., 2006; Schlenger et al., 2002; Schuster et al., 2001), most of the studies have failed to reveal high rates of posttraumatic stress disorder (PTSD; see reviews in Silver et al., 2005; and Vázquez, 2005), or concomitant increases in the use of mental health services (Rosenheck & Fontana, 2003) and psychotropics (McCarter & Goldman, 2002).

In fact, the pattern of the general population is more often one of resilience than of vulnerability to terrorist acts. Resilience has been defined as "the ability . . . to maintain a relatively stable, healthy level of psychological functioning" in the face of highly adverse events (Bonanno, 2004, pp. 20–21) or "the adult capacity to maintain healthy, symptom-free functioning" (Bonanno, Galea, Bucciarelli, & Vlahov, 2006, p. 81). Although resilience to trauma has conventionally been thought to be rare, only emerging in psychologically exceptional individuals (McFarlane & Yehuda, 1996), the data show that most people who face potentially traumatic situations react without displaying signs of major psychopathologies (Kessler, Sonnega, Bromet, Hughes, & Nelson, 1995). Many people display no psychological effects, not even short-lived ones. In a prospective study, Bonanno et al. (2006) showed that 65.1% of their probability sample (N = 2,752) of New York area residents had either no PTSD symptoms—as assessed by a checklist administered by telephone—or just one symptom during the 6 months following the 9/11 terrorist attacks. The frequency of resilience, defined as absence of PTSD, was surprisingly high even among people who were in the World Trade Center (N = 22) or who were physically wounded in the attack (N = 59)—53.5% and 32.8%, respectively, showed resilience.

To assess resilience adequately without resorting to a method based exclusively on the absence of clinically significant symptoms, people's daily functioning and their capacity to react adaptively to adversity (Vázquez, Cervellón, Pérez-Sales, Vidales, & Gaborit, 2005), to learn from the experience (United Nations International Strategy for Disaster Reduction [UNISDR], 2005), or to implement capacity-building activities either for themselves or for the community (Pérez-Sales, Cervellón, Vázquez, Vidales, & Gaborit, 2005) must also be taken into account. Most of these aspects are usually neglected in current research on resilience in the context of trauma following terrorist attacks. Moreover, an aspect that should be adequately addressed is that probably not all initial reactions of resilience are beneficial at the long term. In a study on the psychological factors leading to resilience, Bonanno, Rennick, and Dekel (2005) studied a small sample (N = 73) of persons who were near the World Trade Center on September 11, 2001. Their results showed that the people who displayed higher positive biases of self-enhancement (a tendency toward overly positive or unrealistic self-serving biases) 18 months later were rated by their friends and relatives as decreasing in social adjustment and as being less honest. Thus, in some people, resilience may have long-term costs.

Many data suggest that the psychopathological symptoms of changes in the life of the general population after episodic terrorist events are fairly short-lived. Moreover, in situations of continued terrorism, a phenomenon of collective habituation is usually observed. Epidemiological studies on the impact of terrorism in the general population of Northern Ireland have generally shown a minimum effect in psychiatric symptoms, which some authors have interpreted as denial of the violence (Cairns & Wilson, 1989). In Colombia, the report of the People's Ombudsman for the year 2000 stated that, at that time, there was an average of one violent death every four hours and a kidnapping every six hours. Surprisingly, Colombia is systematically one of the countries with the highest rates of subjective happiness in the world. A similar phenomenon is observed in the Basque Country regarding the impact of separatist terrorism. In an extensive sociological survey carried out in 2004 with 2,506 interviews, it was reported that concern about terrorism as the main problem of the nation was lower in the Basque Country (27.9%) than in the rest of Spain (65.5%), which has been interpreted as a kind of normalization of violence and, possibly, a collective survival mechanism.

In addition to these elements of apparent resilience, research has also shown that continued terrorism may not significantly affect aspects of positive functioning. During a short telephone survey of a representative national sample of Israel ($N = 501$) comparing data on the impact of the first (2001) and the second (2004) Palestinian *intifadas*, Bleich, Gelkopf, Melamed, and Solomon (2006) found that the percentage of people who felt optimistic about the future (82%) and who felt self-efficacy about possible future terrorist attacks (76.6%) showed no significant changes. Likewise, in a sample of 747 junior high school students in three Israeli cities, Sharlin, Moin, and Yahav (2006) found that living under the threat of attacks did not seem to have a significant effect on children's emotional, cognitive, or behavioral development. Similar outcomes have been found in Palestinian victims of Israeli attacks (Punamaki, Qouta, & el-Sarraj, 1997).

Therefore, if the aim of attacks on the general population is to create a feeling of continued threat in the citizens, it is not clear whether this aim is easily achieved. The bombing of civil populations during World War II is another example of how such attacks can be integrated with relative ease into daily routines without having the expected negative impact and can even produce positive individual or collective changes (Jones, Woolven, Durodie, & Wessely, 2006).

POSITIVE EFFECTS ON INDIVIDUALS AND SOCIETIES

A majority of the people exposed to trauma report that they have experienced some kind of benefit derived not from the trauma itself but from the coping process linked to the adverse experience, which has been called benefit finding, positive life changes, stress-related growth, or posttraumatic growth (Helgeson, Reynolds, & Tomich, 2006; Linley & Joseph, 2004). Whether such positive experiences are a process, a result, or both (see Zoellner & Maercker, 2006), certain elements related to them can sometimes be observed even from the first moments of impact of a traumatic event (Fredrickson, Tugade, Waugh, & Larkin, 2003). In this section, we focus on the positive aspects—both individual and collective—because, whether they occur as a consequence of the shattering of schemas or as a result of a laborious psychological process (Vázquez, Castilla, & Hervás, 2007), such aspects are of great importance in revealing more comprehensively the diverse consequences of terrorist attacks.

DEVELOPMENT OF STRENGTHS AND NEW ABILITIES

There are many individual and collective testimonies of human groups confronting the impact of violence that include descriptions of processes of individual and group growth. From the biblical Exodus to the resistance in the ghettos or the popular struggles in the successive decolonization wars, the diverse forms of civil resistance and community growth seem to be a constant rather than an exception in the history of humanity:

> We learned to protect ourselves from terror with silence, we learned to protect ourselves with the help of prayer, but this was not enough and so, we [also] learned to protect ourselves from terror by taking decisions together. And we are still doing so. (Testimony of a victim's relative, National Committee of Displaced Persons of Peru, CONDECOREP, pp. 168–169)

Any potentially traumatic situation is a challenge to the people who suffer it. Challenges have the characteristic of making people give more than usual of themselves, and as a result, they can sometimes develop new skills or promote strengths that were to some extent hidden or underdeveloped. Research shows that terrorist attacks can lead to the development of different kinds of strength, at both a personal and a community level.

In El Salvador, almost 2 decades of state terrorism following the policy of razed earth caused the displacement and exile of more than 20,000 people, most of them women and children, to refugee camps in Honduras in the 1980s. In a two-phase retrospective study of a sample of 300 women who returned to the country in 1992 after the peace agreements, a significant increase was observed in the percentage of women who had learned new professions or skills, driven by the situation and their increased feelings of self-efficacy and their perception of personal agency (Vasquez, 2000).

In the case of the 9/11 attacks, a large-scale study over the Internet that included data from more than 4,000 people, compared the data of those who participated in the study before and after the attacks. The results showed that, following the attack, seven character strengths (gratitude, hope, kindness, leadership, love, faith, and teamwork) increased significantly, and moreover, this increase was sustained months later (Peterson & Seligman, 2003). It seems that, in addition to the collective negative impact, many individuals displayed significant positive changes in various strengths in the interpersonal area (kindness, leadership, love, and teamwork), and in aspects concerning the philosophy of life (spirituality), two areas in which improvements are often found after traumatic events (e.g., Ai, Evans-Campbell, Santangelo, & Cascio, 2006; Vázquez et al., 2005). Likewise, increase was observed in the ability to express hope and gratitude, aspects that have important emotional implications.

Despite the novelty of the field, this is not the only study focusing on the development of strengths after a terrorist attack. In a study carried out by our group after the March 11 attacks in Madrid, positive consequences of these attacks were examined (Vázquez, Hervás, et al., 2006). For this purpose, 3 to 4 weeks after the attacks, 502 people (students and general population) were assessed, of whom 20 had been directly exposed to the attacks and 43% knew someone who had been directly affected. Data were gathered about their perception of growth and learning after the attacks, as well as positive and negative emotions experienced, among other measures. The results showed that 31% of the participants perceived positive consequences from the attacks, whereas 61% reported having experienced learning. The area of most frequent growth was feeling closer to others (80% of the total sample), followed by higher social cohesion (79% of the total sample), and, last, feeling personally prepared for similar future situations (31% of the total sample).

It appears that terrorist attacks—originally planned to weaken society—can sometimes act as catalysts to develop strengths related to human relations, to improve social and community aspects, and even philosophical or spiritual aspects.

Altruism and Philanthropic Behaviors

Altruistic behaviors are usually common after disasters (Fischer, 1994). In the case of 9/11, in addition to the usual organizations that work in disasters and emergencies, new foundations were created (e.g., September 11 Fund) to channel assistance funds both at regional and state levels (Foundation Center, 2002; Renz, 2002a, 2002b). The financial aid received was unprecedented and by December 31, 2001, an estimated $1.9 billion had been received from businesses, foundations, and institutions for the recovery efforts (Steinberg & Rooney, 2005).

Although changes in individual philanthropic behaviors are more difficult to analyze, some data point in this direction. The national survey of Schuster et al. (2001), carried out September 14–19, 2001, with 560 participants, found that 36% of the adults interviewed said they had donated blood in response to the attacks. In the survey of the National Tragedy Study (September 13–19), Smith, Rasinski, and Toce (2001) observed that most American citizens engaged in positive civic actions as a response to the terrorist attacks: 59% of the general population performed at least some of these actions (charities, blood donation, or volunteering for organizations). Penner (2004) also verified that visits to the web site www.volunteermatch.org, which offers users a list of organizations in which people can volunteer, tripled in the days following the attacks, compared with the average of previous years, and this effect was maintained for about 5 weeks, at which time, the visits returned to the previous levels. Increase in altruistic behavior was also observed after the March 11, 2004, attacks in Madrid (Conejero, de Rivera, Páez, & Jiménez, 2004), especially in the parts of the country with a stronger feeling of belonging to a national Spanish identity.

Studies carried out with longer time intervals than the first few days after a terrorist attack offer even higher estimations of these kinds of behavior. A poll carried out October 5–8, 2001, found that 70% of Americans reported some type of charitable involvement (Independent Sector, 2001). Likewise, the Center on Philanthropy at Indiana University performed a phone survey ("America Gives"), between October and November 2001 to quantify the help provided by individuals after the 9/11 attacks. A total of 1,304 randomly selected American adults were asked about philanthropic behaviors. A total of 74.4% of the surveyed people responded to the tragedy with some kind of charitable activity (giving money; donating food, clothing, blood; or giving volunteer hours to help the victims; Steinberg & Rooney, 2005).

Again, these results show that terrorist attacks can have positive and unexpected behavioral effects that, although temporary, may be important social cohesion elements and may favor the creation of a more positive shared social script of the events.

SOCIAL SHARING OF EMOTIONS

Talking to others is a common mechanism that is usually displayed when confronting traumatic events, and it may have a positive adaptive value. "Putting emotions into words" may have important social, cognitive, and emotional implications by improving one's own emotional regulation and receiving instrumental information to cope with the effects of the trauma (Zech, Rimé, & Nils, 2004). The disclosure of emotions probably favors social cohesion and the feeling of collective identity that allows people to verify that their own emotions and reactions are also experienced by others and to construct a collective script of the disaster (Gortner & Pennebaker, 2003; Meichenbaum, 2005).

Using a nonintrusive method—an electronic recorder device—Mehl and Pennebaker (2003) recorded conversations of a small sample of U.S. university students in naturalistic settings, starting September 10, 2001, and for

10 days following September 11. An interesting finding of the study is that, although participants did not change in their overall amount of interactions, they gradually shifted from group conversations and phone calls to in-person dyadic interactions. Moreover, whereas 2 days after the attack, 35% to 55% of the conversation topics were related to the attack, 10 days later this topic was only present in 5% of the conversations. The results of the study indicate that when facing a terrorist attack, the social expression of emotions and the way in which they are produced change (from a group format, that indicates more physical proximity and coming physically closer to others, to a dyadic format). Thus, just as the trauma-related symptoms decrease quickly a few weeks after a terrorist attack (Galea et al., 2003), the initial emotional expressions also seem to go back to normal, and have an adaptive value.

Although there may be differences in personality and cognitive style, and gender or cultural differences (see Singh-Manoux, 2001) in the use and effectiveness of social sharing, this could be one of the mechanisms that, in general, facilitate positive processing of trauma (Fredrickson et al., 2003), as long as the right conditions are present, such as having an "appropriate target" (Lepore, Ragan, & Jones, 2000). Obviously, not all social contexts in which terrorist attacks occur favor this possibility. Whereas in attacks like those of Madrid or the United States, talking with anyone and condemning the deeds was possible and probably had positive consequences, in situations of ethnical conflict or of clashes within a community or nation, the expression of emotions may be severely limited, making healthy emotional processing more difficult (e.g., Somasundaram, 2004).

Demonstrations are another interesting kind of social reaction to attacks on a group. This is a frequent phenomenon in some countries (e.g., Spain or Italy) but almost nonexistent in others (e.g., the United States or Israel after suicide attacks), and is beginning to appear in Arab countries (e.g., Lebanon, Palestine). In Spain, after some of the most significant attacks of the terrorist organization ETA or after the attacks by al-Qaeda on March 11, 2001, there were multitudinous demonstrations in which millions of people participated on the same day, and that have become symbolic milestones of the collective chronicle of active resistance to terror (Sabucedo, Rodríguez, & López, 2000). These collective demonstrations of cohesion and social attachment have probably had the instrumental value of increasing the perception of collective control over terrorist violence (Funes, 1998; Tejerina, 2000). Participating in these acts may also have other positive psychological effects. In a sample of 1,650 university students and their acquaintances or relatives, Basabe, Páez, and Rimé (2004) observed that attending demonstrations in the days following the March 11, 2004, terrorist attacks in Madrid predicted a more positive and benevolent image of oneself, of others, and of the world at 3-week and 2-month follow-ups. Therefore, active participation in demonstrations of rejection of violence may also positively affect participants' cognitive schemas.

Changes in Worldviews

The individual and collective effects of terrorism, both in behavioral and in cognitive domains, can be diverse. Torabi and Seo (2004) investigated changes in Americans' lifestyle as a consequence of 9/11, by means of a telephone survey performed between July 23 and September 8, 2002. Using random-digit dialing in a nationally representative sample of 807 U.S. adults, 29% ($N = 236$) of the respondents reported some behavioral changes in their lives, and 7% had experienced severe negative changes due to the 9/11 attacks, and such changes were still affecting their lives at the time of the interview (they had increased their precautions concerning surroundings and people, they avoided crowded areas, felt apprehension about deployment of loved ones, or were reluctant to fly). About 30% reported having experienced more positive than negative changes and, interestingly, most of these changes considered positive by the interviewees were related to the cognitive domain (becoming more appreciative of life and family or reinforcing some aspect of personal identity such as becoming more patriotic, more spiritual, or religious); see also Ai et al. (2006).

The consequences of trauma (e.g., severity and duration of symptoms) may depend on the extent to which traumatic events violate individual assumptions that usually maintain beliefs about justice or perceptions of personal invulnerability and self-efficacy. Perhaps the most well known and extended model of inner representations is that of Janoff-Bulman (1992), who integrates previous related models (e.g., Epstein, 1991). This author proposed that, from early experiences, human beings normally develop a schema of the world based on three core assumptions:

1. The world and other people are benevolent.
2. The world and our personal experience are meaningful.
3. The self is worthy.

When traumatic experiences shatter these assumptions to any degree, psychological effects seem to be more severe. In a study with a sample of survivors of different types of trauma, Goldenberg and Matheson (2005) found that more damage to these inner representations is associated with passive coping strategies (avoidance, wishful thinking, and self-blame), which, in turn, is associated with more severe symptoms of PTSD.

In the tradition of so-called posttraumatic growth, it has been proposed that this shattering of schemas is a factor that can set off other posttraumatic growth processes more easily (Calhoun & Tedeschi, 2005; Tedeschi &

Calhoun, 1995). Although changes in schemas probably often occur gradually and progressively over one's lifetime, some intense experiences, such as terrorist attacks, may shatter these beliefs almost instantaneously (Janoff-Bulman, 1992, 2005), forcing the individual to activate a process of reconstruction that occasionally may lead to an intense experience of growth. Thus, one of the basic issues that should be addressed and which is of enormous importance, is not only psychological but also political: Can terrorism shatter people's core beliefs or assumptions? And, if so, can consequences of the shock also be positive?

Because of its characteristics (intentionality, unpredictability, continuous threat, etc.), terrorism probably directly affects these core assumptions as much or more than other kinds of human-induced violence (e.g., sexual assault, rape, interpersonal violence) that are known to affect inner representations (Goldenberg & Matheson, 2005).

One of the most probable hypotheses of the negative effects of terrorism is that it can shatter a generalized positive image of human beings and of justice and order in the world. Some studies with survivors of the Holocaust have found that, despite difficulties integrating what happened in their life trajectory (Shamai & Levin-Megged, 2006), some survivors say they acquired a deeper viewpoint of the meaning of life (Prager & Solomon, 1995). But the existence of positive consequences in the view of the world and of oneself is a controversial issue. In the only review published to date about the possibility of posttraumatic growth in times of war (Rosner & Powell, 2006), the authors conclude that, in the short term, there does not seem to be any evidence of its existence. Powell, Rosner, Butollo, Tedeschi, and Calhoun (2003) used the Posttraumatic Growth Inventory in two representative samples of adult ex-refugees and displaced people who lived in former Yugoslavia before the war and were currently living in Sarajevo, Bosnia, and Herzegovina, 3.5 years after the war. The authors found that participants' mean scores were much lower than the reported means of survivors of other traumatic situations.

There are few data about the effects of terrorism on the cognitive schemas of the general population. Using the World Assumption Scale (WAS; Janoff-Bulman, 1989), two longitudinal studies in the general population in Spain between 3 and 8 weeks after the March 11 terrorist attacks in Madrid found no changes in participants' benevolent view of the world or in their faith in other people (Techio & Calderón-Prada, 2005; Ubillos, Mayordomo, & Basabé, 2005).

Also using the WAS, Solomon and Laufer (2005) studied the world assumptions of 2,999 Israeli adolescents living in various zones that differed in the degree of exposure to political violence. The study showed that more negative world assumptions were associated with having suffered traumatic events in general, but they had no relation to the exposure to specific terrorist incidents. The best predictors of a positive view of the world was having adequate social support and a high religious and political commitment, rather than the terrorist incidents experienced. This probably suggests a process of habituation to violence.

In the National Tragedy Study (Smith et al., 2001), a nationally representative random telephone survey was performed with 2,126 U.S. residents about the emotional impact of the 9/11 tragedy. This survey was carried out between September 13 and September 27, 2001, and also included some items and indicators from the General Social Surveys from 1972, which makes the analysis of the results of this study especially interesting. Moreover, to analyze changes over time, the authors made a second survey between January 10 and March 4, 2002, reinterviewing a substantial subsample of the participants of the first round (Rasinski, Berktold, Smith, & Albertson, 2002).

Table 4.1 displays some of the more relevant results about positive emotions experienced and variables related to change in schemas of the world and humankind. After the attacks, national pride increased in the general population of the United States, a score that is normally already among the two or three highest in the world (Smith & Kim, 2006). Moreover, pride in specific domains, such as the army and the history of the country increased even more. Thus, the elements of cohesion and national and collective identity apparently underwent a significant increase in American citizens after 9/11. In addition, according to some authors, a decline in public cynicism about the government and higher cohesion between different political parties in those moments of crisis were also observed (Chanley, 2002).

This increased national pride was accompanied by an increase in behaviors such as the use of the national flag in cars, gardens, houses, or workplaces. In fact, between 74% and 82% of Americans engaged in flag-display behaviors, according to several national surveys (see Skikta, 2006). It is not clear whether this exhibition of signs of national identity is an indicator of ostentation of strength, intimidation, or nationalist exaltation (an uncritical acceptance of national superiority and dominant status of one's nation) or, as suggested by Skikta, it is simply a manifestation of positive emotions linked to patriotism and to in-group enhancement. In any case, this kind of patriotic exaltation is not at all a universal reaction. In Spain, after the March 11 attacks, only a minor nationalist response was observed. Interestingly enough, there was also an absence of negative changes in Spanish citizens' attitude toward the Arab-Muslim population (Moya & Morales-Marente, 2005; Techio & Calderón-Prada, 2005), which suggests that the core assumption of the benevolence of humankind was not affected by the al-Qaeda terrorist attacks.

Table 4.1

Changes in National Pride, Confidence in Institutions, Misanthropy, and Worldviews after the September 11 Attacks in the United States

	GSSS[a] 1996–2000 (%)	National Tragedy Study			
		2001[b]		2002[c]	
		National (%)	New York (%)	National (%)	New York (%)
A. National pride (General)					
I would rather be a citizen of America than of any other country in the world. (Agree)	90.4	97.4	92.4	96.7	91.8
Generally speaking, America is a better country than most other countries. (Agree)	80.2	85.3	81.0	86.2	83.3
There are some things about America today that make me feel ashamed of America. (Disagree)	18.4	40.0	46.4	49.1	39.9
B. National pride (Domain-specific: Very proud of America for . . .)					
America's armed forces	47.1	79.5	75.7	83.7	76.2
Its history	47.1	68.3	58.1	55.7	51.3
The way democracy works	26.8	60.6	54.7	55.4	55.4
C. Confidence in institutions (Great confidence in . . .)					
The military	39.7	77.4	68.4	80.7	73.3
Congress	12.7	43.4	43.8	31.3	36.2
Major companies	28.4	31.7	31.2	20.4	19.7
D. Misanthropy (People are . . .)					
Fair	51.6	63.2	61.7	64.1	56.8
Helpful	45.7	66.9	68.7	66.9	71.9
Trustworthy	35.0	41.3	30.9	39.2	32.1
E. Worldviews					
World is filled with evil and sin.	15.0	18.1	16.7	NA	NA
There is much goodness in the world, which hints at God's goodness.	58.0	62.1	57.8	NA	NA

(continued)

Table 4.1 *(Continued)*

	GSSS[a] 1996–2000 (%)	National Tragedy Study			
		2001[b]		2002[c]	
		National (%)	New York (%)	National (%)	New York (%)
Human nature is basically good.	55.4	54.4	53.6	NA	NA
Human nature is fundamentally perverse and corrupt.	18.9	27.5	26.8	NA	NA

[a] General Social Survey data, 1996–2000. Data shown in the table are from the most recent round. *General Social Surveys, 1972–2000: Cumulative Codebook,* by J. A. Davis, T. W. Smith, and P. V. Marsden, 2001, Chicago: National Organization for Research at the University of Chicago.

[b] Data from *America Rebounds: A National Study of Public Responses to the September 11th Terrorist Attacks: Preliminary Findings,* by T. W. Smith, K. A. Rasinski, and M. Toce, 2001, Chicago: National Organization for Research at the University of Chicago. Retrieved June 10, 2002, from www.norc.uchicago.edu/projects/reaction/pubresp.pdf.

[c] Data from *America Recovers: A Follow-Up to a National Study of Public Response to the September 11th Terrorist Attacks,* by K. A. Rasinski, J. Berktold, T. W. Smith, and B. L. Albertson, 2002, Chicago: National Organization for Research at the University of Chicago. Retrieved September 15, 2002, from www.norc.uchicago.edu/projects/reaction/pubresp2.pdf.

NA = Not available.

Taken conjointly, the data suggest that, at least with this kind of exogroup terrorism, terrorist attacks can have an unexpected rebound effect on national self-esteem and intragroup cohesion, which is probably the opposite from the effect intended by the terrorists. It is interesting to verify that, if we analyze the case of the United States, this increase in cohesion and national identity and pride in one's country did not occur at the expense of a decrease in positive core beliefs about humankind and the world. Therefore, in addition to the consistent data about resilience observed in the general population (Bonanno et al., 2006; Silver et al., 2005), beliefs about the goodness of human nature and the world in general remained unchanged and they also resisted the terrorist attacks of 9/11 in the United States. To sum up, at least in the paradigmatic case of the 9/11 terrorism, "national pride, confidence in institutions, and faith in people and human nature all have gained ground, with positive assessments generally outnumbering negative judgments" (Smith et al., 2001, p. 3).

POSITIVE EMOTIONS

Most of the research on the effects of trauma has typically focused on symptoms and adverse reactions (Yehuda, 2002) and hardly any attention has been paid to the presence of positive emotions, which might imply that negative emotions are much more frequent or intense than positive emotions in this kind of situation.

Some interesting exceptions that have addressed directly or indirectly the analysis of positive emotions in the context of these traumatic experiences can provide a different view. In the National Tragedy Study (Smith et al., 2001), the 10-item Bradburn Affect Balance Scale (Bradburn, 1969) was used to measure five positive and five negative feelings and emotions "during the past few weeks." The items included questions about feelings of depression, loneliness, and restlessness as well as feelings of being "on the top of the world," pleased, or proud. Aggregating the data of the study, 69.0% of the participants said they felt positive emotions during that time, and 33.7% felt negative emotions. Moreover, positive emotions were experienced more frequently—feeling "Pleased/Accomplished" (89%) and "Proud" (80%)—whereas the two emotions experienced less frequently were negative—feeling "Upset/Criticized" (24%) and "Lonely/Remote" (26%). It is surprising that, comparing the data of 2001 in the Bradburn Scale after the terrorist attacks with the series of data available since 1963, positive affect was, in general, above previous readings. In fact, looking at historical series of data, being proud of a compliment, being praised for an accomplishment, and feelings that "things were going your way" were at record highs.

In the study carried out by our group (Vazquez, Hervás, et al., 2006) after the March 11, 2004, attacks in Madrid, we found similar results. The most frequently experienced positive emotions were feelings of solidarity (85% of the sample), and the feelings of being a part of a community (82%). It is especially noteworthy that these were the most intense emotions in absolute terms, more than any negative emotion. (The intensity of positive emotions is represented in Table 4.2.)

The existence of positive emotions is not only a positive component itself, but it may also promote growth and the creation of positive meanings for the trauma. In the Madrid study just mentioned, we found that the perception of growth increased with the level of positive emotions experienced on the day of the attacks and following days; however, the feeling of growth had no significant relationship, either positive or negative, with the level of negative emotions experienced. That is, distress and negative emotions do not seem to affect the factors related to posttraumatic growth, but again, the level of positive emotions experienced promotes growth. If we analyze this relation in more detail, we observe that the positive emotions that are more closely associated with the feeling of growth after the event are those of feeling "determined" and "belonging to a nation." The correlations be-

Table 4.2

Mean and Standard Deviation of Intensity of Positive Emotions
after March 11 Madrid Terrorist Attacks

Positive Emotions	Mean	*SD*
Solidarity	3.12	.99
Part of a nation	3.07	1.04
Interested	2.51	1.11
Trust in others	1.77	1.04
Active	1.69	1.14
Strong	1.64	1.11
Peaceful	1.56	1.12
Determined	1.49	1.13
Grateful	1.12	1.37
Proud	1.09	1.34
Optimistic	0.74	0.92
Sense of safety	0.68	0.96
Sense of control	0.59	0.94
Cheerful	0.48	0.77
Inspired	0.42	0.78
Enthusiastic	0.30	0.65

Note: 4-point Likert Scale (ranging from 0 = none or very slightly to 4 = a lot).

Based on *The role of positive emotions on the psychological reactions following the Madrid, March 11, 2004, terrorist attacks,* by C. Vázquez, G. Hervás, and P. Pérez-Sales, 2006. Paper presented at the Third European Conference on Positive Psychology, Braga, Portugal.

tween perceptions of growth and different positive emotions are displayed in Table 4.3.

A similar example of the role of positive emotions is observed in a study that focuses on the positive effects of the 9/11 attacks and specifically analyzes the role of a resilient coping style and of positive emotions (Fredrickson et al., 2003). The most remarkable aspect of this study is that the design employed was both longitudinal and prospective. By coincidence, a few months before the terrorist attacks, 133 students from New York had been assessed on various personality measures such as optimism, resilient coping style, and life satisfaction, among others. The authors gathered data from 47 persons from the original sample (47%) 10 days after the attack. In this study, posttraumatic growth was conceptualized as the positive change in a three-factor variable: life satisfaction, optimism, and tranquility. It was found that resilient people were more apt to experience growth because of

Table 4.3
Zero-Order Correlations between Positive Emotions
and the Growth-Related Index

Positive Emotions	Growth-Related Index
Determined	.28*
Part of a nation	.26*
Attentive	.25*
Strong	.24*
Proud	.21*
Active	.21*
Grateful	.21*
Trust in others	.20*
Interested	.20*
Peaceful	.17*
Solidarity	.16*
Optimistic	.16*
Excited	.11**
Sense of control	.10**

*$p < .001$.

**$p < .05$.

Note: Only significant results reported.

Based on The role of positive emotions on the psychological reactions following the Madrid, March 11, 2004, terrorist attacks, by C. Vázquez, G. Hervás, and P. Pérez-Sales, 2006. Paper presented at the Third European Conference on Positive Psychology, Braga, Portugal.

the attacks and, interestingly, this relation was mediated by the level of positive emotions experienced on the day of the attacks and the following days. That is, resilient people grew more as a result of the attacks because they experienced more positive emotions after the attacks. This means that positive emotions are not only present, but may play a significant role in posttraumatic growth. This finding is coherent with the theory proposed by Fredrickson (2000), according to which, positive emotions promote broadening behavioral repertories and building new resources (the broaden-and-build theory).

The existence of positive aspects after traumatic events does not mean that the negative aspects are negligible. In a study carried out with a Spanish sample after the March 11 attacks, a direct and significant relation was found between the perception of positive and negative changes (Barbero-Val & Linley, 2006). People with more positive changes also reported a high level of negative changes, a fact that was also found in a British sample assessed after the 9/11 attacks in the United States (Linley, Joseph, Cooper, Harris, & Meyer, 2003). Thus, these results show that the existence of positive aspects does not imply the reduction of negative aspects, but, in contrast, they seem to support the idea that, to some extent, people must feel shaken by the traumatic experience before they can generate changes (Calhoun & Tedeschi, 2005). At the social level, the effects of the coexistence of positive and negative elements can also occur. The civil clash experienced in Sri Lanka, although it has had huge individual and social costs, has promoted cooperation and cohesion in groups and community organizations, which has led to some decline in the caste system and more protagonism of women in the social and political life of the country (Somasundaram, 2004).

LIMITATIONS OF CURRENT RESEARCH

Most of the quantitative research on the effects of terrorism comes from Western academic settings (DiMaggio & Galea, 2006), although proportionally, the most frequent form of terrorism is state terrorism in nonwestern countries (e.g., Guatemala, Colombia, Sri Lanka, South Africa, Indonesia, or Peru). This cultural bias is an important issue because, just as it is important to take into account idiosyncratic posttraumatic reactions in diverse cultures (de Jong, 2002), one could assume that the same thing holds true for positive reactions.

Another important limitation of the available literature is that most of it is descriptive and mainly focuses on epidemiological or clinical aspects of terrorist impact (Engdahl, 2005; Yehuda, 2002). There are very few studies about the psychological processes that are deployed in traumatic situations of this kind (see Joseph & Linley, 2006), and there is little information about the relation between clinical variables and psychological protection factors. As noted by Tedeschi (1999), almost all we know about posttraumatic growth comes from studies whose main goal was to determine the negative effects of trauma, mainly in the area of PTSD. Furthermore, few works are directly designed to study prospectively the variables that affect the onset and maintenance of posttraumatic growth or of positive aspects, whatever they may be, related to trauma. Future research should address the study of positive emotions as a goal in itself, for which assessment instruments and appropriate designs are required that would allow researchers to better determine the impact of trauma in multiple areas and domains.

SUMMARY

Throughout this chapter, we have analyzed investigations that share the attribute of showing that terrorist attacks may have unexpected positive consequences, both at an individual and a community level.

An important sociopolitical lesson can be learned. Governments that, reasonably, aim all their efforts and resources toward minimization of the negative effects derived from terrorist attacks, should not forget an important intervention area still to be developed: the promotion of positive aspects and growth (Pérez-Sales & Vázquez, in press; Wessely, 2004). Providing a relevant space for and facilitating the appearance of positive emotions such as solidarity or feelings of union can be an important catalyst of growth. The images of global solidarity with the victims of the 9/11 attacks that were transmitted by all the televisions in the world are a good example of how a space for positive elements may be provided, and together with the data reviewed herein, they are a reminder of how positive experiences can be potentially promoted in extensive levels of the population without having to resort to direct interventions.

The positive elements that can be found in adverse situations cannot just be algebraically subtracted from the negative results. These elements can coexist, offering complex individual and collective sceneries. As concluded by Torabi and Seo (2004) from the data of their study on the changes in lifestyle in American citizens after the 9/11 attacks, although this adverse incident "may have positive effects on individuals' mental and emotional health by having a common enemy, thereupon committing themselves to the common goal in a positive and proactive manner and sharing emotional ties with other people, it may also hurt flexibility and receptivity of individuals as well as society as a whole, which tends to harbor the vicious cycle leading to political violence or conflicts" (p. 188). Moreover, research on the positive aspects of adversity is beginning to show that the effects of benefit finding on health outcomes are not necessarily positive in all the domains of psychological functioning (Bonanno et al., 2005; Helgeson et al., 2006).

Future research should continue to examine the existence of other positive aspects to complete this alternative view about the consequences of terrorist attacks. Research on the individual and collective utility of positive emotions, as well as of the possible mechanisms involved in posttraumatic growth or benefit finding, would provide society as a whole with more resources to cope with situations of terror and political violence.

Summary Points (Practice)

- Positive emotions after terrorist attacks may promote resilience and growth. Thus, it could be helpful to design interventions aimed at the *promotion* of supporting and nourishing the emergence and maintenance of positive reactions in general, and positive emotions in particular.

- Given the role of *altruism* as a way of reacting positively to events, initiatives with the aim of channeling the diverse types of aid to the affected people may promote growth, both of the individuals and of society as a whole.

- Creating *spaces* in which to communicate emotions can have a beneficial effect on positive adaptation to the effects of the trauma.

- As with any other kind of trauma, it is important to assess and provide feedback about the *learning experienced* at the individual and collective level to promote a more complete perspective of the situation.

- *Symbolic elements* (e.g., flags, monuments, demonstrations) seem to be important to the processing of these kinds of events. In-depth research is needed to investigate how to channel these elements to achieve better adaptation.

Summary Points (Research)

- Most of the evidence gathered on the positive effects of traumatic events has been derived from studies whose goal was, paradoxically, to assess the negative impact of trauma. We need a new generation of studies whose chief aim is the direct assessment of individual and collective positive effects of terror, which use a wider and more comprehensive array of measures.

- When exploring positive and negative effects of terrorism, researchers should pay attention to the effects not only in individuals directly or indirectly affected but also in the *general population,* as this kind of violence is often directed at society itself.

- Researchers should analyze the effects of *different types* of terrorism. Most of the current empirical evidence is mainly based on just one type of terrorism that is common in modern Western societies (episodic attacks made by terrorists from other nations). This type of terrorist violence is not representative of the type of terrorism to which most world societies are exposed.

- We need more longitudinal studies on the dynamics of the changes, either positive or negative, induced by terrorist threats. It would be highly relevant to assess the extent to which initial positive emotions (e.g., feelings of social cohesion) are related—and how—to effects typically associated with the concept of posttraumatic growth (e.g., long-term improvements in individual or social functioning, changes in spirituality).

- It is also necessary to analyze whether some apparently positive effects (e.g., upsurge of patriotism) could have *collateral negative effects* (e.g., feelings of revenge).
- Further research is also needed on the extent to which short- or long-term positive reactions generated by terrorist attacks are adaptive or somehow associated with positive health outcomes.

REFERENCES

Agger I., & Buus Jensen, S. (1996). *Trauma and healing under state terrorism.* London: Zed Books.

Ai, A., Evans-Campbell, T., Santangelo, L., & Cascio, T. (2006). The traumatic impact of the September 11, 2001 terrorist attacks and the potential protection of optimism. *Journal of Interpersonal Violence, 21,* 689–700.

Baca, E., Baca-García, E., Pérez-Rodriguez, M., & Cabanas, M. L. (2005). Short- and long-term effects of terrorist attacks in Spain. In Y. Danieli, D. Brom, & J. Sills (Eds.), *The trauma of terrorism* (pp. 157–170). New York: Haworth Press.

Barbero-Val, E., & Linley, P. A. (2006). Posttraumatic growth, positive changes, and negative changes in Madrid residents following the March 11, 2004 Madrid train bombings. *Journal of Loss and Trauma, 11,* 409–424.

Basabé, N., Páez, D., & Rimé, B. (2004). Efectos y procesos psicosociales de la participación en manifestaciones después del atentado del 11 de marzo [Psychosocial effects and processes of the participation in demonstrations after the March 11th attack]. *Ansiedad y Estrés, 10,* 1–11.

Baum, A., & Dougall, A. L. (2002). Terrorism and behavioral medicine. *Current Opinion in Psychiatry, 15,* 617–621.

Bleich, A., Gelkopf, M., Melamed, Y., & Solomon, Z. (2006). Mental health and resiliency following 44 months of terrorism: A survey of an Israeli national representative sample. *BMC Medicine, 4,* 21. Available from www.biomedcentral.com /1741-7015/4/21/.

Bonanno, G. A. (2004). Loss, trauma and human resilience: Have we underestimated the human capacity to thrive after extremely aversive events? *American Psychologist, 59,* 20–28.

Bonanno, G. A., Galea, S., Bucciarelli, A., & Vlahov, D. (2006). Psychological resilience after disaster: New York City in the aftermath of the September 11th terrorist attack. *Psychological Science, 17,* 181–186.

Bonanno, G. A., Rennick, C., & Dekel, S. (2005). Self-enhancement among high-exposure survivors of the September 11th terrorist attack: Resilience or social maladjustment? *Journal of Personality and Social Psychology, 88,* 984–998.

Bradburn, N. M. (1969). *The structure of psychological well-being.* Chicago: Aldine.

Cairns, E., & Wilson, R. (1989). Coping with political violence in Northern Ireland. *Social Science and Medicine, 28,* 621–624.

Calhoun, L. G., & Tedeschi, R. G. (2005). The foundations of posttraumatic growth: An expanded framework. In L. G. Calhoun & R. G. Tedeschi (Eds.),

Handbook of posttraumatic growth: Research and practice (pp. 3–23). Mahwah, NJ: Erlbaum.

Campbell, A., Cairns, E., & Mallett, J. (2004). Northern Ireland: Impact of the troubles. *Journal of Aggression, Maltreatment, and Trauma, 9*, 175–184.

Chanley, V. (2002). Trust in government in the aftermath of 9/11: Determinants and consequences. *Political Psychology, 23*, 469–483.

Chomsky, N. (2004). The new war against terror: Responding to 9/11. In N. Scheper-Hughes & P. Bourgois (Eds.), *Violence in war and peace* (pp. 217–223). Oxford: Blackwell.

Conejero, S., de Rivera, J., Páez, D., & Jiménez, A. (2004). Alteración afectiva personal, atmósfera emocional y clima emocional tras los atentados del 11 de marzo [Personal affective alteration and emotional environment after the March 11th attacks]. *Ansiedad y Estrés, 10*, 1–11.

Corrado, R. R., & Tompkins, E. (1989). A comparative model of the psychological effects on the victims of state and anti-state terrorism. *International Journal of Law and Psychiatry, 12*, 281–293.

Curran, P. S. (1988). Psychiatric aspects of terrorist violence: Northern Ireland 1969–1987. *British Journal of Psychiatry, 153*, 470–475.

Danieli, Y., Brom, D., & Sills, J. (2005). *The trauma of terrorism: Sharing knowledge and shared care—An international handbook.* New York: Haworth Press.

Davis, J. A., Smith, T. W., & Marsden, P. V. (2001). *General Social Surveys, 1972–2000: Cumulative Codebook.* Chicago: National Organization for Research at the University of Chicago.

de Jong, J. (2002). Public mental health, traumatic stress and human rights violations in low-income countries: A culturally appropriate model in times of conflict, disaster, and peace. In J. de Jong (Ed.), *Trauma, war and violence: Public mental health in socio-cultural context* (pp. 1–92). New York: Plenum Press.

Desivilya, H., Gal, R., & Ayalon, O. (1996). Long-term effects of trauma in adolescents: Comparison between survivors of a terrorist attack and control counterparts. *Anxiety, Stress and Coping, 9*, 1135–1150.

DiMaggio, C., & Galea, S. (2006). The behavioral consequences of terrorism: A meta-analysis. *Academy of Emergency Medicine, 13*, 559–566.

Engdahl, B. (2005). International findings on the impact of terrorism. *Journal of Aggression, Maltreatment, and Trauma, 9*, 265–276.

Epstein, S. (1991). The self-concept, the traumatic neurosis, and the structure of personality. In D. Ozer, J. M. Healey, & R. A. Stewart (Eds.), *Perspectives on personality* (Vol. 3, pp. 63–98). Greenwich, CT: JAI Press.

Fischer, H. W. (1994). *Response to disaster: Fact versus fiction and its perpetuation—The sociology of disaster.* Washington, DC: University Press of America.

Foundation Center. (2002). *September 11: Perspectives from the field of philanthropy.* New York: Author. Retrieved January 14, 2005, from http://fdncenter.org/research/911/book.html.

Fredrickson, B. L. (2000). Cultivating positive emotions to optimize health and well-being. *Prevention and Treatment, 3.* Available from http://journals.apa.org/prevention/.

Fredrickson, B. L., Tugade, M. M., Waugh, C. E., & Larkin, G. R. (2003). What good are positive emotions in crises? A prospective study of resilience and emotions following the terrorist attacks on the United States on September 11th, 2001. *Journal of Personality and Social Psychology, 84*, 365–376.

Fullerton, C. S., Ursano, R. J., Norwood, A. E., & Holloway, H. H. (2003). Trauma, terrorism, and disaster. In R. J. Ursano, C. S. Fullerton, & A. E. Norwood (Eds.), *Terrorism and disaster: Individual and community mental health interventions* (pp. 1–20). Cambridge: Cambridge University Press.

Funes, M. (1998). Social responses to political violence in the Basque country: Peace movements and their audience. *Journal of Conflict Resolution, 42*, 493–510.

Galea, S., Ahern, J., Resnick, H., Kilpatrick, D., Bucuvalas, M., Gold, J., et al. (2002). Psychological sequelae of the September 11 terrorist attacks in New York City. *New England Journal of Medicine, 346*, 982–987.

Galea, S., Vlahov, D., Resnick, H., Ahern, J., Susser, E., Gold, J., et al. (2003). Trends of probable post-traumatic stress disorder in New York City after the September 11 terrorist attacks. *American Journal of Epidemiology, 158*, 514–524.

Goldenberg, I., & Matheson, K. (2005). The relation between inner representations and coping in recovering from traumatic experiences. *Basic and Applied Social Psychology, 27*, 361–369.

Gortner, E. M., & Pennebaker, J. (2003). The archival anatomy of a disaster: Media coverage and community-wide health effects of the Texas A&M bonfire tragedy. *Journal of Social and Clinical Psychology, 22*, 580–603.

Helgeson, V. S., Reynolds, K. A., & Tomich, P. L. (2006). A meta-analytic review of benefit finding and growth. *Journal of Consulting and Clinical Psychology, 74*, 797–816.

Independent Sector. (2001). *A survey of charitable giving after September 11th, 2001.* Retrieved January 18, 2002, from www.independentsector.org/sept11/survey.html.

Janoff-Bulman, R. (1989). Assumptive worlds and the stress of traumatic events: Applications of the schema construct. *Social Cognition, 7*, 113–136.

Janoff-Bulman, R. (1992). *Shattered assumptions.* New York: Free Press.

Janoff-Bulman, R. (2005). Schema-change perspectives on posttraumatic growth. In L. G. Calhoun & R. Tedeschi (Eds.), *Handbook of posttraumatic growth: Research and practice* (pp. 81–99). Mahwah, NJ: Erlbaum.

Jones, E., Woolven, R., Durodie, B., & Wessely, S. (2006). Public panic and morale: Second World War civilian responses reexamined in the light of the current anti-terrorist campaign. *Journal of Risk Research, 9*, 57–73.

Joseph, S., & Linley, P. A. (2006). Growth following adversity: Theoretical perspectives and implications for clinical practice. *Clinical Psychology Review, 26*, 1041–1053.

Kessler, R. C., Sonnega, A., Bromet, E., Hughes, M., & Nelson, C. B. (1995). Post-traumatic stress disorder in the National Comorbidity Survey. *Archives of General Psychiatry, 52*, 1048–1060.

Lepore, S. J., Ragan, J. D., & Jones, S. (2000). Talking facilitates cognitive-emotional processes of adaptation to an acute stressor. *Journal of Personality and Social Psychology, 78,* 499–509.

Lifton, R. J. (1993). *The protean self: Human resilience in an age of fragmentation.* New York: Basic Books.

Linley, P. A., & Joseph, S. (2004). Positive change after trauma and adversity: A review. *Journal of Traumatic Stress, 17,* 11–21.

Linley, P. A., Joseph, S., Cooper, R., Harris, S., & Meyer, C. (2003). Positive and negative changes following vicarious exposure to the September 11 terrorist attacks. *Journal of Traumatic Stress, 16,* 481–485.

Lira, E. C. M. (1989). *Psicología de la amenaza política y el miedo* [Psychology of political threat and fear]. Santiago de Chile, South America: ILAS.

Martin Baró, I. (Ed.). (1990). *Psicología social de la guerra: Trauma y terapia* [Social psychology of war: Trauma and therapy]. El Salvador, Central America: UCA Editores.

Martín Beristain, C. (1989). *Afirmación y resistencia: La comunidad como apoyo* [Affirmation and resistence: The community as support]. Barcelona, Spain: Virus.

Martín Beristain, C. (2006). *Humanitarian aid work: A critical approach.* Philadelphia: University of Pennsylvania Press.

McCarter, L., & Goldman, W. (2002). Use of psychotropics in two employee groups directly affected by the events of September 11. *Psychiatric Services, 53,* 1366–1368.

McFarlane, A. C., & Yehuda, R. (1996). Resilience, vulnerability, and the course of posttraumatic reactions. In B. A. Van der Kalk, A. C. McFarlane, & L. Weisaeth (Eds.), *Traumatic stress: The effects of overwhelming experience on mind, body and society* (pp. 155–181). New York: Guilford Press.

Mehl, M. R., & Pennebaker, J. W. (2003). The social dynamics of a cultural upheaval: Social interactions surrounding September 11, 2001. *Psychological Science, 14,* 579–585.

Meichenbaum, D. (2005). Resilience and posttraumatic growth: A constructive narrative perspective. In L. G. Calhoun & R. G. Tedeschi (Eds.), *Handbook of posttraumatic growth: Research and practice* (pp. 355–367). Mahwah, NJ: Erlbaum.

Miguel-Tobal, J. J., Gonzalez-Ordi, H., Cano-Vindel, A., Irurarrizaga, I., Rudenstine, S., Vlahov, D., et al. (2006). Post-traumatic stress and depression after the March 11 terrorist attacks in Madrid. *Journal of Traumatic Stress, 19,* 69–80.

Miller, A. M., & Heldring, M. (2004). Mental health and primary care in a time of terrorism: Psychological impact of terrorist attacks. *Families Systems and Health, 22,* 7–30.

Moya, M., & Morales-Marente, E. (2005). Reacciones psico-políticas ante los ataques terroristas del 11 de marzo del 2004 [Psycho-political reactions to the terrorist attacks of March 11th, 2004]. *Revista de Psicología Social, 20,* 315–330.

Nisbet, R. (1980). *History of the idea of progress.* New York: Basic Books.

Norris, F., Friedman, M., Watson, P., Byrne, C., Diaz, E., & Kaniasty, K. (2002). 60,000 disaster victims speak: Pt. I. An empirical review of the empirical literature, 1981–2001. *Psychiatry, 65,* 207–239.

North, C. S., & Pfefferbaum, B. (2002). Research on the mental health aspects of terrorism. *Journal of the American Medical Association, 288,* 633–636.

Penner, L. (2004). Volunteerism and social problems: Making things better or worse? *Journal of Social Issues, 60,* 645–666.

Pérez-Sales, P., Cervellón, P., Vázquez, C., Vidales, D., & Gaborit, M. (2005). Posttraumatic factors and resilience: The role of shelter management and survivors' attitudes after the earthquakes in El Salvador (2001). *Journal of Community and Applied Social Psychology, 15,* 368–382.

Pérez-Sales, P., & Vázquez, C. (in press). Planning needs and services after collective trauma: Should we look for the symptoms of PTSD? *Intervention: International Journal of Mental Health, Psychosocial Work and Counselling in Areas of Armed Conflict.*

Peterson, C., & Seligman, M. (2003). Character strengths before and after September, 11. *Psychological Science, 14,* 381–384.

Powell, S., Rosner, R., Butollo, W., Tedeschi, R. G., & Calhoun, L. G. (2003). Posttraumatic growth after war: A study with former refugees and displaced people in Sarajevo. *Journal of Clinical Psychology, 59,* 71–83.

Prager, E., & Solomon, Z. (1995). Perceptions of world benevolence, meaningfulness, and self-worth among elderly Israeli holocaust survivors and non-survivors. *Anxiety, Stress and Coping, 8,* 265–277.

Punamaki, R. L., Qouta, S., & el-Sarraj, E. (1997). Models of traumatic experiences and children's psychological adjustment: The roles of perceived parenting and the children's own resources and activity. *Child Development, 68,* 718–728.

Rasinski, K. A., Berktold, J., Smith, T. W., & Albertson, B. L. (2002). *America recovers: A follow-up to a national study of public response to the September 11th terrorist attacks.* Chicago: National Organization for Research at the University of Chicago. Retrieved September 15, 2002, from www.norc.uchicago.edu/projects/reaction /pubresp2.pdf.

Renz, L. (2002a). *Assessing the post-9/11 funding environment: Grantmakers' perspectives.* New York: Foundation Center.

Renz, L. (2002b). *Giving in the aftermath of 9/11: Foundations and corporations respond.* New York: Foundation Center.

Rosenheck, R., & Fontana, A. (2003). Use of mental health services by veterans with PTSD after the terrorist attacks of September 11. *American Journal of Psychiatry, 160,* 1684–1690.

Rosner, R., & Powell, S. (2006). Posttraumatic growth after war. In L. G. Calhoun & R. G. Tedeschi (Eds.), *Handbook of posttraumatic growth: Research and practice* (pp. 197–213). Mahwah, NJ: Erlbaum.

Rubin, G. J., Brewin, C. R., Greenberg, N., Simpson, J., & Wessely, S. (2005). Psychological and behavioral reactions to the 7 July London bombings: A cross-sectional survey of a representative sample of Londoners. *British Medical Journal, 331,* 606–611.

Sabucedo, J. M., Rodríguez, M., & López, W. (2000). Movilización social contra la violencia política: Sus determinantes [Social mobilization against political violence: Its determinants]. *Revista Latinoamericana de Psicología, 32,* 345–359.

Schlenger, W. E., Caddell, J. M., Ebert, L., Jordan, B. K., Rourke, K. M., Wilson, D., et al. (2002). Psychological reactions to terrorist attacks: Findings from the National Study of Americans' Reactions to September 11. *Journal of the American Medical Association, 288,* 581–588.

Schuster, M. A., Stein, B. D., Jaycox, L., Collins, R. L., Marshall, G. N., Elliott, M. N., et al. (2001). A national survey of stress reactions after the September 11, 2001 terrorist attacks. *New England Journal of Medicine, 345,* 1507–1512.

Shamai, M., & Levin-Megged, O. (2006). The myth of creating an integrative story: The therapeutic experience of holocaust survivors. *Qualitative Health Research, 16,* 692–712.

Sharlin, S. A., Moin, V., & Yahav, R. (2006). When disaster becomes commonplace: Reaction of children and adolescents to prolonged terrorist attacks in Israel. *Social Work in Health Care, 43,* 95–114.

Silver, R. C., Holman, E. A., McIntosh, D. N., Poulin, M., & Gil-Rivas, V. (2002). Nationwide longitudinal study of psychological responses to September 11. *Journal of the American Medical Association, 288,* 1235–1244.

Silver, R. C., Poulin, M., Holman, E. A., McIntosh, D. N., Gil-Rivas, V., & Pizarro, J. (2005). Exploring the myths of coping with a national trauma: A longitudinal study of responses to the September 11th terrorist attacks. In Y. Danieli, D. Brom, & J. Sills (Eds.), *The trauma of terrorism* (pp. 129–141). New York: Haworth Press.

Singh-Manoux, A. (2001). Cultural variations in social sharing of emotions. *Journal of Cross-Cultural Psychology, 32,* 647–661.

Skikta, L. J. (2006). Patriotism or nationalism? Understanding post-September 11, 2001 flag-display behavior. *Journal of Applied Social Psychology, 35,* 1995–2011.

Smith, T. W., & Kim, S. (2006). National pride in comparative perspective: 1995/96 and 2003/04. *International Journal of Public Opinion Research, 18,* 127–136.

Smith, T. W., Rasinski, K. A., & Toce, M. (2001). *America rebounds: A national study of public responses to the September 11th terrorist attacks—Preliminary findings.* Chicago: National Organization for Research at the University of Chicago. Retrieved June 10, 2002, from www.norc.uchicago.edu/projects/reaction/pubresp.pdf.

Solomon, Z., & Laufer, A. (2005). In the shadow of terror: Changes in world assumptions in Israeli youth. *Journal of Aggression, Maltreatment, and Trauma, 9,* 353–364.

Somasundaram, D. (2004). Short- and long-term effects on the victims of terror in Sri Lanka. *Journal of Aggression, Maltreatment, and Trauma, 9,* 215–228.

Steinberg, K., & Rooney, P. (2005). America gives: A survey of American's generosity after September 11. *Nonprofit and Voluntary Sector Quarterly, 31,* 110–135.

Techio, E., & Calderón-Prada, A. (2005). Relaciones intergrupales, valores, identidad social y prejuicio en España después del atentado terrorista del 11 de Marzo [Intergroup relations, values, social identity and prejudice in Spain after the terrorist attack of March 11th]. *Revista de Psicología Social, 20,* 277–287.

Tedeschi, R. G. (1999). Violence transformed: Posttraumatic growth in survivors and their societies. *Aggression and Violent Behavior, 4,* 319–341.

Tedeschi, R. G., & Calhoun, L. G. (1995). *Trauma and transformation: Growing in the aftermath of suffering*. Thousand Oaks, CA: Sage.

Tejerina, B. (2000). Civil society, political violence and social movements: The case of the Basque country. *Papeles de Oñate/Oñate Papers*, 121–147.

Torabi, M. R., & Seo, D. C. (2004). National study of behavioral and life changes since September 11. *Health Education and Behavior, 31*, 179–192.

Ubillos, S., Mayordomo, S., & Basabé, N. (2005). Percepción de riesgo, reacciones emocionales y el impacto del 11-M [Perception of risk, emotional reactions and the impact of March 11th]. *Revista de Psicología Social, 20*, 289–300.

United Nations. (1999). *International convention for the suppression of the financing of terrorism*. Adopted by the General Assembly of the United Nations in Resolution 54/109 of 9 December 1999.

United Nations International Strategy for Disaster Reduction. (2005). *Hyogo framework for action 2005–2015: Building the resilience of nations and communities to disasters*. Available from www.unisdr.org/eng/hfa/docs/Hyogo-framework-for-action-english.pdf.

Vasquez, N. (2000). *Las mujeres refugiadas y retornadas: Las habilidades adquiridas en el exilio y su aplicación en tiempos de paz* [The women who fled and returned: Skills acquired in exile and their application in times of peace]. El Salvador, Central America: Las Dignas.

Vázquez, C. (2005). Stress reactions of the general population after the terrorist attacks of S11 (USA) and M11 (Madrid, Spain): Myths and realities. *Annuary of Clinical and Health Psychology, 1*, 9–25. Available from www.us.es/apcs/vol1esp.htm.

Vázquez, C., Castilla, C., & Hervás, G. (2007). Reacciones frente al trauma: Vulnerabilidad, resistencia y crecimiento [Reactions to trauma: Vulnerability, resilience and growth]. In E. Fernández-Abascal (Ed.), *Emociones positivas* [Positive emotions]. Madrid, Spain: Pirámide.

Vázquez, C., Cervellón, P., Pérez-Sales, P., Vidales, D., & Gaborit, M. (2005). Positive emotions in earthquake survivors in El Salvador (2001). *Journal of Anxiety Disorders, 19*, 313–328.

Vázquez, C., Hervás, G., & Pérez-Sales, P. (2006, July). *The role of positive emotions on the psychological reactions following the Madrid March 11, 2004 terrorist attacks*. Paper presented at the Third European Conference on Positive Psychology, Braga, Portugal.

Vázquez, C., Pérez-Sales, P., & Matt, G. (2006). Post-traumatic stress reactions following the Madrid March 11, 2004 terrorist attacks in a Madrid community sample: A cautionary note about the measurement of psychological trauma. *Spanish Journal of Psychology, 9*, 61–74.

Wessely, S. (2004). When being upset is not a mental health problem. *Psychiatry, 67*, 153–157.

Whalen, C., Henker, B., King, P., Jamner, L., & Levine, L. (2004). Adolescents react to the events of September 11, 2001: Focused versus ambient impact. *Journal of Abnormal Child Psychology, 32*, 1–11.

World Health Organization. (2002). *World report on violence and health.* Geneva, Switzerland: Author.

Yehuda, R. (2002). Post-traumatic stress disorder. *New England Journal of Medicine, 346,* 108–114.

Zech, E., Rimé, B., & Nils, F. (2004). Social sharing of emotion, emotional recovery, and interpersonal aspects. In P. Philippot & R. Feldman (Eds.), *The regulation of emotion* (pp. 157–185). New York: Erlbaum.

Zoellner, T., & Maercker, A. (2006). Posttraumatic growth in clinical psychology: A critical review and introduction of a two component model. *Clinical Psychology Review, 26,* 626–653.

CHAPTER 5

Posttraumatic Growth and Immigration: Theory, Research, and Practice Implications

TZIPI WEISS and RONI BERGER

Now the Lord said unto Abram: "Get thee out of thy country, and from thy kindred, and from thy father's house, unto the land that I will show thee."

—Genesis 12

LEAVING ONE'S COUNTRY for a new land involves multiple losses of familiarity with physical and cultural environment, economic and social status and resources, language and identity, as well as a sense of community. Even when immigration results in improved economic, educational, employment, medical, and personal safety conditions, immigrants may lose their sense of identity and what their place is in the world. Consequently, the immigration experience is highly stressful and potentially traumatic (Berger, 2004; Drachman & Shen-Ryan, 1991; Harper & Lantz, 1996). The concept of posttraumatic growth as related to immigration is beginning to receive scholarly attention (Berger & Weiss, 2002, 2006; Weiss & Berger, 2006).

Worldwide, there are over 191 million documented immigrants and refugees (United Nations, 2006), requiring the helping professions to develop new ways of thinking about working with these populations not only toward reduction of distress but also toward facilitating personal growth. To do so successfully, practitioners need to be informed about theoretical, empirical, and clinical knowledge that pertains to posttraumatic growth in the context of immigration. To address this need, Chapter 5 has three parts. First, theoretical aspects of posttraumatic growth in relation to the immigration experience are reviewed. Second, empirical findings relative to posttraumatic growth in immigration are presented. Finally, principles for posttraumatic growth-informed practice with immigrants and refugees are discussed and illustrated.

THEORETICAL ASPECTS

The posttraumatic growth model postulates personal growth as an outcome of cognitive-emotional processing of challenges triggered by a stressor event. These challenges include responding to trauma-related emotional distress, to threats to basic assumptions about self and the world and to the disruption in life narrative. These challenges are affected by the pretrauma qualities of the individual and characteristics of the stressor events. The cognitive engagement with these challenges includes automatic as well as deliberate rumination, which may involve writing and talking about trauma-related content (Calhoun & Tedeschi, 2006).

Both distal (macro) and proximate (micro/mezzo) sociocultural aspects of the environment provide the context for individual rumination about trauma-related experiences and the development of posttraumatic growth. Distal aspects refer to predominant values, themes, narratives, and ways of constructing the world in the society at large. Proximate aspects describe family, friends, religious congregations and peers who represent "the small communities and social networks of people with whom an individual interacts" (Calhoun & Tedeschi, 2006, p. 12) and constitute one's primary reference group. Availability of social support and models of posttraumatic growth, the degree of corumination (the degree to which the rumination can be shared with another individual), and the responses to disclosure of trauma-related thoughts and indications of growth are likely to influence individual rumination processes as well as the level and characteristics of posttraumatic growth.

In their original conceptual model, Tedeschi and Calhoun (1995) identified, on the basis of an extensive literature review, three domains of posttraumatic growth: *changed perception of self, changed sense of relating to others, and changed philosophy of life.* Changed perception of self refers to an individual's recognition of both increased vulnerability and strengths, of a greater capacity to cope with adversities as well as the emergence of new possibilities in life. Changed sense of relating to others describes increased readiness to invest in relationships, greater compassion and closeness, and freedom to be oneself. Changed philosophy of life pertains to changes in priorities, clarification of values, appreciation of life and spirituality.

Tedeschi and Calhoun (1996) further developed a scale to allow the study of posttraumatic growth (the Posttraumatic Growth Inventory, PTGI). Using the PTGI, they identified five factors of posttraumatic growth: *personal strength, new possibilities, relating to others, appreciation of life,* and *spiritual change.* Empirical studies in diverse cultural contexts varied in the degree to which they replicated the original factor structure (Ho, Chan, & Ho, 2004; Kilic, 2006; Linley, Andrews, & Joseph, 2007; Maercker, 2006; Powell, Rosner, Butollo, Tedeschi, & Calhoun, 2003; Weiss & Berger, 2006), leaving the statistical delineation of the factor structure of the PTGI open to further investigation (Calhoun & Tedeschi, 2006).

The posttraumatic growth model, with its attention to qualities of the stressor event, the individual involved, multiple challenges, rumination, and the social context, has been discussed in the context of immigration (Berger & Weiss, 2002, 2006). The immigration experience as a stressor event has three common characteristics. First, immigration as a stressor presents a threat mostly to cognitive and emotional integrity, although in some situations (e.g., illegal immigrants, refugees, and asylum seekers) a threat to life or physical integrity may also be present because the immigrants may be at risk of harm in their home country, which has forced them to flee, or may face difficult circumstances in the country to which they have relocated.

Second, unlike most traumatic stressors, which are unpredictable and uncontrollable, immigration most often involves an element of choice. In this sense, the immigration experience resembles divorce and remarriage, where the loss is by choice at least for some of the people involved (Berger & Weiss, 2002). The fact that one can choose whether to immigrate contributes to society's failure to recognize it as a traumatic stressor and disenfranchises the related grief, leaving some people to be potentially unsympathetic to the immigrants' plight (e.g., "Nobody forced you to come here. You could go back").

Third, like divorce and life-threatening illness, immigration comprises a series of stressful events along a multiphased prolonged period rather than a distinct event such as an earthquake or a motor vehicle accident (Berger & Weiss, 2002). These phases are *departure, transit,* and *resettlement.* Stressors in the *departure* phase, where deliberation, planning, and preparations take place, are related to separation from people, places, and possessions; fears of the unknown; emotional conflicts; and increased familial discord (Halberstadt, 1992). For refugees and immigrants from hostile countries, when relocation is irreversible, departure represents a particularly stressful phase. Stressors in the *transit* phase, where the actual relocation occurs, are related to the complicated logistics of moving for all immigrants, dangers of border crossing for illegal immigrants, and prolonged periods in camps for refugees. Stressors in the *resettlement* phase are typically related to unfamiliar rules, norms, and language as well as issues related to housing, employment, and the need to reinvent oneself in a new environment (Berger & Weiss, 2002; Garza-Guerrero, 1974; Stewart, 1986).

Because of these stressor events, immigrants face the challenges of managing emotional distress as well as coping with the threats to their fundamental beliefs about their identity and their place in the world. The emotional distress in immigration initially peaks at the *departure* phase when a great sense of loss is experienced as the person separates from the familiar. The level of emotional distress is highly variable during the *transit* phase and often peaks again during the *resettlement* phase when an intense sense of loss emerges after the first several months of euphoria (Berger & Weiss, 2002). The grief work commonly involved in coming to terms with immigration-related losses may last for years, though its intensity gradually subsides (Berger, 2004). The challenges facing immigrants are influenced also by prerelocation qualities of the individual such as successful coping with previous stressor events.

The emotional distress previously described both triggers and sustains rumination, which is critical for the development of posttraumatic growth. Rumination includes four patterns of recurrent thinking—making sense, solving problems, reminiscing, and anticipating (Martin & Tesser, 1996). In the context of immigration, rumination involves recurrent comparisons of life before and after the transition. A recent immigrant from Siberia to New York exhibited reminiscing saying, "even the smell of apples was not the same. There you would go into the home and a fresh and sweet smell of the apples displayed on the table would hit you. Here they have a synthetic smell, like everything else" (Berger, 2004, p. 8).

The degree to which the rumination process culminates in posttraumatic growth is related to the immediate as well as the broader sociocultural contexts. Defining macro sociocultural contexts in immigration is complex because it requires understating both the culture of origin and the culture of relocation in terms of their position on the individualism-familism-collectivism continuum. This position affects the similarity or difference in values between the two cultures, especially in relation to stress, trauma, and coping, which impacts the degree of stress experienced by individuals and consequently their engagement in cognitive rumination. The greater the difference, the higher the probability for culture shock (the subjective experience of immigration-related anxiety) in response to the objective culture loss (Stewart, 1986). This greater degree of stress is likely to trigger the rumination that leads to posttraumatic growth (Tedeschi & Calhoun, 2004).

The micro/mezzo sociocultural context of immigration is also unique. Typical proximate elements such as immediate and extended family may not be available (e.g., when one immigrates leaving behind a spouse, children, and parents). Furthermore, even when they are available physically, they may not be available psychologically if they are overwhelmed by their own struggle with immigration-related stressors. Compatriots and other immigrant groups, which often serve as substitute family, represent particularly important mezzo-level factors in successful immigration because they may offer instrumental and emotional support and models of growth (Glassman & Skolnik, 1984).

EMPIRICAL KNOWLEDGE

Although posttraumatic growth has been identified in survivors of war, accidents, medical conditions such as life-threatening illnesses and infertility, birth of a seriously sick or disabled child, substance abuse, death of a loved one, childhood sexual abuse, rape, natural and technological disasters (see Linley & Joseph, 2004; Tedeschi & Calhoun, 2004, for reviews), and has been studied in diverse sociocultural contexts including the United States (Cordova, Cunningham, Carlson, & Andrykowski, 2001); China (Ho et al., 2004); Turkey (Kilic, 2006); Israel (Lev-Wiesel & Amir, 2003); Germany (Maercker & Herrle, 2003); South Africa (Polatinsky & Esprey, 2000); Bosnia (Powell et al., 2003); Australia (Shakespeare-Finch & Copping, 2006); Japan (Taku, 2006); and the United Kingdom (Linley, Joseph, Cooper, Harris, & Meyer, 2003). Only two studies have examined posttraumatic growth in immigration (Berger & Weiss, 2006; Powell et al., 2003).

Powell et al. (2003) examined posttraumatic growth in individuals who became refugees (crossed international borders) or displaced (relocated within their own country) during the war in Bosnia. Their sample experienced "not one but several traumatic events—moreover in a particularly stressful and threatening war and post war environment over a period of several years" (pp. 73–74) and reported a relatively low level of posttraumatic growth.

Berger and Weiss (2006) explored posttraumatic growth in Latina immigrants to the United States. Their sample reported a moderately high level of stress and the level of stressfulness was related to type of separation, specifically to the question of who was left behind. Severe stressors encountered by the Latina immigrants were risks of drowning, exposure to wild animals, starvation, physical and sexual assaults, and exploitation. For 17% of the sample, the stressor event met *DSM-IV* criteria for traumatic stressor. Unlike Powell et al., Berger and Weiss found a considerable level of self-reported personal growth. A number of factors may explain these differences including gender composition of samples (female only in Berger &

Weiss; males and females in Powell et al.), cultural issues (Latino culture was associated with greater reporting of posttraumatic growth in a study by Tomich & Helgeson, 2004), and types of stressor events (all participants in the Powell et al. study were exposed to pre-relocation war-related trauma, whereas in the Berger and Weiss sample only a minority of participants had such experiences). Both studies failed to document any association between level of stress and overall reports of posttraumatic growth.

Findings regarding correlates of posttraumatic growth also varied between the two immigration-related studies. Powell et al. (2003) identified age but not gender as significantly related to posttraumatic growth, whereas in the Berger and Weiss (2006) study, age was unrelated to posttraumatic growth (gender was irrelevant because all participants were women). Berger and Weiss also found that posttraumatic growth was related to participation in counseling and to a limited degree to the importance of religion in the person's life.

Culture-specific manifestations of posttraumatic growth as well as the relationship between qualities of the distal social environment and posttraumatic growth are yet to be fully explored empirically. One exception is Maercker's (2006) finding that the lack of social acknowledgment of the pain related to the experience of stressor event negatively affects posttraumatic growth. In relation to proximate sociocultural aspects, findings are mixed. In the context of breast cancer, Weiss (2004a, 2004b) found an association between posttraumatic growth and social context variables such as general social support, quality of marital relationships, and contact with individuals who modeled posttraumatic growth, whereas Cordova et al. (2001) did not find a direct connection between proximate social context variables and posttraumatic growth. The role of these variables as related to posttraumatic growth in the context of immigration has not been studied.

PRACTICE IMPLICATIONS

Practicing from a posttraumatic growth perspective does not imply using a specialized intervention method; rather it involves integrating the growth perspective into commonly used strategies for change such as cognitive-behavioral therapy (Calhoun & Tedeschi, 2006). Consistent with the aforementioned components of the posttraumatic growth model, immigration-related assessment and intervention efforts should address the challenges, cognitive processing, and sociocultural contexts while considering pretrauma qualities of the immigrant and adjusting the role of the practitioner accordingly (Berger & Weiss, 2002).

To grieve immigration-related losses, which are often overlooked or rejected by broader society, and engage in productive cognitive processing, immigrants need recognition of the losses they perceive, validation of the accompanying pain, and permission to mourn. This requires the practitioner to assess the degree to which the proximate and distal natural social environments provide such opportunities. Does a spouse allow the necessary space for contemplating the loss of the country-of-origin language or does he or she minimize the meaning of the loss and is pushing to embrace the new language and "move on"? On the macro level, does the community of compatriots support loss-related expressions and provide opportunities to sustain some of the immigrants' original culture?

The practitioner thus potentially needs to intervene on multiple levels. On the macro level, the practitioner needs to work with communities (e.g., via collaboration with natural leaders), to enhance understanding of the importance of recognizing and processing losses because the absence of such acknowledgment may negatively affect posttraumatic growth (Maercker, 2006). On the micro/mezzo level, the practitioner may have to provide culturally sensitive individual and familial counseling services. The initial focus of the intervention needs to be on validation and normalization of immigrants' reactions. Including a psycho-educational component on loss and trauma in the context of immigration could help immigrants with emotional regulation.

To develop posttraumatic growth in response to the pain and turmoil of immigration, individuals need to engage in constructive rumination rather than in the "brooding" type (constantly revisiting the traumatic events in detail; Calhoun & Tedeschi, 2006). Therefore, the role of the practitioner is to create conditions that enhance constructive rumination. This goal can be accomplished through helping the immigrant redefine basic concepts such as strengths and identify past instances of successful coping with traumatic events (Calhoun & Tedeschi, 1999). Other means for facilitating constructive rumination include encouraging engagement in family rituals such as storytelling about the immigration experience, creative writing, nonverbal techniques, community theater, and additional expressive strategies (Berger, 2004).

In the process of rumination, individuals tend to struggle with existential and spiritual questions, and therefore, the practitioner needs to be open and attentive to indications of these issues and make them part of the conversation. This readiness on the part of the practitioner is particularly indicated in light of the finding that among Latina immigrants, the importance of religion in one's life is related to some aspects of posttraumatic growth (Weiss & Berger, 2006).

Practitioners need to avoid imposing expectations for growth on immigrant clients. Instead, they should help clients rebuild their damaged or shattered worldviews and develop new life narratives that incorporate loss in a meaningful way. Practitioners must listen carefully, to identify and highlight client statements that hint of positive changes (Calhoun & Tedeschi, 2006). Practitioners' receptivity to growth is especially important when social expectations for continuing grief discourage relating positive changes to the trauma. Refugees who escaped war, natural disaster, and political strife tend to hesitate and feel guilty when experiencing positive changes.

Furthermore, practitioners need to recognize that the development of posttraumatic growth may be a lengthy process (Lepore & Revenson, 2006) and thus be patient and also teach the immigrant client to be patient. In struggling with immigration-related stressors, posttraumatic growth may appear later than in the context of other stressors. The extensive logistic and practical activities immigrants must deal with during the postmigration phase—learning a new language and finding proper housing and employment (Drachman & Paulino, 2005)—may delay the cognitive engagement with losses and thus postpone the emergence of posttraumatic growth.

Immigrants are more likely to develop posttraumatic growth if during their struggle they have contact with others who experienced a similar trauma and perceived benefits (Weiss, 2004b). There are various ways to create such contact. First, the practitioner might be an immigrant who experienced posttraumatic growth and can model it, with proper timing, to the client. Second, the immigrant might be involved in group experiences with other immigrants, some of whom maybe further along in the struggle and already perceiving some benefits from it. The group may create a context for cognitive processing and emotional support that further contribute to posttraumatic growth. A third way to connect immigrants with a posttraumatic growth model might be through partnering them with other immigrants who can serve as role models.

SUMMARY

In the immigration literature, the major emphasis is on the immigrant's experience as a trauma with accompanying negative effects, whereas strengths, resilience, and potential salutary effects are neglected. Although the empirical study of posttraumatic growth in immigration is in its infancy, the positive findings of the few studies available on personal growth among immigrants and refugees support the application of the conceptual model and its related practice interventions to these populations. Much more effort is needed to increase the understanding of immigration-related posttraumatic growth and to acquire the knowledge to inform development of practice guidelines for facilitating posttraumatic growth among the swelling ranks of immigrants.

Much evidence has been accumulated on posttraumatic growth correlates in connection with many stressor events as predicted by the posttraumatic growth model. Stressor event, individual, and social context characteristics have been found to play a role in posttraumatic growth following many different life events, and therefore, pursuing such connections in immigration might be a fruitful direction for research. Because posttraumatic growth is associated with characteristics of the stressor event, studying posttraumatic growth as it relates to the type and circumstances of immigration is indicated. One typology pertains to the legal status and subsequent eligibilities of immigrants, which affect levels of stress and social acceptance. An individual may be a legal immigrant, refugee, asylum seeker, immigrant in a refugee-like situation or undocumented. Studies that look at the association between level and domain of posttraumatic growth and immigration status can provide category-specific interventions for enhancing posttraumatic growth.

Another direction for research of differential posttraumatic growth refers to demographic characteristics such as culture of origin and developmental phase. Cross-cultural studies indicated the universality of posttraumatic growth as well as its culture-specific meaning (Weiss & Berger, 2006). Therefore, it is very important to study posttraumatic growth in immigrants from different cultures of origin. Posttraumatic growth in immigrants who relocate from a familial to an individualistic society such as from a Latin country to the United States may be different than posttraumatic growth in immigrants relocating from a collectivistic society such as the former Soviet Union to a country in the Western world. Equally important is researching posttraumatic growth along the life span and the intersection of developmental challenges with other stressors in immigrants. Thus, studying posttraumatic growth in children, adolescents, adults, and the aged immigrants may yield knowledge that can offer useful guidelines for the design and delivery of services that address unique age-related needs.

Understanding the association between the social environment of the immigrant and posttraumatic growth is a wide-open field for exploration. Are there differences in posttraumatic growth between immigrants who live in a homogeneous ethnic enclave and those who live in a socially diverse environment? In light of the role that social acceptance plays in posttraumatic growth, how does receivership by the establishment, other immigrant groups, and compatriots affect it?

Finally, because posttraumatic growth was found to be related to counseling in Latina immigrants (Berger & Weiss, 2006), examination of the connection between posttraumatic growth and counseling in other immigrant populations is called for. Studies designed to understand exactly what aspects of counseling are effective in facilitating posttraumatic growth and which ones are inhibiting are also necessary.

Summary Points (Practice)

- Integrate the posttraumatic growth perspective in all intervention approaches.
- Allow for mourning of immigration-related losses.
- Consider micro, mezzo, and macro interventions.
- Support constructive rumination.
- Allow existential and spiritual contemplation.
- Refrain from imposing expectations for posttraumatic growth.
- Listen carefully and highlight intimations of growth.
- Be patient.
- Provide posttraumatic growth role models.

Summary Points (Research)

- Posttraumatic growth and immigration status: Is posttraumatic growth differentially prevalent across different immigrant groups?
- Posttraumatic growth and culture of origin: Does the experience of posttraumatic growth differ by country of origin?
- Posttraumatic growth in immigration along the life span: Is the experience of posttraumatic growth through immigration affected by life span factors?
- Posttraumatic growth and the homogeneity of the social context: Is the experience and degree of posttraumatic growth affected by the social context?
- Posttraumatic growth and social receivership: Is the experience of posttraumatic growth affected by the extent of an immigrant's integration into the new society?
- Posttraumatic growth and counseling: Are there particular therapeutic approaches that facilitate growth?

REFERENCES

Berger, R. (2004). *Immigrant women tell their stories.* New York: Haworth Press.

Berger, R., & Weiss, T. (2002). Immigration and posttraumatic growth: A missing link. *Journal of Immigrant and Refugee Services, 1,* 21–39.

Berger, R., & Weiss, T. (2006). Posttraumatic growth in Latina immigrants. *Journal of Immigrant and Refugee Studies, 4,* 55–72.

Calhoun, L. G., & Tedeschi, R. G. (1999). *Facilitating posttraumatic growth: A clinician's guide.* Mahwah, NJ: Erlbaum.

Calhoun, L. G., & Tedeschi, R. G. (Eds.). (2006). *Handbook of posttraumatic growth.* Mahwah, NJ: Erlbaum.

Cordova, M. J., Cunningham, L. L. C., Carlson, C. R., & Andrykowski, M. (2001). Posttraumatic growth following breast cancer: A controlled comparison study. *Health Psychology, 20,* 176–185.

Drachman, D., & Paulino, A. (Eds.). (2005). *Immigrants and social work.* New York: Haworth Press.

Drachman, D., & Shen-Ryan, A. (1991). Immigrants and refugees. In A. Gitterman (Ed.), *Social work practice with vulnerable populations* (pp. 618–646). New York: Columbia University Press.

Garza-Guerrero, A. C. (1974). Culture shock: Its mourning and the vicissitudes of identity. *Journal of the American Psychoanalytic Association, 22,* 408–429.

Glassman, U., & Skolnik, L. (1984). The role of social group work in refugee resettlement. *Social Work with Groups, 7,* 45–62.

Halberstadt, A. (1992). The Soviet Jewish family: A cultural perspective. *Grand Rounds, 1,* 2–12.

Harper, K. V., & Lantz, J. (1996). *Cross-cultural practice: Social work with diverse populations.* Chicago, IL: Lyceum.

Ho, S. M. Y., Chan, C. L. W., & Ho, R. T. H. (2004). Posttraumatic growth in Chinese cancer survivors. *Psycho-Oncology, 13,* 377–389.

Kilic, C. (2006, November 6). *Posttraumatic Growth Inventory: Response of earthquake survivors on the Turkish version.* Paper presented at the twenty-second annual International Society for Traumatic Stress Studies meeting, Los Angeles.

Lepore, S. J., & Revenson, T. A. (2006). Resilience and posttraumatic growth: Recovery, resistance, and reconfiguration. In L. G. Calhoun & R. G. Tedeschi (Eds.), *Handbook of posttraumatic growth: Research and practice* (pp. 24–46). Mahwah, NJ: Erlbaum.

Lev-Wiesel, R., & Amir, M. (2003). Posttraumatic growth among holocaust child survivors. *Journal of Loss and Trauma, 8,* 229–237.

Linley, P. A., Andrews, L., & Joseph, S. (2007). Confirmatory factor analysis of the Posttraumatic Growth Inventory. *Journal of Loss and Trauma, 12,* 321–332.

Linley, P. A., & Joseph, S. (2004). Positive change following trauma and adversity: A review. *Journal of Traumatic Stress, 17,* 11–21.

Linley, P. A., Joseph, S., Cooper, R., Harris, S., & Meyer, C. (2003). Positive and negative changes following vicarious exposure to the September 11, 2001, terrorist attacks. *Journal of Traumatic Stress, 16,* 481–485.

Maercker, A. (2006, November 6). *The German version of the Post Traumatic Growth Inventory.* Paper presented at the twenty-second annual International Society for Traumatic Stress Studies meeting, Los Angeles.

Maercker, A., & Herrle, J. (2003). Long-term effects of the Dresden bombing: Relationships to control beliefs, religious belief, and personal growth. *Journal of Traumatic Stress, 16,* 579–587.

Martin, L. L., & Tesser, A. (1996). Clarifying our thoughts. In R. S. Wyer (Ed.), *Ruminative thought: Vol. 9. Advances in social cognition* (pp. 189–209). Mahwah, NJ: Erlbaum.

Polatinsky, S., & Esprey, Y. (2000). An assessment of gender differences in the perception of benefit resulting from the loss of a child. *Journal of Traumatic Stress, 1,* 709–718.

Powell, S., Rosner, R., Butollo, W., Tedeschi, R. G., & Calhoun, L. G. (2003). Posttraumatic growth after war: A study with former refugees and displaced people in Sarajevo. *Journal of Clinical Psychology, 59,* 71–83.

Shakespeare-Finch, J., & Copping, A. (2006). A grounded theory approach to understanding cultural differences in posttraumatic growth. *Journal of Loss and Trauma, 11,* 355–371.

Stewart, E. C. P. (1986). The survival stage of intercultural communication. *International Christian University Bulletin, 1,* 109–121.

Taku, K. (2006, November 6). *The Japanese version of the posttraumatic growth inventory.* Paper presented at the twenty-second annual International Society for Traumatic Stress Studies meeting, Los Angeles.

Tedeschi, R. G., & Calhoun, L. G. (1995). *Trauma and transformation: Growing in the aftermath of suffering.* Thousand Oaks, CA: Sage.

Tedeschi, R. G., & Calhoun, L. G. (1996). The Posttraumatic Growth Inventory: Measuring the positive legacy of trauma. *Journal of Traumatic Stress, 9,* 455–471.

Tedeschi, R. G., & Calhoun, L. G. (2004). Posttraumatic growth: Conceptual foundations and empirical evidence. *Psychological Inquiry, 15,* 1–18.

Tomich, P. L., & Helgeson, V. S. (2004). Is finding something good is the bad always good? Benefit finding among women with breast cancer. *Health Psychology, 23,* 16–23.

United Nations. (2006). *International migration.* New York: Department of Economic and Social Affairs Population Division. Retrieved January 29, 2007, from www.un.org/esa/population/publications/2006Migration/.

Weiss, T. (2004a). Correlates of posttraumatic growth in husbands of breast cancer survivors. *Psycho-Oncology, 13,* 260–268.

Weiss, T. (2004b). Correlates of posttraumatic growth in married breast cancer survivors. *Journal of Social and Clinical Psychology, 23,* 733–746.

Weiss, T., & Berger, R. (2006). Reliability and validity of a Spanish version of the Posttraumatic Growth Inventory. *Research on Social Work Practice, 16,* 191–199.

CHAPTER 6

Broken Vows: Divorce as a Spiritual Trauma and Its Implications for Growth and Decline

ANNETTE MAHONEY, ELIZABETH J. KRUMREI,
and KENNETH I. PARGAMENT

AN ENDURING WONDER of human nature is that many people respond to tragic events by experiencing posttraumatic growth (Linley & Joseph, 2004). They often become stronger personally and deepen their connections to other people as well as their faith life. Individuals commonly attribute such psychological, social, and spiritual growth to spiritual resources, such as having a loving relationship with God, engaging in spiritual exercises, or obtaining support from fellow believers (Pargament & Ano, 2004). However, traveling down a spiritual road to triumph over profound stressors is not necessarily straightforward or easy. Such a journey can be thwarted when spirituality itself creates roadblocks. One such roadblock occurs when traumatic events are interpreted as a violation or a loss of something sacred to the individual. Individuals who view stressful events not only as unpredictable and devastating, but also as negative spiritual experiences suffer what we refer to as a *spiritual trauma*. On the one hand, spiritual trauma can mire people in painful spiritual struggles, as illustrated by a divorcee who is unable to move beyond feelings of betrayal by God for the loss of a once sacred marriage. On the other hand, the deep discomfort created by spiritual traumas and struggles may push people to seek out new, or draw on well-worn, spiritual resources rather than turn away from the spiritual realm altogether. Such efforts may facilitate long-range psychological as well as spiritual growth in the healing process.

In this chapter, we elaborate a dynamic model of spiritual coping to help scholars and practitioners appreciate spirituality's potential to facilitate growth when disaster strikes, as well as many of the pitfalls in this process. Our hope is to move researchers beyond simplistic views on spirituality's role in trauma and to help therapists guide clients out of spiritual quagmires and toward growth when faced with devastation. We focus on divorce to illustrate the model's clinical usefulness in applied settings and we relay new findings about spiritual coping with divorce to inspire researchers interested in spirituality and trauma.

Divorce is well suited to our purposes because, like other traumatic events, it can unexpectedly occur and severely disrupt every aspect of an individual's life. Studies have long documented the psychological problems that can accompany this life transition such as depression, anxiety, emotional distress, and identity crises (e.g., Bloom, Asher, & White, 1978; Kitson & Raschke, 1981; Weiss, 1975). Furthermore, divorce unfolds against a backdrop in which marriage has been elevated to the position of a paramount sacred institution (Mahoney & Tarakeshwar, 2005). Divorce causes marital relationships to fall from this sacred pedestal and thus may often be appraised in an intensely negative spiritual light. Furthermore, religious institutions offer divorcing individuals little in the way of spiritual teachings, scriptural stories, or rituals that could facilitate effective spiritual coping responses with this painful transition. This was highlighted by Smith and Smith (2000) who found that the religious organizations of 343 laypeople living in the greater New York area did not provide much support and assistance specific to coping with divorce. As a result, divorce can leave people mired in spiritual struggles, unable to find healthy spiritual responses to this event. Nevertheless, those who can turn to their faith in positive ways may reap rich rewards.

Remarkably, the complex interplay of divorce and spiritual coping has received little empirical scrutiny. We located only three published studies that directly examine this topic. Greeff and Merwe (2004) studied resiliency factors as reported by either one parent or one adolescent from 98 divorced families. In 51% of the cases, faith was identified as an important coping resource, especially by parents. Blomquist (1985) and Nathanson (1995) each qualitatively interviewed a handful of divorcing individuals about spirituality's role in divorce, and both found that spirituality facilitated postdivorce adjustment and growth. Given these initial findings as well as estimates that nearly half of the roughly 90% of married Americans with a religious group affiliation are likely to divorce (Mahoney, Pargament, Tarakeshwar, & Swank, 2001), spirituality's role in facilitating or hindering divorce adjustment merits far more attention (Ladd & Zvonkovic, 1995). With this goal in mind, we recently conducted a study of 100 adults who had filed for divorce within the past 6 months and collected both quantitative data and qualitative written comments about their views of their divorce (Krumrei, Mahoney, & Pargament, 2007). In this chapter, we highlight findings from this initial effort to examine spiritual coping with divorce. Because of the scarcity of research aimed directly at this topic, we also offer many clinical examples to flesh out our conceptual model, hoping that others will follow suit by researching these ideas.

MODEL OF SPIRITUAL COPING WITH TRAUMA AND SUBSEQUENT GROWTH: DIVORCE AS AN ILLUSTRATION

We begin by offering our basic definition of *spirituality*. We conceptualize spirituality as "the search for the sacred" (Pargament & Mahoney, 2002). Concepts of God, divinity, and transcendent reality are at the center of our definition of the sacred. However, virtually any aspect of life can become part of the sacred by its association with, or representation of, divinity (Pargament & Mahoney, 2002, 2005). Therefore, spirituality includes the many means that people use to incorporate the sacred into their lives, including the beliefs, experiences, rituals, and communities that they associate with supernatural forces.

In turn, *spiritual coping* integrates the search for the sacred into Lazarus and Folkman's (1984) classic tripartite theory of coping consisting of (1) primary and secondary appraisals of a stressor, (2) cognitive or behavioral strategies to deal the event, and (3) sought-after outcomes of coping. The concept of the sacred sets spiritual coping apart from secular forms of coping because a spiritual dimension is folded into the other elements. This conceptualization reflects Pargament's definition of *religious coping* as "a search for significance in times of stress in ways related to the sacred." Pargament (1997) theorized that life events can be interpreted in spiritual terms (spiritual coping appraisals), that unique spiritual pathways are available to cope with stress (spiritual coping processes), and that the destinations people strive to reach through coping processes can be imbued with sacred significance. Although Pargament has previously labeled this process as religious coping, we use the term spiritual coping here for two reasons. First, the field of the psychology of religion has increasingly deemphasized the role of formal, institutional religion in peoples' lives and, second, modern people are increasingly pursuing nontraditional routes as well as traditional pathways in their searches for the sacred.

Spiritual Traumas and Negative Spiritual Appraisals

Parameters of a Spiritual Trauma   Naturally, a person must experience a traumatic event to cope with it and then grow. The first question is, what constitutes a traumatic event? Consistent with prior research, we adhere to Calhoun and Tedeschi's (2006, p. 3) view of the terms "trauma, crisis, major stressor, and related terms as essentially synonymous expressions to describe circumstances that significantly challenge or invalidate important components of the individual's assumptive world." Such events profoundly disrupt the ability of people to understand, predict, or control their life. The more pervasive the implications of the event, the more traumatic it is. Divorce is a potentially traumatic event. Few get married with the expectation that their marriage will fail, despite recent Census Bureau estimates that as many as 50% of married individuals who are now in their 40s will or have experienced divorce (Kreider, 2005). Further, most couples build a life together, with the accompanying personal sacrifices in career, personal, or home life, based on the premise that the relationship will be permanent. Divorce violates such expectations, bringing with it widespread changes in assumptions people have about the course of their entire life. In addition, divorce usually triggers major disruption, at least temporarily, across multiple domains of life including social, financial, parental, residential, and vocational (e.g., Amato, 2000; Brown, Felton, Whiteman, & Manela, 1980; Kitson, Barbri, Roach, & Placidi, 1989; Walters-Chapman, Price, & Serovich, 1995).

Of particular interest here are the ways that life crises such as divorce challenge or invalidate certain spiritually based assumptions about how the world operates. Extending Calhoun and Tedeschi's view of trauma, we propose that a spiritual trauma occurs when an event severely disrupts the individual's spiritual orienting system, which refers to a generalized set of spiritual beliefs, practices, and relationships. Further, we extend Lazarus and Folkman's premises that a person's appraisals of an event shape the degree to which that event is experienced as traumatic. Thus, a spiritual trauma occurs to the degree to which an event is viewed as threatening and damaging to an individual's core spiritual values and goals (primary coping appraisal), accompanied by an appraisal of spiritual resources available to manage the stressor (secondary coping appraisal). A sufficiently distressing event provokes subsequent spiritual coping methods to reestablish an individual's spiritual foundation. In our model, we have identified two spiritual appraisals of stressful events that constitute a serious challenge or invalidation of spiritual expectations and that would intensify the perceived threat and damage by the event: sacred loss and desecration. To set the stage for a discussion of these pernicious spiritual appraisals, we must first review the meaning of another concept—sanctification.

Sanctification   The term *sanctification* refers to perceiving an aspect of life as having divine character and significance (Mahoney et al., 1999; Pargament & Mahoney, in press). Two such processes have been identified in prior research. *Theistic* sanctification refers to viewing an aspect of life as being a manifestation of one's images, beliefs, or experience of God. *Non-theistic* sanctification occurs without reference to a specific deity and takes place when an aspect of life is imbued with divine qualities such as bound-lessness, ultimate value, and transcendence. One study found that most husbands and wives view their marriage through a spiritual lens (Mahoney et al., 1999). Sanctification extends the realm of the sacred beyond concepts of God, the divine, and transcendence and embeds seemingly mundane as-pects of life within a rich spiritual landscape. Events that shatter the web of beliefs woven around sacred objects, especially family relations, may be particularly threatening and damaging (Mahoney, Pargament, Murray-Swank & Murray-Swank, 2003; Pargament & Mahoney, 2005).

Sacred Loss and Desecration Appraisals Sacred loss and desecration both consist of a negative primary spiritual appraisal wherein an event takes on a powerful spiritual meaning because it is seen as adversely affecting a sanctified aspect of life (Pargament, Magyar, Benore, & Mahoney, 2005). Sa-cred loss appraisals occur when one perceives the loss of something once viewed as a manifestation of God or invested with sacred qualities. Here are examples of such appraisals: "Something I held as sacred is no longer present in my life"; "Something of sacred importance in my life disap-peared when this event took place"; "I lost something I thought God wanted for me"; and "Something that connected me to God is gone." Dese-cration appraisals refer to perceiving a sanctified aspect of life as having been violated (Pargament et al., 2005). Examples are "A part of my life that God made sacred was attacked"; "Something that was sacred to me was de-stroyed"; "This event ruined a blessing from God"; and "Something that was sacred to me was destroyed."

Although both sacred loss and desecration appraisals involve the disso-lution of a perceived point of connection between the human and transcen-dent reality, the two types of appraisals differ in an important respect. Desecration appraisals incriminate someone or something as being respon-sible for violating the sacred. In contrast, sacred loss appraisals do not nec-essarily involve attributions of blame since a loss can be perceived as accidental, inevitable, or outside human or divine control. Nevertheless, in many instances, the two types of appraisal may go hand in hand. Divorce appears to be a case in point. In our study of 100 adults who filed for a di-vorce in the past 6 months, we found a very high covariation of these ap-praisals ($r = .82$; Krumrei et al., 2007). Further, three-quarters of divorcees indicated that descriptions of sacred loss and desecration applied to their divorce to some degree.

Psychological Impact of Sacred Loss and Desecration Appraisals   The next question is whether perceived sacred losses and desecrations exacerbate post-traumatic distress. Three lines of reasoning suggest this could be the case. First, assumptions that people make about sanctified aspects of life represent critical ingredients of their worldview (Pargament & Mahoney, 2005). Sacred objects, such as marital bonds, may often be presumed to be ever-lasting and deserving of absolute commitment, sacrifice, and reverence. Others may assume that sanctified objects hold a special power and are guarded by divine forces that will prevent their loss or harm. Even if only held implicitly, threats to such assumptions can be psychologically powerful. Infidelity may be terribly shocking because it shakes profound spiritual assumptions about marriage. Listen to this woman: "I could not comprehend the level of ongoing purposeful deceit on the part of my significant other. [It was] unimaginable that an 'upstanding, prominent, religious, moral, preaching' person could be so utterly deceitful in so many ways for such an extended period of time" (48-year-old woman after discovering that her partner had been maintaining 3-year affair with a mutual friend; Pargament et al., 2005).

Second, the sacred may be central to the stories and themes people live by. Narrative theorists have described how people lend meaning to their lives by structuring their experiences into "macronarratives," encompassing life stories, and "micronarratives," smaller stories (Neimeyer & Levitt, 2001, p. 48). Narratives that are interwoven with a sacred dimension may be particularly compelling. In the case of marriage, many may believe that finding their spouse fulfills a long sought-after hope to find a soul mate. The marital ceremony may often be seen as transforming this bond into an eternal, transcendent union that reflects a larger spiritual plan for one's life. The loss or violation of such sacred narrative themes is likely to disrupt the flow of one's life. Events like divorce may be even more painful when individuals cannot find religious teachings that help them make sense of the shattering of the old sacred story line or enable them to construct a new tale.

Third, research indicates that people work harder to preserve and protect, and derive greater benefits from that which they perceive as sacred. Husbands and wives who sanctify their marriages tend to be more protective of their relationships; they respond to conflict with better problem-solving strategies such as more collaboration, less verbal aggression, and less stalemating. In terms of benefits, greater sanctification of the marriage is tied to greater marital satisfaction and more commitment (Mahoney et al., 1999). Similar findings regarding investments and benefits associated with sanctification have emerged for major life strivings, parenting, physical well-being, and the environment (Pargament &

Mahoney, 2005). Overall, sanctification appears to raise the psychological and spiritual stakes tied to an aspect of life. Though people may have much to gain by sanctifying their marriages, they also have more to lose when the marriage fails.

Empirical Evidence on Links between Spiritual Trauma and Distress   Consistent with these lines of reasoning, emerging research indicates that people who view their tragedies through a negative spiritual lens are likely to report higher levels of distress. Higher perceptions of sacred loss and desecration have been linked to greater psychological and spiritual distress for college students recently hurt in a romantic relationship (Magyar, Pargament, & Mahoney, 2000), for adults reflecting on the most negative event in their lives in the past 2 years (Pargament et al., 2005), and for coeds from Ohio and New York in response to the 9/11 terrorists attacks in the United States (Mahoney et al., 2002). Our recent study (Krumrei et al., 2007) on divorce reinforces that experiencing a spiritual trauma is tied to greater distress. The more divorcing individuals viewed their divorce as a sacred loss or desecration, the greater their experience of depression, posttraumatic anxiety, anger, and spiritual distress. Qualitatively, participants also relayed in their own words that viewing their divorce through a negative sacred lens heightened their distress. One person conveyed feelings of sadness, anger, and spiritual turmoil in this way: "I feel ashamed to even go to Church. . . . I feel like a failure to my ex and to God and to my family and to every human on the planet. I feel like I have done something unforgivable to my ex-spouse. This sometimes angers me."

SPIRITUAL TRAUMA AND SPIRITUAL STRUGGLES

Three Types of Spiritual Struggles   Spiritual traumas often disrupt an individual's spiritual orienting system, or generalized set of spiritual beliefs, practices, and relationships. Spiritual struggles can be defined as signs of a spiritual orienting system under stress; the struggles represent efforts to conserve or transform a spirituality that has been threatened or harmed (Pargament, Desai, & McConnell, 2006). Based on research using a 100-item, multidimensional measure of religious coping (the RCOPE), Pargament and others have reliably identified seven distinct spiritual struggles experienced by adults (Pargament, Smith, Koenig, & Perez, 1998). For the purposes of this chapter, we group these methods into three categories of spiritual struggles: divine, intrapersonal, and interpersonal.

DIVINE SPIRITUAL STRUGGLES   Divine spiritual struggles center on an individual's relationship, thoughts, and feelings toward God. Any traumatic event can pose a threat to views of God as an all-loving, omnipotent being who ensures that good things will happen to good people. In response to a crisis, the individual may feel abandoned or betrayed by God, feel angry with God, punished by an angry God, or question God's power. These struggles may be especially potent for spiritual traumas that bring expectations about God under fire. A divorcing person may wonder how God allowed a sacred aspect of life to be lost or violated, followed by turmoil for what this means for the person's relationship with God. Listen to the anguished words of one divorcee: "Equating the union of marriage with the union with God can be devastating for people going through a divorce. If the marriage has been a metaphor for union with God, then the obvious sequel is that the divorce symbolizes separation from God. The broken relationship with spouse is experienced as broken relationship with God" (Livingston, 1985, p. 246). Divorced individuals may also reason that because they could not be perfectly accepting, giving, and healing to one another in their marriage, they deserve to be cut off from the presence of God (Livingston, 1985) and redefine the divorce as a divine punishment. As one participant in our study said about his ex-wife, "I am so sorry I hurt her the way I did. I know that God was not and is not looking out for me." In addition, those who take a passive spiritual stance with God may feel painfully bewildered, questioning why God ignored their pleas for divine intervention to save their marriage. Finally, individuals may reappraise God's power, coming to see God as less able to control or intervene than previously assumed.

INTRAPERSONAL SPIRITUAL STRUGGLES   Intrapersonal spiritual struggles refer to internal questions, doubts, and uncertainties about spiritual matters. Although any crisis may trigger intrapersonal struggles, perceptions of sacred loss and desecration may exacerbate spiritual struggles within the self. One intrapersonal spiritual struggle focuses on questions about one's ultimate purpose in life. People may enter marriage believing they are wisely following an inner spiritual voice toward their highest spiritual destiny, particularly if this decision was preceded by much spiritual reflection. A subsequent divorce would raise serious doubts about the soundness of their inner spiritual compass and leave these people existentially adrift, wondering where they should have been headed and where to go next. Another intrapersonal struggle involves conflicts between desires to gratify human appetites and desires to be virtuous (Exline, 2002). In the case of divorce, a person may desperately want to exit a lifeless marriage in hopes of fulfilling unmet needs for sexual gratification, emotional intimacy, or financial security with a different partner down the road. Such desires, however, clash with the premise that a sacred marriage demands lifelong perseverance despite personal costs. Significant guilt may ensue as the person wrestles to spiritually justify ending a marriage for these reasons. Intrapersonal struggles may also focus on religious systems of belief and practice. Those who violate the parameters that they believe surround a sacred marriage may be unable to forgive themselves for breaking their vows to be sexually or emotionally faithful.

INTERPERSONAL SPIRITUAL STRUGGLES   Interpersonal spiritual struggles involve spiritual tensions and conflicts with family, friends, congregations, and communities, and may be especially prominent during interpersonal crises. Interpersonal spiritual struggles can occur when members of one's social system disagree with that person's spiritual interpretation of, or response to, trauma. Interpersonal disagreements may be especially toxic when people perceive the sacred in different ways. Less spiritually oriented family members may be unable to grasp that a divorcee experiences the breakup of a marriage as a sacred loss or desecration, and then fail to express appropriate levels of empathy. Alternatively, an individual who feels alienated from a religious institution that condemns divorce may also end up feeling alienated from family members or fellow believers who urge the use of spiritual resources (e.g., participation in worship services or traditional religious rituals) that are no longer meaningful to the individual. On a related note, divorced individuals are more likely to apostatize their religion than nondivorced people (Lawton & Bures, 2001). Thus, for some, divorce means not only cutting ties to one's spouse but also one's religious community.

Another set of interpersonal spiritual struggles can occur when the individuals feel blamed or judged for the divorce by their religious community. Various participants in our study (Krumrei et al., 2007) said things such as, "I felt that there was a lot of judgment on the part of the church toward my divorce and no support or grace. . . . Friends from the church could not see past the scripture of divorce being a sin. . . . If there's one message I would want to communicate, it's that those going through a divorce need compassion and grace, not judgment, from the church." Some may also experience spiritual penalties as a consequence of getting divorced. Some religious institutions exclude divorced individuals from religious rituals (e.g., divorced Catholics who do not seek or are not granted an annulment are technically barred from receiving communion) or the community altogether (e.g., religious shunning of divorcees).

Finally, interpersonal spiritual struggles can occur when the perpetrator of the trauma is viewed as being influenced by supernatural evil forces. We have labeled such an attribution as "demonization of the perpetrator." This involves believing that the individual(s) deemed responsible for a sacred loss or desecration wittingly or unwittingly operated under the influence of the devil or possesses demonic (e.g., satanic, demonic, evil) qualities. In the context of divorce, an individual may believe that actions of the self or the partner that precipitated the divorce were influenced by evil forces. Demonizing an ex-spouse could have a polarizing effect on already painful negotiations that are necessary to finalize a divorce or to manage ongoing custody arrangements that require minimal trust in the moral integrity of one's ex-spouse. Demonizing oneself in relation to an ex-partner could lead one to accept a blatantly unfair divorce settlement or to abdicate parental rights and responsibilities out of a sense of worthlessness, which then jeopardizes healthy parent-child relationships after the divorce.

INTERPLAY AMONG SPIRITUAL STRUGGLES   Despite useful conceptual distinctions, the three highlighted types of spiritual struggle are likely to co-occur and interact in complex ways. Divorces marked by desecrations that break religiously rooted wedding vows raise a host of intersecting spiritual dilemmas. Individuals whose spouses persist in infidelity, substance abuse, or domestic violence may struggle with how much God wants them to sacrifice their own well-being to remain married (divine struggle). Such individuals may also feel inner turmoil about whether to follow perceived mandates from God or their religious community to remain married, especially if these directives clash with their inner spiritual intuitions (intrapersonal struggle). Further, offending spouses may accuse partners who refuse to tolerate desecrations of being spiritually inferior for not being unconditionally forgiving (interpersonal struggle). Even more difficult dilemmas may occur when the boundaries between acceptable and unacceptable behavior on the part of a spouse are ambiguous, such as instances in which the individual feels chronically emotionally abandoned or neglected by his or her spouse.

Empirical Research on Spiritual Struggles and Divorce   Studies have shown clear and consistent links between the three types of spiritual struggles reviewed previously and indicators of distress. Ano and Vasconcelles (2005) conducted a meta-analysis of 49 studies of religious coping and reported that divine spiritual struggles were consistently tied to greater psychological maladjustment. Furthermore, divine struggles have been longitudinally related to poorer medical and psychological functioning (Pargament et al., 2006; Pargament, Koenig, Tarakeshwar, & Hahn, in press). While studied less often, intrapersonal and interpersonal spiritual struggles also correlate with more distress (e.g., Exline, Yali, & Sanderson, 2000; Krause, Ingersoll-Dayton, Ellison, & Wulff, 1999; Pargament et al., 1998). Little research has involved spiritual coping with interpersonal stressors, such as divorce, or events that are perceived as spiritual traumas. Further, although some anecdotal evidence (e.g., Spaniol & Lannan, 1985) and small qualitative studies suggest (Blomquist, 1985; Nathanson, 1985) that divorce elicits spiritual struggles, our study appears to be the first to examine this issue quantitatively. Notably, 71% of our participants reported experiencing some type of spiritual struggle over their divorce. Further, higher levels of spiritual struggles were strongly tied to greater depression, anger, and posttraumatic anxiety symptoms, even after taking into account demographics and access to adaptive spiritual and nonspiritual coping resources (Krumrei et al., 2007).

Spiritual Traumas and Spiritual Resources

Ample research shows that adaptive use of spiritual resources (positive spiritual coping methods) offer unique benefits to people, even after controlling for other resources, when they face a host of life stressors. This includes the death of a loved one, terminal illness, major surgery, imprisonment, physical abuse, war, racism, flooding, car accidents, and adjustment to college (Pargament et al., 2006). Over time, such strategies decrease emotional stress, and increase well-being and spiritual growth (Pargament & Ano, 2004; Pargament, Koenig, Tarakeshwar, & Hahn, 2001; Pargament et al., 1998). Spirituality can likewise be a vital, perhaps even the most relevant, place to turn to recover from spiritual traumas. However, cross-sectional research reveals an important paradox about spiritual resources. At the time of a crisis, greater use of spiritual resources is often linked with greater psychological distress (e.g., anxiety, depression, and anger) and spiritual struggles (e.g., anger or doubts about God). This effect has been coined a *stress mobilization effect.* Nevertheless, even at the time of a crisis, greater positive spiritual coping is tied to self-reports of stress-related psychological and spiritual growth (the individual's perception that a particular stressor has been helpful in making positive changes in life). Taken together, these findings indicate that psychic and spiritual struggles motivate many people to turn to their faith as a means to grow through their pain. We now discuss specific spiritual resources that could facilitate postdivorce adjustment.

Spiritual Resources to Cope with Sacred Traumas   Pargament and others have reliably identified 10 distinct spiritual coping strategies employed by adults that predict desirable functioning (Pargament et al., 1998). For the purposes of this chapter, we group these methods into three categories that parallel our discussion of spiritual struggles: divine, intrapersonal, and interpersonal.

Adaptive Divine/God-Oriented Spiritual Coping Methods   This set of spiritual coping strategies directly centers on an individual's relationship, thoughts, and feelings toward God. One such strategy involves proactively seeking a sense of control and relief through building a partnership with God (collaborative spiritual coping). Listen to this woman's description of collaborating with God to sort through her emotions and thoughts about her divorce: "Coping for me came through spending time alone journaling and praying honestly to God. . . . I have learned a lot about judging others, and I have discovered a great insight into myself." A related strategy is making a conscious decision to relinquish control over a situation to God after doing all in one's power to influence the situation (active spiritual surrender). Divorcing persons might have sought counseling, read self-help books, tried to bargain and negotiate with their spouse, and made all compromises short of those violating their core personal integrity, but still have been unable to stop a divorce. Here it could be adaptive to give control up to God, saying "I have done my best and must leave the rest up to God." Another God-centered strategy is to search for comfort and reassurance through God's love and care. One participant spoke of growing closer to God through the divorce saying, "God has been present in my life for many years . . . but I've never felt closer to Him than I do now. . . . Sometimes I feel like God is the only one who can help me now." Finally, an individual may reinterpret a stressful situation in a positive spiritual light (referred to as *benevolent spiritual reappraisal*). This strategy may be especially useful to combat perceptions of sacred loss and desecration. An individual might try to view the divorce as part of God's plan and means by which God is trying to strengthen the person. The following comment from one of our participants illustrates this process: "My divorce was swift, not my choice, and has broken my heart. But praying and believing that God, or some higher power, has a hand in this and there is a grand plan for my life, has helped me focus, even in my darkest hours."

ADAPTIVE INTRAPERSONAL POSITIVE SPIRITUAL COPING METHODS   Another set of spiritual resources centers on people's attempts to discover, access, or reestablish elements of their internal spiritual orienting system beyond a God figure (although God may still be relevant). Individuals can engage in spiritual activities to shift focus from the stressor. In the case of divorce, they may engage in prayer, private spiritual rituals, or public worship services to get their mind off problems and transcend feelings of anger, hurt, and fear. Efforts to seek spiritual purification constitute another way to regroup interior spiritual life, particularly if individuals feel some responsibility for the sacred trauma. A person may choose to confess to oneself, clergy, fellow believers or God personal failings that contributed to the divorce and resolve to avoid similar transgressions in the future. This may free the person from debilitating guilt and reestablish a sense of spiritual integrity. Another strategy is to seek out a sense of connectedness with forces that transcend the self as a means to free oneself from suffocating isolation. In a divorce, one can seek spiritual intimacy with others (e.g., share feelings of spiritual trauma with another), attempt to feel part of a larger, transcendent force (e.g., nature walks) or search for a closer connection with a higher power (e.g., meditation).

The preceding methods may often reflect much used tools within a well-integrated spiritual orienting system. However, trauma can also open people to reformulate their sense of spiritual meaning, direction, and purpose. Divorcing individuals may come to believe that their commitment to their marriage led them astray from their deepest values. Chronic conflict over issues that often lead to divorce (e.g., money, sex, religion, morals, child-rearing) can be rooted in fundamentally differing visions between partners of what is spiritually desirable (Mahoney, 2005). Being freed from a spouse who pushes against or discourages the other partner's spiritual values could be experienced as a wonderfully liberating opportunity to return to, or discover anew, one's core spiritual vision for life.

On a related note, some divorcing individuals may undergo a spiritual conversion marked by a radical shift in what constitutes their highest priorities in life (Mahoney & Pargament, 2004). One such spiritual conversion fits the classic Christian motif where a prideful focus on one's power and superiority is replaced by humble recognition that the sacred should be at the center of one's existence. A divorce may cause a person who had taken arrogant pride in constructing a "perfect marriage" to see the sacred not as superfluous, but of central importance. Another type of spiritual conversion, rooted in Christian feminism, involves replacing an excessive need of others' approval with a healthy sense of empowerment rooted in bonding with the sacred. A divorce may help a person realize that unchecked emotional dependency on the ex-spouse led to abuse and helped create a failed marriage. A divorce may draw the person inward, searching for a sense that the sacred resides both within and outside the self, which then provides a fundamental sense of worthiness.

INTERPERSONAL POSITIVE SPIRITUAL COPING   Family, friends, congregations, and communities play a central role in this set of spiritual resources. One method is to search for comfort through the love and care of congregation members and clergy. Here two of our divorcing participants describe seeking spiritual support from others, with one saying: "the [church] members have supported and helped me immensely," and another noting: "I work in a religious facility and have turned to the Sisters here for much support. . . . The Sisters here have been my biggest connection to God." Conversely, some cope with trauma by attempting to provide spiritual support and comfort to others. In the case of divorce, one may pray for or with friends or family members who are affected by the divorce, and try to give them spiritual strength by being a healthy, spiritual role model and listening compassionately to their spiritual struggles. Finally, one may seek out spiritually based forgiveness for wrongdoing by the ex-partner or self in the marriage. This includes using spiritual rituals and God as a resource to let go of anger, resentment, and bitterness. One participant told us, "I have a long way to go before I can heal from this. But by the grace of God, I will heal and forgive—one day."

Empirical Research on Use of Religious Resources and Divorce Adjustment   Our findings about positive methods of spiritual coping to deal with divorce mirror those found for other major life stressors. Consistent with stress-mobilization effects discussed earlier, greater use of positive religious coping methods was cross-sectionally related to higher levels of posttraumatic anxiety, depression, anger, and negative spiritual appraisals and spiritual struggles. However, the more participants turned to their faith in healthy ways to cope with the divorce, the more they reported experiencing posttraumatic and spiritual growth (Krumrei et al., 2007). Thus, the more individuals feel distressed by their divorce, the more they may mobilize their spiritual resources, which are tied to greater growth. It is also important to note that positive religious coping strategies partially or fully accounted for associations between sacred loss and desecration appraisals, and spiritual struggles. This implies that access to adaptive forms of spiritual coping can help resolve the troubling spiritual doubts or concerns that divorce engenders. Longitudinal research with divorcing individuals is needed to confirm this sequential chain of events that has been found for other major life stressors. Finally, we found that spiritual coping makes a difference for personal growth beyond any such benefits gained by using nonspiritual coping.

SUMMARY

In this chapter, we have presented a conceptual model on the role that spirituality plays in promoting trauma-related growth. We have argued that a potentially traumatic experience, such as divorce, can be experienced as a sacred loss or desecration. Such perceptions and feelings reflect a unique and additive dimension of an already intensely stressful experience, rendering it a spiritual trauma. Spiritual traumas may often trigger painful spiritual struggles, but such perceptions can also facilitate long-range psychological and spiritual growth. Many individuals may be highly motivated to grow rather than entirely abandon a spiritual frame of reference.

Further, spirituality offers numerous adaptive resources to help an individual recover from spiritual traumas and overcome the suffering associated with spiritual struggles.

Divorce may often raise profound spiritual issues that are relevant to how a person construes and adjusts to divorce. The following Summary Points provide sample questions for clinicians who are helping clients constructively resolve spiritual struggles and capitalize on past or new spiritual resources.

Summary Points

- Gain background information about clients' spiritual frame of reference:
  - —First, obtain basic information about clients' current spiritual orienting system. Three opening questions are, "In what ways, if any, do you see yourself as a spiritual or religious person?" "Do you believe in God or a Higher Power? If so, how do you envision or think about God?" and, "Are you affiliated with a religious denomination and how active are you in that group?" Many individuals will elaborate on their spiritual backgrounds from these questions. After acquiring a basic understanding of a client's spirituality, the clinician can focus on the intersection of divorce and spirituality.
- Gain information about clients' spiritual frame of reference for their marriage and divorce:
  - —Ask neutral, global questions about the role of spirituality in the divorce. An example is, "Has your spirituality, or your religious beliefs or background, entered into your thoughts or feelings about your divorce?"
  - —Ask questions about positive spiritual appraisals individuals may have had about their marriage. A nontheistic question is, "Have you ever experienced your marriage as a spiritual experience or sacred in any way?" A theistically oriented question would be, "Have you ever believed that your marriage was somehow connected to God or a Higher Power?"
- Help clients articulate if and how much they experience their divorce as a spiritual trauma:
  - —Help clients identify and express feelings of sacred loss or desecration in connection with their divorce. "Sacred loss" and "desecrations" probes could be, respectively, "How much do you feel you lost something of spiritual importance because of the divorce?" and "How much did your divorce violate your expectations of the spiritual nature of your marriage?"

—Help normalize and reduce stigma about clients viewing their divorce as a sacred loss and desecration.

—Explore what, if any, psychological and spiritual distress clients feel because of experiencing the divorce as a trauma that threatens or damages their spiritual worldview.

• Help clients articulate spiritual struggles caused by divorce:

—Open with a general question such as, "Have you found yourself feeling confused or having more questions and doubts about spirituality because of your divorce?"

—Follow up with questions about divine, intrapsychic, and interpersonal spiritual struggles. Sample probes are, "Has your divorce created negative thoughts and feelings for you about the nature of God?" "Has your divorce led you to have questions, doubts, or uncertainties about your spiritual journey in life?" and "Have you experienced tension between yourself and others about your divorce because of spiritual or religious issues?"

—Explore how divorce may have led to a decline in clients' level of satisfaction with their spiritual life and decline in any spiritual or religious activity that was previously helpful.

• Identify when clients have used adaptive spiritual coping in the past to deal with the divorce or other traumas:

—Explore if and when clients have dealt successfully with a stressful event using spiritual resources. An example question is, "In what ways has your spirituality or involvement in religion helped you deal with your divorce or another major challenge in your life?"

—Explore specific attempts clients have made to turn to their faith to deal with the divorce. Probe in the areas of relating to God (e.g., "Have you found yourself turning to God for support?"), individual spiritual practices (e.g., "Have you read about or tried new spiritual exercises or rituals to help you deal with your divorce?"), and interpersonal spiritual coping (e.g., "Have you talked to others who might understand what you are going through both emotionally and spiritually?").

—Ask clients about the extent to which they feel these efforts have been helpful. If not helpful, explore what the barriers are in this situation compared with others where spiritual resources have worked effectively.

• Explore with clients possible ways the divorce has or could trigger spiritual growth:

—Explore clients' attempts to reformulate their spiritual thinking or operating to accommodate the divorce.

—Ask clients to imagine what spiritual growth due to the divorce might look like.

—Explore clients' examples and offer the client examples of how others have found their faith tested but strengthened by personal crises.

REFERENCES

Amato, P. R. (2000). The consequences of divorce for adults and children. *Journal of Marriage and the Family, 62*, 1269–1287.

Ano, G. G., & Vasconcelles, E. B. (2005). Religious coping and psychological adjustment to stress: A meta-analysis. *Journal of Clinical Psychology, 61*, 461–480.

Blomquist, J. M. (1985). The effect of the divorce experience on spiritual growth. *Pastoral Psychology, 34*, 82–91.

Bloom, B. L., Asher, S. H., & White, S. W. (1978). Marital disruption as a stressor: A review and analyses. *Psychological Bulletin, 85*, 867–894.

Brown, P., Felton, B. J., Whiteman, V., & Manela, R. (1980). Attachment and distress following marital separation. *Journal of Divorce, 3*, 303–317.

Calhoun, L. G., & Tedeschi, R. G. (2006). The foundations of posttraumatic growth: An expanded framework. In L. G. Calhoun & R. G. Tedeschi (Eds.), *Handbook of posttraumatic growth: Research and practice* (pp. 3–23). Mahwah, NJ: Erlbaum.

Exline, J. J. (2002). Stumbling blocks on the religious road: Fractured relationships, nagging vices, and the inner struggle to believe. *Psychological Inquiry, 13*, 182–189.

Exline, J. J., Yali, A. M., & Sanderson, W. C. (2000). Guilt, discord, and alienation: The role of religious strain in depression and suicidality. *Journal of Clinical Psychology, 56*, 1481–1496.

Greeff, A. P., & Merwe, S. (2004). Variables associated with resilience in divorced families. *Social Indicators Research, 68*, 59–75.

Kitson, G. C., Barbri, K. B., Roach, M. J., & Placidi, K. S. (1989). Adjustment to widowhood and divorce: A review. *Journal of Family Issues, 10*, 5–32.

Kitson, G. C., & Raschke, H. J. (1981). Divorce research: What we know, what we need to know. *Journal of Divorce, 4*, 1–37.

Krause, N., Ingersoll-Dayton, B., Ellison, C. G., & Wulff, K. M. (1999). Aging, religious doubt, and psychological well-being. *Gerontologist, 39*, 525–533.

Kreider, R. M. (2005). *Number, timing, and duration of marriages and divorces: 2001* (Current Population Reports, 70–97). Washington, DC: U.S. Census Bureau.

Krumrei, E. J., Mahoney, A., & Pargament, K. I. (2007). *Divorce and the Divine: The role of spiritual appraisals, coping, and struggles for adults' post-divorce adjustment.* Manuscript submitted for publication.

Ladd, L. D., & Zvonkovic, A. (1995). Single mothers with custody following divorce. *Marriage and Family Review, 20*, 189–211.

Lazarus, R. S., & Folkman, S. (1984). *Stress, appraisals, and coping.* New York: Springer.

Lawton, L. E., & Bures, R. (2001). Parental divorce and the "switching" of religious identity. *Journal for the Scientific Study of Religion, 40,* 99–111.

Linley, P. A., & Joseph, S. (2004). Positive change following trauma and adversity: A review. *Journal of Traumatic Stress, 17,* 11–21.

Livingston, P. H. (1985). Union and disunion. *Studies in Formative Spirituality, 6,* 241–253.

Magyar, G. M., Pargament, K. I., & Mahoney, A. (2000, August). *Violating the sacred: A study of desecration among college students.* Paper presented at the annual meeting of the American Psychological Association, Washington, DC.

Mahoney, A. (2005). Religion and conflict in family relationships. *Journal of Social Issues, 61,* 689–706.

Mahoney, A., & Pargament, K. I. (2004). Sacred changes: Spiritual conversion and transformation. *Journal of Clinical Psychology, 60,* 481–492.

Mahoney, A., Pargament, K. I., Ano, G., Lynn, Q., Magyar, G., McCarthy, S., et al. (2002, August). *The devil made them do it? Demonization and the 9/11 attacks.* Paper presented at the annual meeting of the American Psychological Association, Chicago.

Mahoney, A., Pargament, K. I., Jewell, T., Swank, A. B., Scott, E., Emery, E., et al. (1999). Marriage and the spiritual realm: The role of proximal and distal religious constructs in marital functioning. *Journal of Family Psychology, 13,* 321–338.

Mahoney, A., Pargament, K. I., Murray-Swank, A., & Murray-Swank, N. (2003). Religion and the sanctification of family relationships. *Review of Religious Research, 40,* 220–236.

Mahoney, A., Pargament, K. I., Tarakeshwar, N., & Swank, A. (2001). Religion in the home in the 1980s and 1990s: A meta-analytic review and conceptual analysis of religion, marriage, and parenting. *Journal of Family Psychology, 15,* 559–596.

Mahoney, A., & Tarakeshwar, N. (2005). Religion's role in marital and family relationships. In R. F. Paloutzian & C. L. Park (Eds.), *Handbook of the psychology of religion* (pp. 177–198). New York: Guilford Press.

Nathanson, I. G. (1995). Divorce and women's spirituality. *Journal of Divorce and Remarriage, 22,* 179–188.

Neimeyer, R. A., & Levitt, H. (2001). Coping and coherence: A narrative perspective on resilience. In C. R. Snyder (Ed.), *Coping with stress: Effective people and processes* (pp. 46–67). New York: Oxford University Press.

Pargament, K. I. (1997). *The psychology of religion and coping: Theory, research, practice.* New York: Guilford Press.

Pargament, K. I., & Ano, G. (2004). Empirical advances in the psychology of religion and coping. In K. W. Schaie, N. Krause, & A. Booth (Eds.), *Religious influences on health and well-being in the elderly* (pp. 114–140). New York: Springer.

Pargament, K. I., Desai, K., & McConnell, K. M. (2006). Spirituality: A pathway to posttraumatic growth or decline? In R. Tedeschi & L. Calhoun (Eds.), *Handbook of posttraumatic growth: Research and practice* (pp. 121–137). Mahwah, NJ: Erlbaum.

Pargament, K. I., Koenig, H. G., Tarakeshwar, N., & Hahn, J. (2001). Religious struggle as a predictor of mortality among medically ill elderly patients: A two-year longitudinal study. *Archives of Internal Medicine, 161,* 1881–1885.

Pargament, K. I., Koenig, H. G., Tarakeshwar, N., & Hahn, J. (in press). Religious coping methods as predictors of psychological, physical, and spiritual outcomes among medically ill elderly patients: A two-year longitudinal study. *Journal of Health Psychology.*

Pargament, K. I., Magyar, G. M., Benore, E., & Mahoney, A. (2005). Sacrilege: A study of sacred loss and desecration and their implications for health and well-being in a community sample. *Journal of Personality and Social Psychology, 44,* 59–78.

Pargament, K. I., & Mahoney, A. (2002). Spirituality: Discovering and conserving the sacred. In C. R. Snyder (Ed.), *Handbook of positive psychology* (pp. 646–675). Washington, DC: American Psychological Association.

Pargament, K. I., & Mahoney, A. (2005). Sacred matters: Sanctification as vital topic for the psychology of religion. *International Journal of the Psychology of Religion, 15,* 179–198.

Pargament, K. I., McConnell, K., Mahoney, A., & Silberman, I. (in press). They killed our Lord: The perception of Jews as desecrators of Christianity as a predictor of anti-Semitism. *Journal for the Scientific Study of Religion.*

Pargament, K. I., Smith, B. W., Koenig, H. G., & Perez, L. (1998). Patterns of positive and negative religious coping with major life stressors. *Journal of the Scientific Study of Religion, 37,* 711–725.

Smith, J. A., & Smith, A. H. (2000). Parishioner attitudes toward the divorced/separated: Awareness seminars as counseling interventions. *Counseling and Values, 45,* 17–27.

Spaniol, L., & Lannan, P. (1985). Divorce and spirituality. *Studies in Formative Spirituality, 6,* 399–405.

Walters-Chapman, S. F., Price, S. J., & Serovich, J. M. (1995). The effects of guilt on divorce adjustment. *Journal of Divorce and Remarriage, 22,* 163–177.

Weiss, R. (1975). *Marital separation.* New York: Basic Books.

CHAPTER 7

Growth through Loss and Adversity in Close Relationships

JOHN H. HARVEY

I
N THIS CHAPTER, I review evidence and case studies of persons who have experienced growth through adversity and loss in their close relationships. Two specific groups are targeted in this analysis. One is children of divorce. We know from an extensive literature that many children of divorce are adversely affected by their parents' divorce. However, as documented by Harvey and Fine (2004), many other young persons also grow, mature, and become stronger in their outreach to others based on their experiences in a divorcing family. In this chapter, I address some of those growth experiences and provide narrative illustrations from young persons' reports of how their parents' divorce affected them.

A second focus of this chapter is on persons who have lost parents. Narrative evidence also is presented for persons who have experienced such losses (Harvey & Chavis, 2006). Like the children of divorce, people who have lost parents may experience major impacts such as anger, depression, difficulties in relationships and work life, and changes in how they see themselves and their merits and meaning as human beings. The final part of this chapter deals with how this evidence might be useful to practitioners and to others coping with their own losses in similar situations.

THEORETICAL FOUNDATION

The theoretical basis for the narrative evidence discussed in this work is account-making theory. An account is defined as a storylike statement (written or oral) that attempts to describe, explain, and possibly just vent about some complex and emotionally involving pattern of events (Harvey, Weber,

& Orbuch, 1990; Orbuch, 1997). To understand what is meant by an account-making perspective, it is first important to realize that we are all storytellers. That is our bedrock capacity as human beings (Coles, 1989). As noted by Bochner, Ellis, and Tillmann-Healy (1997), people rely on stories to make sense out of their ongoing lived experience. Furthermore, stories both reflect the objective realities of what we experience and shape our interpretations of our experiences. Thus, stories both represent and shape experience (Bochner et al., 1997).

It is argued in account-making theory that confiding accounts of major events such as losses of close others can be restorative to the human psyche. This act of confiding helps a person gain perspective, achieve catharsis, and feel connected to others who have suffered similar losses or who care deeply about one's experiences (Harvey et al., 1990). In large measure, the following sections on narrative evidence about loss speak to this role of confiding parts of one's account in adaptation to the new realities that major loss brings to a person's life.

PERVASIVENESS OF DIVORCE

In most Western countries, there has been a great increase in the divorce rate from 3 out of 10 marriages ending in divorce in 1960 to 5 out of 10 by 1975 and a continued high rate into the twenty-first century. This increase has had many untoward effects on society (Whitehead, 1996). Economically, marital dissolution is hard on all parties, but especially so on women (Hetherington & Kelly, 2002; McLanahan, 1999). Compared with children whose parents remain married, children of divorced parents also experience higher rates of several problems, such as internalizing behaviors (e.g., anxiety, depression), externalizing problems (e.g., behavior problems), and poor school performance (particularly dropping out of school; Emery, 1999; Fine, 2000).

The implications of the rapid rise in the divorce rate extend beyond the single-family unit to affect such areas as government policy, the provision of mental health services, and society as a whole. In this context of relatively high divorce rates, federal policy has been drafted to attempt to improve child support compliance rates and to address other political issues relevant to the family (Bogenschneider, 2000). Some states in the United States have adopted Covenant Marriage legislation, which attempts to make the process of divorce more difficult for couples (e.g., usually involves a 2-year wait from filing to granting of a divorce). In addition, there has been a tremendous increase in the number of mental health professionals working on relationships and divorce issues in the past 3 decades, to the point where divorce-related intervention programs, such as mediation and parent education programs for divorcing parents, have become increasingly popular and often mandated (P. Feng & Fine, 2000).

THE EFFECTS ON CHILDREN

The effects of divorce on children is a prime, timely topic because in the early twenty-first century, Census Bureau data indicate that at least 50% to 60% of the children in the United States will spend some period of time before they reach 18 in a home in which divorce has occurred. One-third or more of the children in this country will live in a stepfamily by the time they reach 18. Statistically, parental divorce is strongly associated with adult children's divorces (Amato & Booth, 1997), a phenomenon commonly known as the "intergenerational transmission of divorce." Amato and De-Boer (2001) found that parental divorce approximately doubled the chances that offspring would divorce as adults.

There is an abundance of literature on the intergenerational transmission of divorce. Factors such as education, income, family and social support systems, and individual attitudes and expectations have been implicated as explaining why offspring of divorced parents are more likely to divorce as adults (D. Feng, Giarrusso, Bengtson, & Frye, 1999). Compared with children from first-married families, children of divorced parents have been found to have lower income and educational attainment, to marry at younger ages, and to be more likely to cohabit prior to marriage (Furstenberg & Teitler, 1994). Amato and DeBoer (2001) concluded that children from divorced families have a higher likelihood of divorcing because they hold a "comparatively weak commitment to the norm of lifelong marriage" (p. 1038). The types of reported negative effects of divorce on children are diverse and numerous. An August 1999 news story (AP wire story) suggested that teen boys who have had limited or negative interaction histories with their fathers, often in connection with divorce, are at higher risk for smoking, drinking, and illegal drug usage than are teen boys with strong relationships with a single mother. Children of divorce often report that they have been placed in the middle of interparental conflict, bitter struggles about money, new dating partners, wrongs such as infidelities at the time of their parents' breakups, and the like (Harvey & Fine, 2004).

Semischolarly books providing data and perspective on the effects of divorce on children and adults have been published by well-known scholars such as Wallerstein, Lewis, and Blakeslee (2000) and Hetherington and Kelly (2002). Because Hetherington and Wallerstein have quite different views on the effects of divorce on children, their divergent views received considerable national attention in such magazines as *Newsweek* and *Time.*

The Hetherington-Wallerstein debate highlights a frustrating aspect of the divorce literature—scholars often reach conflicting conclusions about how harmful divorce can be to children. Hetherington and colleagues found that while there was initial turmoil in the lives of the children, their lives had become more normal by the second year after divorce and that there were few substantial long-term differences between these children and their counterparts from first-marriage families. By contrast, Wallerstein and her colleagues concluded that as many as one-half of the young men and women they studied entered adulthood as worried, underachieving, self-deprecating, and sometimes angry people because of their parents' divorces.

In an attempt to understand why scholars often reach different conclusions about the effects of divorce on family members, Fine and Demo (2000) argued that researchers' different theoretical perspectives, values, disciplines, and training often lead them in divergent research directions and, ultimately, to the generation of different conclusions, sometimes from the very same data.

EMERY'S RAPPROCHEMENT TO THE CONTROVERSY

How can one make sense of these different threads in the literature—with some investigators emphasizing long-term pain and sadness, whereas others are emphasizing resilience and strength? A synthesis of the literature by Emery (1999) may be helpful in resolving these apparently disparate conclusions. Emery has proposed five facts related to how divorce affects children:

1. Divorce causes a great deal of stress for children.
2. Divorce increases the risk (often doubling it, depending on the dimension studied) of psychological problems.
3. Despite the increased risk, most children from divorced families function as well as do children from first-marriage families.
4. Children whose parents divorce report considerable pain, unhappy memories, and continued distress.
5. Individual differences in children's postdivorce adjustment are influenced by aspects of postdivorce family life, particularly the quality of the child's relationship with the residential parent, the nature of interparental conflict, the family's financial standing, and the relationship between the child and the nonresidential parent.

According to Emery, some investigators, particularly Wallerstein, focus on the fourth point without adequately considering the others, whereas others tend to minimize the stress and pain experienced by these children and young adults. In a sense, some scholars are blinded by looking at only one or two aspects of the proverbial multifeatured elephant.

VOICES OF HOPE

Harvey and Fine (2004) analyzed hundreds of narratives by children of divorce, persons between the ages of 18 and 27. A general conclusion from this work was that while many children experience great hurt and pain when their parents divorce, others grow and learn new roles and perspectives. These latter children epitomize the functioning group in Emery's (1999) third category. They show lots of hope and maturity about the complexities of adult close relationships. Consider the following illustrative excerpt from Harvey and Fine's evidence:

> I think that I did grow up emotionally faster than a lot of my friends, but I don't necessarily believe this is such a bad quality. I learned to do things on my own, and I learned that life does not always go the way that you expect it to go. Having to deal with the unexpected brings character, and it makes you see things for what they really are, not just what you see on the surface. So, I can honestly say that I have forgiven both of them and I don't place blame on either one of them (22-year-old woman's comments on the positives deriving from her parents' divorce).

A set of fuller narratives further attest to the positive possibilities both for parents and children. These narratives suggest the wilderness course that children of divorce must navigate between valleys of pain and loss and mountains of new experience and growth. First, a 21-year-old woman:

> Divorce is such a commonality—especially in the United States anymore. It is reported that 51% of the people in this country have been divorced. I think people really need to take that statistic into account and realize that marriage is not something you just jump into or do for fun. Marriage, like anything else will have its negatives. And I feel that people need to be aware of that before they do anything pertaining to marriage. It just seems to me that people are not wanting to assume marital responsibility anymore and the only way to get out of that responsibility is by getting a divorce.
>
> First, I will give you a little of my maternal family history concerning divorces. My grandmother and grandfather were married before they married each other. They were both at age 18 when they got married to their previous spouses. My aunt, my mother's sister, was married 10 years when her husband decided to leave her for another woman. And my mother got married 23 years ago to my biological father. She gave birth to me a year after they

were married. He, not being ready to faithfully be a husband or a father, decided to leave my mother when I was 6 months old. With the divorce, he took everything—even jewelry and a car that was my mother's. My mother had lost almost all the things she owned—except her clothes, the house, and yours truly. As a matter of fact, he wanted nothing to do with me after they divorced, which didn't affect me too much because I did not know the man anyway. But, my mother was another story. Not only did she lose many of her personal belongings, but she lost her partner and a man she loved very much. She was ready for the marriage, but he was not.

Thankfully, a year or so later, my mother started dating my "dad," and he has been my dad ever since. My parents got married when I was 5 years old and 6 months later my brother was born. You're probably thinking, "Hmm, that's a pretty happy ending . . ." but to be honest with you, it is a little more complicated than that. My mom had lost her first husband, so it took her 5 years for her to gain the courage back to trust another man in matrimony. I remember there were nights when my dad would be gone at work on the midnight shift when I was a small child, and my mother had just had a nightmare. I could just tell by the look on her face and by the words she said that it was about my father. I would just hug and hold her until she stopped crying.

Since divorce runs in my family like water through a hose, I hope to be the one to break that chain when/if I ever do get married. I look at the marriage my mom and dad have, and all in all, it is a good one. Through their arguments and disputes, they've managed to be married for 16 years.

I've witnessed some pretty ugly conflict, but they endured the hardships and have done the best job they could. I really take pride in that because you don't see that too often anymore. To be honest, I'm tired of viewing marriages as delicate when they should be rock solid. The vows of "til death do us part" should be taken into account. In conclusion, I feel that marriage is not something to be taken for granted or dealt with as a game. Marriage is a lifelong commitment. And until people start believing that, the United States will probably continue to climb the trend of divorce. I feel that doing all that is possible to save marriages is what needs to be done, and divorce should only be considered as a last resort.

Another 21-year-old woman also reveals strength after enduring much loss associated with her parents' divorce:

Divorce is a very hard concept, something that affects everyone involved. I am a victim of divorce. My parents divorced when I was 13, probably the most crucial time in my life. I was experiencing so many new things, starting a new school (middle school) making new friends, going through puberty, and I was also diagnosed with diabetes that same year. I helplessly felt that my life was falling apart. Two years previous to my parents' divorce, my father had an affair with another lady, one of my mother's friends actually, who my father worked with.

My parents tried to work it out, they seemed to be happier than I ever remembered following that. However, my mother then found my father and the lady he was having an affair with together again a year and a half later. That is when they decided to call it quits.

Divorce has changed my life. My siblings and I moved with my mother. Thankfully my parents still got along well enough that they mutually agreed that when my father wanted to see us he could, there were no strict regulations as to child custody. I missed our family all being together. My older brother and sister were in high school and were never home at all it seemed like, probably because they felt that it was not really home without all of us together. Dinner time was always when my family would sit down together and talk about each other's day and just reminisce, we no longer had that, we did, but it was only my mother, little sister and me usually. Being from a small town, everyone knew everything that was going on with my family, I was so embarrassed I remember.

Out of all of my friends, I was now the only one whose parents were divorced. When I would go to my friends' houses and see a happy family bonding, I would hurt, long for that once again. Everyone was so supportive though, thank god. My mother and I formed a very close bond, she became my best friend, she needed me, and I needed her. I was also still very close to my father and continue to be today. I was always Daddy's little girl, and when he did this to my family, it was so hard for me to understand it. Fortunately, I am a very forgiving person, and decided I needed to put the past behind me, and rather live for today and the future.

I have struggled throughout life since the divorce, but it has only made me a better, stronger person. I have learned responsibility, learned how to be a hard worker (I have had a job since I was 14 and am now putting myself through college!) I am a very grateful person; I am content and very happy-go-lucky. I realize that divorce was the best thing for my family right now. I often wonder what it would have been like if my parents would not have gotten divorced, but then think to myself, everything happens for a reason, and I am who I am today because of what has happened to me in the past, and made me that much more of a better person!

As is evident from these stories, young people have to work hard to find positive aspects of the trying circumstances of their parents' divorce. The first respondent provided a classic line in this project when she said, "Since divorce runs in my family like water through a hose," reflecting the intergenerational (and intragenerational) transmission of divorce. Still, both writers show perspective and strength in meeting these challenges and believing that they can handle other events that no doubt will be part of their long-term adjustment to divorce in their family.

A final "wilderness to hope" story is provided by this 20-year-old woman, who muses about how divorce at any point in a child's life can be devastating. But then, the person has to get up off the ground and go on, and, in survival, the person may see that the long-range outcome is better than if the divorce had not occurred:

Divorce is a very traumatic event—it's difficult for everyone involved. Each family member is impacted, whether it is the parents or the children. I often wonder what the best age is for a child to experience divorce. Would it be easier for a 6-year-old, a 16-year-old, or a 26-year-old? I guess it depends on the circumstances, but I think that it would have been hardest for me as a teenager. Going through my parents' divorce was very difficult for me, and I was away at college 90% of the time. I could not imagine what it would have been like if I still was living at home.

When my parents announced that they were going to get a divorce, I felt that my parents owed it to me and my brothers to stay together no matter what. I was not going to allow it to happen. I remember everything about that day, what went on, where I was, and my initial reactions. I had just finished my freshman year of college, and returned home for the summer. My parents gathered us around the kitchen table, and told us that their relationship was over. The conversation began with my father saying, "Your mother and I have something very important to talk to you guys about. What I am about to tell you has been the most difficult decision that we have ever had to make." At that exact moment, I knew what they were going to say. After my parents finished telling us what they needed to tell us, I became extremely upset claiming that this was not going to happen. I didn't care what it took, divorce was not an option. I felt it was the easy way out, and the effects would be too severe.

Basically all of my close relationships changed following my parents' divorce. The relationship that I have with my brothers and father is stronger than it has ever been. The relationship that I have with my mother and girlfriend (now ex-girlfriend) has weakened. It was amazing to me how different my views on life and relationships have changed because of the divorce. I think that I am a very different person now, and see the world in a different way.

Recovery is an important part of the grieving process and I feel recovered. Life has its ups and downs, but I truly believe that everything happens for a reason. For some unknown reason, I was supposed to experience divorce; maybe it was to strengthen who I was; maybe it was to open my eyes regarding relationships; maybe it was to bring me closer to my brothers; maybe it was to forever change the relationship that I have with my dad. When I say that I am recovered from my parents' divorce; this does not mean that I am "over" my parents' divorce. I don't think that I will ever be over it. How could I get over it? It was a traumatic event of my adolescence, and it permanently altered who I am. Life does go on, however, and I am continuing to play the cards that were dealt to me. I am a different person now compared to when my parents were still together, but I would like to think that it is for the better. I have grown a lot from my experience with divorce, and I think that I am a stronger person because of it.

More generally, the following positive themes emerged in Harvey and Fine's (2004) work:

- Divorces can be civil and friendly.
- Divorces can lead to better parenting, including that provided by stepfathers.
- There are many and varied consequences of divorce, but the net result can be positive for all concerned.
- There may be a period of great despair, but with work a more constructive, hopeful period can follow.
- There can be a lot of growth deriving from this time of pain and sorrow.
- Parents should not stay in a conflicted marriage simply for the sake of the children.

PARENT LOSS

In this section, I discuss narrative evidence from a study by Harvey and Chavis (2006) of parent loss. Again, hundreds of narratives were analyzed for major themes about how people reacted to and coped with the loss of their parent.

DeSpelder and Strickland (2002) outlined variables that affect grieving and adaptation to the loss of a loved one, including the loss of a parent. Examples are personality (e.g., people with so-called hardy, resilient personalities are assumed to deal more effectively with major loss), whether the person believes the loved one has been relieved of suffering or that the death could have been avoided, the perceived relationship with the deceased (respondents reporting a close, ongoing relationship or a relationship that required work—unfinished business—often mentioned their difficulty in adjusting), and conflicting memories of experiences with the deceased loved ones. In general, ambivalence is a stark reality of the grieving process for the loss of a parent.

Most of the respondents in the Harvey and Chavis (2006) study found their grieving and adjustment to be challenging. They agreed to participate in the hopes that writing about their loss would help in their eventual adjustment and in finding greater peace. They also had the objective of helping others, educating others, and increasing general awareness of this phenomenon, which ultimately can translate to increased societal support for parental loss.

GROWTH AFTER THE LOSS OF A PARENT

Growth after the loss of a loved one occurs in the context of the griever's feeling that he or she can readily remember the loved one (maybe by memorializing the life and accomplishments) and give back to others based on what he or she gained from the loved one.

People cope and memorialize the loss of loved ones in many ways. Central to most coping mechanisms appears to be the act of remembering (and maybe telling the story of) the loved one. That is the essence of the memorial act (e.g., setting up a cross to designate a place along a highway where a loved one died). We do not want the world to forget that our loved one lived and made certain contributions to others.

As important as coping to many people is using the loss as a springboard to give back to others in some positive way. Erikson (1963) was a pioneer in articulating how people can grow through the act of giving back to future generations. As illustrated by many valuable human creations, major losses are energizing forces in this act. The following is what one young woman said about her desire to give back based on the loss of her dad at an early age:

> I have been able to positively use the tragedy of my father in many instances. I am able to bring this situation up to people who have lost a parent or other significant people in their lives as a commonality and thus they have felt more comfortable confiding in me. While again, totally different situations, this bond has allowed me to be there to listen to those that have gone through loses because they have added comfort in confiding in me. This has been a wonderful gift and I am blessed that I have that to give.
>
> Maybe that has led me to volunteering for organizations like crisis intervention lines and mediation groups. And I am sure it has influenced my desire to work in social work in the future and applying for my master's in social work.

In the following excerpt, a woman describes how she often misses her deceased mother, who would be her confidante about the swirling events in life as a 20-something young person. The honoring of her mother in this excerpt attests to this ongoing love:

> Being 25 and single in the city, so often I have longed for my mom's wisdom and generous ear to help me through the dating world. Not too long ago, I had some pretty high expectations regarding a relationship dashed and I was just devastated. The only thing I could think of was how badly I wanted to share this with my mom. There was no one else I wanted to talk to but her and I just had to cry it out for a while until I finally called a friend.

There is not a day that has gone by in the past 7 years that I haven't thought of or missed my mom. In many ways, she is always on my mind because various things throughout each day will trigger a thought of her. You don't "get over" the loss of someone you loved so deeply; the grieving gets better and becomes livable, but it never fully goes away. Honoring my mother as her legacy is very important to me. There is no greater compliment than when someone says, you really look like your mom or you remind me of her. She was just the most beautiful, kind, nonjudgmental, and loving soul I have ever met and for myself and those who loved her, because of her life and death, we are forever changed. There is a quote I came across a while ago and it really touched me: "As is the mother, so is her daughter." I really hope so.

A male respondent addressed his own cycle of grieving and remembering:

I was 20 when my father died, and now I'm 34. He was 49. I think about him from time to time; I memorialize him on his death day every August by thinking about him and what he might think of what I'm doing with myself, what I've done with myself over the preceding year. And on some cycle, the timing of which is a mystery to me, I wonder intensely about him, and about who I am through him. I guess these are periods of grieving. I don't know how resolved I am about having lost my father, or how I would know that I am.

The following excerpt came from a long account by a woman of the death of her mother (from cancer) and also of a boyfriend (from drowning) in the same period of time. She wrote of her own desperate struggles, involving suicide attempts and alienation from her father and his new wife. In the long run, she shows both continuing powerful emotions and feelings of loss, but also remarkable clarity about how she needed to continue to wage battle against the impacts of these losses. This battle included her seeking therapy:

Those are the things that I wish for the most. I wish I could see her again, and tell her how sorry I am that I was too self-involved to spend much time with her before she died. I want her to meet my boyfriend, the man I know I'm going to marry. He is the first person to make me happy in years. I am angry that she can't meet him, and that he will never know her laugh or see her face. Sure, he's seen her in pictures, but that is in no way even close to the same. I wish she could see my sister now that she's 16. I wish that she could come to my wedding, and be there for my brother and sister-in-law's new baby due in January 2003. I guess on some level, I think she will be there for all of that because it's very possible she can be a spectator of earth from wherever she is right now. I just wish she could have a backstage pass so we could meet once again. One thing that my mother's death (along with every other loss) taught me was to not take people for granted. It made me aware of just how short time can be with someone. Nobody is guaranteed a certain number of hours here on earth, and that is the hardest. Since 1995, I have been terrified of people I love dying. Every time the phone rings, especially late at night, I think that someone must have died. It's so morbid, but I can't help it.

I started therapy again about 8 months ago, and it's the first time that I've really worked on the issues that, at times, still consume me. I am working on my fear of abandonment and death.

In the last excerpt, another complex story unfolds. A young man lost both of his parents early in life. This double loss precipitated many secondary losses, including great feelings of loneliness and isolation. He also documented a history of other losses that would challenge anyone's coping capacity. This story is important not only because it documents some of the secondary losses people who lose both parents experience, it also shows this young man's resilience and will to persevere:

My first year [after the loss of his parents] I felt nothing, I knew no love, no peace. . . . I was a fearful child scared to death. My home was gone, both of my parents were dead, my childhood was over, and I would not be able to rest that deep rest of comfort and childhood ever again. I would forever be unable to forget that the worst was possible. I was very lonely. I cried, I cried a stifled and pathetic cry. . . .

Between the death of my mother and my father, my paternal grandmother, whom I grew up seeing on a daily basis, died from cancer. My senior year at boarding school, the fathers of two of my classmates died. A year after the death of my father, a family from the church I used to attend got into a big car accident and two of their four children died. . . . The deaths never seemed to end. Although I was not scared of death, it worried me a lot: Would my friends come back after the summer, or would they die in summer car accidents? Thoughts like that dominated my mind while I was in boarding school. . . . I had the belief that death before age 19 was my fate. I felt like I was the prophet of my own doom. I thought that maybe killing myself would finally free me of the knowledge of death, of the knowledge that all things degrade and are eventually destroyed.

I never did kill myself, obviously, but I never formally tried either. I knew that if I was going to do it that I was not going to fail. I eventually came to see my thinking that I wouldn't make it to my 18th birthday was actually a masked desire to be reborn. I wanted to die at age 18 without all of the pain and without all of this hurt and suffering—I wanted to leave it all behind me, I needed a rite of passage. . . . There was one night the summer before I went to college that I sat with an open knife and contemplated suicide. I sat for hours feeling the blood flow to the lower parts of my body as I became cold and frozen. I thought about many things, about the fantasies of suicide and my own funeral. I had a girlfriend at the time, my first, and I imagined her at my funeral weeping. I imagined the scene when my brother and his wife came in the next day and saw me dead in a pool of blood that extended all across the carpet. . . .

Looking back at all of these things now from the age of 23, I have come a little distance from my old self and would like to note in closing a few things I have observed. I can see that I lost my parents before I was ready to live in the world as an independent person. I sought surrogates for my parents.

There was a part of me as a child that was lost. I later turned the fear that the worst would happen into a reason to cherish everything good in my life, to spend time with my friends, and to share with them as much as I could. I am engaged to be married now and try to pour everything into each day that I spend with my partner. I still have the fear that I will come home and have a message in my answering machine saying that she has been killed by a car while biking home from work, or something like that. I have been thinking that way less and less, though. I still know that anytime she may die, but I don't worry about it like the way I used to. Death, if it can be said to do so, has taught me this very important lesson about life, and I have never forgotten the lesson. It informs all of my life, nearly everything I do.

CONCLUSIONS ON LOSS OF PARENT NARRATIVE EVIDENCE

This work on the loss of a parent focused on the story lines and images that are common across this type of profound loss. The stories only hint at the complex lives that are being represented. It is amazing how long-lasting emotions surrounding the death of a parent can continue to influence the lives of survivors. The stories reported were filled with much continuing angst. It is left to the living to sort out the issues and feelings, a job we, too, will take to our dying days. The loss of a parent almost always diminishes the self (Harvey, 2002). But it also can, with work, make the self stronger. The words in the title of Harvey and Chavis's (2006) article, "still but unquiet voices," seem to capture the essence of what our respondents often were saying. Their dead parent lived on in their minds and reactions to many aspects of living. These voices would not be stilled until the child also died. Novelist Joyce Carol Oates noted in an interview (*O Magazine*, January 2001) about the death of her mother that there is an eternal cycle both of children and parents requiring the love of their parents, however old or long deceased.

TOWARD THEORETICAL SYNTHESIS

What are some overarching theoretical ideas that help us understand the collective evidence on the effects on children of divorce and parent loss? Joseph and Linley (2005) present a useful theoretical analysis, referred to as organismic valuing theory of growth through adversity that comports well with much of the evidence presented in these studies. Joseph and Linley's theory posits that people are intrinsically motivated toward rebuilding their assumptive world in a direction consistent with their innate tendency toward actualization. Growth inevitably occurs in facilitative environments. In this analysis, people are motivated to engage in a realistic reappraisal of the meaning of the event and its existential implications and to move toward greater authenticity in living, a process leading to greater psychological well-being.

Consistent with Joseph and Linley's (2005) argument, many of the respondents in the Harvey and Fine (2004) and Harvey and Chavis (2006) studies indicated that their growth from loss occurred intrinsically and gradually over time; individual differences in how and when growth unfolded also were evident. As Joseph and Linley also hypothesized, a majority of the respondents in these studies were working toward a new schematic understanding of their social world in light of their loss, and this understanding was facilitating a greater actualization of their life mission. The last account in the Parent Loss section illustrates this reasoning. This story attests to this young man's battle to make sense of what has been a daunting, changing landscape of loss (with multiple deaths of key loved ones), or in Joseph and Linley's (2005) terms to accommodate new traumatic information. Yet, he is finding ways to make his voice heard and to make his life more meaningful, building on the lessons of such profound losses. Many respondents in both studies indicated that their choice of careers and overall life missions were very much guided by these landmark losses in their lives and their quest to give back based on what they learned. They are, therefore, more open to the existential possibilities forced on them by their losses (Yalom & Lieberman, 1991). Fortunately, for the majority of respondents in both studies, the respondents were supported by environments of close others facilitating their account making and coping activities.

In terms of future research, it is obvious that not all people emerge from the throes of great loss to achieve growth, or even modest movement. Some people give up hope and sometimes end their lives prematurely when they perceive the burdens and implications of loss as being too great (Shneidman, 1996). A central research question for the future, therefore, is what are the determining conditions for the different outcomes associated with their different types of major loss? There has been inadequate descriptive and hypothesis-testing work on types of major losses, individual differences in coping, different coping approaches, and the social conditions that influence patterns of reaction to loss (Harvey & Miller, 1998).

In terms of the studies presented here, why and how do some children thrive fairly soon after their parents' divorces, whereas others feel devastated and work for years to understand divorce in their family and how to respond constructively to it? Although we know a lot about the role of the actual implementation of the divorce (e.g., the civility and cooperation exhibited by the parents) on postdivorce patterns (Ahrons, 1994), we do not have integrative theories that accommodate the diverse data about how children react to divorce. A similar line of questions may be asked by people's responses to parent loss. Certainly, factors such as the age of the child and the parent and the extent to which their lives are close and intertwined are obviously important to understanding reactions and coping attempts. However, neither integrative theory nor fine-grained descriptive work exists to help us begin to understand the full set of factors involved, or range of long-term reactions shown in these situations.

In concert with broadly integrative conceptions such as the one advanced by Joseph and Linley (2005), the account-making approach (Harvey et al., 1990) has promise for helping us better understand the diversity of responses to different loss situations. For many of us, account making about our major losses is a lifelong process with new implications and new subjective shapes and contours over time. Theoretically, people develop subaccounts within overall master accounts (e.g., the divorce of a person's parents and that person's own divorce, are both subaccounts that feed into the master account of losses that have led to who and where the person is at midlife). We know too little about how these subaccounts and master accounts are related, especially as people age and experience what they may perceive as a pileup of losses.

The account-making approach emphasizes not only the acts of cognitive and emotional work directed at understanding, expression, and edification about life's dilemmas, it also stresses the role of confidants and social interaction as integral to successful account making (account making that leads the account maker to feel some degree of completion in the articulation of what happened, why it happened, and learning based on these events).

What needs much attention in the realm of empirical work is the role that confidants and loved ones play in people's construction of these accounts and how the accounts are connected with account-relevant action over time. As Orbuch (1997) argues, it is likely that long-term psychological health is greatly affected by having at least one close confidant who cares about a person's ongoing major life events and important stories, and who is there to listen to the person's oft-telling of these stories. A confidant's act of omission in not being there to listen to an account maker, or being dismissive or rejecting of the account maker's stories, also appears to have a powerful negative impact in social interaction about major life events (Orbuch, Harvey, & Davis, & Merbach, 1994).

SUMMARY

As revealed in recent writing (e.g., Snyder & Lopez, 2002), a great variety of topics may be usefully pursued within the purview of positive psychology. The study of how people cope with major losses certainly fits within this area of work. Combining the studies of loss described in this chapter, a set of five conclusions about growth after loss and adversity emerge:

1. Loss occurs within ongoing contexts, such as family life and the development of young people. The effects of loss often ripple across the generations of families and affect people's development for much of their lives. Research is needed that treats loss and trauma and their effects in this broader set of considerations.
2. Consistent with a theme of positive psychology, people may grow and prosper after experiencing major loss (Tedeschi & Calhoun, 1995). However, their passage may be unsteady and involve years of struggle. Accordingly, research that follows people over extended periods of time will better reflect these changes and the ultimate new identities and strengths that emerge.
3. In the midst of the stories described in this chapter was the notion that sometimes just hanging on or movement was a victory in the context of major loss. "Just keep on going" is another outcome that is common and relatively positive (Harvey, Barnett, & Rupe, 2006). It probably is not growth as much as it is movement—not giving up, not wallowing in despair, not becoming abjectly depressed. It is, plainly put, surviving psychologically. Future research might better distinguish this type of positive movement from what is often referred to as posttraumatic growth.
4. Movement, then, can be seen as being akin to resilience, which Tedeschi and Calhoun (2003) describe as the "ability to go on with life after hardship and adversity" (p. 10). They point out that posttraumatic growth is different from this concept in that, unlike resiliency, it involves a qualitative change in functioning. However, "movement" after a loss or traumatic event would also require a qualitative change in functioning. To attempt to live life exactly as it had been before such a pivotal event would not only be an attempt at something impossible, it would most likely be counterproductive as well. To "just keep on going," it is necessary to recognize what has happened, realize that there is no return to life as it was once known, and adjust

daily functioning accordingly. This adjustment would not necessarily be positive in nature, but a qualitative change nevertheless.

5. People who have experienced major loss cope best when they have a forum to express their emotions and thoughts about their losses. In this vein, the role of confidants who care about one's story and who listen and are there for persons in their darkest moments is inestimable in the course of adaptation to major loss.

Summary Points

- Divorce is becoming increasingly common with one third of American children living in a stepfamily by the age of 18.
- Children of divorce can be adversely affected as evidenced by social, economic, and psychological indicators. But recent narrative research also shows that many children experience growth.
- Theoretical perspective influences how we interpret data and whether we emphasize the negative or positive outcomes.
- Parental loss is associated with adverse outcomes, but narrative research also shows evidence for growth.
- Growth from loss often seems to occur intrinsically and gradually over time. Individual differences are important.
- Account-making theory provides a framework for understanding how adverse experiences can lead to growth.
- Account making emphasizes the role of cognitive and emotional work, and also very importantly the role of social interaction processes.
- The importance of confidants who listen and care about the person's story in their darkest moments must be strongly emphasized as central to account making and growth-related processes.

REFERENCES

Ahrons, C. (1994). *The good divorce.* New York: HarperCollins.

Amato, P. R., & Booth, A. (1997). *A generation at risk: Growing up in an era of family upheaval.* Cambridge, MA: Harvard University Press.

Amato, P. R., & DeBoer, D. D. (2001). The transmission of marital instability across generations: Relationship skills or commitment to marriage. *Journal of Marriage and the Family, 63,* 1038–1051.

Bochner, A. P., Ellis, C., & Tillmann-Healy, L. M. (1997). Relationships as stories. In S. Duck (Ed.), *Handbook of personal relationships* (2nd ed., pp. 307–324). Chichester, West Sussex, England: Wiley.

Bogenschneider, K. (2000). Has family policy come of age? A decade review of the state of U.S. family policy in the 1990s. *Journal of Marriage and the Family, 62,* 1136–1159.

Coles, R. (1989). *The call of stories.* Boston: Houghton Mifflin.

DeSpelder, L. A., & Strickland, A. L. (2002). *The last dance: Encountering death and dying* (6th ed.). New York: McGraw-Hill. .

Emery, R. E. (1999). *Marriage, divorce, and children's adjustment.* Thousand Oaks, CA: Sage.

Erikson, E. (1963). *Childhood and society* (2nd ed.). New York: Norton.

Feng, D., Giarrusso, R., Bengston, V. L., & Frye, N. (1999). Intergenerational transmission of marital quality and marital instability. *Journal of Marriage and the Family, 61,* 451–463.

Feng, P., & Fine, M. A. (2000). Evaluation of a research-based parenting education program for divorcing parents: The Focus on Kids program. *Journal of Divorce and Remarriage, 34,* 1–23.

Fine, M. A. (2000). Divorce and single parenting. In C. Hendrick & S. S. Hendrick (Eds.), *Sourcebook of close relationships* (pp. 139–152). Newbury Park, CA: Sage.

Fine, M. A., & Demo, D. H. (2000). Divorce: Societal ill or normative transition? In R. M. Milardo & S. W. Duck (Eds.), *Families as relationships* (pp. 135–156). Chichester, West Sussex, England: Wiley.

Furstenberg, F. F., & Teitler, J. O. (1994). Reconsidering the effects of marital disruption: What happens to children of divorce in early childhood? *Journal of Family Psychology, 11,* 489–502.

Harvey, J. H. (2002). *Perspectives on loss and trauma: Assaults on the self.* Thousand Oaks, CA: Sage.

Harvey, J. H., Barnett, K., & Rupe, S. (2006). Perspectives on traumatic growth and outcomes associated with major loss. In L. Calhoun & J. Tedeschi (Eds.), *Handbook of posttraumatic growth* (pp. 100–117). Mahwah, NJ: Erlbaum.

Harvey, J. H., & Chavis, A. Z. (2006). Stilled but unquiet voices: The loss of a parent. *Journal of Loss and Trauma, 11,* 181–199.

Harvey, J. H., & Fine, M. (2004). *Children of divorce: Stories of loss and growth.* Mahwah, NJ: Erlbaum.

Harvey, J. H., & Miller, E. (1998). Toward a psychology of loss. *Psychological Science, 9,* 429–434.

Harvey, J. H., Weber, A. L., & Orbuch, T. L. (1990). *Interpersonal accounts: A social psychological perspective.* Oxford: Blackwell.

Hetherington, E. M., & Kelly, J. (2002). *For better or for worse: Divorce reconsidered.* New York: Norton.

Joseph, S., & Linley, P. A. (2005). Positive adjustment to threatening events: An organismic valuing theory of growth through adversity. *Review of General Psychology, 9,* 262–280.

McLanahan, S. S. (1999). Father absence and the welfare of children. In E. M. Hetherington (Ed.), *Coping with divorce, single parenting, and remarriage: A risk and resilience perspective* (pp. 117–145). Mahwah, NJ: Erlbaum.

Oats, J. C. (2001, January). Interview, p. 21. *O Magazine.*

Orbuch, T. L. (1997). People's accounts count: The sociology of accounts. *Annual Review of Sociology, 23,* 455–478.

Orbuch, T. L., Harvey, J. H., Davis, S. H., & Merbach, N. (1994). Account-making and confiding as acts of meaning in response to sexual assault. *Journal of Family Violence, 9,* 249–264.

Shneidman, E. (1996). *The suicidal mind.* New York: Oxford University Press.

Snyder, C. R., & Lopez, S. J. (Eds.). (2002). *Handbook of positive psychology.* New York: Oxford University Press.

Tedeschi, R. G., & Calhoun, L. G. (1995). *Trauma and transformation: Growing in the aftermath of suffering.* Thousand Oaks, CA: Sage.

Tedeschi, R. G., & Calhoun, L. G. (2003). Posttraumatic growth: Conceptual foundations and empirical evidence. *Psychological Inquiry, 15,* 1–18.

Wallerstein, J. S., Lewis, J. M., & Blakeslee, S. (2000). *The unexpected legacy of divorce: A 25-year landmark study.* New York: Hyperion.

Whitehead, B. D. (1996). *The divorce culture.* New York: Vintage.

Yalom, I. D., & Lieberman, M. A. (1991). Bereavement and heightened existential awareness. *Psychiatry, 54,* 334–345.

CHAPTER 8

Beyond Survival: Growing Out of Childhood Sexual Abuse

RACHEL LEV-WIESEL

FROM THE TIME she was 3 years old until the age of 13, Norma was sexually abused by her father. When beginning therapy, she said, "At first you are overwhelmed, humiliated, and helpless . . . don't know what to do . . . then you start to hate him . . . fear the next time he will approach you . . . then you get used to it. It becomes part of your life . . . you can't see yourself as a nonvictim . . . finally it [the abuse] becomes the essence of your life."

Three months later, she said, "I could not understand why he did that to me . . . now I do. He was twisted, sick . . . it had nothing to do with me . . . it had to do with his own drives. He was unable to see me as a person and had psychopathic tendencies."

At the end of the therapy, Norma concluded, "I know I can help other girls to cope with it . . . help them differentiate themselves from the perpetrator . . . it has become the mission of my life, to help others by telling my story . . . helping others is actually helping myself. . . . I have learned that one should be good to other people . . . maybe my experience, without lessening the suffering, contributed to my life in a sense that I am a better person today."

The search for meaning in the backdrop of suffering has been conceptualized in numerous ways in scientific literature, including terms such as "the search for meaning," "meaning making," "perception of benefits," "stress-related growth," "posttraumatic growth," and "thriving." No matter what terminology is used, there are two main processes whereby individuals seek to attribute meaning to their experience. The first such process involves searching for an explanation or reason for the event, and the second entails perceiving positive changes as a result of their coping efforts. Norma succeeded in both processes. She realized that she was not to blame or responsible for her father's behavior; both the blame and responsibility were his. This comprehension contributed to finding a meaning exhibited by devoting herself to helping other survivors of sexual abuse. In fact, her comment at the commencement of therapy that, in time, the abuse is transformed into the essence of the victim's life was reframed into the positive utilization of the abusive experience to help others.

By helping others, Norma has posttraumatically developed beyond the role of childhood sexual abuse survivor. The concept of posttraumatic growth (PTG) is often referred to as a positive psychological outcome of a traumatic event (Yalom & Lieberman, 1991), stress-related growth (Park, Cohen, & Murch, 1996), thriving (O'Leary, Alday, & Ickovics, 1998), and resilience (Sigal, 1998). It is regarded as both a process and an outcome in which people not only bounce back from trauma but manage to further develop and grow (Tedeschi, Park, & Calhoun, 1998). In other words, they do not merely survive but rather, transform the experience so that it holds some benefit for them. Such transformation does not imply that they do not suffer from posttraumatic stress symptomatology but rather, that such symptomatology coexists with positive changes (Lev-Wiesel & Amir, 2003).

According to Janoff-Bulman (1992), traumatic events instigate change through the shattering and rebuilding of assumptive worlds. Individuals' attempts to understand a traumatic event and its repercussions on their lives are crucial to resolving the trauma (Frankl, 1963; Janoff-Bulman, 1992; Taylor, 1983; Tedeschi & Calhoun, 1995, 2004). Some people, like Norma, manage to establish new psychological constructs that incorporate the possibility of such traumas, and better ways to cope with them.

Posttraumatic growth can be seen as the antithesis of posttraumatic stress disorder (Greenberg, 1995). Yet, data on the relationship of growth domains (changes in perception of self, changed relationships with others, and changed philosophy of life) and psychological well-being after childhood sexual abuse trauma are scarce (Calhoun & Tedeschi, 1998). This chapter discusses the concept of posttraumatic growth in childhood sexual abuse survivors. A literature review focusing on the long-term effects of childhood sexual abuse and the concept of posttraumatic growth is followed by the presentation of two studies that examined explanations given to the abuse by incestuous survivors in relation to personal resources, and posttraumatic growth in survivors of sexual abuse (Lev-Wiesel, Amir, & Besser, 2005).

CHILDHOOD SEXUAL ABUSE, POSTTRAUMATIC GROWTH

Children are physically and emotionally dependant on their family framework. Therefore, physical or sexual abuse perpetrated by a family member is likely to shake the entire emotional existence of the child. The home becomes a place of terror rather than a place of comfort and security (Davis, Petretic-Jackson, & Ting, 2001). Reviews of the vast array of studies examining the long-term sequel of all kinds of childhood abuse (e.g., Neumann, Houskamp, Pollock, & Briere, 1996) list numerous psychological, behavioral, and social difficulties in adults, such as depression, anxiety, guilt, sleep disturbances, poor appetite, heart palpitations, obsessive thoughts about the victimization (e.g., Janoff-Bulman & McPharson-Frantz, 1997), and posttraumatic stress disorder (American Psychiatric Association, 1994). Survivors of traumatic childhood experiences such as sexual abuse, physical abuse, rape, or domestic violence, often report a lasting sense of terror, horror, vulnerability and betrayal that interferes with their intimate relationships in adulthood.

Recognizing that child-abuse experiences are not all alike, some writers examine the influences that contribute to differences in individuals' adjustment following victimization. Factors related to aspects of the abusive situation itself such as severity, use of force, relationship to the offender, perpetrator substance abuse, and victim's age all appear to predict adjustment in the former victims of child abuse (Browne & Finkelhor, 1987; Faust, Runyon, & Kenny, 1995; Higgins & McCabe, 1994; Runtz & Schallow, 1997; Spaccarelli, 1994).

With regard to situational factors during childhood, parental warmth (Wind & Silvern, 1994), social support (Irwin, 1996; Runtz & Schallow, 1997), violence between spouses and poor marital quality (O'Keefe, 1995), family functioning (Koverola, Proulx, Battle, & Hanna, 1996), and support from the nonoffending parent (Everson, Hunter, Runyan, Edelsohn, & Coulter, 1989; Zimrin, 1989) appear to be important determinants of the long-term impact of child abuse.

PERSONAL RESOURCES

In studies of coping with general life stress, personal resources have been found to be more effective than other resources such as social support (Antonovsky, 1979; Ben-Sira, 1985, 1991). Personal resources are strengths or traits the individual has such as potency (Ben-Sira, 1993), hardiness (Kobasa, 1979), and a sense of coherence (Antonovsky, 1979). Numerous studies have reported evidence for the stress-buffering effects of personal resources (Ben-Sira, 1985, 1991; Lefcourt, Miller, Ware, & Sherk, 1981; Wheaton, 1985). Others have reported that irrespective of the level of stress, personal resources are associated with psychological well-being (Cohen et al., 1982; Holahan & Moos, 1986; Kobasa, Maddi, & Kahn, 1982; Nelson & Cohen, 1983). With regard to abusive experiences during childhood, potency is a particularly useful concept in studying well-being because it reflects the ability of maintaining one's emotional homeostasis in conditions where other resources lose their effectiveness. Activated after a previous failure in coping, potency is defined as an enduring confidence in one's own capabilities, and confidence in and commitment to one's social environment, perceived as a basically meaningful order and by a reliable and just distribution of rewards (Ben-Sira, 1993). Empirical evidence renders inferential support to the stress-buffering and readjustment promoting functions of potency in society-at-large and among disabled persons (Ben-Sira, 1985).

In relation to survivors of childhood sexual abuse, Fromuth (1986) found, in a sample of college women, that many aspects of the relationship between childhood sexual abuse and later psychological and sexual adjustment were accounted for by perceived parental support, which led the author to conclude that the relationship was not due to child sexual abuse per se, but, rather, to the confounding effect of family background. However, abused children may not accurately recall their parent's actual level of support, and the perception of support (or lack of it) may be a function of one's personal coping resources and coping style.

FEELINGS TOWARD THE PERPETRATOR—EXPLAINING THE ABUSE

Numerous studies have discussed incest survivors' feelings about themselves (Bruckner & Johnson, 1987; Derek, 1989). Extremely low self-esteem and self-hatred are common among survivors (Briere, 1989; Russel, 1986). They often hold the distorted belief that they are responsible for the abuse perpetrated against them; a misconception that results in feelings of self-blame. Most abusers tell children that it is their fault for being abused, shifting the blame away from their own behaviors and placing it on the child (Bass & Davis, 1988; Derek, 1989).

Hoglund and Nicholas (1995) examined the relationship between an abusive family environment and proneness to shame, guilt, anger, and hostility. They found that greater exposure to emotional abusiveness was significantly linked to higher rates of shame, overt and covert hostility, and a tendency to experience anger without a specific provoking factor. Women were found to have greater feelings of shame and guilt that were related to covert hostility and unexpressed anger; whereas men reported higher levels of overt hostility and expressed anger.

Sternberg, Lamb, Greenbaum, and Dawud (1994) assessed the effects of various types of domestic violence on children's perceptions of their parents, all of whom were living with their children at the time of the study. Physically abused children perceived their parents more negatively than nonabused children, but also retained positive perceptions of their parents.

Forward (1990) emphasized the importance of enabling adult survivors of child abuse to free themselves from the responsibility of the abusive behavior by analyzing and understanding the perpetrator's personality. Adults who were abused as children often have difficulties commencing therapy, since they fear their own vulnerability and cannot believe that anyone would want to help them or could understand them. The abusive experiences have reinforced their shame and guilt and keep them convinced that they are not worthy of help (Brandis, 1996). According to Forward (1990), successful adjustment is achieved by expressing the negative feelings toward the parent—a process that ultimately leads to forgiveness. This process enables adult survivors to preserve positive feelings or at least to alleviate negative feelings toward the perpetrator, which thereby leads to coming to terms with the past (since preoccupation with negative feelings toward either oneself or another person prevents one from investing energy in self-actualization).

POSTTRAUMATIC GROWTH IN SURVIVORS OF CHILD SEXUAL ABUSE

Certain individual differences in the cognitive processing of the abusive experience, such as causal attributions (Gold, 1986) and feelings of stigma and self-blame (Coffey, Leitenburg, Henning, Turner, & Bennet, 1996) were found to influence recovery from childhood maltreatment. Some of these studies have even suggested that cognitive, social, and environmental factors may be more important than the characteristics of the abuse in predicting the adjustment of former victims of childhood abuse.

Findings of a study conducted on women who had suffered childhood sexual abuse revealed that 49% of the participants reported positive outcomes, while 88% of them also reported negative impacts on their lives (McMillen, Rideout, & Zuravin, 1995). Positive changes among the female survivors included the impression of being a stronger person (Draucker, 1992, 2001; McMillen et al., 1995), and of knowing/understanding oneself better (Draucker, 1992; Himelein & McElrath, 1996; Woodward & Joseph, 2003), the willingness to help other survivors (Draucker, 1992), the commitment to protect their own children (Draucker, 1992, 2001; McMillen et al., 1995), greater religious faith (Himelein & McElrath, 1996), and a healthier understanding of interpersonal relationships (Himelein & McElrath, 1996). In another study, Frazier, Conlon, and Glaser (2001) who examined the long-term effects of rape found that 80% of the women reported empathy for other victims, an improvement in family relations, and a greater appreciation of life 2 weeks after the assault. However, the same percentage of women also confirmed negative changes in terms of their mental health and their sense of safety and justice in the world.

Healing therefore, entails forgiving or at least understanding the abusive experience, which includes disengagement from the pileup of negative feelings toward the self and toward the offender-parent. To overcome personal difficulties, adult survivors of child abuse need at their disposal coping resources such as potency, which is developed through life experience especially during childhood.

Study 1: Why Did Dad Sexually Abuse Me?   This study[1] of adult survivors of childhood sexual abuse examined perceptions of quality of life in regard to the explanation given by them to the abuse experience. Fifty-two adult survivors (15 men, 37 women) of childhood paternal sexual abuse who had completed therapy were qualitatively interviewed about their past and current life. In addition, the following quantitative measures were used: Explanation for abusive behavior scale (Lev-Wiesel, 1999), feelings toward offender scale (Lev-Wiesel, 1999), Quality of Life (Amir, 1998), and Potency (Ben-Sira, 1985).

The qualitative analysis of the interviews revealed three types of explanation given by adult survivors of incest for their father's abusive behavior:

1. The abuse was attributed to the parent's personality. The abuse was attributed either to the parent's sadistic traits or evilness, or alternatively, to the parent's mental illness. The survivor's feelings toward the offender who blamed his or her parents (both the mother and the father) were anger, hostility, hatred, and a desire for revenge.

   As "S" stated, " 'Mother'—This word should refer to all that is good, warm, and loving. Not my mother. She was never a mother. In order to hear a kind word, or look, I did so much, I agreed to endure everything. She knew but kept silent, for it was for her own benefit. I hate my mother, I hate her so much. I feel like strangling her. My rage is enormous. She allowed my father to rape me, bite me, to humiliate me. She called me a liar. I was the pervert. They remained the symbol of honesty and innocence. Well, they are criminals. They don't know

---

[1] The study was first published in 1999, *Child and Adolescents Social Work Journal*, 16(4), 291–304.

what parenthood means. How can they look at themselves in the mirror? She is a whore, a pervert. I will make her pay for her crimes. I wish her sleepless nights, to be frightened more than I was. I will trample her, hurt her, make fun of her tears, and see that she suffers the rest of her life."

2. Another explanatory category provided by survivors was self-blame or in other words, that he or she was responsible for the victimization either because of his or her bad personality (inappropriate behaviors) or seductive manner (i.e., the victim was the seducer). The feelings accompanying cases of self-blame were self-hatred, low self-esteem, low self-appreciation, helplessness, powerless, self-destructiveness, and suicidal thoughts.

   As "Y," who was abused physically and verbally by her mother, and sexually by her father stated, "I have dreamt that I am skinny. It felt wonderful. Why did I feel it in the dream instead of in real life? I am fed up with punishing myself. My life at my parents' house was one horrible punishment. Why did I deserve it? I notice I can't talk when my mother humiliates me. She treats me as if I am nothing. I am a human being who managed to survive through hell. I know I need to free myself from her influence, to vomit her, to stop being afraid of her, yet, it's so hard. I know how much she suffered and I pity her so. It's so difficult for me to see her unhappy. I am afraid I will harm anyone I love. I am afraid to lose my mind. I am afraid the feelings inside me will burst out with no control. I tried so hard to be my mother's mother, her sister, or her friend, but failed. I was punished for this failure. I feel so bad, I blame myself constantly."

3. The third category constructed by survivors involves the attribution of the abusive behavior to circumstantial conditions such as unemployment, marital problems (the mother rejecting the father), or the death of one parent's spouse. In such cases, there was no one to blame. Consequently, the feelings reported were confusion, ambivalence, distrust, high levels of anxiety, paranoid perspectives, difficulties making decisions, pessimism, and an inability to form positive relationships.

   As "U" stated, "My father was so helpless. . . . He was unemployed for such a long time. There was no one who could help us. Sometimes I wonder if life could have been different, but I don't really believe it could. Though I know I should blame my father for what he did, I feel only pity for him. Most of the time I try not to think of what happened, it is so confusing."

Analysis of interviews revealed that 26.7% of male and 21.6% of female survivors attributed the abuse entirely to the offender's personality, 40.0%

of male and 18.9% of female survivors claimed they were responsible for the abuse, and 26.7% of male and 24.3% of female survivors believed the abuse occurred as a result of negative circumstances. The remainder, 6.6% of male and 35.2% of female survivors both blamed themselves and attributed the abuse to the abuser's personality or the circumstances.

Analysis of variance comparing the levels of satisfaction from life dimensions between male and female survivors (ANOVA) revealed that female survivors had significantly higher levels of satisfaction in their family, professional, and social lives compared with the male survivors. In addition, among those who attributed the abuse to their parent's personality or to circumstances, it was found that a higher percentage of female survivors reported a high or moderate degree of satisfaction from the family, professional, and social dimensions of life than did male survivors. None of the survivors, male or female, who attributed the abuse to their own personalities, reported having high or moderate levels of satisfaction in their family life. In regard to male survivors, none of those who attributed the abuse to their personality, to circumstantial, or to combined explanations reported satisfaction, moderate or high, in their professional or social life. Also, 30.7% of female and none of the male survivors who attributed the abuse to combined explanations reported being moderately or highly satisfied in their family life.

Some female survivors who attributed the abuse to the offender's personality described their current life as happy and challenging, and maintained that this state enhances their self-esteem. For example, "S" said, "No one can guess what I was going through. In a way, the awful experience I went through strengthened me. I decided to succeed in both my marriage and my work, and I did. I am quite satisfied with my life."

Many participants who blamed themselves or circumstances reported having a wide range of difficulties in everyday life, in terms of relationships with family and friends, and in the area of work. As "Y" said, "Sometimes when I feel so bad, I try to remind myself of my friends who participated in group therapy with me and I think to myself that if they didn't deserve to be abused by their parents, maybe I didn't deserve it either." Another woman ("U"), said, "I am never satisfied with anything. For example, I am so afraid of losing my job, though there is no sign of this happening, and if it did it would force me to find something I might be more satisfied with. You know, you should not trust other people. People often compliment me on the good job I do, but I know they don't really mean it."

Furthermore, the results from the quantitative measures revealed that a higher percentage of survivors who attributed the abuse to the offender's characteristics managed to keep their self-esteem fairly intact and enjoyed a higher quality of life than survivors who bore the full burden of blame on themselves or blamed situational factors. In addition, a relationship was found among explanations given for the abusive behavior, potency, and the level of negative feelings toward the offender-parent. Results indicated that attributing responsibility for the abusive behavior to the offenders' personality increased the level of negative feelings toward the offender-parent, while attributing the abusive behavior to the victim's personality was found to have no effect on feelings toward the offender. It should be mentioned that empirical research affirms that believing the abusive behavior to be one's own fault decreases the victim's self-esteem (Briere, 1989; Russel, 1986). Potency was found to decrease the level of negative feelings toward the offender-parent. This demonstrates the important role potency plays in the survivor's adjustment in adulthood.

Study 2: Posttraumatic Growth among Female Survivors of Childhood Abuse in Relation to the Perpetrator's Identity   The objective of this study[2] was to examine the extent of posttraumatic stress disorder (PTSD) symptomatology and posttraumatic growth in young adult female survivors of childhood abuse in relation to the identity of the perpetrator. Self-report questionnaires with regard to negative life events, PTSD symptoms, and posttraumatic growth were administered to 246 nonclinical adult female survivors of childhood abuse. A sample of 93 participants who reported having been sexually or physically abused during childhood either by a family member or a stranger were drawn for the study purpose. Participants were administered a self-report questionnaire that consisted of the following measures: Traumatic Events Questionnaire (Norris, 1992), PTSD-Scale (Horowitz, Wilner, & Alvarez, 1979), and The Posttraumatic Growth Inventory (PTGI; Tedeschi & Calhoun, 1996). The findings revealed that the levels of both PTSD and posttraumatic growth were higher among survivors who were sexually or physically abused by a family member compared with those who were sexually or physically abused by a stranger. In addition, mediational analysis revealed that levels of PTSD mediated the identity of the perpetrator effect on posttraumatic growth. In sum, the findings indicated that survivors of domestic abuse had higher levels of PTSD and higher levels of PTG compared with those who were abused by a nonfamily member.

DISCUSSION

As the literature review and the two presented studies reveal, the relationship among childhood sexual abuse experiences, posttraumatic symptomatology, and posttraumatic growth involves complex mechanisms that entail

---

[2] The paper was first published in 2005 in the *Journal of Loss and Trauma*, 10(1), 7–18, coauthored by R. Lev-Wiesel, M. Amir, and A. Besser.

personal resources, explanations for the abuse and situational factors. The first study suggested that attributing responsibility for the abusive behavior on the offenders' personality increased the level of negative feelings toward the offender-parent, whereas attributing the abusive behavior to the victim's personality was found to have no effect on feelings toward the offender. This is consistent with previous findings indicating that believing the abusive behavior to be one's own fault decreases the victim's self-esteem (Briere, 1989; Russel, 1986). The fact that potency decreased the level of negative feelings toward the offender-parent demonstrates the important role potency plays in the survivor's adjustment in adulthood. Potency reflects not only self-confidence but also the commitment and belief in society's inherent order and meaning, which may relieve feelings of hostility and revenge. Survivors possessing high levels of potency are apt to relate to others with more trust than those with lower potency levels—a phenomenon that may lead to more fulfilling interpersonal relations.

The first interpersonal relationship that humans encounter is the child-parent relationship, which subsequently serves as the basic model for interpersonal relationships in adulthood. Through subconscious and conscious processes, children internalize significant others, thereby creating or destroying their ability to react to other people with trust and confidence. As Battegay (1992) pointed out, the symbiotic-narcissistic basic relationship of early childhood is reactivated in every later object relation. All active ego performances along with the individual's differentiation from the object are constructed on this basis. Being occupied or overwhelmed with negative feelings toward an offender-parent may prevent the individual from investing energy in self-actualization and hinder the ability and confidence to interact with others.

An interesting question remains concerning the factors that determine successful adjustment in adulthood. Why do some survivors successfully adjust, manage to find meaning in the abuse, and grow beyond survival, whereas others who report less traumatic experiences fail to do so? This question raises the inquiry as to the origin of potency. Does potency develop through childhood experiences, as Ben-Sira (1991) stated, or is it a heredity trait (based on one's pain threshold and stress tolerance)? Assuming that growth is a hereditary and common trait in humans, could the level of posttraumatic growth be contingent on the level of potency?

According to M. Klien (1976), positive maternal experiences in early childhood (the schizoparanoid stage) enhance the ability of the child to differentiate himself/herself from the mother through the development of basic trust and self-control. This theory indicates that a fulfilling relationship with a parent at an early stage may function as a protective factor (integrated with potency) against future abusive experiences. Practical experience reveals that adults tend to report the ages of incurred abuse. One client said: "Everything was fine till my mother gave birth to my sister. I was 5 then. That was the first time he (the father) came to my room (she was sexually abused by her father since she was 5 years old)." If she had a good relationship with her parents previously, she might have acquired potency that would help her recover from the trauma in adulthood. Similarly, literature regarding the psychological adjustment of Holocaust survivors indicated that good and fulfilling relationships existing previously to the traumatic experiences contributed to recovery (Kestenberg & Brenner, 1996; H. Klien, 1974). In addition, the age at which the survivor experienced the abuse may influence the level of potency acquired. Other factors such as the severity of abuse, frequency, and social support, which have all been found to affect posttraumatic stress reactions (Yehuda & McFarlane, 1997), still have to be examined in relation to potency and posttraumatic growth.

Adult survivors with this personal resource at their disposal were more liberated from their negative feelings toward the offender-parent than others. Could it be that some of the survivors enhanced their potency when they succeeded in differentiating themselves from their traumatic experiences and their offending parents? In a previous study, Lev-Wiesel and Amir (2003) speculated that, like the biological role of vagal functions to regulate the energy balance and energy content in the body in a state of hunger in order to track food (Szekely, 2000), anxiety is externalized into activity (Hanney & Kozlowska, 2002) and transforms into "doing," similar to Bandura's (1993) concept of self-efficacy. This process is likely to enhance feelings of mastery and competence—or the sense of growth.

As previously mentioned, recovery from child abuse may be seen as a process of moving from denial to identification as a victim and eventually from victim identification to identification as a survivor. Acknowledgment that victimization indeed occurred involves the overcoming of feelings relating to denial, powerlessness and vulnerability associated with being victimized. It is both a cognitive and an emotional experience. Healing means placing victimization in its historical context through exploring and understanding the elements that contributed to its occurrence (e.g., explaining the abusive behavior). By recognizing the elements in the past that influence current reactions and finding ways to minimize the influence of no longer functional feelings and behaviors, the survivor learns to separate the past from the present. This means taking charge of one's life by developing a new self; strengthening individual self-confidence, locus of control, and self-esteem; and regaining belief in order and meaning in society—all of which are elements of potency and are fundamental to posttraumatic growth.

SUMMARY

Based on these findings, it seems that two groups of adult survivors of child abuse may have more difficulties in adjustment than others: the first are those who blame themselves for being abused; the second are those who blame their parents for the abuse and have low levels of potency. As for the first group, self-blame may prevent survivors from allowing themselves to feel anger, hostility, and hatred (which are normal feelings toward someone who hurts us) toward the offender-parent, and instead direct those negative feelings against themselves, an act which in turn, will lower their self-worth. DiBlasio and Proctor (1993) suggested that recovery demands dealing with the hurt (the pain that was suffered because of the offender) and the resentment toward the offender for causing this pain. Recovery means giving up the resentment. Successful therapy is viewed, therefore, as a process in which an abused person heals the wounds of hurt and hate, disconnects from the unhealthy connection (physical or mental) with the offender, and is freed to pursue healthy and growth-promoting activities (Walton, 2005).

Female survivors of childhood sexual abuse can grow beyond mere survival. The process of posttraumatic growth and creation of a resilient self does not mean eliminating the trauma or its symptoms altogether, but rather, creating new aspects of self and experience, both contributing to a felt sense of well-being and strength—from denial of the abuse through self-blame, or by investing negative feelings of hate and resentment in the abuser, into an active change process of reorganizing those aspects of self, feelings, personal meanings, somatic meanings, and relationships that were constructed through the abuse.

Summary Points

- Childhood abuse is associated with numerous subsequent psychological, behavioral, and social difficulties in adulthood, including depression, anxiety, guilt, sleep disturbances, eating pathology, health problems, obsessive thoughts, and posttraumatic stress disorder.
- Factors related to aspects of the abusive situation itself such as severity, use of force, relationship to the offender, perpetrator substance abuse, and victim age all appear to predict adjustment in the former victims of child abuse.
- Situational factors such as parental warmth, social support, and marital quality appear to be important determinants of the long-term impact of child abuse.
- Adults who are abused as children often have difficulties commencing therapy, since they fear their own vulnerability and cannot believe that anyone would want to help them or could understand them.

- Positive changes have been documented among female survivors: They appear to be stronger individuals, know or understand themselves better, are willing to help other survivors, are committed to protecting their own children, have greater religious faith, and show a healthier understanding of interpersonal relationships.
- Research indicates that two groups of adult survivors of child abuse may have more difficulties in adjustment than others: The first are those who blame themselves for being abused; the second are those who blame their parents for the abuse and have low levels of potency.

REFERENCES

American Psychiatric Association. (1994). *Diagnostic and statistical manual of mental disorders* (4th ed.). Washington, DC: Author.

Amir, M. (1998). WHOQOL group: The World Health Organization Quality of Life Assessment (WHOQOL)—Development and general psychometric properties. *Social Science and Medicine, 46*, 1569–1585.

Antonovsky, A. (1979). *Health stress and coping.* San Francisco: Jossey-Bass.

Bandura, A. (1993). Perceived self-efficacy in cognitive development and functioning. *Educational Psychologist, 28*(2), 117–148.

Bass, E., & Davis, L. (1988). *The courage to heal* (p. 217). New York: Harper & Row.

Battegay, R. (1992). The tactile-symbiotic relationship as the earlier phase of child development. *Zeitschrift fur Psychosomatische Medizin und Psychoanalise, 38*(2), 115–128.

Ben-Sira, Z. (1985). Potency: A stress buffering link in the coping-stress-disease relationship—Social. *Science Medicine, 21*(4), 397–406.

Ben-Sira, Z. (1991). *Regression, stress and readjustment aging.* New York: Praeger.

Ben-Sira, Z. (1993). *Zionism at the close of the twentieth century.* Lewiston, NY: Edwin Mellen Press.

Brandis, A. (1996). *Adult survivors of abuse.* Atlanta, GA: Psychological Associates.

Briere, J. (1989). *Therapy for adults molested as children.* New York: Springer.

Browne, A., & Finkelhor, D. (1987). Impact of child sexual abuse: A review of the research. *Annual Progress in Child Psychology and Child Development,* 555–584.

Bruckner, D. F., & Johnson, P. E. (1987, February). Treatment for survivors of childhood sexual abuse. *Social Casework, 87,* 81–87.

Calhoun, L. G., & Tedeschi, R. G. (1998). Beyond recovery from trauma: Implications for clinical practice and research. *Journal of Social Issues, 54,* 323–337.

Coffey, P., Leitenberg, H., Henning, K., Turner, T., & Bennet, R. T. (1996). Mediators of the long-term impact of child sexual abuse: Perceived stigma, betrayal, powerlessness, and self-blame. *Child Abuse and Neglect, 20,* 447–455.

Cohen, P., Struening, E. L., Muhlin, G. L., Genevie, L. E., Kaplan, S. R., & Peck, H. B. (1982). Community stressors mediating conditions and well-being in urban neighborhoods. *Journal of Community Psychology, 10*, 377–391.

Davis, J. L., Petretic-Jackson, P. A., & Ting, L. (2001). Intimacy dysfunction and trauma symptomatology: Long-term correlates of different types of child abuse. *Journal of Traumatic Stress, 14*(1), 63–80.

Derek, J. (1989). Mood disturbances among women clients sexually abused during childhood. *Journal of Interpersonal Violence, 4*(2), 122–133.

DiBlasio, F. A., & Proctor, J. H. (1993). Therapists and the clinical use of forgiveness. *American Journal of Family Therapy, 21*, 175–184.

Draucker, C. B. (1992). Construing benefit from a negative experience of incest. *Western Journal of Nursing Research, 14*, 343–357.

Draucker, C. B. (2001). Learning the harsh realities of life: Sexual violence, disillusionment, and meaning. *Health Care for Women International, 22*, 67–84.

Everson, M., Hunter, W., Runyan, D., Edelsohn, G., & Coulter, M. (1989). Maternal support following disclosure of incest. *American Journal of Orthopsychiatry, 59*, 197–207.

Faust, J., Runyon, M. K., & Kenny, M. C. (1995). Family variables associated with the onset and impact of intra-familial childhood sexual abuse [Special issue: The impact of the family on child adjustment and psychopathology]. *Clinical Psychology Review, 15*(5), 443–456.

Forward, S. (1990). *Toxic parents.* Tel Aviv, Israel: Matar (Hebrew).

Frankl, V. E. (1963). *Man's search for meaning: An introduction to logotherapy.* New York: Washington Square Books.

Frazier, P., Conlon, A., & Glaser, T. (2001). Positive and negative life changes following sexual assault. *Journal of Consulting and Clinical Psychology, 69*, 1048–1055.

Fromuth, M. E. (1986). The relationship of childhood sexual abuse with later psychological and sexual adjustment in a sample of college women. *Child Abuse and Neglect, 10*, 5–15.

Gold, E. (1986). Long-term effects of sexual victimization in childhood: An attributional approach. *Journal of Consulting and Clinical Psychology, 54*, 471–475.

Greenberg, M. A. (1995). Cognitive processing of traumas: The role of intrusive thoughts and reappraisals. *Journal of Applied Social Psychology, 25*, 1262–1296.

Hanney, L., & Kozlowska, K. (2002). Healing traumatized children: Creating illustrated storybooks in family therapy. *Family Process, 41*(1), 37–65.

Higgins, D. J., & McCabe, M. P. (1994). The relationship of child sexual abuse and family violence to adult adjustment: Toward an integrated risk-sequelae model. *Journal of Sex Research, 31*(4), 255–266.

Himelein, M. J., & McElrath, J. A. V. (1996). Resilient child sexual abuse survivors: Cognitive coping and illusion. *Child Abuse and Neglect, 20*, 747–758.

Hoglund, C. L., & Nicholas, K. B. (1995). Shame, guilt, and anger in college students exposed to abusive family environments. *Journal of Family Violence, 10*(2), 141–157.

Holahan, C. J., & Moos, R. H. (1986). Personality, coping and family resources in stress resistance: A longitudinal analysis. *Journal of Personality and Social Psychology, 51*, 389–395.

Horowitz, M., Wilner, N., & Alvarez, W. (1979). Impact of Event Scale: Measure of subjective stress. *Psychosomatic Medicine, 41,* 209–218.

Irwin, H. J. (1996). Traumatic childhood events, perceived availability of emotional support, and the development of dissociative tendencies. *Child Abuse and Neglect, 20*(8), 701–707.

Janoff-Bulman, R. (1992). *Shattered assumptions: Towards a new psychology of trauma.* New York: Free Press.

Janoff-Bulman, R., & McPharson-Frantz, C. (1997). The impact of trauma on meaning: From meaningless world to meaningful life. In M. J. Power & C. R. Brewin (Eds.), *The transformation of meaning in psychological therapies: Integrating theory and practice* (pp. 91–106). New York: Wiley.

Kestenberg, J. S., & Brenner, I. (1996). *The last witness: The child survivor of the Holocaust.* Washington, DC: American Psychiatric Press.

Klien, H. (1974). Child victims of the Holocaust. *Journal of Clinical Child Psychology, 2,* 44–47.

Klien, M. (1976). *Contributions to psycho-analysis.* London: Hogarth Press.

Kobasa, S. C. (1979). Stressful life events, personality, and health: An inquiry into hardiness. *Journal of Personality and Social Psychology, 37,* 1–12.

Kobasa, S. C., Maddi, S. R., & Kahn, S. (1982). Hardiness and health: A prospective study. *Journal of Personality and Social Psychology, 42,* 168–177.

Koverola, C., Proulx, J., Battle, P., & Hanna, C. (1996). Family functioning as predictors of distress in revictimized sexual abuse survivors. *Journal of Interpersonal Violence, 11,* 263–280.

Lefcourt, H. M., Miller, R., Ware, E. E., & Sherk, D. (1981). Locus of control as a modifier of the relationship between stressors and moods. *Journal of Personality and Social Psychology, 41,* 457–369.

Lev-Wiesel, R. (1999). Feelings of adult survivors of child abuse feelings toward their offender-parents. *Child and Adolescents Social Work Journal, 16*(4), 291–304.

Lev-Wiesel, R., & Amir, M. (2003). Post-traumatic growth among Holocaust child survivors. *Journal of Loss and Trauma, 8*(4), 229–237.

Lev-Wiesel, R., Amir, M., & Besser, A. (2005). Posttraumatic growth among female survivors of childhood abuse in relation to the perpetrator identity. *Journal of Loss and Trauma, 10*(1), 7–18.

McMillen, C., Rideout, G. R., & Zuravin, S. (1995). Perceived benefit from child sexual abuse. *Journal of Consulting and Clinical Psychology, 63,* 1037–1043.

Nelson, D. W., & Cohen, L. H. (1983). Locus of control perceptions and the relationship between life stress and psychological disorder. *American Journal of Community Psychology, 11,* 705–722.

Neumann, D. A., Houskamp, B. M., Pollock, V. E., & Briere, J. (1996). The long-term sequel of childhood sexual abuse in women: A meta-analytic review. *Child Maltreatment, 1,* 6–16.

Norris, F. H. (1992). Epidemiology of trauma: Frequency and impact of different potentially traumatic events on different demographic groups. *Journal of Consulting and Clinical Psychology, 60,* 409–418.

O'Keefe, M. (1995). Predictors of child abuse in maritally violent families. *Journal of Interpersonal Violence, 10*(1), 3–25.

O'Leary, V. E., Alday, C. S., & Ickovics, J. R. (1998). Models of life change and post-traumatic growth. In R. G. Tedeschi, C. L. Park, & L. G. Calhoun (Eds.), *Post-traumatic growth: Positive changes in the aftermath of crisis* (pp. 127–151). Mahwah, NJ: Erlbaum.

Park, C. L., Cohen, L. H., & Murch, R. (1996). Assessment and prediction of stress-related growth. *Journal of Personality, 64,* 71–105.

Runtz, M., & Schallow, J. R. (1997). Social support and coping strategies as mediators of adult adjustment following childhood maltreatment. *Child Abuse and Neglect, 21*(2), 211–226.

Russel, D. E. H. (1986). *The secret trauma: Incest in the women.* New York: Basic Books.

Sigal, J. J. (1998). Long-term effects of the Holocaust: Empirical evidence for re-silience in the first, second, and third generation. *Psychoanalytic Review, 85*(4), 579–585.

Spaccarelli, S. (1994). Stress, appraisal, and coping in child sexual abuse: A theoretical and empirical review. *Psychological Bulletin, 116,* 1–23.

Sternberg, K. J., Lamb, M. E., Greenbaum, C., & Dawud, S. (1994). The effects of domestic violence on children's perceptions of their perpetrating and non per-petrating parents. *International Journal of Behavioral Development, 17*(4), 779–795.

Szekely, M. (2000). The vagus nerve in thermoregulation and energy metabolism. *Autonomic Neuroscience Basic and Clinical, 85*(1/3), 26–38.

Taylor, S. E. (1983). Adjustment to threatening of events: A theory of cognitive adaptation. *American Psychologist, 38,* 1161–1173.

Tedeschi, R. G., & Calhoun, L. G. (1996). The posttraumatic Growth Inventory: Measuring the positive legacy of trauma. *Journal of Traumatic Stress, 9,* 455–471.

Tedeschi, R. G., & Calhoun, L. G. (2004). Posttraumatic growth: Conceptual foundations and empirical evidence. *Psychological Inquiry, 15,* 1–18.

Tedeschi, R. G., Park, C. L., & Calhoun, L. G. (1998). *Posttraumatic growth: Positive changes in the aftermath of crisis.* Mahwah, NJ: Erlbaum.

Walton, E. (2005). Therapeutic forgiveness: Developing a model for empowering victims of sexual abuse. *Clinical Social Work Journal, 33*(2), 193–207.

Wheaton, B. (1985). Models for the stress-buffering functions of coping resources. *Journal of Health and Social Behavior, 26,* 352–364.

Wind, T. W., & Silvern, L. (1994). Parenting and family stress as mediators of the long-term effects of child abuse. *Child Abuse and Neglect, 18*(5), 439–453.

Woodward, C., & Joseph, S. (2003). Positive change processes and post-traumatic growth in people who experienced childhood abuse: Understanding vehicle of change. *Psychology and Psychotherapy: Theory, Research and Practice, 76,* 267–283.

Yalom, I. D., & Lieberman, M. A. (1991). Bereavement and heightened existential awareness. *Psychiatry: Journal for the Study of Interpersonal Processes, 54*(4), 334–345.

Yehuda, R., & McFarlane, A. C. (Eds.). (1997). Psychobiology of posttraumatic stress disorder. *Annals of the New York Academy of Sciences, 821.*

Zimrin, H. (1989). *Battered children: A multidimensional problem.* Tel Aviv, Israel: Oren (Hebrew).

CHAPTER 9

Posttraumatic Growth Following Sexual Assault

PATRICIA A. FRAZIER and MARGIT I. BERMAN

S URVEYS OF COMMUNITY samples (e.g., Breslau et al., 1998) indicate that most individuals experience a major traumatic event in their lives. It thus is not surprising that the psychological effects of trauma have been the focus of much research attention. Most research has focused on the negative consequences of traumatic events, such as Posttraumatic Stress Disorder (PTSD). However, a growing body of research demonstrates that many survivors report positive life changes following traumatic events. This phenomenon is referred to by several names, including posttraumatic growth (PTG), positive life change, stress-related growth, and perceived benefits or benefit-finding.[1] Common areas of growth reported by trauma survivors reflect changes in three general life domains: sense of self (e.g., increased strength and maturity), relationships (e.g., increased closeness to others), and spirituality or life philosophy (e.g., increased sense of purpose in life). Additionally, trauma survivors often report greater empathy with others' suffering. While not denying the distress associated with traumatic events, research on PTG reflects the potential for traumatic events to serve as the impetus for positive life changes.

In our work, we have chosen to focus on PTG following sexual assault for several reasons. First, sexual assault is an unfortunately common traumatic event, experienced by approximately 20% of women in the United States (Tjaden & Thoennes, 2000). Second, sexual assault is associated with higher rates of PTSD than many other traumas (e.g., Kessler, Sonnega, Bromet,

---

[1] Although these terms often are used interchangeably, measures of these constructs are sometimes uncorrelated and have different correlates (Sears, Stanton, & Danoff-Burg, 2003).

Hughes, & Nelson, 1995). Third, sexual assault differs from other events typically examined in the PTG literature (e.g., health problems) because it involves intentional harm and greater stigma. Despite this, few studies have examined PTG following sexual assault. The purpose of this chapter is to review findings from our program of research on PTG following sexual assault, including (1) the prevalence, timing, and course of PTG; (2) the relations among PTG and posttrauma distress and well-being; and (3) the correlates of PTG. Unlike much research on PTG that focuses exclusively on positive changes, we include findings regarding both positive and negative life changes (e.g., negative changes in beliefs about the safety of the world), which provides a more comprehensive picture of the aftermath of traumatic events. Within each section, we compare our findings to other research on PTG following sexual assault and to the broader PTG literature. Although limited space does not permit a comprehensive review of the broader literature (see Helgeson, Reynolds, & Tomich, 2006; and Zoellner & Maercker, 2006, for recent reviews), in each section we discuss how some of our key findings compare to the broader literature. We conclude with a discussion of clinical implications and directions for future research.

PREVALENCE, TIMING, AND COURSE OF POSTTRAUMATIC GROWTH

Our research in this area began in the mid-1980s. Prior to that time, to our knowledge, the only mention of PTG following sexual assault in the research literature was a chapter by Veronen and Kilpatrick (1983). Their clinical work with sexual assault survivors suggested that many women may be prompted by an assault to make positive changes in their lives. They described four models by which rape could lead to positive life change: a life threat to life appreciation model, where the rape leads women to reassess life priorities and goals and take better care of themselves; a system-mediated change model, where rape prompts access to needed psychosocial services; a rape as a consciousness-raising experience model, where rape and involvement with rape-crisis helpers alerts a woman to other forms of oppression she may be experiencing, prompting increased assertiveness and improved life outcomes; and a rape as challenge model, where stereotypes about women coping poorly with rape provide a beneficial downward social comparison that some women may use to promote recovery and positive coping efforts. Although the chapter is intriguing, no data are presented on the prevalence of growth or the prevalence of these various pathways to growth.

To assess the prevalence of growth, our first study included one open-ended question that asked the rape survivors in our sample whether the rape had caused any positive changes in their lives and, if so, what those changes had been. Data were collected at 3 days postrape from 67 women who had sought help at a hospital-based rape crisis program. To our surprise, more than half (57%) of the victims reported some positive change in their life as a result of the rape, even at 3 days postrape (Frazier & Burnett, 1994). Their responses were coded into nine categories. The most frequent positive change reported was that they were now more cautious (e.g., "It taught me to be more cautious and alert," 22%). The other categories were each reported by fewer than 10% of the sample: appreciate life more (e.g., "I appreciate my children and my life more"), changed my relationships in positive ways (e.g., "It brought me closer to my husband than ever before"), reevaluate life and goals (e.g., "I have been forced to look at myself, my life, my relationships, and work"), take better care of myself (e.g., "I've quit drinking"), more assertive (e.g., "It taught me to be more assertive and a little less trusting"), realize strengths (e.g., "I've learned to like myself better and realize how strong I am"), choose different types of men (e.g., "I no longer will date men or associate with men who cannot express emotion or be supportive"), and closer to God (e.g., "I've drawn closer to God").

Because the majority of the rape survivors in this first study reported positive life changes, we developed a more structured measure of positive (and negative) life changes to assess these changes more systematically. This measure included 17 items tapping the listed domains (as well as some additional items) that were ultimately grouped into four categories reflecting the categories of change identified in the broader PTG literature: changes in self (7 items; e.g., ability to be assertive); changes in spirituality/life philosophy (4 items; e.g., appreciation of life); changes in relationships (2 items; relationships with friends and family), and changes in empathy (1 item; concern for others in similar situations). Each item was rated on a 5-point bipolar scale so that participants could report either positive or negative change in each area. In addition, three items were included that reflected changes in beliefs we thought typically would change in the negative direction (e.g., beliefs about the safety of the world). To assess the prevalence of positive and negative life changes, we counted the number of life areas that were rated as changed for the better (4 or 5 on a 5-point scale) and the number of life areas that were rated as changed for the worse (1 or 2 on a 5-point scale).

We used this measure in a study of 171 rape survivors who sought help at the same rape crisis program mentioned earlier. In this study, survivors completed surveys assessing positive and negative life changes, distress, and various potential correlates of distress and growth at 2 weeks, and 2, 6, and 12 months post-assault (Frazier, Conlon, & Glaser, 2001; Frazier, Tashiro, Berman, Steger, & Long, 2004). Because we gathered data on positive and negative change soon after the assault and at three additional times, we could assess some key assumptions in the literature regarding the timing and course of PTG. Specifically, theories regarding the PTG process, although acknowledging that growth can occur soon after a trauma, generally assume that it is the result of a long recovery process (Calhoun & Tedeschi, 1998; Schaefer & Moos, 1998). Consistent with this notion, many researchers have studied PTG among survivors of traumas that occurred months or years previously. In addition, many theoretical models assume that the number of positive life changes survivors report generally increases over time (see O'Leary, Alday, & Ickovics, 1998, for a review). For example, according to Tedeschi and Calhoun's (1995) model, the initial response to a trauma is characterized by unmanageable distress, which triggers rumination processes. These rumination processes are followed by an initial stage of growth and then a final stage of *further* growth and wisdom. However, because most studies have assessed positive life changes at one time, we know very little about how the process of growth unfolds.

Contrary to the notion that growth necessarily takes months or years to develop, at 2 weeks post-assault, 91% of the survivors in our sample described at least one positive life change that resulted from the assault (Frazier et al., 2001). The average number of positive changes reported was 4.59 (SD = 3.99). The most common positive changes at the 2-week period were more concern for others in similar situations (80%), better relationships with family (46%), and greater appreciation of life (46%). However, 95% also reported negative life changes 2 weeks following the assault (M = 9.16, SD = 4.90). The most common negative changes were in mental health (84%) and beliefs about the safety and fairness of the world (81% to 83%).

In terms of the course of posttraumatic change over time, increased empathy occurred early and was the most commonly endorsed area of positive change at all four time periods (72% to 81%). Positive changes in relationships also occurred soon after the assault and remained relatively stable through the 1-year assessment (37% to 43% across time). Positive changes in self (e.g., increased ability to recognize one's own strengths) and spirituality (e.g., increased spiritual well-being) were less common 2 weeks after the assault than at subsequent assessments. The interval between the 2-week and 2-month assessments appeared to be a time of significant change in these domains. For example, positive self-changes increased from 20% of the sample at 2 weeks to 39% at 2 months, and then remained stable. As mentioned, negative changes in beliefs about the fairness and safety of the world were common at the 2-week assessment and remained relatively common throughout the study (65% to 83%). Negative changes in beliefs about the goodness of other people also were common across all four time periods (60% to 74%). The average number of positive and negative changes reported at 12 months post-assault was 6.34 (SD = 5.07) and 6.12 (SD = 4.99), respectively.

Because not all survivors completed all four assessments, we next examined changes in the average number of positive and negative changes
reported at adjacent time periods (e.g., from 2 weeks to 2 months post-
assault) using paired *t*-tests. These analyses only included those who
had data from both time points. These analyses revealed that positive
changes increased and negative changes decreased over time, with the
interval from 2 weeks to 2 months post-assault being the period of greatest change.

However, generalizations about the posttrauma recovery process derived
from the paired *t*-tests may not accurately capture individual differences in
posttrauma recovery. Therefore, we also analyzed the data using hierarchical linear modeling (HLM), which allowed us to assess individual differences in rates of change. These analyses revealed that survivors differed
significantly from each other in the pattern of positive and negative
changes they reported over time. Thus, although the paired *t*-tests revealed
that, on average, positive changes increased and negative changes decreased over time, these averages mask significant individual variability revealed in the HLM analyses. For example, some individuals (24%) reported
fewer positive changes and *more* negative changes at 1 year than at 2 weeks
post-assault.

Although these first two studies provided useful data regarding posttrauma life change among sexual assault survivors, they also were limited
in various respects. First, all participants had reported to the emergency
room following the assault and hence were not necessarily representative of
most sexual assault survivors. Moreover, both studies focused exclusively
on recent victims, which precluded investigation of long-term changes resulting from sexual assault.

Thus, in our next study, we identified 135 rape survivors from an urban
Midwestern community via a random-digit dialing phone survey (Frazier,
Conlon, Steger, Tashiro, & Glaser, 2006). Interested participants completed
mailed surveys of positive and negative life changes resulting from the assault, distress, well-being, and potential correlates of distress and well-
being. With regard to life changes, the assault survivors in this study
reported an average of approximately seven positive changes and four negative changes resulting from the assault an average of 16 years post-assault.
Increased empathy for others in similar situations was the most commonly
reported positive change (78%). A considerable percentage of respondents
also reported positive changes in self such as increased assertiveness (60%)
and a greater ability to recognize their strengths (61%). Similarly, positive
changes in spirituality were frequently reported, such as appreciation of
life (56%) and spiritual well-being (47%). Slightly less than one-third of respondents reported that their relationships with friends (29%) and family

(31%) had changed positively as a result of the assault. Finally, a substantial proportion of the sample reported negative changes in beliefs about the fairness and safety of the world (44 to 48%) and in mental health (44%).

Despite the differences between the ER-based and community samples, the prevalence of positive change is remarkably similar across the two studies. The mean number of positive changes reported an average of 16 years post-assault (6.94) was comparable to that reported at 1-year post-assault in the longitudinal study (6.31) although the average number of negative changes reported is slightly lower (4.15 versus 6.12) in the community sample. The frequency of the various types of changes reported in the current sample also is quite similar across the two studies. In both studies, increased empathy is the most common positive change. After increased empathy, the three most common positive changes years after the assault are in the areas of self (increases in assertiveness and ability to recognize personal strengths) and spirituality (greater appreciation of life), consistent with the findings from the longitudinal study. Positive changes in relationships were slightly less common among the nonrecent assault survivors than among the recent assault survivors. This suggests that the impact of a trauma on relationships may fade over time whereas the impact on the self and spirituality may be more enduring. Alternatively, unlike the participants in the longitudinal study who sought help immediately following the assault, women in the community sample may not have told anyone about the assault and thus their relationships may not have been positively affected. Thus, if victims do not disclose an assault to friends and family, they may miss the opportunity to experience increased closeness in those relationships.

The most common negative changes reported by survivors in the community sample are with regard to beliefs about the safety and fairness of the world. Again, despite differences between the two samples, these also were the most commonly reported negative changes in the longitudinal study. However, negative changes in beliefs are less common an average of 16 years post-assault than in the year following the assault. Nonetheless, a substantial proportion of nonrecent survivors continue to report negative changes in their views regarding the benevolence of the world. This is consistent with other findings that basic assumptions about the world can remain shattered for years posttrauma (Janoff-Bulman, 1989).

COMPARISONS WITH OTHER SEXUAL ASSAULT STUDIES

Apart from our own program of research, we are aware of only two quantitative studies that have examined PTG following adult sexual assault. Burt and Katz (1987) surveyed 113 rape survivors, most of whom had been raped several years previously, about changes that had occurred in their lives since the rape, using a study-designed measure of 28 items that could be endorsed to reflect either positive or negative change. At least half of the sample reported at least "a little" positive change on 15 of the 28 items (and 25% or more reported moderate to a great deal of positive change on these items). The types of positive changes reported were similar to those reported by our samples, including positive changes in self ("I trust myself more"), relationships ("I know more who my real friends are"), life philosophy ("My life has more meaning"), and empathy ("I'm more interested in helping sexual assault victims"). In fact, 30% reported being more involved in social or political action since the rape (although recruiting at rape crisis centers may have selected for women who were more socially active). The other study (Kennedy, Davis, & Taylor, 1998) only assessed increases or decreases in spirituality since the assault, which had occurred 9 to 24 months previously. Among the 70 mostly African American rape survivors, 60% reported increased spirituality since the rape, and 47% reported increased well-being, whereas 20% reported decreased spirituality and 47% reported decreased well-being.

Consistent with our research, both studies suggest that PTG following sexual assault is common. However, because both studies were cross-sectional and assessed survivors several months to years postrape, they do not provide information on whether PTG can occur soon after an assault (timing) or how it might change over time (course). They did both assess the relation between time since the assault and reported growth, with inconsistent results: Burt and Katz (1987) reported that positive changes were associated with increased time since the rape whereas Kennedy et al. (1998) found no association.

Comparisons with the Broader Literature

One important finding from our research concerns the types of positive changes reported by sexual assault survivors. Although the survivors in our samples report many of the same kinds of growth reported by survivors of other traumatic events (e.g., greater life appreciation, closer relationships), they also report some unique types of change, such as being more cautious. Similar changes were reported by survivors of child sexual abuse (McMillen, Zuravin, & Rideout, 1995). These event-specific changes are not generally captured by standard growth measures (e.g., Tedeschi & Calhoun, 1996). The political and social action reported by the sexual assault survivors in the Burt and Katz (1987) study is another category not well-represented on standard measures although it also is reported by survivors of other traumas, often in terms of helping or educating others (e.g., Davis, Nolen-Hoeksema, & Larson, 1998; Updegraff, Taylor, Kemeny, & Wyatt, 2002).

Other important findings from our longitudinal data suggest that reports of PTG can occur soon after a trauma and that they generally—but not always—increase over time. The few others studies that assess early reports of PTG also find that it is reported by the majority of participants within a few weeks after an event (e.g., Affleck, Tennen, & Croog, 1987; McMillen et al., 1995), although we assessed PTG sooner than most studies. Regarding the course of PTG, only one other study of which we are aware has used HLM to assess trajectories of growth over time (Manne et al., 2004). Like us, they found that positive changes generally increased over time; however, distinct from our findings, they found no significant individual differences in growth trajectories. Nonetheless, other researchers have reported decreases in self-reported PTG over time (Davis et al., 1998; McMillen et al., 1995; Milam, 2004) or negative correlations between growth and time since the event (e.g., Weiss, 2004). For example, in McMillen et al.'s (1995) study of disaster survivors assessed 4 to 6 weeks and 3 years postevent, the number who reported increased closeness to others decreased from 45% to 25% over time. Positive changes that disappear over time hardly seem to qualify as "growth."

POSTTRAUMATIC GROWTH, DISTRESS, AND WELL-BEING

Perhaps more important than questions regarding the prevalence, timing, and course of PTG are questions regarding whether and how reports of growth are associated with recovery from the negative effects of trauma events, such as PTSD. That is, do survivors who report that there was some positive aspect of the trauma also report less distress? Or, can one report positive life change, yet still feel depressed or anxious as a result of the trauma? We addressed these issues in both the longitudinal study of recent survivors and the community sample of nonrecent survivors. The longitudinal study allowed us to assess the relation between early reports of growth and both concurrent and subsequent distress. Because most studies of growth have been conducted with survivors of traumas that occurred several years previously, we do not know whether it is adaptive for survivors to report positive life changes soon after a trauma. Some argue that early reports of change may reflect denial (Cohen, Hettler, & Pane, 1998). Given that survivors must process the event in order to recover (Foa & Rothbaum, 1998), denial is not likely to be helpful. Conversely, others argue that growth may be more likely for those who find it rapidly (Calhoun & Tedeschi, 1998).

Analyses of cross-sectional data from the longitudinal study (Frazier et al., 2001) indicated that survivors who reported more positive life changes reported lower levels of depression at both 2 weeks and 1 year post-assault, and fewer PTSD symptoms at 2 weeks but not 1 year post-assault. Those who reported more negative life changes reported more symptoms of depression and PTSD at both time periods. The relations among negative changes and distress generally were stronger than those among positive changes and distress.

Because some survivors reported fewer positive changes at 2 weeks than at 12 months post-assault, we also examined how patterns of self-reported positive changes over time were associated with distress levels at 12 months post-assault. To do this, we first created four groups of survivors based on the number of positive changes they reported at 2 weeks and 12 months post-assault: (1) those who reported "low" levels of positive changes at 2 weeks post-assault and "high" levels at 12 months post-assault ("gained positive changes"); (2) those who reported high levels at 2 weeks and low levels at 12 months ("lost positive changes"); (3) those who reported low levels at both points ("never had positive changes"), and (4) those who reported high levels at both points ("always had positive changes"). "Low" and "high" levels were defined via a median split on the PTG measure; the median number of positive changes reported was three at 2 weeks post-assault and five at 12 months. The survivors who reported the *lowest* levels of depression and PTSD at 12 months after the assault were those who reported positive life changes at 2 weeks after the assault and maintained those changes over time. Survivors who reported the *highest* levels of depression and PTSD were those who never reported positive life changes. Interestingly, those who reported positive life changes at 2 weeks after the assault, but not at 12 months post-assault ("lost positive changes"), were as distressed as those who never reported positive life changes. Those who "gained" positive changes did not differ in 12-month distress levels from those who never reported positive life changes.

Thus, in the longitudinal study, survivors who reported more positive life changes generally reported less distress, particularly on a measure of depressive symptoms. We sought to replicate and extend these findings in a community sample of nonrecent survivors by examining the relations among posttrauma life change and a broader range of outcomes, including life satisfaction and perceived health, and by accounting for the effects of recent life stressors and personality on these relationships. Given that most participants had been sexually assaulted several years previously, it seemed important to account for the contribution of recent life events to current adjustment. Similarly, because variability in adjustment may be accounted for partly by personality traits (Watson & Hubbard, 1996), we examined the associations between positive life change and adjustment controlling for both neuroticism and extraversion. These are considered the

"Big Two" personality traits and have received the most attention in the stress and coping literature (Watson & Hubbard, 1996). Although we hypothesized that accounting for these variables would decrease the strength of the correlations among positive change and adjustment measures, we anticipated that self-reported positive life change would still account for unique variance in distress, life satisfaction, and perceived health.

Correlations among the positive life change scale and measures of depression, anxiety, PTSD, life satisfaction, and perceived health all were significant (Frazier et al., 2006). Survivors who reported more positive life changes reported fewer symptoms of depression, anxiety, and PTSD, with correlations in the medium to large range ($r = -.37$ to $-.51$). There also was a large correlation between positive life change and life satisfaction ($r = .49$). The correlation with better-perceived health was significant but small ($r = .18$). All correlations were reduced after controlling for the previous year's stressors and personality ($r = -.18$ to $-.32$ for distress measures; $r = .32$ for life satisfaction) although they remained significant (except for perceived health; $r = .05$).

Comparisons with Other Sexual Assault Studies

As mentioned, only two other studies have examined PTG following sexual assault. In the Burt and Katz (1987) study, reporting positive changes was correlated with self-rated recovery from rape, but not with a negative symptom measure formed by combining scores on four standard symptom inventories. When three separate types of positive changes were examined, changes in the self were associated with fewer psychological symptoms whereas positive actions and changes in interpersonal skills were not associated with symptoms. In the Kennedy et al. study (1998), positive changes in spirituality were associated with positive changes in well-being, although decreases in spirituality were more associated with decreased well-being than increases in spirituality were associated with increases in well-being. In other words, negative changes hurt more than positive changes helped.

Comparisons with the Broader Literature

Our two key results with regard to the relationship between PTG and distress include findings relating early reports of PTG to later distress, and patterns of PTG over time and distress. Specifically, in our longitudinal study (Frazier et al., 2001), individuals who reported positive changes early on, and who retained those positive changes over time, reported the fewest symptoms of PTSD and depression 1 year after the assault. Two other longitudinal studies also suggest that perceiving benefits soon after the trauma is associated with better subsequent adjustment (Affleck et al., 1987; McMillen, Smith, & Fisher, 1997). However, another study found that benefit finding soon after a trauma was associated with better subsequent outcomes only for those who were higher in dispositional optimism (Rini et al., 2004). In fact, among those lower in optimism, those who reported more benefits had somewhat poorer subsequent adjustment than those who reported fewer benefits initially. Similarly, Tomich and Helgeson (2004) found that early benefit finding was associated with poorer subsequent adjustment among breast cancer patients with more severe disease.

Studies assessing changes in reported PTG over time also are scarce but also indicate that early reports of growth may be adaptive under some circumstances. Two other studies examined subsequent (time 2) distress as a function of whether survivors kept, lost, gained, or never reported positive changes (Davis et al., 1998; Milam, 2004). Similar to our results, those who never reported PTG reported the highest levels of distress at time 2, followed by those who "lost" benefits over time, followed by those who gained benefits over time, followed by those who always reported growth. In both studies, as well as our own, those who lost benefits actually became more distressed over time. However, using a simple change score, Rini et al. (2004) did not find a significant relation between change in benefit finding and subsequent adjustment.

CORRELATES OF POSTTRAUMATIC GROWTH

Given that many survivors report positive life changes following an assault, and that these self-reported changes are associated with lower distress levels, an important goal is to identify factors that are related to reporting positive life changes following a traumatic event like a sexual assault. Several researchers have developed models of factors that may either facilitate or hinder positive life change following traumatic events (see O'Leary et al., 1998, for a review). These include personal resources, environmental resources, and the individual's coping strategies and appraisal of the event.

In the longitudinal study described previously (Frazier et al., 2004), we assessed the relations among variables in each of these categories and both early reports of PTG and changes in self-reported PTG over time, both of which predict later distress levels, as discussed previously. The categories and specific correlates measured were: personal characteristics (prior sexual victimization, ethnicity), environmental resources (social support), coping (approach, avoidant, and religious), and control appraisals (behavioral self-blame [past control], control over the recovery process [present control], and taking precautions to prevent future assaults [future control]). The environmental, coping, and control appraisal measures were gathered at all four time points.

The significant correlates of early (2 week) positive change were higher early levels of social support, approach coping, religious coping, and control over the recovery process. With regard to predictors of patterns of PTG over time, the trajectories of social support, approach coping, religious coping, control over the recovery process, and taking precautions were all positively associated with PTG trajectories, suggesting that, within individuals, increases in these variables were associated with increases in self-reported PTG over time. Avoidant coping and behavioral self-blame trajectories were negatively associated with PTG trajectories, suggesting that decreases in avoidant coping and behavioral self-blame were associated with increases in self-reported PTG over time.

Consistent with Schaefer and Moos' (1998) model, we also assessed whether the significant relations among the three personal (i.e., ethnicity, prior victimization) and environmental (i.e., social support) resource variables and PTG were mediated by coping and control appraisals. Of these three variables, only social support was significantly related to PTG. The potential mediators (i.e., variables related to both social support and PTG) were approach and avoidant coping, taking precautions, and control over the recovery process. Regression analyses revealed that control over the recovery process was the strongest mediator of the relation between social support and PTG trajectories. In other words, the primary reason that increases in social support were associated with increases in self-reported PTG was because increases in social support were associated with increased control over the recovery process.

In the community sample of nonrecent survivors, we again attempted to replicate and expand on this work, primarily by assessing a broader range of potential correlates of self-reported growth (Frazier et al., 2006). We included several of the same variables as in the longitudinal study, including social support, religious coping, and the three types of control appraisals. We assessed the same types of coping but examined them separately rather than as combined measures of approach and avoidant coping. With regard to personal characteristics, we assessed three basic personality traits—extraversion, openness to experience, and neuroticism—that may be more important determinants of responses to stressful life events than ethnicity or prior victimization. Finally, as in the longitudinal study, when any of the personal (personality traits) or environmental (social support) resources were associated with self-reported PTG, we assessed whether those relations were mediated by coping strategies or control appraisals.

Correlations revealed that reporting more positive changes was associated as hypothesized with less neuroticism, more extraversion, more social support, more cognitive restructuring and expressing emotions, and less problem avoidance and social withdrawal, greater religious coping, and more perceived control over the recovery process. These correlations generally were in the small to medium range ($r = .19$ to $.44$). The strongest correlates were neuroticism (which was negatively associated with self-reported PTG) and perceived control over the recovery process (which was positively related to PTG). Contrary to predictions, three variables—openness, behavioral self-blame, and taking precautions—were not associated with self-reported positive change. Mediation analyses suggested that (a) social withdrawal partially mediated the relation between extraversion and PTG, (b) perceived control over the recovery process partially mediated the relations among both neuroticism and social support and PTG, and (c) religious coping partially mediated the relation between social support and PTG.

COMPARISONS WITH OTHER SEXUAL ASSAULT STUDIES

Neither of the two other studies of PTG following sexual assault focused much on the question of who is likely to report growth. Although Burt and Katz (1987) reported a positive correlation between postrape positive changes and self-esteem, because both constructs were measured at one time years postrape, we cannot necessarily conclude that having higher self-esteem contributes to the ability to find benefits. Kennedy et al. (1998) examined race, assault severity (injuries, perceived danger), and intrinsic religiosity as correlates of change in spirituality and well-being. Positive changes in spirituality were more often reported by African American women (71%) than by Hispanic (54%) or White (38%) women. Assault severity was not associated with changes in well-being (although there was little variability in perceived danger). Intrinsic religiosity was associated with increased spirituality and well-being although, as with the Burt and Katz study, the direction of the relation was unclear.

COMPARISONS WITH THE BROADER LITERATURE

The key findings from our research into the specific correlates of PTG confirm existing findings and also suggests important variables that deserve more attention. In Helgeson et al.'s (2006) recent meta-analysis of the correlates of PTG, the largest relations were between PTG and optimism ($r = .27$) and positive reappraisal ($r = .38$). Similarly, in our longitudinal study, approach coping (which includes positive reappraisal) predicted early reports of growth, and increases in approach coping over time were associated with increases in PTG over time (Frazier et al., 2004). Positive reappraisal (cognitive restructuring) also was associated with more self-reported PTG in our cross-sectional study (Frazier et al., 2006). Two important correlates of PTG in our research *not* examined in Helgeson et al.'s meta-analysis were perceived control over the recovery process and social support. Control over the recovery process seems particularly important to assess because changes in perceived control had the strongest relations with PTG trajectories in the longitudinal study as well as the strongest relations with PTG in the cross-sectional study. Perceived control also warrants more research attention because it may be more amenable to clinical change than some variables that have been more widely researched, such as personality traits, demographic characteristics, or characteristics of the trauma.

Another key finding of our research was that the cross-sectional correlates of PTG differed somewhat from the correlates of PTG trajectories. For example, initial levels of social support, approach coping (which includes positive reappraisal and expressing emotions), religious coping, and control over the recovery process were associated with initial levels of PTG but not PTG trajectories. However, *changes* in these and other (e.g., avoidant coping, self-blame) variables did predict PTG trajectories (Frazier et al., 2004). Few other studies have assessed correlates of PTG trajectories. In one study of women recently diagnosed with breast cancer and their partners, increases in growth trajectories over time occurred most among women who initially thought more about why they might have developed breast cancer and who engaged in more attempts to search for meaning in breast cancer (Manne et al., 2004). In addition, trajectories of change in expressing emotions covaried with growth trajectories, such that women who expressed their emotions more over time also reported more growth over time. Finally, women whose partners expressed more of their own emotions over time also reported more growth (Manne et al., 2004). In another study of breast cancer patients, Helgeson, Snyder, and Seltman (2004) identified trajectories of changes in mental health, which included groups that both increased and decreased in mental health over time. The variables that distinguished among these two groups were personal resources (which included perceived control) and social resources (which included social support). Specifically, women with more personal and social resources were more likely to have improved mental health over time. Thus, the results of these three longitudinal studies suggest that expressing emotions, having more social support, and having more perceived control are all associated with more positive recovery trajectories.

CLINICAL IMPLICATIONS

Our research on PTG following sexual assault suggests several points relevant to clinical work with rape survivors. First, rape survivors are able to identify positive changes in their lives resulting from the rape even soon after the rape occurred. Normative data on the prevalence of positive changes in the early posttrauma period are important for clinicians working with trauma survivors, who may focus exclusively on the more recognized negative effects of trauma (e.g., PTSD), and ignore potential positive life changes. Rape crisis counselors seeing clients in the immediate aftermath of rape may wish to assess for PTG and perceived benefits even soon after the assault, while simultaneously avoiding the implication that women should feel benefits or that rape is in some way beneficial. Tedeschi and Kilmer (2005) have discussed methods for assessing PTG in clinical practice and the benefits of doing so in greater detail.

Additionally, those who found benefits soon after the rape and still saw themselves as reaping those benefits a year later had the least distress, whereas individuals who either never saw benefits, or reported benefits early but then "lost" them (i.e., no longer identified benefits at 1-year posttrape) had significantly poorer psychological health. These findings suggest that counselors should help clients to find or create benefits out of traumatic events (an issue discussed further later), but also that counselors should work to bolster whatever positive changes clients identify soon after a rape, so that these are not "lost" over time. For example, perceived social support is an important correlate of both PTG and psychological well-being, and improved relationships are an area where rape victims often report positive change (e.g., "I never knew how good other people could be"). However, friends and family who provide warm support in the immediate aftermath of a rape may be at risk of "compassion fatigue" (Figley, 1995) over time, leading to a risk of lost perceived positive change in relationships for the victim. Helping victims to bolster their social support networks might thus be one important means by which counselors can help victims prevent benefit losses over time.

How might counselors encourage PTG in clients, particularly for those who cannot see any benefits to themselves in the experience, or who perceive themselves as unable to grow beyond a traumatic rape? Although few relevant data specific to sexual assault are available, the broader literature on PTG does provide some clues. One study (Weiss, 2004) found that rates of PTG were higher among breast cancer survivors who had contact with other women who had survived breast cancer and experienced PTG. These "PTG models" included both women who the participants had met in natural social contexts and through psychosocial intervention. However, Weiss noted that there was no significant relationship between being in counseling or in a support group and having a PTG model available, nor any significant relationship between counseling and support group participation and greater PTG. Collectively, these data suggest that clients may benefit if counselors facilitate their exposure to PTG models who have used rape or sexual abuse as a catalyst for positive change in their lives.

In addition, several studies suggest that writing about perceived benefits from stressful experiences and chronic illness (generally over several sessions) is associated with better physical health outcomes, including fewer health center visits, medical appointments, and reported physical symptoms (e.g., Stanton et al., 2002). Writing about stressful events has been extensively researched where the goal of the writing is emotional expression and disclosure (usually of negative emotion), and this paradigm is known to be beneficial (Frattaroli, 2006). Research on writing about positive experiences and benefits of a stressful experience is more novel, but also appears beneficial (Frattaroli, 2006).

FUTURE RESEARCH

In this section, we focus on important research directions with PTG in general, although they also apply to research on PTG following sexual assault. These include increased attention to the validity of self-reported PTG, additional longitudinal research, and developing and testing increasingly sophisticated models of the growth process.

Because virtually all data on PTG consist of survivors' reports that they have experienced various positive life changes, concerns about the validity of these self-reports (i.e., whether they are reflected in actual life changes) are increasingly being raised (e.g., Tomich & Helgeson, 2004). There are several reasons to suspect that self-reports of growth may not represent actual life changes. First, as mentioned, longitudinal studies suggest that some survivors actually report decreases over time in self-reported growth (Davis et al., 1998; Frazier et al., 2001; McMillen et al., 1995; Milam, 2004). The term *growth* suggests a permanent enrichment or change in the individual; if a change does not last, it seems inappropriate to call it growth. Second, people may describe the positives that came out of a stressor because they want to appear to be coping well (Carver, 2005), or because they think that is what their social network members want to hear (Wortman, 2004). Self-reports of growth also may reflect adherence to a cultural script, as suggested by the finding that reports of growth following terrorist events were higher in the United States than in Spain (Steger, Frazier, & Zacchanini, in press). Third, self-reported PTG may represent illusory perceptions motivated by the desire to alleviate distressing feelings. Across four studies, McFarland and Alvaro (2000) presented convincing evidence that people report PTG not because they have actually grown but because they derogate their past selves. Finally, people generally are not very accurate in assessing the degree to which they have changed over time, which calls into question the accuracy of self-reports of growth (Tennen & Affleck, 2005). Reinforcing these concerns, in three recent studies, we found little evidence for the validity of self-reported PTG (Frazier & Kaler, 2006).

In a previous paper (Frazier & Kaler, 2006), we outlined an agenda for future research on the validity of PTG. Specifically, we recommended that researchers conduct prospective studies of traumatic events, assess whether self-reports of growth are evident in actual behaviors either in laboratory or real-life situations, and examine whether individuals who report that they have grown from a stressful event are better able to cope with and are less affected by future stressors. We are currently conducting a multisite prospective study of the effects of traumatic life events, conducted by following a large group of undergraduate students over time, some of whom will experience traumatic events over the course of the study. In that way, we can assess actual life change pre- to posttrauma. We also assess behaviors oriented toward helping others, an area of growth that has been neglected and warrants additional research.

Given the findings from our longitudinal study, we also see a need for more research on the process of PTG over time. In particular, our research suggests the need to assess early reports of growth, trajectories of self-reported growth over time, how both early reports of growth and growth trajectories are related to subsequent distress levels, and factors that predict both early growth and growth trajectories. One factor that deserves increased attention is perceived control, particularly perceived control over the recovery process (Frazier, 2003). Although our focus here is on PTG, we believe that future longitudinal research should include measures of posttrauma distress and address all the previous questions with regard to both growth and distress. For example, the factors that lead to growth likely differ from those that decrease distress, which has important implications for interventions.

SUMMARY

Studies of the relations among measures of growth and distress or well-being need to test more sophisticated models, including mediator and moderator models. For example, existing data suggest that measures of perceived growth may be more strongly related to outcomes for some people (e.g., racial minorities) than for others (Helgeson et al., 2006), and that the relation between perceived growth and outcomes may be curvilinear rather than linear (Lechner, Carver, Antoni, Weaver, & Phillips, 2006). If these more complex relations are not taken into account, research relating growth and outcomes will continue to be inconsistent. Additional research also should examine mediators of the relation between PTG and other outcomes, in addition to examining mediators of the relations between personal and environmental resources and PTG as we did in the longitudinal study (Frazier et al., 2004). At this point, we know little about why self-reported PTG is associated with less subsequent distress and better health. Stanton et al. (2002) found that writing about one's deepest thoughts and feelings and writing about positive feelings were equally effective in promoting health and well-being among cancer patients, although the mechanisms underlying the effectiveness of the two interventions differed (Low, Stanton, & Danoff-Burg, 2006). Moreover, Low et al. were unsuccessful in identifying the mediators of the health benefits of writing about positive thoughts and feelings.

Summary Points (Practice)

- Assess PTG even soon after traumatic events.
- Bolster whatever positive changes clients identify so that they are maintained over time.
- Help clients to find PTG models—others who have used trauma as a catalyst for positive change.

Summary Points (Research)

- Validate self-reports of PTG using prospective designs and behavioral measures.
- Conduct longitudinal studies of posttrauma recovery including measures of PTG and distress.
- Test increasingly sophisticated models of the growth process, including mediators and moderators.

REFERENCES

Affleck, G., Tennen, H., & Croog, S. (1987). Causal attribution, perceived benefits, and morbidity after a heart attack: An 8-year study. *Journal of Consulting and Clinical Psychology, 55,* 29–35.

Breslau, N., Kessler, R., Chilcoat, H., Schultz, L., Davis, G., & Andreski, P. (1998). Trauma and posttraumatic stress disorder in the community: The 1996 Detroit area survey of trauma. *Archives of General Psychiatry, 55,* 626–632.

Burt, M. R., & Katz, B. L. (1987). Dimensions of recovery from rape: Focus on growth outcomes. *Journal of Interpersonal Violence, 2,* 57–81.

Calhoun, L., & Tedeschi, R. (1998). Posttraumatic growth: Future directions. In R. Tedeschi, C. Park, & L. Calhoun (Eds.), *Posttraumatic growth: Positive changes in the aftermath of crisis* (pp. 215–238). Mahwah, NJ: Erlbaum.

Carver, C. (2005, May). *Positive changes after adversity: One phenomenon or diverse phenomena?* Paper presented at the Positive Life Changes, Benefit-Finding and Growth Following Illness Conference, Storrs, CT.

Cohen, L., Hettler, T., & Pane, N. (1998). Assessment of posttraumatic growth. In R. Tedeschi, C. Park, & L. Calhoun (Eds.), *Posttraumatic growth: Positive changes in the aftermath of crisis* (pp. 23–42). Mahwah, NJ: Erlbaum.

Davis, C., Nolen-Hoeksema, S., & Larson, J. (1998). Making sense of loss and benefiting from the experience: Two construals of meaning. *Journal of Personality and Social Psychology, 75,* 561–574.

Figley, C. R. (1995). Compassion fatigue as secondary traumatic stress disorder: An overview. In C. R. Figley (Ed.), *Compassion fatigue: Coping with secondary traumatic stress disorder in those who treat the traumatized* (pp. 1–20). New York: Brunner-Routledge.

Foa, E., & Rothbaum, B. (1998). *Treating the trauma of rape: Cognitive behavioral therapy for PTSD.* New York: Guilford Press.

Frattaroli, J. (2006). Experimental disclosure and its moderators: A meta-analysis. *Psychological Bulletin, 132,* 823–865.

Frazier, P. (2003). Perceived control and distress following sexual assault: A longitudinal test of a new model. *Journal of Personality and Social Psychology, 84,* 1257–1269.

Frazier, P., & Burnett, J. (1994). Immediate coping strategies among rape victims. *Journal of Counseling and Development, 72,* 633–639.

Frazier, P., Conlon, A., & Glaser, T. (2001). Positive and negative life changes following sexual assault. *Journal of Consulting and Clinical Psychology, 69,* 1048–1055.

Frazier, P., Conlon, A., Steger, M., Tashiro, T., & Glaser, T. (2006). Positive life changes following sexual assault: A replication and extension. In F. Columbo (Ed.), *Post-traumatic stress: New research* (pp. 1–22). Hauppauge, NY: Nova Science.

Frazier, P., & Kaler, M. E. (2006). Assessing the validity of self-reported stress-related growth. *Journal of Consulting and Clinical Psychology, 74,* 859–869.

Frazier, P., Tashiro, T., Berman, M., Steger, M., & Long, J. (2004). Correlates of levels and patterns of PTG among sexual assault survivors. *Journal of Consulting and Clinical Psychology, 72,* 19–30.

Helgeson, V., Reynolds, K., & Tomich, P. (2006). A meta-analytic review of benefit finding and growth. *Journal of Consulting and Clinical Psychology, 74,* 797–816.

Helgeson, V., Snyder, P., & Seltman, H. (2004). Psychological and physical adjustment to breast cancer over 4 years: Identifying distinct trajectories of change. *Health Psychology, 23,* 3–15.

Janoff-Bulman, R. (1989). Assumptive worlds and the stress of traumatic events: Applications of the schema construct. *Social Cognition, 7,* 113–136.

Kennedy, J. E., Davis, R. C., & Taylor, B. G. (1998). Changes in spirituality and well-being among victims of sexual assault. *Journal for the Scientific Study of Religion, 37,* 322–329.

Kessler, R., Sonnega, A., Bromet, E., Hughes, M., & Nelson, C. (1995). Posttraumatic stress disorder in the national comorbidity survey. *Archives of General Psychiatry, 52,* 1048–1060.

Lechner, S., Carver, C., Antoni, M., Weaver, K., & Phillips, K. (2006). Curvilinear associations between benefit finding and psychosocial adjustment to breast cancer. *Journal of Consulting and Clinical Psychology, 74,* 828–840.

Low, C. A., Stanton, A. L., & Danoff-Burg, S. (2006). Expressive disclosure and benefit finding among breast cancer patients: Mechanisms for positive health effects. *Health Psychology, 25,* 181–189.

Manne, S., Ostroff, J., Winkel, G., Goldstein, L., Fox, K., & Grana, G. (2004). Post-traumatic growth after breast cancer: Patient, partner, and couple perspectives. *Psychosomatic Medicine, 66,* 442–454.

McFarland, C., & Alvaro, C. (2000). The impact of motivation on temporal comparisons: Coping with traumatic events by perceiving personal growth. *Journal of Personality and Social Psychology, 79,* 327–343.

McMillen, J. C., Smith, E., & Fisher, R. (1997). Perceived benefit and mental health after three types of disaster. *Journal of Consulting and Clinical Psychology, 65,* 733–739.

McMillen, J. C., Zuravin, S., & Rideout, G. (1995). Perceived benefit from child sexual abuse. *Journal of Consulting and Clinical Psychology, 63,* 1037–1043.

Milam, J. E. (2004). Posttraumatic growth among HIV/AIDS patients. *Journal of Applied and Social Psychology, 34,* 2353–2376.

O'Leary, V., Alday, C., & Ickovics, J. (1998). Models of life change and posttraumatic growth. In R. Tedeschi, C. Park, & L. Calhoun (Eds.), *Posttraumatic growth: Positive changes in the aftermath of crisis* (pp. 127–151). Mahwah, NJ: Erlbaum.

Rini, C., Manne, S., DuHamel, K. N., Austin, J., Ostroff, J., Boulad, F., et al. (2004). Mothers' perceptions of benefit following pediatric stem cell transplantation: A longitudinal investigation of the roles of optimism, medical risk, and sociodemographic resources. *Annals of Behavioral Medicine, 28,* 132–141.

Schaefer, J., & Moos, R. (1998). The context for posttraumatic growth: Life crises, individual and social resources, and coping. In R. Tedeschi, C. Park, & L. Calhoun (Eds.), *Posttraumatic growth: Positive changes in the aftermath of crisis* (pp. 99–126). Mahwah, NJ: Erlbaum.

Sears, S. R., Stanton, A. L., & Danoff-Burg, S. (2003). The yellow brick road and the emerald city: Benefit finding, positive reappraisal coping, and posttraumatic growth in women with early-stage breast cancer. *Health Psychology, 22,* 487–497.

Stanton, A. L., Danoff-Burg, S., Sworowski, L. A., Collins, C. A., Branstetter, A. D., Rodriguez-Hanley, A., et al. (2002). Randomized, controlled trial of written emotional expression and benefit finding in breast cancer patients. *Journal of Clinical Oncology, 20,* 4160–4168.

Steger, M., Frazier, P., & Zacchanini, J. L. (in press). Terrorism in two cultures: Stress and growth following September 11th and the Madrid train bombings. *Journal of Loss and Trauma.*

Tedeschi, R. G., & Calhoun, L. G. (1995). *Trauma and transformation: Growing in the aftermath of suffering.* Thousand Oaks, CA: Sage.

Tedeschi, R. G., & Calhoun, L. G. (1996). The Posttraumatic Growth Inventory: Measuring the positive legacy of trauma. *Journal of Traumatic Stress, 9,* 455–471.

Tedeschi, R. G., & Kilmer, R. P. (2005). Assessing strengths, resilience, and growth to guide clinical interventions. *Professional Psychology: Research and Practice, 36,* 230–237.

Tennen, H., & Affleck, G. (2005, May). *Positive change following adversity: In search of novel theories, meticulous methods, and precise analytic strategies.* Paper presented at the Positive Life Changes, Benefit-Finding, and Growth Following Illness Conference, Storrs, CT.

Tjaden, P., & Thoennes, N. (2000). *Full report of the prevalence, incidence, and consequences of violence against women.* Washington, DC: U.S. Department of Justice.

Tomich, P. L., & Helgeson, V. S. (2004). Is finding something good in the bad always good? Benefit finding among women with breast cancer. *Health Psychology, 23,* 16–23.

Updegraff, J. A., Taylor, S. E., Kemeny, M. E., & Wyatt, G. E. (2002). Positive and negative effects of HIV infection in women with low socioeconomic resources. *Personality and Social Psychology Bulletin, 28,* 382–394.

Veronen, L. J., & Kilpatrick, D. G. (1983). Rape: A precursor of change. In E. J. Callahan & K. A. McCluskey (Eds.), *Life-span developmental psychology: Nonnormative life events* (pp. 167–190). New York: Academic Press.

Watson, D., & Hubbard, B. (1996). Adaptational style and dispositional structure: Coping in the context of the five-factor model. *Journal of Personality, 64,* 737–774.

Weiss, T. (2004). Correlates of posttraumatic growth in married breast cancer survivors. *Journal of Social and Clinical Psychology, 23,* 733–746.

Wortman, C. B. (2004). Posttraumatic growth: Progress and problems. *Psychological Inquiry, 15,* 81–90.

Zoellner, T., & Maercker, A. (2006). Posttraumatic growth in clinical psychology: A critical review and introduction of a two component model. *Clinical Psychology Review, 26,* 626–653.

PART III

CLINICAL APPROACHES AND THERAPEUTIC EXPERIENCES OF MANAGING DISTRESS AND FACILITATING GROWTH

CHAPTER 10

Facilitating Posttraumatic Growth Following Cancer

MATTHEW J. CORDOVA

> Since cancer, what is important to me has changed. Little things
> that used to worry me don't anymore, and I am clearer about what
> matters. For the first time in my life, I believe I am a very strong
> person. It's strange to say, but cancer has actually led to some very
> good things for me.
>
> —50-year-old woman with metastatic lung cancer

WHILE A VAST body of literature has documented the negative psychosocial impact of cancer (Kornblith, 1998), there is also considerable evidence of the potential for positive life changes in those
facing malignant disease (Stanton, Bower, & Low, 2006). General approaches for facilitating posttraumatic growth (PTG) have been offered
(Calhoun & Tedeschi, 2000), but empirical evidence that specific strategies
are effective in helping those with cancer experience such growth is limited. This chapter reviews: (1) the potentially traumatic aspects of the cancer experience, (2) the literature on cancer-related posttraumatic stress,
(3) the literature on PTG following cancer, (4) theoretical frameworks that
may inform efforts to facilitate PTG, (5) suggestions for working with individuals facing cancer, and (6) directions for future research.

CANCER AS A TRAUMATIC STRESSOR

In many ways, cancer parallels other traumatic stressors. The diagnosis
may be sudden and unexpected, the disease and treatment may pose

185

threats to one's life, and the experience may evoke intense emotional responses of fear and helplessness. Further, diagnosis with cancer may undermine one's assumptions about control, invulnerability, safety, and predictability (Green, Epstein, Krupnick, & Rowland, 1997).

At the same time, having cancer is not a discrete, singular stressful experience, but rather entails a cascade of unfolding threats and stressors (Gurevich, Devins, & Rodin, 2002; Kangas, Henry, & Bryant, 2002). Beginning with detection, work-up, and initial diagnosis, individuals experience a great deal of stress as they try to process complex medical information and make treatment decisions in the context of heightened emotions (Stanton & Snider, 1993). Cancer treatment and its side effects can be extremely demanding. Surgical treatment can be invasive, painful, and disfiguring (Jacobsen, Roth, & Holland, 1998). Daily radiation therapy for weeks on end may cause fatigue, skin irritation, gastrointestinal problems, and disruption of daily schedule and activities (Johnson, Lauver, & Nail, 1989). Chemotherapy may cause nausea, vomiting, hair loss, fatigue, risk of bleeding problems, and susceptibility to infection (Redd, Jacobsen, & Andrykowski, 1989). Hormone therapies may cause hot flashes, cognitive difficulties, and various physical changes (Knobf, Pasacreta, Valentine, & McCorkle, 1998). While receiving active treatment, many people stop working, apply for disability support, and experience social isolation and financial strain (Wright, 2002). Treatment completion can be quite stressful because the individual must cope with less frequent medical monitoring and try to resume "normal" activities. After treatment, individuals may face a number of ongoing stressors, including persistent treatment side effects and posttreatment effects (e.g., fatigue, cognitive changes); altered body image; concerns about work, insurance, and finances; interpersonal problems; sexual dysfunction; and fears of recurrence (Kornblith, 2003). Those living with progressive or advanced cancer may chronically be coping with disease symptoms, treatment side effects, and immediate concerns about dying. Even in the best circumstances, when treatment has been successful and the disease is in remission, the combination of physical, emotional, social, informational, practical, and financial demands on cancer patients can be overwhelming.

Cumulatively, these experiences constitute a traumatic stressor for many with cancer. In two studies, more than 60% of primary breast cancer patients reported that they perceived their cancer as a threat to their life and that they responded with fear, helplessness, or horror (Andrykowski, Cordova, Studts, & Miller, 1998; Cordova, Cunningham, Carlson, & Andrykowski, 2001). In a heterogeneous sample of cancer patients, 33% were likely to meet diagnostic criteria for Acute Stress Disorder in the month following diagnosis (McGarvey et al., 1998). Given the potentially traumatic nature of the cancer experience, it is not surprising that a growing literature has examined posttraumatic stress responses in this population.

CANCER-RELATED POSTTRAUMATIC STRESS

Since diagnosis with a life-threatening illness was included in the *Diagnostic and Statistical Manual of Mental Disorders,* 4th Ed. (*DSM-IV;* American Psychiatric Association, 1994) as a stressor that could potentially elicit Posttraumatic Stress Disorder (PTSD), a substantial literature has developed on cancer-related posttraumatic stress (Gurevich et al., 2002; Kangas et al., 2002). Prevalence of cancer-related PTSD ranges from 5% to 35% (Kangas et al., 2002). It is common for cancer survivors to report subdiagnostic levels of intrusive ideation and avoidance, and such reports have been associated with poorer quality of life (Kangas et al., 2002).

Several correlates of cancer-related posttraumatic stress symptoms have been identified. Demographic and personality factors, such as younger age (Green et al., 1998), lower income (Cordova et al., 1995), less education (Jacobsen, Widows, et al., 1998), and greater emotional reactivity (Tjemsland, Soreide, & Malt, 1998) have been associated with greater PTSD symptomatology. Historical characteristics, such as greater past trauma (Green et al., 2000) and a history of emotional problems (Mundy et al., 2000) have also been identified as risk factors. Concurrent factors, such as greater life stressors (Butler, Koopman, Classen, & Spiegel, 1999), poorer social support (Andrykowski & Cordova, 1998), higher social constraints (Lepore & Helgeson, 1998; Manne, 1999), less knowledge of disease stage (Naidich & Motta, 2000), greater dissociative symptoms at the time of diagnosis (Kangas, Henry, & Bryant, 2005), and greater fear of recurrence (Black & White, 2005) have been linked to greater symptomatology. Finally, disease and treatment variables, such as shorter time since diagnosis or treatment completion (Andrykowski & Cordova, 1998), greater disease severity (Jacobsen, Widows, et al., 1998), and recurrent disease (Butler et al., 1999) have shown relationships to greater cancer-related posttraumatic stress symptoms. In summary, it appears that the greater threats posed by cancer, and the fewer resources to cope with those threats, predict greater posttraumatic stress reactions to the disease.

As with other traumatic experiences, cancer has the potential to elicit enduring and impairing posttraumatic stress reactions. There is evidence that cancer-related PTSD symptoms do not dissipate over time (Andrykowski, Cordova, Kenady, McGrath, & Sloan, 2000), are associated with decrements in quality of life (Cordova et al., 1995), and do not simply reflect global distress (Cordova, Studts, Hann, Jacobsen, & Andrykowski, 2000).

CANCER-RELATED POSTTRAUMATIC GROWTH

Some characteristics of the cancer experience may provide opportunities for PTG. First, the primary threat posed by cancer, death, is future-oriented (Green et al., 1997). Whereas survivors of more time-limited traumatic experiences must learn to recognize that the danger they experienced no longer poses a threat, it is realistic for those with cancer to worry that the disease will progress and shorten their life. In this way, cancer patients are never really "posttrauma"—many describe trying to live while "waiting for the other shoe to drop." While this uncertainty can be highly anxiety-provoking, it also may prompt the individual to consider, "What do I want out of the time I have left, however long that is?" This questioning may lead to a shift in priorities and values, and to a different appreciation of and approach to day-to-day life.

Second, cancer and its treatment disrupt "life as usual" for a prolonged period of time. For months on end, those with cancer may forgo or adapt "normal" activities due to fatigue, nausea, pain, busy appointment schedules, financial strain, or emotional distress. Over time, individuals are faced with constructing a "new normal" and making decisions about what aspects of their life they want to resume, give-up, alter, or prioritize differently. Again, this may lead to an enhanced sense of direction, appreciation, and meaning in life.

Third, many with cancer need more physical care, practical assistance, and emotional support than usual from friends and family. Whereas some in their social network are able to meet these needs, it is common for patients to experience social withdrawal or more overt rejection from those they turn to for support (Lepore, 2001). Positive and negative interpersonal experiences may prompt cancer patients to re-evaluate their connections with others, potentially intensifying their appreciation of, and improving their satisfaction with, some relationships.

Fourth, cancer confronts people with their mortality. In considering dying, many reflect on life's meaning, their purpose in the world, their belief (or lack thereof) in God, and spirituality (Tedeschi & Calhoun, 1995). For some, these existential considerations result in an increased appreciation of life and stronger or clearer sense of spirituality. In sum, cancer can be profoundly stressful, disruptive, and distressing, but may also lead people to reexamine their priorities, their relationships, and themselves and experience a sense of personal growth and positive change.

It appears that the majority of cancer patients identify positive life changes due to their cancer experience. Benefits have been identified by 50% to 90% of breast cancer patients (Colllins, Taylor, & Skokan, 1990;

Petrie, Buick, Weinman, & Booth, 1999; Sears, Stanton, & Danoff-Burg, 2003; Taylor, 1983; Taylor, Lichtman, & Wood, 1984; Zemore & Shepel, 1989), 76% of testicular cancer patients (Rieker, Edbril, & Garnick, 1985), and 60% to 95% of survivors of childhood/adolescent cancer (Fritz & Williams, 1988; Wasserman, Thompson, Wilimas, & Fairclough, 1987). Across a multitude of other studies, those with cancer have reported positive changes in satisfaction with life and in the meaning of life, in self-confidence and a sense of personal strength, in life priorities and goals, in sense of spirituality, in compassion for others, and in relationships with friends and family (Andrykowski, Brady, & Hunt, 1993; Antoni et al., 2001; Bellizzi, 2004; Bower et al., 2005; Carpenter, Brockopp, & Andrykowski, 1999; Carver & Antoni, 2004; Cordova et al., 2001; Fromm, Andrykowski, & Hunt, 1996; Ho, Chan, & Ho, 2004; Lechner et al., 2003; Manne, Ostroff, & Winkel, 2004; Schulz & Mohamed, 2004; Spiegel, Bloom, & Yalom, 1981; Stanton et al., 2002; Thornton, 2002; Thornton & Perez, 2006; Tomich & Helgeson, 2002, 2004; Weiss, 2004; Widows, Jacobsen, Booth-Jones, & Fields, 2005).

Although attempts have been made to identify factors that may predict or promote PTG following cancer, findings have been somewhat inconsistent. Sociodemographic variables, such as higher SES (Widows et al., 2005); minority ethnicity (Tomich & Helgeson, 2004); younger age (Bellizzi, 2004); and being married, employed, and with higher education (Bellizzi & Blank, 2006) have been linked with reports of positive life change after cancer. Greater PTG has also been associated with a range of social, cognitive, and personality factors, such as greater social support (Lechner, Antoni, & Zakowski, in press; Schulz & Mohamed, 2004; Weiss, 2004), greater optimism (Antoni et al., 2001), and greater perceived stressfulness of cancer (Cordova et al., 2001; Lechner et al., 2003; Sears et al., 2003; Widows et al., 2005). Coping styles, such as positive reframing (Sears et al., 2003; Thornton & Perez, 2006), acceptance (Schulz & Mohamed, 2004), and cognitive and emotional processing (Antoni et al., 2001; Manne et al., 2004) have been linked with greater likelihood of PTG. Medical variables, such as greater disease severity (Andrykowski et al., 1996) and longer time since diagnosis (Manne et al., 2004; Sears et al., 2003) have also been linked with greater perceptions of growth in patients with cancer. Considered together, these findings suggest that greater perception of threat posed by cancer, greater resources to cope with that threat, and greater intentional attempts to engage with and process the experience, may be associated with greater cancer-related PTG.

Attempts to identify links between cancer-related PTG and indices of distress have yielded inconsistent findings. Some cross-sectional investigations have found perception of positive change to be associated with better adjustment (e.g., Ho et al., 2004; Katz, Flasher, Cacciapaglia, & Nelson, 2001; Taylor et al., 1984; Urcuyo, Boyers, Carver, & Antoni, 2005), whereas others have found these outcomes to be unrelated (e.g., Andrykowski et al., 1993; Fromm et al., 1996). Longitudinal studies have yielded similar results. Some have found perceived benefits of cancer to be associated with better later adjustment (Carver & Antoni, 2004), whereas others have linked such perceptions to poorer later adjustment (Tomich & Helgeson, 2004). Still other studies have found no significant relationship between early benefit finding and later distress (Sears et al., 2003; Widows et al., 2005). Multidimensional models of emotional well-being would suggest that positive and negative adjustment may be multifaceted and independent of one another, such that distress and PTG are not mutually exclusive (Calhoun & Tedeschi, 2006).

THEORETICAL FRAMEWORKS

Several theoretical frameworks may inform efforts to facilitate PTG in those with cancer. Parkes' (1971) construct of "psychosocial transition" describes major life events that cause an individual to reformulate their expectations and plans for the future and their view of the world; successful negotiation of such transitions may entail both distress and a sense of personal growth. Janoff-Bulman (1992, 2004, 2006) holds that as "shattered assumptions" are recast and new skills are developed to cope with massive life disruption, individuals may experience a sense of personal growth. By facing threats of death, loss of connection with others, and loss of control, one may emerge with a greater sense of appreciation of and meaning in life, relationships, and personal competence (Janoff-Bulman & Berger, 2000). Existential theory suggests that directly confronting one's mortality may elicit a reevaluation and redefinition of life goals and priorities (Spiegel & Classen, 2000; Yalom, 1980). Together with comprehensive frameworks of the development of PTG (Calhoun & Tedeschi, 2006), these viewpoints suggest that PTG following cancer may be facilitated by helping patients directly engage with threats, manage emotional distress, express and intentionally process emotional and cognitive reactions to their illness, develop a coherent story about what has occurred, and revise beliefs and goals for the future.

There is some initial evidence that therapeutic approaches based on these concepts may enhance cancer patients' perception of benefits. Antoni et al. (2001) and McGregor et al. (2004) found that a 10-week, group-based cognitive-behavioral stress management (CBSM) intervention (Antoni, 2003) increased benefit finding among women with primary breast cancer. Penedo et al. (2006) demonstrated that men with localized prostate cancer who received the CBSM intervention reported increased benefit finding, and that these improvements were mediated by development of stress management skills. Based on these studies, it appears that cognitive-behavioral intervention components, such as education, relaxation and meditation training, and cognitive restructuring may facilitate PTG among cancer patients.

Supportive expressive therapy (SET; Spiegel & Classen, 2000), an existential, emotion-focused group intervention, emphasizes helping patients directly face and express emotions about the losses they have experienced, confront their concerns about the future, reevaluate their priorities, and focus on meaningful activities and relationships. Although SET has demonstrated efficacy in reducing distress in cancer patients (Classen et al., 2001; Goodwin et al., 2001; Spiegel et al., 1981), and although participants in SET groups routinely report that this therapy has enhanced their sense of personal growth (Spiegel & Classen, 2000), the impact of SET on PTG or related outcomes has not been formally assessed in published studies to date.

Theoretical frameworks and some experimental and anecdotal data suggest that clinicians may facilitate PTG in those with cancer. Based on these approaches, some specific strategies for working with cancer patients can be identified. But first, a few caveats warrant discussion.

CAVEATS

Caution should be taken in working with cancer patients to facilitate PTG. First, it is not at all clear that cancer patients need help in this regard. The majority of patients spontaneously experience positive life changes, suggesting that this may be a natural process that does not require clinical facilitation. Overzealous intervention attempts may undermine the natural experience. Second, our understanding of the meaning of reports of PTG is still developing. Some view such perceptions as illusory, attempts at positive self-presentation, or attempts to cope with distress. It may be that we do not yet know enough to forge ahead in attempts to promote this process. Third, given the burdensome pressure cancer patients perceive to "stay positive," actively prescribing identification of benefits from cancer may be perceived as invalidating, leading them to suppress or inhibit expressions of distress. With these caveats, what follows are suggestions for helping patients reflect on and understand their experience and make decisions about how they want to approach the challenge of living well in the face of uncertainty.

WORKING WITH INDIVIDUALS FACING CANCER

WHERE

Given that only a minority of cancer patients meet criteria for a formal psychiatric disorder, identify the need for formal mental health services, or have the resources to attend appointments beyond their medical visits, clinicians working in integrated, multidisciplinary oncology/hematology settings are ideally situated to employ the strategies described here. Such settings enable clinicians to establish contact in a nonthreatening way and meet with a full-range of patients, some with diagnosable psychopathology and others experiencing "within normal limits" distress, who may benefit from conversations that may facilitate PTG. That said, the approaches that follow can be utilized in contacts with cancer patients in office-based therapy visits, group therapy sessions, or other consultations.

WHO AND WHEN

Many studies of PTG and cancer focused on patients with early stage disease, who had completed treatment, and who were years postdiagnosis. While these patients may be experiencing continued stressors, they may not be as encumbered by physical and practical demands as those still in the midst of treatment or facing active disease, and thus may have a better perspective from which to report positive changes. However, there are not sufficient data to suggest that this is the ideal population or window in which to intervene to facilitate PTG. It could be argued that those facing active treatment or progressive disease may be in a better position to benefit from intervention. Thus, it is not possible to make conclusive statements regarding when and with whom facilitation of PTG should be attempted.

HOW

Based on the empirical and theoretical literature reviewed previously, and grounded in the author's clinical experience as a psychologist working in oncology/hematology settings, the following suggestions for facilitating PTG are offered:

- *Provide education and normalize the full-range of emotional reactions:* The experience of having cancer evokes a wide-range of affective responses, including fear, anxiety, sadness, anger, hopelessness, confusion, guilt, and shame. It is common for patients and their family members to feel anxious and preoccupied with what is happening, and to try to avoid thinking about it to reduce emotional arousal. This avoidance is further reinforced by the previously mentioned pressures to "stay positive." Rigid avoidance increases intrusive ideation, worry, and distress. One man with pancreatic cancer said, "The more I push it away and try to be upbeat, the more upset I become." Educating all involved about these common reactions and helping them redefine what is means to "stay positive" can them develop greater acceptance of and flexibility regarding emotions, which can better enable them to process and cope with what is happening.

- *Facilitate disclosure and communication:* It is common for patients and those around them to attempt to conceal emotional reactions to avoid upsetting each other or being accused of losing "hope." Every time a woman with ovarian cancer expressed anxiety about the future, her spouse told her, "Don't talk like that, you're going to beat this." The cumulative result of these common responses is often that patients and family members are experiencing the same worries and emotions in isolation and without the support they both need. Orienting patients and families to these common dynamics and teaching them skills to communicate more openly can enhance mutual support and improve their relationship satisfaction.

- *Guide patients to tell the story of their cancer to someone:* Some patients liken being diagnosed with cancer to getting on a moving roller-coaster. Because of how rapidly the process of detection, work-up, diagnosis, treatment decision making, and treatment onset can unfold, and because it can be extremely anxiety-provoking to reflect on the details of these stressors, many patients look back at that period as a "blur" that they would just as soon forget. A breast cancer patient who was 2 months posttreatment completion stated, "I still haven't let myself think about all that has happened." Helping patients construct a coherent narrative about what they have been through can help them develop a sense of understanding and control. Telling this story in detail can help patients access, process, and habituate to strong affective reactions linked with this tumultuous period, and emerge feeling stronger for it.

- *Ask patients to talk about their lives before cancer:* Having cancer often leaves people feeling like full-time patients, undermining their sense of normalcy and challenging their identity. A man with lymphoma stated, "It's hard to remember who I was before cancer." Asking patients about their upbringing, family, friends, education, work history, hobbies, travels, sense of spirituality, triumphs, losses, goals, and values can help increase their self-awareness and help them view their experience with greater continuity. It can also serve as a baseline against which they can consider the impact of cancer on who they are and what is important to them.

- *Encourage patients to take inventory of what they have and haven't lost:* Helping patients examine what has and hasn't changed can enable them to identify and process losses and recognize who they are still. Some losses are quite obvious (e.g., impaired physical functioning, role changes), while others are more subtle (e.g., sense of competence and invulnerability). It is common to meet patients who have not reflected on these changes due to being in "survival mode" or due to strict rules they (or others) have set about "focusing on the positive." Helping patients identify what has changed and express related sadness, anger, and anxiety can help them both mourn losses and orient to what hasn't been lost. Many of us define who we are by what we can do. It is common for patients to feel as if their essential qualities are being stripped away one by one. A man with leukemia stated, "I've always been the guy my friends came to for help with projects, but right now I can't lift a hammer." Helping patients identifying enduring qualities, abilities, and roles can help them emerge with a strengthened sense of who they are.

- *Give patients opportunities to talk directly about their ultimate worries and concerns:* Many patients and family members believe that if they talk about their worries it will make them depressed, cause the worries to "become true," represent a lack of hope, or burden others. The goal for many is to "just stay focused on the present." However, most patients also admit that they have a number of worries about the future that are sources of great anxiety and preoccupation. One man with head and neck cancer said, "It all hits me at night when everyone is asleep and I let myself think about what might happen." Difficulty facing worries about the future undermines the goal of focusing on life in the present. Helping patients identify and process concerns can give them opportunities to break worries down into solvable problems, face uncertainty, and make important decisions. For example, it is common for patients to worry about pain and suffering, burdening their family, losing control and dignity, dying, and how their loved ones will carry on. Talking openly about these fears can help them identify solutions (e.g., pain management, palliative/hospice care, anticipate coping strategies, financial/legal planning), express and process emotions, and decide how they want to maximize their time so that they can live well now.

- *Teach cognitive-behavioral coping skills:* The intensity and chronicity of stress experienced by those with cancer is often sufficient to overwhelm existing coping resources. For many, high levels of physiological arousal are obstacles to expressing emotions, problem solving, and considering topics that may further exacerbate anxiety. A man with multiple myeloma described, "I'm a bundle of nerves—I feel totally out of control." Further, preexisting negative schemas and unrealistic, extreme, or distorted appraisals of the current situation can exacerbate distress and undermine one's sense of control and self-efficacy to manage day-to-day life. Teaching patients skills, such as progressive muscle relaxation, diaphragmatic breathing, imagery, self-hypnosis, and mindfulness meditation, can increase their sense of control over their bodies and enhance their ability to observe, tolerate, and at times regulate their thoughts and emotional reactions. Introducing a framework for identifying and challenging negative thoughts and generating more realistic self-talk can increase cognitive flexibility and lead to more positive appraisals. Care should be taken in utilizing these cognitive strategies because they run the risk of being perceived as "mind games" or "spin control." Cancer patients have many experiences that can rationally be viewed as "negative"—attempting to recast them otherwise can feel invalidating. However, most patients are receptive to the rationale that at times our thinking patterns can make a difficult situation worse. Equipping them with these strategies can enhance their sense of personal strength and their ability to process their experience more directly.

- *Help patients clarify and live according to their values, priorities, and goals:* Faced with threats of loss, limited energy, and compressed time, many cancer patients recognize that "life as normal" must change. Given limited resources, they realize that they have to prioritize. A patient with thyroid cancer said, "I now need to focus on people and activities that nurture me." Asking patients about the principles they want to live by, their goals, and the people, activities, and causes that are most important to them can help them determine how they want to spend their time and energy. Through overt behavioral changes (e.g., spending more time with certain people or hobbies) and less observable shifts (e.g., greater spiritual engagement, more time spent "in the moment"), patients may emerge with a greater sense of meaning and clarity in their lives.

Michael's Story

Michael's story illustrates many of the processes of PTG and the strategies for working with patients facing cancer. Michael was a 51-year-old man who had been diagnosed with unresectable liver cancer. He was told that he had at most 1 to 2 years to live and that treatment options were limited due to his comorbid medical conditions. He was offered chemotherapy and told that there was a low probability of it slowing his disease or reducing his symptoms of abdominal pain, fatigue, and shortness of breath.

When approached in the clinic a few weeks into treatment, Michael was suspicious about meeting with a psychologist, angrily stating that he wasn't "crazy" and could handle things on his own. After the rationale for the meeting was explained ("People here are pretty stressed—my job is to see how you're doing and if I can be useful to you"), Michael softened and shared that he hadn't been sleeping well. He had been thinking about his father's difficult death from lung cancer and feeling anxious—when he tried to push these thoughts out of his mind, they returned "with a vengeance." He was trying to "maintain hope," but was feeling angry and scared. Michael was receptive to normalization of these emotions. He was encouraged to spend less energy fighting his reactions and instead to acknowledge them and let them pass on their own.

Michael reported that he was a "recovering alcoholic" and had been sober for 9 years. He had been divorced for 20 years and had little contact with his 21-year-old son. He was living with his girlfriend of 3 years, Penny, and they were thinking about getting married. Michael worked as a mechanic and enjoyed riding motorcycles, fishing, and hiking. At the end of this contact, Michael agreed to touch base when he returned to the clinic to "see how things are going."

Michael returned to clinic accompanied by Penny, and there was clearly tension between them. He stated that everything was going fine, but Penny was tearful and stated that she had been extremely worried about him and their future. On further discussion, Michael admitted to similar anxieties and stated that he didn't want to upset Penny by talking about the possibility of dying. Both were receptive to validation of their reactions, observation of their similar concerns, and education regarding ways they could talk together about their worries without feeling like "cancer" invaded their every moment together. Michael talked about the rapid weight loss, abdominal pain, and overwhelming fatigue that prompted him to see his primary care physician, his shock and fear when imaging studies and a biopsy confirmed the diagnosis, and his feelings of hopelessness and transient thoughts of suicide when told of his prognosis. Penny expressed sadness at the possibility of losing Michael and confusion regarding the best way to support him. Both admitted to feeling "on edge all the time," and were receptive to learning a relaxation exercise involving breathing and imagery. In addition, both were able to identify ways that their negative self-talk about their emotional reactions was influencing their behavior and contributing to their mutual sense of isolation. They agreed to be more mindful of their thought patterns and to check out their expectations with one another. At the end of this meeting, Michael reported feeling "lighter," more in control, and more "on the same page" with Penny.

In subsequent meetings over the next few months, Michael talked about his life and identity before cancer, what was changing, and what was still the same. He had survived an abusive childhood and worked to put himself through trade school. He was married briefly before a bitter divorce, and had always regretted not maintaining closer contact with his son. He overcame severe alcohol dependence to become clean and sober and build a successful business as a mechanic. He had a fierce sense of independence and self-sufficiency; he didn't like the idea of depending on others, both due to concerns about burdening them and due to fears that they would let him down. He had always been proud of his mechanical abilities, physical strength, and endurance. He was gregarious and was known within his social network as the person to go to when you had a problem. Michael admitted to struggling with the losses due to his cancer, "I'm not sure who I am anymore." Due to fatigue and pain, he was forced to go on disability and was seldom feeling well enough to go hiking. No longer spending time at his auto shop, he missed the satisfaction of fixing cars and motorcycles and serving customers. At the same time, Michael was able to identify enduring qualities that were not touched by his disease. He recognized that he continued to be a fair, caring, and supportive friend, and a loving, sensitive partner to Penny. He continued to value his sobriety and enjoy time outdoors, even if this meant fishing from the dock rather than hiking to a remote lake or stream.

Michael also began to talk more about his worries about death and dying. He had watched his mother care for his father as he was dying of lung cancer, and was extremely fearful of being in severe pain, not being able to care for himself, losing "control," and the uncertainty of "being dead." He worried about the burden of caregiving on Penny and the impact his death would have on her emotionally and financially. He felt a great deal of guilt about his "failure" as a father and a sense of urgency to "set things right" with his son. Michael reported that these concerns were "always in the back of my mind, but they only pop up when I let my guard down." He reported that talking directly about them reduced his anxiety, helped him consider his priorities, and begin to actively problem solve about things within his control.

In reflecting on his values and priorities, Michael identified a number of actions he wanted to take. First, he and Penny decided to proceed with their plans to be married, to formalize their commitment to one another and to simplify financial/legal issues for her after his death. Second, he decided to stop chemotherapy, which had provided little benefit, and initiate home hospice services. This enabled him to spend less time going to and from the hospital and recovering from treatment side effects, and more quality time with Penny and his friends. It also gave him a sense of security that Penny would be well-supported practically and emotionally and that he would be able to die at home with maximum symptom relief. Third, Michael arranged to sell his business to two of his friends, who agreed to retain the name of the garage and to keep Penny on as an employee, giving him a sense that the product of his hard work would be carried on, and that Penny would be taken care of. Finally, Michael contacted his son and arranged to visit him. Although their meeting involved some conflict, Michael was able to explain the factors that impacted his "absenteeism" over the years, and express his care and hopes for his son. Over the course of 3 additional meetings at Michael's home, he and his son established a deepened sense of closeness and respect. Michael stated, "I think we're squared away now."

In a telephone conversation 3 weeks before Michael's death, 10 months after his diagnosis, he shared his perception of how his life had changed due to his cancer. He stated, "I realize that I'm stronger than I thought. I used to think that I was only as good as the last job I did, but that has changed. I now know who I am, what I want, and who is important to me. Whether I live for another 3 months or 3 years, I'm satisfied with where I'm at."

Michael's story reflects many of the aspects of PTG and approaches to working with cancer patients described in this chapter. It is notable that his story does not represent a "happy ending" and that the growth he experienced was intermingled with pain and distress. However, his ability to confront painful emotions, face losses and fears, reflect on his essential qualities and values, and translate these into action improved the quality of both his life and his death.

FUTURE RESEARCH

Despite the emergence of a growing volume of research on PTG and related constructs over the past 2 decades, our understanding of this phenomenon is still relatively limited and empirical study of ways to facilitate PTG is in its infancy. The few intervention studies that have demonstrated changes in PTG in cancer patients were not necessarily designed with this goal (Antoni et al., 2001; McGregor et al., 2004; Penedo et al., 2006) and included a therapeutic approach with multiple components, making it difficult to determine the active ingredients (although per Penedo et al., 2006, development of stress management skills appears at least partially implicated).

Further, studies of therapeutic approaches that are theoretically well-designed to impact PTG, such as SET, have not assessed such outcomes. Future research should be sensitive to the possibility of PTG, in design of interventions and in assessment of outcomes. Studies should monitor intervention content and process variables to facilitate identification of components linked to PTG.

It is also notable that little is known about the most appropriate timing or population of cancer patients in which to introduce such interventions. Most studies to date have focused on primary or limited stage cancer patients, some of whom were still receiving treatment and most of whom had relatively good prognoses. It is unclear whether different therapeutic approaches are called for in attempting to facilitate PTG in early versus advanced cancer patients, or those who are still receiving treatment versus those who are posttreatment. Future studies might compare the impact of the same treatment approach delivered at different time points with regard to diagnosis/treatment and with different populations with regard to disease severity.

Finally, to date the primary method of PTG assessment has been via self-report measures. It is possible that in efforts to establish psychometric rigor and to quantify outcomes, valuable information has been lost that may yield clinical insights. Use of both qualitative and quantitative methodology may improve sensitivity to and understanding of PTG outcomes.

SUMMARY

Understanding and facilitating PTG outcomes in cancer patients is a work in progress. This chapter described the state of the literature and offered suggestions for both sensible clinical approaches and future empirical study.

Summary Points (Practice)

- Cancer is experienced as a traumatic stressor for many patients.
- Cancer patients commonly report intrusions and avoidance.
- The majority of cancer patients identify benefits from their experience.
- Existential and cognitive theories suggest that direct engagement and active processing of the cancer experience may facilitate PTG.
- Be cautious: Do not prescribe or expect PTG.
- Provide education and normalize the full-range of emotional reactions.
- Facilitate disclosure and communication.
- Guide patients to tell the story of their cancer experience.
- Ask patients to talk about their lives before cancer.

- Encourage patients to take inventory of what they have and haven't lost.
- Give patients opportunities to talk directly about their ultimate worries and concerns.
- Teach cognitive-behavioral coping skills.
- Help patients clarify and live according to their values, priorities, and goals.

Summary Points (Research)

- Monitoring intervention content and process variables linked to PTG.
- Comparing interventions at different time points with regard to diagnosis/treatment and with different populations with regard to disease severity.
- Use of both qualitative and quantitative methodology may improve sensitivity to and understanding of PTG outcomes.

REFERENCES

American Psychiatric Association. (1994). *Diagnostic and statistical manual of mental disorders* (4th ed.). Washington, DC: Author.

Andrykowski, M. A., Brady, M. J., & Hunt, J. W. (1993). Positive psychosocial adjustment in potential bone marrow transplant recipients: Cancer as a psychosocial transition. *Psycho-Oncology, 2,* 261–276.

Andrykowski, M. A., & Cordova, M. J. (1998). Factors associated with PTSD symptoms following treatment for breast cancer: A test of the Andersen model. *Journal of Traumatic Stress, 11,* 189–203.

Andrykowski, M. A., Cordova, M. J., Kenady, D. E., McGrath, P. C., & Sloan, D. A. (2000). Stability and change in PTSD symptoms following breast cancer treatment: A one year follow-up. *Psycho-Oncology, 9,* 69–78.

Andrykowski, M. A., Cordova, M. J., Studts, J. L., & Miller, T. (1998). Posttraumatic stress disorder after treatment for breast cancer: Prevalence of diagnosis and use of the PTSD Checklist-Civilian Version (PCL-C) as a screening instrument. *Journal of Consulting and Clinical Psychology, 66,* 586–590.

Andrykowski, M. A., Curran, S. L., Studts, J. L., Cunningham, L., Carpenter, J. S., McGrath, P. C., et al. (1996). Psychosocial adjustment and quality of life in women with breast cancer and benign breast problems: A controlled comparison. *Journal of Clinical Epidemiology, 49,* 827–834.

Antoni, M. H. (2003). *Stress management intervention for women with breast cancer.* Washington, DC: American Psychological Association.

Antoni, M. H., Lehman, J. M., Kilbourn, K. M., Boyes, A. E., Culver, J. L., Alferi, S. M., et al. (2001). Cognitive-behavioral stress-management intervention decreases the prevalence of depression and enhances benefit-finding among women under treatment for early-stage breast cancer. *Health Psychology, 20,* 20–32.

Bellizzi, K. M. (2004). Expressions of generativity and posttraumatic growth in adult cancer survivors. *International Journal of Aging and Human Development, 58,* 267–287.

Bellizzi, K. M., & Blank, T. O. (2006). Predicting posttraumatic growth in breast cancer survivors. *Health Psychology, 25,* 47–56.

Black, E. K., & White, C. A. (2005). Fear of recurrence, sense of coherence, and posttraumatic stress disorder in hematological cancer survivors. *Psycho-Oncology, 14,* 510–515.

Bower, J. E., Meyerowitz, B. E., Desmond, K. A., Bernaards, C. A., Rowland, J. H., & Ganz, P. A. (2005). Perceptions of positive meaning and vulnerability following breast cancer: Predictors and outcomes among long-term breast cancer survivors. *Annals of Behavioral Medicine, 29,* 236–245.

Butler, L. D., Koopman, C., Classen, C., & Spiegel, D. (1999). Traumatic stress, life events, and emotional support in women with metastatic breast cancer: Cancer-related traumatic stress symptoms associated with past and current stressors. *Health Psychology, 18,* 555–560.

Calhoun, L. G., & Tedeschi, R. G. (2000). *Facilitating posttraumatic growth: A clinician's guide.* Mahwah, NJ: Erlbaum.

Calhoun, L. G., & Tedeschi, R. G. (2006). The foundations of posttraumatic growth: An expanded framework. In L. G. Calhoun & R. G. Tedeschi (Eds.), *Handbook of posttraumatic growth: Research and practice* (pp. 1–23). Mahwah, NJ: Erlbaum.

Carpenter, J. S., Brockopp, D. Y., & Andrykowski, M. A. (1999). Self-transformation as a factor in the self-esteem and well-being of breast cancer survivors. *Journal of Advanced Nursing, 29,* 1402–1411.

Carver, C. S., & Antoni, M. H. (2004). Finding benefit in breast cancer during the year after diagnosis predicts better adjustment 5 to 8 years after diagnosis. *Health Psychology, 23,* 595–598.

Classen, C., Butler, L. D., Koopman, C., Miller, E., DiMiceli, S., Giese-Davis, J., et al. (2001). Supportive-expressive group therapy and distress in patients with metastatic breast cancer. *American Journal of Psychiatry, 58,* 494–501.

Collins, R. L., Taylor, S. E., & Skokan, L. A. (1990). A better world or a shattered vision? Changes in perspectives following victimization. *Social Cognition, 8,* 263–285.

Cordova, M. J., Andrykowski, M. A., Kenady, D. E., McGrath, P. C., Sloan, D. A., & Redd, W. H. (1995). Frequency and correlates of PTSD-like symptoms following treatment for breast cancer. *Journal of Consulting and Clinical Psychology, 63,* 981–986.

Cordova, M. J., Cunningham, L. L. C., Carlson, C. R., & Andrykowski, M. A. (2001). Posttraumatic growth following breast cancer: A controlled comparison study. *Health Psychology, 20,* 176–185.

Cordova, M. J., Studts, J. L., Hann, D. M., Jacobsen, P. B., & Andrykowski, M. A. (2000). Symptom structure of PTSD following breast cancer. *Journal of Traumatic Stress, 13,* 301–319.

Fritz, G. K., & Williams, J. R. (1988). Issues of adolescent development for survivors of childhood cancer. *Journal of the American Academy of Child and Adolescent Psychiatry, 27,* 712–715.

Fromm, K., Andrykowski, M. A., & Hunt, J. (1996). Positive and negative psychosocial sequelae of bone marrow transplantation: Implications for quality of life assessment. *Journal of Behavioral Medicine, 19,* 221–240.

Goodwin, P. J., Leszcz, M., Ennis, M., Koopmans, J., Vincent, L., Guther, H., et al. (2001). The effect of group psychosocial support on survival in metastatic breast cancer. *New England Journal of Medicine, 13,* 1719–1726.

Green, B. L., Epstein, S. A., Krupnick, J. L., & Rowland, J. H. (1997). Trauma and medical-illness: Assessing trauma-related disorders in medical settings. In J. P. Wilson & T. M. Keane (Eds.), *Assessing psychological trauma and PTSD* (pp. 160–191). New York: Guilford Press.

Green, B. L., Krupnick, J. L., Rowland, J. H., Epstein, S. A., Stockton, P., Spertus, I. L., et al. (2000). Trauma history as a predictor of psychologic symptoms in women with breast cancer. *Journal of Clinical Oncology, 18,* 1084–1093.

Green, B. L., Rowland, J. H., Krupnick, J. L., Epstein, S. A., Stockton, P., Stern, N. M., et al. (1998). Prevalence of posttraumatic stress disorder (PTSD) in women with breast cancer. *Psychosomatics, 32,* 102–111.

Gurevich, M., Devins, G. M., & Rodin, G. M. (2002). Stress response syndromes and cancer: Conceptual and assessment issues. *Psychosomatics, 43,* 259–281.

Ho, S. M., Chan, C. L. W., & Ho, R. T. H. (2004). Posttraumatic growth in Chinese cancer survivors. *Psycho-Oncology, 13,* 377–389.

Jacobsen, P. B., Roth, A. J., & Holland, J. C. (1998). Surgery. In J. C. Holland (Ed.) & W. Breitbart, P. B. Jacobsen, M. S. Lederberg, M. Loscalzo, M. J. Massie, & R. McCorkle (Assoc. Eds.), *Psycho-Oncology* (pp. 257–268). New York: Oxford University Press.

Jacobsen, P. B., Widows, M. R., Hann, D. M., Andrykowski, M. A., Kronish, L. E., & Fields, K. K. (1998). Posttraumatic stress disorder symptoms following bone marrow transplantation for breast cancer. *Psychosomatic Medicine, 60,* 366–371.

Janoff-Bulman, R. (1992). *Shattered assumptions: Towards a new psychology of trauma.* New York: Free Press.

Janoff-Bulman, R. (2004). Posttraumatic growth: Three explanatory models. *Psychological Inquiry, 15,* 30–34.

Janoff-Bulman, R. (2006). Schema-change perspectives on posttraumatic growth. In L. G. Calhoun & R. G. Tedeschi (Eds.), *Handbook of posttraumatic growth: Research and practice* (pp. 81–99). Mahwah, NJ: Erlbaum.

Janoff-Bulman, R., & Berger, A. (2000). The other side of trauma: Towards a psychology of appreciation. In J. H. Harvey & E. D. Miller (Eds.), *Loss and trauma: General and close relationship perspectives* (pp. 29–44). Philadelphia: Brunner/Mazel.

Johnson, J. E., Lauver, D. R., & Nail, L. M. (1989). Process of coping with radiation therapy. *Journal of Consulting and Clinical Psychology, 57,* 358–364.

Kangas, M., Henry, J. L., & Bryant, R. A. (2002). Posttraumatic stress disorder following cancer: A conceptual and empirical review. *Clinical Psychology Review, 22,* 499–524.

Kangas, M., Henry, J. L., & Bryant, R. A. (2005). Predictors of posttraumatic stress disorder following cancer. *Health Psychology, 24,* 579–585.

Katz, R. C., Flasher, L., Cacciapaglia, H., & Nelson, S. (2001). The psychosocial impact of cancer and lupus: A cross-validational study that extends the generality of "benefit-finding" in patients with chronic disease. *Journal of Behavioral Medicine, 24,* 561–571.

Knobf, M. T., Pasacreta, J. V., Valentine, A., & McCorkle, R. (1998). Psychosocial adaptation of cancer survivors. In J. C. Holland (Ed.) & W. Breitbart, P. B. Jacobsen, M. S. Lederberg, M. Loscalzo, M. J. Massie, & R. McCorkle (Assoc. Eds.), *Psycho-Oncology* (pp. 277–288). New York: Oxford University Press.

Kornblith, A. B. (1998). Psychosocial adaptation of cancer survivors. In J. C. Holland (Ed.) & W. Breitbart, P. B. Jacobsen, M. S. Lederberg, M. Loscalzo, M. J. Massie, & R. McCorkle (Assoc. Eds.), *Psycho-Oncology* (pp. 223–256). New York: Oxford University Press.

Kornblith, A. B. (2003). Psychosocial and sexual functioning of survivors of breast cancer. *Seminars in Oncology, 30,* 799–813.

Lechner, S. C., Antoni, M. H., & Zakowski, S. G. (in press). Coping mediates the relationship between social support and finding benefit in the experience of cancer. *Psycho-Oncology.*

Lechner, S. C., Zakowski, S. G., Antoni, M. H., Greenhawt, M., Block, K., & Block, P. (2003). Do sociodemographic and disease-related variables influence benefit-finding in cancer patients? *Psycho-Oncology, 12,* 491–499.

Lepore, S. J. (2001). A social-cognitive processing model of emotional adjustment to cancer. In A. Baum & B. L. Andersen (Eds.), *Psychosocial interventions for cancer* (pp. 99–116). Washington, DC: American Psychological Association.

Lepore, S. J., & Helgeson, V. S. (1998). Social constraints, intrusive thoughts, and mental health after prostate cancer. *Journal of Social and Clinical Psychology, 17,* 89–106.

Manne, S. (1999). Intrusive thoughts and psychological distress among cancer patients: The role of spouse avoidance and criticism. *Journal of Consulting and Clinical Psychology, 67,* 539–546.

Manne, S., Ostroff, J., & Winkel, G. (2004). Posttraumatic growth after breast cancer: Patient, partner, and couple perspectives. *Psychosomatic Medicine, 66,* 442–454.

McGarvey, E. L., Canterbury, R. J., Koopman, C., Clavet, G. J., Cohen, R., Largay, K., et al. (1998). Acute stress disorder following diagnosis of cancer. *International Journal of Rehabilitation and Health, 4,* 1–15.

McGregor, B. A., Antoni, M. H., Boyers, A., Alferi, S. M., Blomberg, B. B., & Carver, C. S. (2004). Cognitive-behavioral stress management increases benefit finding and immune function among women with early-stage breast cancer. *Journal of Psychosomatic Research, 56,* 1–8.

Mundy, E. A., Blanchard, E. B., Cirenza, E., Gargiulo, J., Maloy, B., & Blanchard, C. G. (2000). Posttraumatic stress disorder in breast cancer patients following autologous bone marrow transplantation or conventional cancer treatments. *Behaviour Research and Therapy, 38,* 1015–1027.

Naidich, J. B., & Motta, R. W. (2000). PTSD-related symptoms in women with breast cancer. *Journal of Psychotherapy in Independent Practice, 1,* 35–54.

Parkes, C. M. (1971). Psychosocial transitions: A field for study. *Social Science and Medicine, 5,* 101–115.

Penedo, F. J., Molton, I., Dahn, J. R., Shen, B., Kinsinger, D., Traeger, L., et al. (2006). A randomized clinical trial of group-based cognitive-behavioral stress management in localized prostate cancer: Development of stress management skills improves quality of life and benefit finding. *Annals of Behavioral Medicine, 31,* 261–270.

Petrie, K. J., Buick, D. L., Weinman, J., & Booth, R. J. (1999). Positive effects of illness reported by myocardial infarction and breast cancer patients. *Journal of Psychosomatic Research, 47,* 537–543.

Redd, W. H., Jacobsen, P. B., & Andrykowski, M. A. (1989). Behavioral side effects of adjuvant chemotherapy. *Recent Results in Cancer Research, 115,* 272–278.

Rieker, P. P., Edbril, S. D., & Garnick, M. B. (1985). Curative testis cancer therapy: Psychosocial sequelae. *Journal of Clinical Oncology, 3,* 1117–1126.

Schulz, U., & Mohamed, N. E. (2004). Turning the tide: Benefit finding after cancer surgery. *Social Science and Medicine, 59,* 653–662.

Sears, S. R., Stanton, A. L., & Danoff-Burg, S. (2003). The yellow brick road and the emerald city: Benefit-finding, positive reappraisal coping, and posttraumatic growth in women with early-stage breast cancer. *Health Psychology, 22,* 487–497.

Spiegel, D., Bloom, J. R., & Yalom, I. (1981). Group support for patients with metastatic cancer: A randomized outcome study. *Archives of General Psychiatry, 38,* 527–533.

Spiegel, D., & Classen, C. (2000). *Group therapy for cancer patients: A research-based handbook of psychosocial care.* New York: Basic Books.

Stanton, A. L., Bower, J. E., & Low, C. A. (2006). Posttraumatic growth after cancer. In L. G. Calhoun & R. G. Tedeschi (Eds.), *Handbook of posttraumatic growth: Research and practice* (pp. 138–175). Mahwah, NJ: Erlbaum.

Stanton, A. L., Danoff-Burg, S., Sworowski, L. A., Collins, C. A., Branstetter, A., Rodriguez-Hanley, A., et al. (2002). Randomized, controlled trial of written emotional expression and benefit finding in breast cancer patients. *Journal of Clinical Oncology, 20,* 4160–4168.

Stanton, A. L., & Snider, P. R. (1993). Coping with a breast cancer diagnosis: A prospective study. *Health Psychology, 12,* 16–23.

Taylor, S. E. (1983). Adjustment to threatening events: A theory of cognitive adaptation. *American Psychologist, 38,* 1161–1173.

Taylor, S. E., Lichtman, R. R., & Wood, J. V. (1984). Attributions, beliefs about control, and adjustment to breast cancer. *Journal of Personality and Social Psychology, 46,* 489–502.

Tedeschi, R. G., & Calhoun, L. G. (1995). *Trauma and transformation: Growing in the aftermath of suffering.* Thousand Oaks, CA: Sage.

Thornton, A. A. (2002). Perceiving benefits in the cancer experience. *Journal of Clinical Psychology in Medical Settings, 9,* 153–165.

Thornton, A. A., & Perez, M. A. (2006). Posttraumatic growth in prostate cancer survivors and their partners. *Psycho-Oncology, 15,* 285–296.

Tjemsland, L., Soreide, J. A., & Malt, U. F. (1998). Posttraumatic distress symptoms in operable breast cancer III: Status one year after surgery. *Breast Cancer Research and Treatment, 47,* 141–151.

Tomich, P. L., & Helgeson, V. S. (2002). Five years later: A cross-sectional comparison of breast cancer survivors with healthy women. *Psycho-Oncology, 11,* 154–169.

Tomich, P. L., & Helgeson, V. S. (2004). Is finding something good in the bad always good? Benefit finding among women with breast cancer. *Health Psychology, 23,* 16–23.

Urcuyo, K. R., Boyers, A. E., Carver, C. S., & Antoni, M. H. (2005). Finding benefit in breast cancer: Relations with personality, coping, and concurrent well-being. *Psychology and Health, 20,* 175–192.

Wasserman, A. L., Thompson, E. I., Wilimas, J. A., & Fairclough, D. L. (1987). The psychological status of childhood/adolescent Hodgkin's disease. *American Journal of Diseases in Children, 141,* 626–631.

Weiss, T. (2004). Correlates of posttraumatic growth in married breast cancer survivors. *Journal of Social and Clinical Psychology, 23,* 733–746.

Widows, M. R., Jacobsen, P. B., Booth-Jones, M., & Fields, K. K. (2005). Predictors of posttraumatic growth following bone marrow transplantation for cancer. *Health Psychology, 24,* 266–273.

Wright, E. P. (2002). Social problems in oncology. *British Journal of Cancer, 87,* 1099–1104.

Yalom, I. D. (1980). *Existential psychotherapy.* New York: Basic Books.

Zemore, R., & Shepel, L. F. (1989). Effects of breast cancer and mastectomy on emotional support and adjustment. *Social Science and Medicine, 28,* 19–27.

CHAPTER 11

Group-Based Therapies for Benefit Finding in Cancer

SUZANNE C. LECHNER, BRENDA L. STOELB, and MICHAEL H. ANTONI

INTEREST IN THE positive consequences of traumatic life events has burgeoned over the past decade. Whereas in 1996, there were only a handful of articles on the topic, there are now dozens of published articles and chapters. As the research literature has grown, so has interest in the clinical applications of the research and theory on the phenomenon. In this chapter, we highlight some topic areas that are of interest to clinicians specifically.

First, a note on terminology: There are at least a dozen terms used to refer to the positive changes that occur following a traumatic or stressful life event. Posttraumatic growth, stress-related growth, benefit finding, and adversarial growth are among the many descriptors of this phenomenon (Antoni et al., 2001; Linley & Joseph, 2004; Park, Cohen, & Murch, 1996; Tedeschi & Calhoun, 1995). In a recent brainstorming session at a conference on positive life changes following illness, there was a consensus that greater specificity is needed to differentiate the terms (Aldwin et al., 2005). In this chapter, *benefit finding* (BF) and *growth* are used to refer to the belief that positive changes have resulted from one's experience with cancer.

INTERVENTIONS AND BENEFIT FINDING

Psycho-oncology interventions are typically designed to foster a return to precancer psychosocial functioning (Antoni, 2003). There are a number of

---

This work was supported by a grant from the National Cancer Institute R03 CA113096, National Cancer Institute R01 CA064710, and the Braman Family Breast Cancer Institute of the UM Sylvester Comprehensive Cancer Center at the University of Miami Miller School of Medicine. We thank Jessica Tocco for her assistance with manuscript preparation.

group-based interventions that have shown promising results in improving mood, distress, quality of life, and other markers of adjustment (Andersen et al., 2004; Antoni et al., 2001, 2006; Spiegel, Kraemer, Bloom, & Gottheil, 1989). One aspect of adjustment may be the perception of benefits arising from having cancer. Some patients report that having cancer has led them to appreciate life more. Others feel that they are stronger and more capable of handling life's challenges. Many patients notice that they relate to others on a different level and note enhanced relationships with family and friends. Increased feelings of spirituality and religiosity are often cited. Finally, some patients see having cancer as the impetus to change their lifestyle and adopt health behaviors (Fromm, Andrykowski, & Hunt, 1996).

Case Study

Inpatient treatment unit at a cancer center where patients receive high doses of clinical trial chemotherapy medications for end-stage cancer. Psychology trainee SL greets one of her first oncology patients:

SL: How are you feeling today?

PATIENT: I'm fine. [smiles] Breast cancer is the best thing that ever happened to me.

SL: Tell me more about that. What led you to feel this way? [The novice therapist is inwardly shocked, and wondering if the patient has a somewhat distorted sense of reality.]

PATIENT: Around the time that I was diagnosed, I was working very hard in a large law firm. I rarely spent good, quality time with my children. My husband was raising them alone and I was miserable. I hadn't seen my sister in 3 years. Breast cancer gave me the opportunity to reevaluate all that.

SL: How did that come about?

PATIENT: Chemotherapy was hard, I mean really hard. I was so fatigued and tired I just could not drag myself to work. I sat on the couch and my husband, kids, and friends had to do everything for me. It was really tough on me because I am an independent person and I had to rely on other people for the first time in a long time. And I came to see how much they loved me and cared about me, all because I let them. I let myself be vulnerable because I did not have a choice.

SL: What you're saying reminds me of the old saying about "every cloud has a silver lining."

PATIENT: Yes, but don't get me wrong, it wasn't an easy process. I did a lot of soul-searching. I was miserable for a long time, crying every day, tired all of the time, I didn't want to see anyone because I looked terrible. But over time I've come to see that I have people in my life who really care for me and have my best interests at heart. I missed out on so much of my kids growing up. I am not going to miss out on any more of it. I still work, but for a smaller firm and I work normal hours. My husband and I go out on dates, I've been to my daughter's piano recital and a bunch of my son's baseball games. I smile much more now.

Witnessing the process of meaning making, benefit finding, and growth in a patient can be an extremely rewarding experience for a therapist. Sometimes, life crises can offer a unique opportunity for an individual to reevaluate his or her life. Traumas interrupt routines and prevailing thinking patterns. This creates a sense of vulnerability, but also provides new avenues for patients to explore in therapy. The trauma-induced disruption can sometimes lead to the process of searching for meaning in life's events. By asking the questions "Why did this happen?" and "What are the implications for my life if I make it through this?" some patients identify areas that need changing or recognize strengths they did not realize they had. The process of dealing with any trauma, especially being diagnosed with a potentially life-threatening illness, is often arduous. Many therapists have been trained to look for pathology and to identify negative sequelae. The focus on BF has helped many to shift their perspective to look at psychological health, thriving, and optimal adjustment. Many therapists even describe a sense of vicarious growth (Calhoun & Tedeschi, 1999) whereby the therapist begins to reevaluate his or her own experiences (see also Linley & Joseph, 2007; Linley, Joseph, & Loumidis, 2005).

Few intervention studies have included BF as an endpoint. Antoni et al. (2001, 2006) and Penedo et al. (2006) are the only studies that we are aware of that examined BF as an outcome in psycho-oncology intervention trials. These studies employed the cognitive-behavioral stress management (CBSM) and relaxation skills training intervention model. This form of intervention aims to reduce distress and improve quality of life using a multimodal intervention (Antoni, 2003). In one study, we tested the effects of a CBSM group intervention for women who had recently been diagnosed with and treated surgically for early stage breast cancer (Antoni et al., 2001). Women were randomized into a 10-week CBSM intervention or a 1-day stress management seminar. The baseline psychosocial assessment took place within 2 months of surgery; women were reassessed at postintervention, at 6-months postsurgery, and again roughly 1-year postsurgery. The goal of the intervention was to reduce stress and distress by teaching participants behavioral and cognitive strategies in a supportive group atmosphere. We had the following aims: to improve awareness of stress and provide tools to reduce it; increase the use of adaptive coping strategies; preserve and augment participants' social support networks; disprove myths about the disease; create a safe space for the expression of concerns and feelings; encourage use of relaxation techniques; and promote hope and a positive self-image. Our findings revealed that participants in the CBSM intervention condition showed a significant increase in BF at postintervention (which was maintained at both follow-up assessment points) as compared to women in the control condition who showed no significant change over time. Although our intervention was not designed to promote BF per se, we believe it may have had such an effect because it targeted many of the factors identified as key components in the development of BF in Tedeschi and Calhoun's (1995) theoretical model. For example, the supportive group climate may have inadvertently promoted BF by facilitating emotional expression, a process commonly thought to be an important ingredient in the development of BF. Similarly, other factors tied to relaxation training (decreased vigilance and anxiety) may have helped individuals to be more open to alternative ways of thinking, while cognitive restructuring techniques may have offered them the methods for changing appraisals allowing them to positively reframe ongoing life experiences.

Other interventions such as supportive-expressive therapy, which targets feelings of isolation and distress by examining fears and existential issues directly in a group forum, may also unwittingly enhance evolution of BF. In a ground-breaking study of women with metastatic breast cancer, Spiegel and his colleagues (1989) developed a group-based, supportive-expressive therapy intervention that focused on addressing existential issues, coping with breast cancer, and using meditation and self-hypnosis techniques to reduce pain. As with our CBSM groups, the psychological processes targeted by this intervention were also identified as precursors of BF according to Tedeschi & Calhoun's (1996) model. Clinical reports of the participants' spontaneous comments reveal that the women had indeed found meaning and grew from their experiences with breast cancer. It is unfortunate, therefore, that Spiegel and his colleagues did not include a measure of BF in this study. What is most remarkable about the study, however, is that the women in the intervention condition lived 18 months longer than controls. Women in the intervention condition also demonstrated significant improvements in psychological outcomes. While survival benefits were not observed in a replication study by another group (Goodwin et al., 2001), psychological gains were again evident.

There are few published reports of group-based interventions *that were specifically designed to promote BF*. In a later section of this chapter, we suggest that there are many reasons why *group-based* therapies should not yet be developed to promote BF in cancer patients. We strongly be-

lieve in the efficacy and utility of clinical interventions that can help foster recovery from trauma, and carefully designed interventions may be
able to utilize the trauma-induced disruption in the person's life to promote psychological health and thriving. We envision these interventions
would encompass many of the characteristics that are described in the
following section.

THERAPEUTIC AGENTS: GROUPS ARE A POTENTIALLY FERTILE GROUND FOR THE DEVELOPMENT OF BENEFIT FINDING

A number of group characteristics or processes may contribute to the development of BF, even when this is not the primary aim or goal of the group
in question. Some of these characteristics are often considered to be intrinsic aspects of the group milieu (Yalom, 1995), while others are intra- and interpersonal variables that are frequently targeted as part of group-based
interventions. For example, in addition to social support and learning more
effective cognitive coping skills (e.g., reframing), group features or aims
such as enhancing hope and optimism, encouraging emotional expression
and/or processing, acceptance, and other approach-related efforts (Stanton
et al., 2000) may accelerate the working-through process after a traumatic
or stressful event. According to current theory (e.g., Tedeschi & Calhoun,
2004), certain interpersonal and intrapersonal variables should affect
whether the search for meaning is undertaken, as well as the effectiveness
of that search. For example, BF has been empirically linked to variables including (but not limited to) emotional expressiveness, emotional processing, and coping in prior studies of cancer patients. Although we recognize
that many of the aforementioned variables may exert a reciprocal influence
on one another and on BF, we consider those that are believed to have the
greatest impact on BF in a group setting: supportive environment/social
support; schema revision/cognitive processing; emotional expression and
emotional processing; and coping.

SUPPORTIVE ENVIRONMENT AND SOCIAL SUPPORT FROM OTHER GROUP MEMBERS

Support from other people is considered to be especially important during
highly stressful or traumatic life events (Janoff-Bulman, 1992; Park & Folkman, 1997; Tedeschi & Calhoun, 1995). In addition to evidence that suggests
that social support can moderate the deleterious effects of trauma (e.g., Ren,
Skinner, Lee, & Kazis, 1999), individuals who are able to share their experience with concerned others, and who perceive adequate instrumental and informational support should be more likely to begin searching for meaning

and to successfully find positive meaning (Schaefer & Moos, 1998; Tedeschi & Calhoun, 1996). Drawing on theories of attachment, support from significant others may provide a safe "base" from which the individual can explore the consequences or ramifications of the traumatic event. Although research is limited, a positive relationship has been found between social support and BF in medical and health-related populations including husbands of women with breast cancer (Weiss, 2004a), bereaved HIV/AIDS caregivers (Cadell, Regehr, & Hemsworth, 2003), and women living with HIV/AIDS (Siegel, Schrimshaw, & Pretter, 2005). Encouraging findings have also emerged from the few empirical studies that have investigated the relationship between social support and BF specifically among cancer patients. For example, Fife (1995) observed a strong positive relationship between BF and social support from family, friends, and health-care professionals in a sample of 422 patients with a variety of stages and types of cancer. Cordova, Cunningham, Carlson, and Andrykowski (2001) found that discussing cancer with other people was related to greater BF, yet there was no relationship between BF and emotional and tangible social support as measured by the Duke Social Support Questionnaire. In a sample of mixed cancer patients (Lechner, 2000), we found that BF was positively correlated with emotional support as measured by the Interpersonal Support Evaluation List (ISEL; Cohen & Hoberman, 1983).

Unfortunately, individuals coping with cancer may not always receive the amount or type of support they need from spouses, family, or friends. For this very reason, group-based interventions may play a critical role in fostering BF for those patients with limited or inadequate social support. Often, significant others do not know how to respond to their loved one's cancer-related worries or concerns and may inadvertently withdraw or provide inappropriate or unhelpful support. Although this is usually done unintentionally, individuals living with cancer may then be reluctant to disclose their thoughts and feelings with others, thereby preventing them from seeking the additional support they need. Similarly, fears about not wanting to be a burden to friends or family members present the cancer patient with another barrier to accessing social support. But group members who have been through similar cancer-related experiences and challenges can quickly relate to one another and provide an understanding, supportive atmosphere in which it is safe to disclose one's hopes and fears. We have noticed this dynamic take place in our CBSM intervention groups with men and women with cancer, as well as with individuals living with HIV/AIDS. Many of our HIV-positive participants commented on how the other group members had become "their family," and some maintained relationships with one another even after the intervention had ended. Based in part on their own experiences with the familial atmosphere of bereaved parent support groups, Tedeschi and Calhoun (2004) have emphasized this concept of "mutual support" and the pivotal role it may play in BF.

REVISION OF SCHEMAS/COGNITIVE PROCESSING

Because undergoing a challenging or traumatic event may disrupt previously held beliefs about one's self and the world, the revision of schemas is hypothesized to be the active ingredient in the development of BF. Briefly, schema revision is achieved through cognitive processing of the stressful or traumatic event. Cognitive processing involves reflecting on the event in a deliberate or effortful manner and coming to terms with the changes that the event has manifested in one's life. As Tedeschi and Calhoun (2004) have stated, "It is precisely this struggle with the new reality in the aftermath of trauma that is crucial in determining the extent to which BF occurs" (p. 5). Emerging research has lent support to this theory; among men with HIV who had lost a partner or close friend to AIDS, those who reported finding meaning from the death were also classified as high in cognitive processing (Bower, Kemeny, Taylor, & Fahey, 1998). Although beyond the scope of this chapter, it deserves mention that BF researchers make a distinction between productive cognitive processing and anxious or depressogenic rumination about a stressful or traumatic event (Tedeschi & Calhoun, 2004), the latter of which are often associated with less advantageous outcomes such as PTSD or Major Depressive Disorder.

Both clinical anecdotes and empirical findings suggest that group-based interventions may play a critical role in schema revision for individuals with cancer. For example, group facilitators anticipate that different group members will have already completed some cognitive processing on their own prior to meeting with the group, and thus, participants may begin the group with varying levels of BF. Those who have already found benefits and experienced growth can serve as role models for others. The growth process leads to changes in life narrative that can influence others and be enhanced by a supportive group setting, thereby affecting both the persons with high levels of growth as well as individuals who have not yet found any benefit from their cancer experience. Part of this very dynamic has been documented by Weiss (2004b), who discovered that women reporting contact with a breast cancer survivor who perceived benefits from the experience noted significantly greater BF than women who did not have such contact. This notion is also similar to Yalom's notion of "vicarious learning."

The group members' shared cancer experience also provides a secure atmosphere in which participants are allowed to process painful thoughts and emotions. According to the social cognitive processing model (Lepore, 2001), talking with others promotes the cognitive and emotional processing of traumatic events; hence, the inclusive and nurturing group environment may encourage increased self-disclosure and ultimately lead to BF. Findings from a number of studies have lent support to the connection between self-disclosure and BF (such as Cordova et al., 2001 and Stoelb, 2006). Moreover, while the group facilitator is obviously a critical piece in any successful intervention, group members may be particularly sensitive to a clinician's attempts to promote BF. It appears that when clinicians who are not survivors broach this topic, group members may perceive it as being insensitive to the patient's experience. Other group members may be more credible than the clinician in talking about different aspects of the cancer experience and BF.

Finally, the group setting provides group members with a forum to discuss varying perspectives, offer new beliefs, and have them reinforced by individuals who are experiencing a similar stressful life event. However, while shared experience allows fellow group members to challenge one another and provide feedback in a way that the group facilitator often cannot, we suggest that unstructured or unsupervised "venting" may actually do participants more harm than good. Therefore, a skilled group facilitator is necessary for optimal group functioning. A clinician trained to deliver a group-based CBSM intervention may be especially adept at aiding schema revision due to the intervention's emphasis on challenging overly negative or distorted thoughts/beliefs and replacing them with more rational or balanced ones.

EMOTIONAL EXPRESSION/EMOTIONAL PROCESSING

According to theorists and researchers, emotional expression or the processing of trauma-related emotions is a critical piece in the development of BF (e.g., Tennen & Affleck, 2002). In Tedeschi and Calhoun's (2004) model, the ability to manage distressing, trauma-related emotions is necessary for effective cognitive processing and subsequent schema change to occur. Research has begun to support the hypothesized link between emotional expression/emotional processing and BF. In a longitudinal study of 167 women with breast cancer and their partners, patient BF was predicted by the patient's greater emotional expression at the initial time point, while partner BF was predicted by the partner's greater use of emotional processing at the initial time point (Manne et al., 2004).

One of the major roles of a group-based intervention is to allow the participants to explore and process their emotions in an understanding, supportive environment; hence, such groups may promote development of BF. Of course, participants vary in the extent to which they feel comfortable with this task. Data from one of our studies revealed that women who reported engaging in higher levels of emotional processing also reported greater BF at the initial assessment, at the posttreatment assessment, and at the two postintervention follow-up assessments (3- and 9-month; r's ranging from .23 to .32). However, in examining whether emotional processing could prospectively predict BF, results showed that emotional processing at earlier time points did not predict subsequent BF scores, contrary to Manne et al.'s (2004) findings. We could only conclude, therefore, that emotional processing at a given point in time was associated with BF at the same time, but emotional processing did not contribute to BF at later assessment points. It may be that greater emotional processing early on is a necessary ingredient in promoting BF, but that other, perhaps cognitive changes are the sufficient condition for sustaining BF over longer periods.

In addition to the expression/processing of negative or difficult emotions, the group's ability to foster and maintain the experience of positive emotions among its members may further help to promote BF. Although this aspect of group-based interventions has received less attention in the literature, some emerging data has linked positive affect to the development of BF (see Linley & Joseph, 2004). From our clinical experience, group members not only cry together, they laugh together as well. The group often becomes a place where positive experiences and emotions such as joy, courage, and pride are shared—and encouraged—among participants. Tedeschi and Calhoun (2004) have alluded to two factors that may explain why positive affect may be a critical piece in the development of BF. First, the ability to experience positive affect may be reflective of more stable personality traits such as Dispositional, Hope, or Optimism; some of these traits may predispose individuals to experience or report more BF (which is discussed further later). Second, experiencing positive affect may aid in more effective cognitive processing of the traumatic event (Aspinwall, 1998). Being able to experience positive emotions in the context of a trauma or crisis may help an individual to manage overwhelming or distressing emotions and engage in productive or fruitful cognitive processing without getting "stuck" or "bogged down" in depressogenic ruminations. In support of Tedeschi and Calhoun's (2004) theory, some evidence has demonstrated that experiencing positive emotions in the wake of a traumatic event (i.e., 9/11) is related to subsequent postcrisis growth in psychological resources (Fredrickson, Tugade, Waugh, & Larkin, 2003).

COPING

Using adaptive coping strategies is a critical component in the development of BF (Tedeschi & Calhoun, 1996). The manner in which an individual copes with life events is a factor that may influence the extent to which a person experiences or reports BF. In a review of the literature, problem-focused, acceptance, and positive reinterpretation coping strategies were consistently associated with positive change following various forms of trauma or adversity (see Linley & Joseph, 2004). Similar patterns have been found among cancer-specific samples, with positive reframing (Urcuyo, Boyers, Carver, & Antoni, 2005), positive reappraisal/reinterpretation (Sears, Stanton, & Danoff-Burg, 2003; Widows, Jacobsen, Booth-Jones, & Fields, 2005), and active coping (Bellizzi & Blank, 2006; Kinsinger et al., 2006) being significantly related to BF. Because coping has been consistently linked to positive psychological outcomes such as BF, it is often targeted for modification in group-based interventions. In our research, we have examined coping using two conceptually different models of coping, namely Carver, Scheier, and Weintraub's (1989) COPE scale, which regards coping as a response that is initiated when a stressor is appraised as exceeding the individual's ability to meet the demands of a situation (Lazarus & Folkman, 1984); and the Mental Adjustment to Cancer construct, which includes both cognitive and behavioral responses to having cancer (Watson, Greer, Young, & Inayat, 1988).

COPE SCALE

In a separate study of women with early stage breast cancer (i.e., controls in the aforementioned CBSM trial), we explored relationships between BF, coping (using Carver's Brief COPE; Carver, 1997), and emotional approach coping (Emotional Approach Coping Scale; Stanton et al., 2000). Our analyses revealed that during the early period of dealing with a breast cancer diagnosis and treatment, BF was associated with greater positive reframing, religious coping, self-distraction, substance use, emotional processing, and less seeking social support. By the middle of medical (typically chemotherapy or radiation) treatment (3-months postsurgery), however, active coping and religious coping were important correlates of BF. After treatment completion (6-months), greater active coping, emotional processing, greater use of seeking social support, religious coping, and reduced use of acceptance coping was related to higher BF. One year postsurgery, using positive reframing coping and planning coping were associated with greater BF. These data suggest that positive growth and finding cancer-related benefits may be differentially related to the coping strategies women employ at different time points during the illness trajectory. We believe this relationship is dynamic and may reflect the nature of the stressors that are being encountered at a given time. It may also be a reflection of an individual's process of coming to terms with a cancer diagnosis, regardless of time since diagnosis per se. Alternating approach-avoidance cognitive or coping strategies may signal that productive information processing is taking place and may, in fact, be associated with "healthy" or adaptive outcomes. Stroebe and Schut (1999) have discussed just such a model of oscillation between confrontation and avoidance with regard to coping with bereavement (i.e., the dual process model). In other words, an individual's endorsement or use of avoidant coping strategies at a given point in time (e.g., substance use) may not necessarily indicate that he or she has failed to "come to terms" with his or her illness; it may simply mirror his or her place in the adjustment process. Thus, psychosocial interventions that are designed to augment BF via impacting coping efforts should consider time since diagnosis, adjustment phase, and the specific stressors being encountered by participants so as to maximize the intervention's effects.

Mental Adjustment to Cancer Construct

Authors of the Mental Adjustment to Cancer construct identified a series of cancer-specific coping strategies, such as adopting a "fighting spirit," hopelessness/helplessness, fatalism, anxious preoccupation, and denial. These aspects of coping with cancer are believed to tap into appraisal processes, but also include behavioral and cognitive responses as well (Greer, Morris, & Pettingale, 1979; Watson, Greer, Pruyn, & Van den Borne, 1990; Watson, Greer, Rowden, & Gorman, 1991; Watson et al., 1988). With regard to BF, we hypothesized that the active, information-seeking nature of individuals who report high levels of fighting spirit coping would drive them to undertake a search for meaning as a result of having cancer. In a sample of individuals with various types of cancer, we found that having a fighting spirit was positively associated with greater reports of BF (Lechner, 2006). Other, less adaptive, aspects of cancer-specific coping (e.g., adopting a hopeless/helpless response, becoming fatalistic, feeling anxiously preoccupied with the disease) were hypothesized to reduce possibilities for growth. For example, when an individual feels hopeless, he or she may lack the motivation to search for meaning in the event, or to deal with the situation effectively, thereby possibly impeding the development of BF (Schaefer & Moos, 1998). In our mixed cancer sample, BF was related to lower hopelessness/helplessness, but unrelated to anxious preoccupation, denial, and fatalism (Lechner, 2006). Again, it is important to stress that when patients occasionally use less adaptive or avoidant coping strategies, this may not be an indicator of poor adjustment to a cancer diagnosis; rather, it may simply be part of the oscillating adjustment process itself.

INFLUENCE OF SOCIODEMOGRAPHIC AND DISEASE-RELATED CHARACTERISTICS IN A GROUP SETTING

A number of studies have explored the relationships between factors such as age, gender, race/ethnicity, education level, disease stage, and BF; not much work, however, has investigated how these variables may interact with the content or process of a group-based intervention. Although the exact nature of these interactions remains unclear and merits further exploration, certain group participants may be more likely to exhibit growth.

Sociodemographic Variables

Age   Younger participants reported significantly higher levels of benefit finding in our sample of women with early stage breast cancer and in our sample of cancer patients with various forms of cancer. These findings are consistent with results from a number of other studies that also found younger age to be significantly associated with greater BF among cancer-related samples (e.g., Bellizzi, 2004; Manne et al., 2004; Widows et al., 2005). Younger people may be more prone to growth for a number of theorized reasons including greater openness to learning and change (Tedeschi & Calhoun, 2004) and increased cognitive flexibility (Stoelb, 2006). Given their vast experience, older individuals may have already learned significant life lessons and achieved a sense of wisdom, or reached some level of acceptance with existential issues that could preclude a focus on BF (Linley & Joseph, 2004; Tedeschi & Calhoun, 2004; see also Ford, Tennen, & Albert, this volume).

Gender   Some evidence suggests that women are more likely than men to find benefit in a stressful or traumatic event. This is difficult to evaluate in the cancer-BF literature because studies have focused primarily on samples of women (e.g., breast cancer survivors). In studies that have looked at both sexes' reports of cancer-related BF, results have been mixed. Women with breast cancer reported higher levels of BF than did their husbands (Weiss, 2002) and women also reported more positive growth on four out of five BF domains in a sample of adult cancer survivors (Bellizzi, 2004). In our sample of mixed cancer patients, however, gender was not significantly related to BF. To our knowledge, no theories to date have been put forth to explain the relationship between gender and BF; it appears further studies involving both sexes need to be conducted before any conclusions can be drawn.

Education Level, Income, and Employment   The relationships among education level, income, employment, and BF are inconsistent. Higher education and income levels have been linked to greater levels of BF in two noncancer-related samples (see Linley & Joseph, 2004); individuals exposed to war zone trauma (Fontana & Rosenheck, 1998), and low SES women living with HIV (Updegraff, Taylor, Kemeny, & Wyatt, 2002). A positive relationship was also found between income and BF in a group of breast cancer survivors (Cordova et al., 2001). On the contrary, less education and/or lower SES/income was associated with greater BF among men treated for localized prostate cancer (Kinsinger et al., 2006), married breast cancer survivors (Weiss, 2004b), women with breast cancer (Tomich & Helgeson, 2004), and individuals undergoing bone marrow transplantation for cancer (Widows et al., 2005). In our sample of mixed cancer patients, education, income level, and employment status were not significantly related to BF. It seems there is not enough evidence to make definitive statements regarding the role of education level, income, or employment in the development of BF. These variables may interact with other sociodemographic or disease-related factors, accounting for the inconsistencies across studies. In our personal experience, we have seen individuals from a wide range of education and SES levels benefit from group-based interventions and ultimately grow from or find meaning in their illness. Group facilitators need to keep in mind that the delivery of the intervention or participant materials may need to be altered slightly for those of differing education levels.

Race/Ethnicity Typically, non-White race has been associated with higher levels of BF. Unfortunately, a review of the literature reveals very few studies that have looked at relationships between race/ethnicity and BF in cancer, and even fewer that have had adequate numbers of minorities to examine for differences. To date, the majority of work in this area has been conducted with other medical populations such as men and women living with HIV/AIDS (e.g., Siegel & Schrimshaw, 2000). This may be due to the fact that samples in many cancer-related studies have been drawn from less ethnically/racially diverse populations (e.g., Caucasian women with breast cancer). In our sample of women with early stage breast cancer, non-White ethnicity was associated with higher perceptions of found meaning. Kinsinger et al. (2006) also found that Hispanics and non-Hispanic Blacks endorsed higher levels of BF than did non-Hispanic Whites in a sample of men treated for localized prostate cancer. Cultural scripts or norms that place more emphasis on "strength through adversity" or finding meaning in negative life circumstances may account for some of the observed ethnic/racial differences observed in BF. For example, the notion of *aguantar* (to tolerate, to bear) is a common value or coping strategy in many Hispanic/Latino cultural contexts, and the stereotyped gender role of *Marianismo* emphasizes that Latin women surrender to God's will and endure suffering, while believing they will be rewarded for their hardships in the afterlife. BF may further be prompted by the disadvantaged place in society that many ethnic or racial minority groups unfortunately occupy. Facing hardships such as racism, discrimination, community violence, and economic difficulties may be sufficiently stressful or traumatic to provoke a search for meaning in one's life or place in the world. Given all of these reasons, the ethnic or cultural composition of the group should be kept in mind when designing or delivering interventions as certain cultural values or norms could enhance or diminish the development of BF.

Religiosity/Spirituality In general, religiousness and spirituality have shown positive associations with BF among various illness and trauma populations (see Linley & Joseph, 2004; Shaw, Joseph, & Linley, 2005). Although data is relatively scarce, some findings from cancer-specific investigations reflect this pattern (Cordova et al., 2001; Sandoval, 2005; Urcuyo et al., 2005). A number of qualitative or descriptive studies have also focused on the importance of spirituality in the meaning-making process for individuals with cancer (e.g., Breitbart, Gibson, Poppito, & Berg, 2004; McGrath, 2004; Parry & Chesler, 2005). Because many world religions or spiritual practices teach the importance of personal growth through hardship or learning valuable life lessons from misfortune, it seems logical that religiosity/spirituality would be positively associated with BF. It must be kept in mind, however, that this relationship could be confounded by race/ethnicity because minority groups, such as Hispanics or African Americans, tend to endorse higher rates of intrinsic religiosity/spirituality or greater use of religious/spiritual coping strategies than do their White counterparts (e.g., Bourjolly, 1998).

DISEASE-RELATED VARIABLES

Disease Stage The seriousness of the traumatic or stressful event is similarly thought to be an important determinant of BF (Fromm et al., 1996; McFarland & Alvaro, 2000; Tedeschi & Calhoun, 1995). As such, an event must be significantly intense to provoke schema change. If there is too low a threat, schemas may not be shaken or shattered, whereas too great a threat may prove overwhelming and hinder one's search for meaning. To explore this question, we investigated the relationship between BF and disease stage, an objective measure of cancer severity (Lechner et al., 2003). Based on a threshold model, we hypothesized that very low levels of objective life threat (i.e., Stage 0 or I disease) may not be sufficiently threatening to prompt a reexamination of one's life and thus would be associated with lower BF scores. We presumed that schema disruption would be less likely when the risk of dying from cancer was small, whereas very high levels of threat (i.e., Stage IV disease) could inhibit BF due to the intense anxiety associated with discovering that one's illness is potentially fatal. We therefore hypothesized that those individuals whose cancer was moderately life-threatening and whose prognosis was perhaps more ambiguous (i.e., those with Stage II/III disease) would be most likely to search for meaning in life and in the cancer experience. In support of this hypothesis, we discovered that individuals with different disease stages did indeed differ on BF scores, and that this relationship was quadratic, such that individuals with Stage I and Stage IV disease had the lowest BF scores and individuals with Stage II disease exhibited the highest BF scores. Stage III patients did not differ significantly from the other groups. From these findings, we concluded that very high levels of life threat (and/or an unambiguous negative prognosis) could result in a cognitive "shutting down," whereby individuals are so overwhelmed by the experience that they cannot tolerate contemplating the consequences of the illness, and therefore do not undertake a search for meaning. Or if individuals do undertake such a search, they may be unsuccessful in assimilating the negative ramifications of the disease into their long-held schemas and may thus be unable to find positive meaning. While our finding is slightly inconsistent with reports of a linear relationship between BF and trauma severity or perceived life threat (Barakat, Alderfer, & Kazak, 2006; McFarland & Alvaro, 2000; McMillen, Smith, & Fisher, 1997; Tomich & Helgeson, 2004), other studies do support the notion of a curvilinear relationship between psychological benefits and trauma exposure wherein benefits are stronger at intermediate versus high or low levels of exposure (see Linley & Joseph, 2004).

The aforementioned findings have important clinical implications for psycho-oncology. For example, interventions may need to be designed for or target patients in the late stages of the disease who have given up hope and may require assistance in finding meaning. Furthermore, when treating patients of different disease stages in the same group intervention, facilitators should be aware that discernable discrepancies in levels of BF may exist between participants with differing disease severities.

Time since Diagnosis   It is generally accepted that adjusting to a cancer diagnosis is a process that takes time. Initially, patients may experience a great deal of shock and disbelief on hearing the news that they have cancer. According to Tedeschi and Calhoun's (2004) model, cognitions are more likely to be intrusive and/or ruminative during the early stages of response to trauma as schemas are shaken and individuals attempt to make sense of what has happened to them. The authors also refer to the "grief work" in which persons may engage following a crisis or trauma as a means of gradually accepting the losses that have resulted from their experience. They indicate that this period is often lengthy and marked by distress, but may be critical for optimum BF to take place. However, individuals vary greatly with regard to the amount of time needed postdiagnosis to adjust to their illness due to factors such as the type of cancer one is diagnosed with, disease stage or severity, and personal coping styles and resources. Despite this, it makes clinical sense that persons are unlikely to cite true BF immediately after receiving their diagnosis because at least some time is required for adequate emotional and cognitive processing to occur.

A handful of empirical studies have explored the relationship between time since diagnosis and reported BF in cancer-related populations, and the results are mixed. In a cross-sectional sample of breast cancer survivors, Cordova et al. (2001) discovered that posttraumatic growth (PTG) was positively associated with time since diagnosis, whereas Weiss (2004a, 2004b) found that PTG was inversely related to time since diagnosis in a sample of early stage survivors of breast cancer, as well as in a sample of spouses of breast cancer survivors. Our data revealed no such association between time since diagnosis and BF (Lechner et al., 2003). One plausible reason for the discrepancy is that the range of time since diagnosis in these studies was not equivalent across studies 0 to 172 months *postdiagnosis* in Lechner et al. (2003) versus 2 to 58 months *posttreatment* in Cordova et al. (2001). While additional research is needed to elucidate these relationships, time since diagnosis should be taken into account when designing or delivering any psycho-oncology intervention because this is likely to influence the extent to which participants have found meaning or benefit.

PERSONALITY CHARACTERISTICS

In any group-based intervention, the facilitator will naturally assume that each participant will enter into the group with his or her own characteristic style of interacting with the world. Some personality traits may be adaptive and could augment the group's mission, whereas others may not. Likewise, some personality traits are malleable and could be modified through a group intervention, whereas others are certainly more stable and resistant to change. To date, research has shown that certain personality traits or dispositional characteristics are also more likely to either contribute to or be associated with BF. In general, findings from various studies suggest that personality traits such as Extraversion, Conscientiousness, Hardiness, and Openness to Experience are positively related to BF, while Neuroticism is inversely related to BF (see Linley & Joseph, 2004). However, rather than discussing the myriad personality traits and their individual relationships with BF, we focus specifically on Optimism because it is perhaps the most frequently studied trait in this context. Furthermore, while Optimism often shows a strong, positive relationship with BF, it is important to note that data suggest that Optimism and BF are distinct constructs (Tedeschi & Calhoun, 2004).

Optimism and Benefit Finding   Dispositional optimism has been identified as one variable that could enhance perceptions of BF and evidence suggests that trait optimism is linked to BF in samples of cancer patients and their families (e.g., Rini et al., 2004; Urcuyo et al., 2005). Our cross-sectional research has yielded strong correlations between optimism and BF in a sample of mixed cancer patients (Lechner, 2000), yet we have also found the relationship between optimism and BF to be dynamic in nature. Among women with early stage breast cancer entering a CBSM intervention trial, optimism and BF were not significantly correlated at baseline and post-treatment, but changes in these two variables tracked each other moderately well over time: changes from baseline for optimism and BF correlated .46 at the 3-month follow-up and .58 for changes from baseline to the 9-month follow-up, with corresponding correlations in the control condition being nonsignificant. Similarly, Sandoval (2005) found that over time, within-person changes in optimism were associated with within-person changes in BF in a sample of men treated for early stage prostate cancer. In terms of what this evidence means for group-based interventions, it is certainly reasonable to assume that an intervention will not shape or modify individuals' core personality structure, as alluded to previously. However, certain traits or styles may be amenable to small or even moderate change given the right group atmosphere and support. BF theorists suggest that individuals already possessing high levels of traits such as hardiness or optimism may experience less psychological growth after a trauma due to the fact that these individuals are already "very fit" and may not have much room for additional improvement (Tedeschi & Calhoun, 2004). Therefore, persons who possess lower levels of these traits may actually benefit most from a group-based intervention. Our work shows some support for this notion; in a sample of women with early stage breast cancer, the CBSM intervention had its greatest impact on BF at 3-month follow-up for those women who were lowest in optimism at baseline (Antoni et al., 2001).

To summarize, there may be a set of personal characteristics that promotes or hinders BF, and certain people will benefit more from psycho-oncology interventions. CBSM intervention holds promise as a modality that can improve well-being and promote positive adjustment to cancer and other illnesses. New interventions are being developed, and there are two additional therapies that warrant mention for their links to BF, namely expressive writing and personal narrative therapies.

OTHER MODALITIES AND INTERVENTION STYLES

We have been impressed by two sets of interventions that require less intensive attention from a psychotherapist. Expressive writing programs (e.g., Pennebaker, 1994), in which the survivors write about their feelings and thoughts on a topic, have been used to enhance well-being and BF. Stanton et al. (2002) conducted a writing intervention where participants wrote about either (a) their deepest thoughts and feelings about breast cancer, (b) the benefits found in the breast cancer experience, or (c) related the facts of their breast cancer treatment experience (the control condition). Results showed that participating in the active intervention conditions had beneficial effects on health.

Another format that holds promise as an intervention that may facilitate growth is the development of a personal narrative (Neimeyer, 2004). This form of intervention encourages patients to form a cohesive life story of lived experiences. Through the telling and retelling of one's life story, narrative therapy is best described as a set of techniques that can encourage the process of meaning making that presumably precedes the development of BF.

CAVEAT: SOCIAL PRESSURE AND THE TYRANNY OF POSITIVE THINKING

As clinicians who have focused on working with individuals with a variety of illnesses and psychological traumas, we have become acutely aware of what Jimmie Holland and Sheldon Lewis have termed the "Tyranny of Positive Thinking." In their book (2001), they suggest that individuals who are diagnosed with cancer are pressured to "stay positive," "have a positive outlook," and "look on the bright side of things." The popular literature and media have elaborated on the movement to empower cancer patients to be active partners in their own recovery by expounding the notion that the only way to survive cancer is to always show a positive attitude, even when one is feeling sad or discouraged. For many patients, this pressure is an additional burden of the cancer experience. Presenting a positive façade, particularly while one is anticipating unpleasant medical procedures and treatments or contemplating one's mortality is clearly stressful. This distress can be compounded by the sense of isolation that this pressure causes. If all of the members of a patient's social support network insist that she remains positive at all times, the patient may not feel supported by her social support system. In addition, there is no empirical support that repressing so-called negative emotions will enhance adjustment or longevity. Intervention studies (e.g., Spiegel et al., 1989) have shown that appropriate expression of negative feelings may actually contribute to longevity and better quality of life.

As discussed earlier, clinicians have long been aware that patients respond defensively when they are prompted to contemplate an issue too early in the therapeutic process. A group setting may be a particularly dangerous venue for the tyranny of positive thinking. Clinically, we have observed that the topic of positive thinking is inevitably raised by participants in our groups, and it is clear from conversations that there are strong social motivations to report growth and to acquiesce to the popular culture. Cancer-related support groups are commonly offered in both hospital and outpatient settings, and while these groups are immensely helpful in a number of ways, we have found that they can also prescribe positive thinking for group members. In that context, it is important for the group facilitator to allow patients to introduce the topic of BF and growth, and to make it safe for members of the group to disagree. Interventions delivered in an individual format will be less susceptible to these issues.

Also, given such concerns about the tyranny of positive thinking, we wondered if BF might be related to this pressure to pretend to be positive. Using a cross-sectional design, we asked a sample of men and women with various forms of cancer about the extent to which they felt that they must always present a positive attitude even when they weren't feeling positive. Analyses showed that pretending to adopt a positive attitude was significantly related to higher BF scores (Yanez & Lechner, 2005). This suggests that individuals who experience high levels of pressure to be positive may feel the need to report that they have grown from their experience. Similarly, the relationship between BF and pressure to be positive would suggest that finding meaning in illness could be an artifact of the desire to present oneself as a "positive person." Of course, these issues need to be resolved empirically. However, since peer pressure to be positive is often evident in groups, such issues may be more relevant in group therapy than in an individual therapy context.

Why Not Develop Group-Based Interventions to Specifically Enhance Benefit Finding? There are a number of reasons why group-based interventions to specifically promote BF are not warranted—yet. There are risks when clinicians attempt to promote BF, or when there is pressure to endorse BF in a group setting. As many clinicians know, good therapy is often client-driven and works within the patient's framework (Calhoun & Tedeschi, 1999). Proposing benefits too early before the patient is ready to contemplate "making lemonade from lemons" can erode the therapeutic relationship.

In addition to this concern, Park and Helgeson (2006) pointed out in the Introduction to the Special Section on Benefit Finding in the *Journal of Consulting and Clinical Psychology*:

> The field is not yet at a place in basic research to endorse the development of large-scale growth interventions applied to people who have undergone traumatic life events. Until researchers understand more about the origins

of growth, the conditions under which growth is veridical, and the best way to assess growth, links to psychological and physical health will not be fully understood. Without this latter knowledge, it may be ethically irresponsible to attempt growth-based interventions with a highly distressed population. (p. 795)

A group-based therapy to facilitate BF runs the risk of prescribing BF to patients. This would be an unfortunate outcome of the attention being paid to BF. As is clear from the inconsistent and conflicting literature on the relationship between BF and other outcomes, deriving benefits is not a necessary predictor of well-being. For some, finding benefits may not be a necessary or sufficient path toward quality of life or lowered distress, and may not be indicated for some individuals. Given the many unanswered questions and concerns about group-based therapies to promote BF, we suggest that individual therapy with a qualified therapist is the best option at this juncture.

SUMMARY

Despite the lingering questions and directions for future research, this is an exciting time for professionals who wish to fully understand optimal psychological health and thriving before, during, and after cancer treatment.

Summary Points (Practice and Research)

- Studies should identify critical periods of the development of BF in order to provide interventions at optimal times.
- More work is needed to identify how race/ethnicity may act to moderate the development of BF after diagnosis of cancer as well as moderating the effects of psychosocial interventions on BF changes during and after cancer treatment. If race/ethnicity is found to moderate BF changes, it will be important to examine how these differences might contribute to disparities in longer-term quality of life and possibly health disparities as well. Disentangling the contribution of possibly confounding factors such as SES, education, access to care, and religion/spirituality will be key to clarifying the mechanisms underlying the development of BF across different populations.
- The role of BF in the general trauma-adaptation or adjustment process. For example, is BF simply related to decreases in psychological distress long-term, or is it associated with (or a by-product of) the experience of other positive psychological states (e.g., joy, sense of meaning or purpose)?

- How sociodemographic variables influence the development of BF. Are there indeed certain cultural or ethnic scripts that make BF more likely, and if so, what are they?
- Mediators/moderators in the relationship between trauma (i.e., cancer diagnosis and treatment) and found benefit (e.g., use of stress management skills, increased social support).
- When a patient identifies that he or she has grown from his or her cancer experience, how can the clinician enhance or stimulate that process even further—while taking sociodemographic variables into account. Or, if group members independently bring up the topic of BF, when and how should a clinician decide to "intervene."
- Based on current evidence, group-based interventions to develop BF are not yet recommended. The current state of the research suggests that individual therapy with a qualified practitioner is the best approach.

REFERENCES

Aldwin, C. M., Antoni, M. H., Bower, J. E., Carver, C. S., Helgeson, V. S., Lechner, S. C., et al. (2005, May). The state of the science in benefit finding research in health psychology. In S. C. Lechner (Chair), *Health psychology perspectives on positive life changes: Benefit finding and growth following illness.* Symposium conducted at the meeting of Health Psychology Perspectives, Storrs, CT.

Andersen, B. L., Farrar, W. B., Golden-Kreutz, D. M., Glaser, R., Emery, C. F., Crespin, T. R., et al. (2004). Psychological, behavioral, and immune changes after a psychological intervention: A clinical trial. *Journal of Clinical Oncology, 22,* 3570–3580.

Antoni, M. H. (2003). *Stress management intervention for women with breast cancer.* Washington, DC: American Psychological Association.

Antoni, M. H., Lehman, J. M., Klibourn, K. M., Boyers, A. E., Culver, J. L., Alferi, S. M., et al. (2001). Cognitive-behavioral stress management intervention decreases the prevalence of depression and enhances benefit finding among women under treatment for early-stage breast cancer. *Health Psychology, 20,* 20–32.

Antoni, M. H., Wimberly, S. R., Lechner, S. C., Kazi, A., Sifre, T., Urcuyo, K. R., et al. (2006). Reduction of cancer-specific thought intrusions and anxiety symptoms with a stress management intervention among women undergoing treatment for breast cancer. *American Journal of Psychiatry, 163,* 1791–1797.

Aspinwall, L. G. (1998). Rethinking the role of positive affect in self-regulation. *Motivation and Emotion, 22,* 1–32.

Barakat, L. P., Alderfer, M. A., & Kazak, A. E. (2006). Posttraumatic growth in adolescent survivors of cancer and their mothers and fathers. *Journal of Pediatric Psychology, 31,* 413–419.

Bellizzi, K. M. (2004). Expressions of generativity and posttraumatic growth in adult cancer survivors. *International Journal of Aging and Human Development, 58,* 267–287.

Bellizzi, K. M., & Blank, T. O. (2006). Predicting posttraumatic growth in breast cancer survivors. *Health Psychology, 25*, 47–56.

Bourjolly, J. N. (1998). Differences in religiousness among Black and White women with breast cancer. *Social Work in Health Care, 28*, 21–39.

Bower, J. E., Kemeny, M. E., Taylor, S. E., & Fahey, J. L. (1998). Cognitive processing, discovery of meaning, CD4 decline, and AIDS-related mortality among bereaved HIV-seropositive men. *Journal of Consulting and Clinical Psychology, 66*, 979–986.

Breitbart, W., Gibson, C., Poppito, S. R., & Berg, A. (2004). Psychotherapeutic interventions at the end of life: A focus on meaning and spirituality. *Canadian Journal of Psychiatry, 49*, 366–372.

Cadell, S., Regehr, C., & Hemsworth, D. (2003). Factors contributing to posttraumatic growth: A proposed structural equation model. *American Journal of Orthopsychiatry, 73*, 279–287.

Calhoun, L. G., & Tedeschi, R. G. (1999). *Facilitating posttraumatic growth: A clinician's guide.* Mahwah, NJ: Erlbaum.

Carver, C. S. (1997). You want to measure coping but your protocol's too long: Consider the Brief COPE. *International Journal of Behavioral Medicine, 4*, 92–100.

Carver, C. S., Scheier, M. F., & Weintraub, J. K. (1989). Assessing coping strategies: A theoretically based approach. *Journal of Personality and Social Psychology, 56*, 267–283.

Cohen, S., & Hoberman, H. M. (1983). Positive events and social supports as buffers of life change stress. *Journal of Applied Social Psychology, 13*, 99–125.

Cordova, M. J., Cunningham, L. L. C., Carlson, C. R., & Andrykowski, M. A. (2001). Posttraumatic growth following breast cancer: A controlled comparison study. *Health Psychology, 20*, 176–185.

Fife, B. L. (1995). The measurement of meaning in illness. *Social Science and Medicine, 40*, 1021–1028.

Fontana, A., & Rosenheck, R. (1998). Psychological benefits and liabilities of traumatic exposure in the war zone. *Journal of Traumatic Stress, 11*, 485–503.

Fredrickson, B. L., Tugade, M. M., Waugh, C. E., & Larkin, G. R. (2003). What good are positive emotions in crises? A prospective study of resilience and emotions following the terrorist attacks on the United States on September 11th, 2001. *Journal of Personality and Social Psychology, 84*, 365–376.

Fromm, K., Andrykowski, M. A., & Hunt, J. (1996). Positive and negative psychosocial sequelae of bone marrow transplantation: Implications for quality of life assessment. *Journal of Behavioral Medicine, 19*, 221–240.

Goodwin, P. J., Leszcz, M., Ennis, M., Koopmans, J., Vincent, L., Guther, H., et al. (2001). The effect of group psychosocial support on survival in metastatic breast cancer. *New England Journal of Medicine, 345*, 1719–1726.

Greer, S., Morris, T., & Pettingale, K. W. (1979). Psychological response to breast cancer: Effect on outcome. *Lancet, 2*(8146), 785–787.

Holland, J. C., & Lewis, S. (2001). *The human side of cancer: Living with hope, coping with uncertainty.* New York: HarperCollins.

Janoff-Bulman, R. (1992). *Shattered assumptions: Towards a new psychology of trauma.* New York: Free Press.

Kinsinger, D. P., Penedo, F. J., Antoni, M. H., Dahn, J. R., Lechner, S. C., & Schneiderman, N. (2006). Psychosocial and sociodemographic correlates of benefit-finding in men treated for localized prostate cancer. *Psycho-Oncology, 15,* 954–961.

Lazarus, R. S., & Folkman, S. (1984). *Stress, appraisal, and coping.* New York: Springer.

Lechner, S. C. (2000). Found meaning in individuals with cancer (Doctoral dissertation, Finch University of Health Sciences/Chicago Medical School, 2000). *Dissertation Abstracts International, 61*(9B), 4992.

Lechner, S. C. (2006). *Does attitude toward cancer mediate the relationship between social support and finding benefit in the experience of cancer?* Manuscript submitted for publication.

Lechner, S. C., Zakowski, S. G., Antoni, M. H., Greenhawt, M., Block, K., & Block, P. (2003). Do sociodemographic and disease-related variables influence benefit-finding in cancer patients? *Psycho-Oncology, 12,* 491–499.

Lepore, S. J. (2001). A social-cognitive processing model of emotional adjustment to cancer. In A. Baum & B. L. Andersen (Eds.), *Psychosocial interventions for cancer* (pp. 99–116). Washington, DC: American Psychological Association.

Linley, P. A., & Joseph, S. (2004). Positive change following trauma and adversity: A review. *Journal of Traumatic Stress, 17,* 11–21.

Linley, P. A., & Joseph, S. (2007). Therapy work and therapists' positive and negative well-being. *Journal of Social and Clinical Psychology, 26,* 385–403.

Linley, P. A., Joseph, S., & Loumidis, K. (2005). Trauma work, sense of coherence, and positive and negative changes in therapists. *Psychotherapy and Psychosomatics, 74,* 185–188.

Manne, S., Ostroff, J., Winkel, G., Goldstein, L., Fox, K., & Grana, G. (2004). Posttraumatic growth after breast cancer: Patient, partner, and couple perspectives. *Psychosomatic Medicine, 66,* 442–454.

McFarland, C., & Alvaro, C. (2000). The impact of motivation on temporal comparisons: Coping with traumatic events by perceiving personal growth. *Journal of Personality and Social Psychology, 79,* 327–343.

McGrath, P. (2004). Reflections on serious illness as spiritual journey by survivors of hematological malignancies. *European Journal of Cancer Care, 13,* 227–237.

McMillen, J. C., Smith, E. M., & Fisher, R. H. (1997). Perceived benefit and mental health after three types of disaster. *Journal of Consulting and Clinical Psychology, 65,* 733–739.

Neimeyer, R. A. (2004). Fostering posttraumatic growth: A narrative elaboration. *Psychological Inquiry, 15,* 53–59.

Park, C. L., Cohen, L. H., & Murch, R. L. (1996). Assessment and prediction of stress-related growth. *Journal of Personality, 64,* 71–105.

Park, C. L., & Folkman, S. (1997). Meaning in the context of stress and coping. *Review of General Psychology, 1,* 115–144.

Park, C. L., & Helgeson, V. S. (2006). Introduction to the special section: Growth following highly stressful life events—Current status and future directions. *Journal of Consulting and Clinical Psychology, 74,* 791–796.

Parry, C., & Chesler, M. A. (2005). Thematic evidence of psychosocial thriving in childhood cancer survivors. *Qualitative Health Research, 15,* 1055–1073.

Penedo, F. J., Molton, I., Dahn, J. R., Shen, B. J., Kinsinger, D., Traeger, L., et al. (2006). A randomized clinical trial of group-based cognitive-behavioral stress management in localized prostate cancer: Development of stress management skills improves quality of life and benefit finding. *Annals of Behavioral Medicine, 31*, 261–270.

Pennebaker, J. W. (1994). *Hints on running a writing experiment.* Unpublished manual.

Ren, X. S., Skinner, K., Lee, A., & Kazis, L. (1999). Social support, social selection and self-assessed health status: Results from the Veterans Health Study in the United States. *Social Science and Medicine, 48*, 1721–1734.

Rini, C., Manne, S., DuHamel, K. N., Austin, J., Ostroff, J., Boulad, F., et al. (2004). Mothers' perceptions of benefit following pediatric stem cell transplantation: A longitudinal investigation of the roles of optimism, medical risk, and sociodemographic resources. *Annals of Behavioral Medicine, 28*, 132–141.

Sandoval, J. A. (2005). Correlates of benefit finding in men treated for stage I or II prostate cancer (Doctoral dissertation, University of Miami). *Dissertation Abstracts International, 66*(12B), 6934.

Schaefer, J. A., & Moos, R. H. (1998). The context for posttraumatic growth: Life crises, individual and social resources, and coping. In R. G. Tedeschi, C. L. Park, & L. G. Calhoun (Eds.), *Posttraumatic growth: Positive changes in the aftermath of crisis* (pp. 99–125). Mahwah, NJ: Erlbaum.

Sears, S. R., Stanton, A. L., & Danoff-Burg, S. (2003). The yellow brick road and the emerald city: Benefit finding, positive reappraisal coping and posttraumatic growth in women with early-stage breast cancer. *Health Psychology, 22*, 487–497.

Shaw, A., Joseph, S., & Linley, P. A. (2005). Religion, spirituality and posttraumatic growth: A systematic review. *Mental Health, Religion and Culture, 8*, 1–11.

Siegel, K., & Schrimshaw, E. W. (2000). Perceiving benefits in adversity: Stress-related growth in women living with HIV/AIDS. *Social Science and Medicine, 51*, 1543–1554.

Siegel, K., Schrimshaw, E. W., & Pretter, S. (2005). Stress-related growth among women living with HIV/AIDS: Examination of an explanatory model. *Journal of Behavioral Medicine, 28*, 403–414.

Spiegel, D., Kraemer, H. C., Bloom, J. R., & Gottheil, E. (1989). Effect of psychosocial treatment on survival of patients with metastatic breast-cancer. *Lancet, 2*(8668), 888–891.

Stanton, A. L., Danoff-Burg, S., Cameron, C. L., Bishop, M., Collins, C. A., Kirk, S. B., et al. (2000). Emotionally expressive coping predicts psychological and physical adjustment to breast cancer. *Journal of Consulting and Clinical Psychology, 68*, 875–882.

Stanton, A. L., Danoff-Burg, S., Sworowski, L. A., Collins, C. A., Branstetter, A. D., Rodriguez-Hanley, A., et al. (2002). Randomized, controlled trial of written emotional expression and benefit finding in breast cancer patients. *Journal of Clinical Oncology, 20*, 4160–4168.

Stoelb, B. (2006). *Quantitative and qualitative aspects of HIV serostatus self-disclosure: Their relationship to immune function, cortisol, and posttraumatic growth.* Unpublished doctoral dissertation, University of Miami.

Stroebe, M., & Schut, H. (1999). The dual process model of coping with bereavement: Rationale and description. *Death Studies, 23,* 197–224.

Tedeschi, R. G., & Calhoun, L. G. (1995). *Trauma and transformation: Growing in the aftermath of suffering.* Thousand Oaks, CA: Sage.

Tedeschi, R. G., & Calhoun, L. G. (1996). The Posttraumatic Growth Inventory: Measuring the positive legacy of trauma. *Journal of Traumatic Stress, 9,* 455–472.

Tedeschi, R. G., & Calhoun, L. G. (2004). Posttraumatic growth: Conceptual foundations and empirical evidence. *Psychological Inquiry, 15,* 1–18.

Tennen, H., & Affleck, G. (2002). Benefit-finding and benefit-reminding. In S. J. Lopez & C. Snyder (Eds.), *Handbook of positive psychology* (pp. 584–597). New York: Oxford University Press.

Tomich, P. L., & Helgeson, V. S. (2004). Is finding something good in the bad always good? Benefit finding among women with breast cancer. *Health Psychology, 23,* 16–23.

Updegraff, J. A., Taylor, S. E., Kemeny, M. E., & Wyatt, G. E. (2002). Positive and negative effects of HIV infection in women with low socioeconomic resources. *Personality and Social Psychology Bulletin, 28,* 382–394.

Urcuyo, K. R., Boyers, A. E., Carver, C. S., & Antoni, M. H. (2005). Finding benefit in breast cancer: Relations with personality, coping, and concurrent well-being. *Psychology and Health, 20,* 175–192.

Watson, M., Greer, S., Pruyn, J., & Van den Borne, B. (1990). Locus of control and adjustment to cancer. *Psychological Reports, 66,* 39–48.

Watson, M., Greer, S., Rowden, L., & Gorman, C. (1991). Relationships between emotional control, adjustment to cancer and depression and anxiety in breast cancer patients. *Psychological Medicine, 21,* 51–57.

Watson, M., Greer, S., Young, J., & Inayat, Q. (1988). Development of a questionnaire measure of adjustment to cancer: The MAC scale. *Psychological Medicine, 18,* 203–209.

Weiss, T. (2002). Posttraumatic growth in women with breast cancer and their husbands: An intersubjective validation study. *Journal of Psychosocial Oncology, 20*(2), 65–80.

Weiss, T. (2004a). Correlates of posttraumatic growth in husbands of breast cancer survivors. *Psycho-Oncology, 13,* 260–268.

Weiss, T. (2004b). Correlates of posttraumatic growth in married breast cancer survivors. *Journal of Social and Clinical Psychology, 23,* 733–746.

Widows, M. R., Jacobsen, P. B., Booth-Jones, M., & Fields, K. K. (2005). Predictors of posttraumatic growth following bone marrow transplantation for cancer. *Health Psychology, 24,* 266–273.

Yalom, I. D. (1995). *The theory and practice of group psychotherapy* (4th ed.). New York: Basic Books.

Yanez, B., & Lechner, S. C. (2005). Pretending to be positive about cancer is related to poorer psychosocial outcomes. *Annals of Behavioral Medicine, 29,* S181.

CHAPTER 12

Using a Life Span Model to Promote Recovery and Growth in Traumatized Veterans

JUDITH A. LYONS

MANY PEOPLE ENCOUNTER trauma at some point in their life (Kessler, Sonnega, Bromet, Hughes, & Nelson, 1995). Most show no long-term psychiatric impairment even after a horrific event (Bonanno, 2004). European ex-POWs who were tortured during World War II have been found to have adjusted well (Nice, Garland, Hilton, Baggett, & Mitchell, 1996). Similarly, Shmotkin, Blumstein, and Modan (2003) found few differences between Holocaust survivors and a comparison group of other postwar immigrants to Israel.

Recovery is accomplished by many of those who initially developed post-traumatic stress disorder (PTSD). Cognitive behavioral interventions, including exposure therapy, are empirically validated techniques for promoting recovery (return to baseline). Additional strategies may be needed to maximize growth (exceed pretrauma baseline). In this chapter, I discuss the use of personal time lines to facilitate positive appraisal and optimize functioning during the recovery process. Among individuals who develop PTSD, the trauma frequently becomes the focal point of the person's life. Clinicians can help individuals reconnect with their pretrauma past and

This chapter is the result of work supported with resources and the use of facilities at the G. V. (Sonny) Montgomery VA Medical Center, Jackson, Mississippi. The views expressed here represent those of the author and do not necessarily represent the views of the Department of Veterans Affairs or the University of Mississippi Medical Center.

Note: All patient names have been changed and some case examples apply to multiple veterans. For each individual case that is presented, the patient provided a written release approving use of the case material for this chapter.

their future potential through exercises that highlight where in the time line of their life they invest their cognitive and emotional energy. Old coping strategies can become untenable with aging, and developmental milestones can bring with them new reminders of past trauma. Placing the trauma and other stressors within a time line of developmental tasks can normalize what might otherwise be perceived as a discouraging PTSD relapse or delayed onset of PTSD. The chapter includes case examples of individuals who have used these life span perspectives in their effort to overcome PTSD and move forward to positive growth.

Bonanno (2004) distinguishes between *resilience* (those who never succumb; the more common pattern) and *recovery* (the focus of this chapter). Bonanno states, "resilience reflects the ability to maintain a stable equilibrium," (p. 20) whereas "recovery" connotes a lapse in that stable state, followed by a return to baseline. Of those who do develop PTSD, approximately half recover within 3 months (American Psychiatric Association, 2000). Although they are in the minority, this still leaves a large number of individuals who have chronic PTSD and may need professional treatment. Cognitive behavioral interventions, including exposure therapy, are empirically validated techniques for promoting recovery (return to baseline; Foa, Keane, & Freidman, 2000).

Factor analyses by Ruini et al. (2003) show that components of well-being (autonomy, environmental mastery, personal growth, positive relations, purpose in life, self-acceptance) comprise a separate factor from most symptom, distress, and personality measures. It has been demonstrated that patients with mood and anxiety disorders report significantly less well-being and more distress than controls even when their disorder is in remission (Rafanelli et al., 2000). Additional supplemental interventions thus may be needed to maximize growth and well-being.

Fava, Rafanelli, Cazzaro, Conti, and Grandi (1998, p. 479) point out, "There has been little exploration, outside of [sic] psychodynamic realm, of psychological factors affecting progression to full recovery." Indeed, although the current author adheres to a cognitive-behavioral model overall, the work of Erikson (1950/1963) has provided a helpful framework for conceptualizing developmental stages. This chapter discusses the use of a life span perspective to facilitate positive appraisal and optimize functioning during the recovery process. However, the life span perspective used in this chapter is pragmatic and not heavily rooted in a particular theory or model. The implementation of personal time lines is derived from observation of changes spontaneously manifested in patients who were moving from pathology to recovery. Encouraging other clients to consider their situation within the context of similar time lines was found to facilitate the recovery process in those clients also. Readers are urged to integrate these ideas with their own clinical techniques within the context of whichever over-arching theoretical model they use.

WHERE DO CLIENTS INVEST THEIR EMOTIONS AND ENERGY IN THE TIME LINE OF THEIR LIFE?

It has long been asserted that cognitive appraisal plays a major role in positive adjustment and growth following a trauma (e.g., Koss & Burkhart, 1989, regarding rape survivors). It is common to measure our lives relative to major life contexts or events (e.g., before Hurricane Katrina; since 9/11). We segment our lives not only by major disasters, but also by other milestones. We calculate what year something occurred by recalling what car we were driving at the time, which home we lived in, whether the baby was still in diapers then. Among individuals who develop PTSD, the trauma frequently becomes more than a mile marker, it becomes the focal point around which the rest of life revolves.

Although this phenomenon is also observed in nonmilitary trauma, several factors seem to magnify this tendency in veterans. The majority of troops are relatively young. For such individuals, the structure of military life—with its hierarchy, rank, mission, emphasis on peer group attachments—can promote a "pseudo-sense of self-certainty" (Wilson, 1980, p. 137) during the stage of life when they are focused on identity formation. When they leave the military and return to civilian life, the military structure is no longer there to preserve this identity. In reference to World War II veterans, Erikson (1950/1963, p. 42) wrote, "They knew who they were; they had a personal identity. But it was as if, subjectively, their lives no longer hung together—and never would again. There was a central disturbance in what I then started to call ego identity . . . this sense of identity provides the ability to experience one's self as something that has continuity and sameness, and to act accordingly."

Bradshaw, Ohlde, and Horne (1991) offer similar reasons veterans would remain focused on their time in combat: guilt, to honor lost friends, war experiences "were the high point of his life; they symbolized a time when he had felt really important (p. 98)." Consequently, "They relinquish the present to keep the past alive. In the process, they become isolated and fail to continue growing as a member of society (p. 98)." "Now he clings to his pride of having been a combat soldier, but feels overwhelmed at being such a 'lousy civilian'" (p. 101).

USE OF STRUCTURED ASSIGNMENTS TO SHIFT FOCUS

Although it may be obvious to those around them, some individuals with PTSD remain unaware of choices and actions that keep them anchored to the trauma. When the trauma remains the hub around which the rest of life revolves even after completion of exposure therapy or other trauma-focused interventions, individuals may need help to place their trauma in a more adaptive perspective. Exercises that highlight where in the time line of life trauma survivors are investing cognitive and emotional energy can help individuals reconnect with their pretrauma past, current opportunities, and their future potential.

Case Study: Bob

Bob is a Vietnam veteran who presented at the clinic seeking individual therapy approximately 35 years after his service in Vietnam. He displayed his Vietnam service proudly: He was wearing a Vietnam T-shirt and a cap with military insignia and multiple military pins on it, and was carrying a briefcase emblazoned with a large bumper sticker depicting the Vietnam service ribbon. His presenting concern was that he was newly married, multiple past marriages had failed, and the current marriage was faltering. It was difficult to convince him to look at possible behavioral adjustments that might strengthen his marriage because he quickly dismissed each topic with "Well, she just needs to recognize that I'm a Vietnam combat veteran. Us combat veterans just can't . . . [go to crowded public places, be romantic, be patient in traffic, etc.]." Verbal feedback did not yield insight or behavior change. However, a behavioral homework exercise helped Bob recognize the incongruity between his goals and where he focused his attention.

First, Bob was given an opportunity to discuss his Vietnam service. The therapist validated the importance of his service to his country and the huge sacrifices made by him and those with whom he served. He was encouraged to continue to cherish his memories of fallen comrades and his pride in his own military accomplishments. After clearly conveying that the intent was not to minimize his military experience, the therapist asked Bob if he carried any memorabilia related to his marriage (photos, etc.). He had none with him. He was instructed to come to future sessions bearing at least as many mementos of his marriage as of his Vietnam service. He completed the assignment, but needed a rolling cart to carry the pile of framed photos and honeymoon souvenirs he brought to the next session. He was never instructed to reduce the number of Vietnam memorabilia he wore or carried, but these steadily reduced over successive sessions (thus requiring fewer family mementos to balance the score). After only a few sessions, his overall focus had similarly shifted, and the assignment was discontinued. He continues to wear something with a military insignia on it at each session, but such emblems are much less numerous and more discreet. He has become expressive in his marriage, and the relationship has blossomed. He and his wife have become adept at finding ways to enjoy outings within the limits of his chronic PTSD (e.g., attending the Fourth of July barbecue together, with him excusing himself prior to the fireworks). In turn, his wife has gone out of her way (without having been prompted) to acknowledge his military service by donating commemorative artwork to hang in public buildings. His traumas have not been dishonored, but have taken a healthier place in the context of the present.

In implementing such strategic assignments, the goal is to make the veteran aware of how too tight a hold on the past leaves little space in life for the present or future. It is important to remember that lack of societal validation for the life-changing role of the trauma may be maintaining the patient's focus on that trauma (Bradshaw, Ohlde, & Horne, 1991, p. 99). Unless the therapist acknowledges the importance the trauma holds for that individual, the client is apt to resist a shift to other emphases. In Bob's case, the fact that his wife paid public tribute to his military background likely contributed to the intervention's success. Similarly, survivor guilt is a common factor that binds the veteran to the past: "Who will remember if I don't?" In such cases, memorabilia can be incorporated into a memorial shadow box, burial ceremony, and so on, that honors the past but clears the way for increased attention to the present and future.

The gap between past and present can also be bridged by engaging in previously avoided social activities first with fellow veterans then branching out. Cooperative barbecuing for large gatherings is a popular activity among men in our region of the country. Our treatment program installed barbecue grills on a hospital patio, and encouraged residential patients to bring foods to grill together when they return from weekend passes on Sunday nights. This has become a program tradition that tends to expand in complexity over the several weeks each cohort is in the program. By the final weekends, patients often involve family members in menu planning and preparation and they begin to look forward to similar gatherings with extended family after their discharge from the hospital.

Other trauma-related exercises can also segue smoothly into more general growth-promoting assignments. Seligman, Rashid, and Parks (2006) present a sampling of valuable homework suggestions that could be implemented in the non-trauma-specific form the authors present or could be adapted by the clinician to be more trauma-focused.

REINFORCING POSITIVE APPRAISAL OF NATURALLY OCCURRING SITUATIONS

Often, acknowledgment of the trauma can be combined with redirection to the present and future. Directing focus to lessons learned is one of the most common ways to shape adaptive reappraisal of the trauma's role in life. For that reason, even though institutional policy does not require patient consent for use of de-identified case information, I formally requested consent from each patient whose case I have described here. I approached each patient individually, explained the purpose of the chapter, and identified exactly what aspect of their case I thought demonstrated a particular point. I emphasized that their consent was voluntary, yet none declined. Without exception, patients expressed pleasure that their difficult experiences had helped teach the therapist lessons that could benefit other veterans. Some patients revealed additional aspects of their life or treatment that they felt had significantly promoted their recovery. Each such discussion closed with the veteran expressing a sense of meaning and optimism for future growth. The impact of the invitation was especially apparent in the following case.

Case Study: Joe

Joe, a Vietnam veteran who was among the first diagnosed with PTSD nearly 30 years earlier, faxed a letter to the therapist a few days after his consent was requested. "After our last appointment, you made me realize something about myself and our Program." Joe went on the write about the progress he has made and the things he is able to do and enjoy now that he could not before, despite ongoing symptoms. "I'm able to feel joy and pain. The joy takes over, not the pain and guilt." In the letter, Joe repeatedly referred to therapy as "our Program," reflecting a collaborative pride. He also points out that counselors are now on the scene after school shootings and disasters, recognizing that it was Vietnam veterans who helped bring public awareness to the need for trauma services.

Many veterans who could not save buddies or civilians in combat now are compassionate caregivers of family members or volunteer in their community, often in honor of those lost in battle (and some as personally imposed reparation). Similarly, when an acute crisis such as 9/11 or Hurricane Katrina threw most people off balance, many of the veterans in our PTSD clinic remained calm and focused—they were familiar with crisis, had survived past threats and could model for their families and neighbors how to handle such challenges. A study by Bramsen, van der Ploeg, and Boers (2006) revealed a similar pattern. They found that a fireworks disaster in 2000 activated reexperiencing and avoidance reactions in a town that had been heavily bombed during World War II, but such reactions were not specific to people who had PTSD. Those with PTSD symptoms were found to have coped better after the second (fireworks) disaster. I have observed that once people with PTSD have been labeled as "disordered," many of them fail to give themselves credit for ways the trauma has led to resourcefulness and strength. Helping survivors reframe trauma history as growth experiences that have prepared them for current challenges can be tremendously empowering for them.

Taking on a peer leadership or survivor advocacy role allows patients to build something positive in the present. In most cases, this role evolves as the survivors' sense of competence in dealing with their personal trauma develops. Senior members of a trauma group tend to informally mentor newcomers. Such actions are usually adaptive and beneficial for both senior and junior clinic members. Similarly, clinic members tend to be the most effective outreach tool, as they recognize others who are in need of services, provide peer support, and offer encouragement/reassurance about seeking formal help. Many survivors take a more formal advocacy role, becoming formal sponsors, crisis center volunteers, and so on. Therapists can maximize the impact of such steps by reinforcing the significance of such actions and promoting self-appraisal of this role as a sign of growth and competence. Perhaps most importantly, the therapist can help patients brainstorm and proactively prepare for potential pitfalls. This would include respectfully addressing any tendency of patients to jump into care for others before sufficiently dealing with their own trauma.

Men in Joe's family have always served in the military. With a bronze star and other medals, he may be the most highly decorated among them, yet he has been the "black sheep" all his life and has been very lonely. He takes great pride in having recently helped resurrect the chapter (post) of the veterans' organization to which his father had belonged. He goes to work daily at the post doing odd jobs. The post serves as a bridge between him and society—his military deeds are appreciated, his PTSD is understood, his involvement creates a link with his father who never gave him the attention he craved, it opens the door for connection with other estranged members of his military family, and provides a structured role in which to interact with the public who come to play bingo. The many military collectibles that used to adorn the den where he isolated himself at home are now on display at the post. He helps guide new veterans to VA services and other veterans' benefits. He has extreme social anxiety with strangers, but is an entertaining storyteller and is well known by regulars at the post. The increased social network provided by the post has dramatically reduced the frequency of his between-sessions calls to his therapist.

On several occasions, he has gotten agitated about some issue at the post and been ready to quit. Each time, the therapist has helped him examine the pros and cons of continued involvement. This has been sufficient to ventilate his frustrations, and each time, he has expressed satisfaction that he did not resign in haste. With each of these episodes, his social skills are developing and his tolerance for the imperfections of people and institutions is steadily increasing.

In Joe's case, channeling his own past trauma and treatment experiences into present service for others was something that developed gradually and needed ongoing therapist input to shore it up. In other cases, opportunities for service occur more spontaneously and abruptly, but the therapist's aid may be needed to build lasting momentum from the experience.

Case Study: Dan

Dan had been cut off from supplies during a lengthy siege and nearly starved. Since then, he has hoarded food, hiding it in multiple locations in the woods. Obesity has become a life-threatening issue for him, yet he panics when his weight begins to drop. Issues about weight and food have been a central focus of his trauma processing.

When Hurricane Katrina devastated his state, Dan's compassion for others enabled him to donate nearly all his stockpiled food to storm survivors. He also took on the role of distributing other donated food supplies around the region. His efforts were so impressive that he was nominated for the top award given by one of the national service organizations. His own weight continues to fluctuate, and fear of starvation continues to be a topic in therapy. However, his volunteer work has helped offset some of the associated shame, enabling him to finally be honest with his family and primary care providers about what has been impeding his weight reduction.

As Dan's case illustrates, not only can such challenges build the confidence of the survivor and earn the respect of significant others, some situations enable the survivor to master aspects of the prior trauma. This is even clearer in the following two examples.

Case Study: Bill

While in Vietnam, Bill had made a pact with his best buddy. Having seen the corpses of men who had been tortured and mutilated, they each vowed never to let the other fall into the hands of the enemy. When Bill's buddy was mortally wounded and the enemy was closing in, Bill had to quickly decide whether to honor this pact before fleeing for his life. The last thing he could remember was that he was cradling his wounded friend as the friend begged for Bill to shoot him. For years, Bill dissociated whenever he tried to recall whether he had killed his friend or allowed him to be captured. Both options were intolerably repulsive to him. Even the slightest reminder of that situation evoked violence or self-mutilation (early years of this case are presented in Lyons, 1991), and attempts at exposure therapy were therefore abandoned. Other therapies helped him increase his coping and improve relationships, but the extreme reexperiencing of his trauma periodically undermined his efforts to improve his life.

Decades after the war, Bill's family was faced with the quandary of how to care for his father whose dementia was increasing. All the siblings concurred that Dad could no longer safely live outside an institution, but Dad was resisting. The siblings who had been entrusted with Dad's care were waffling, even as Dad's behavior was leading to fires and other serious accidents. Being rather isolated from the family unit by his chronic PTSD, Bill stood back and watched this stalemate with increasing frustration. Finally, he took charge, placed his father in a nursing home, and all his siblings eventually thanked him.

That ended his flashbacks. The challenge of overseeing care of his ailing father primed the cognitive and emotional context that approximated his past trauma. He stated he saw his family's inaction as a choice based in weakness when the situation required decisive action. Having reentered the emotional milieu where painful actions can be better than no action, he could accept both his decision on his father's behalf and his decision on his friend's behalf. Although he never explicitly stated this, the therapist understood his remarks and recovery to imply that he had indeed deliberately shot his friend to prevent him from being tortured, and now accepted that it was the best among bad options.

Such real-life challenges can be pivotal points between decompensation and growth. The cognitive appraisal by the patient appears crucial in setting the direction. The therapist and others can assist by challenging maladaptive appraisals and reinforcing more adaptive thought patterns.

Case Study: Cassandra

Cassandra is a young veteran who was raped. Diagnosed as having concurrent PTSD and somatization disorder, she initially presented in a wheelchair. She had progressed to the point of being able to ambulate freely when, during a college course on public speaking, the instructor assigned a brief speech on a current news topic. He demonstrated this task by giving a sample speech on date rape. Cassandra began to panic, the instructor noticed, and he cut his speech short. Cassandra was mortified that he must have guessed her secret. In subsequent weeks, she reverted to using a wheelchair and her family was seeking to have her hospitalized.

Cassandra felt she had to "disprove" the assumptions her instructor might have made about her. She prepared a speech about the career of a celebrity who was under indictment for rape. Her hope was to demonstrate that she was so disinterested in the rape topic that she could coolly discuss the man's professional accomplishments and "not even notice" the other issues. The therapist was quite skeptical of this plan, but helped her role-play how she would respond if questions were raised about the sexual assault charges pending against this celebrity. The speech went very well and the topic of sexual assault was not raised. Cassandra's acute symptoms abated. However, she remained uncomfortable about her earlier panic reaction in class. Therapy focused on ways her life continued to be constricted by her avoidance of trauma reminders.

Later in the semester, the instructor assigned an impromptu speech on a societal topic of the student's choice. On the spur of the moment, she decided to speak about what she knew all too well: the emotional impact of rape. She stood before the class, told what had happened, how she tried to hide it, the toll it had taken, and how she was learning to deal with it. She received rave reviews from the instructor and classmates and from our women's trauma group when she told them about it that same afternoon. The most powerful praise, however, came from a classmate who pulled her aside, confided that she had also been raped, commended Cassandra on her courage, and thanked Cassandra for the encouragement to no longer hide what had been done to her. Cassandra's rate of progress in therapy accelerated exponentially after this experience. She began to experience her trauma as something that was behind her, not what currently defined her. The knowledge that she had helped a fellow survivor was so reinforcing that she briefly considered shifting her career to rape counseling, but later decided to continue in the field in which she had already trained.

Cassandra is now doing well and is seen only once or twice a year for follow-up. After reading the preceding case description before giving her consent for its inclusion in this chapter, Cassandra reported intense pride in her progress and in the ability to help others by sharing her story. She admitted that an administrator at her school had previously asked if she would tell her story to the whole student body but she had deferred doing so indefinitely. Reading the draft for this chapter led her to decide to call him to say she was ready to speak, and she became enthusiastic about having an opportunity to encourage others that trauma can be overcome. She confided that, while she would not wish a rape on anyone, she is glad in some ways that she did experience trauma, because it has made her a stronger person than she had ever been before.

In the preceding examples, the help extended to others shared clear thematic content with the trauma. However, the link does not have to be so obvious to still be relevant to the patient.

Case Study: Roger

Roger is spearheading a faith-based prison ministry for substance abusers. His personal trauma did not involve crime or addiction. However, he reports that his trauma history helps him relate to inmates who have also known great hardship and it gives his testimony credibility in their eyes.

Similar issues are evident in the case of John.

Case Study: John

John witnessed a phenomenal number of casualties in Vietnam. After intensive individual exposure therapy, his symptoms receded to a chronic but manageable level. Peers in his therapy group look up to him, and he became the unofficial timekeeper. During a past restructuring of treatment groups, an attempt had been made to designate senior group members such as John to be mentors for newcomers. When formally designated in that role, however, John and others became shy, taking less of a leadership role instead of more. However, when situations present naturally that call for his leadership, he rises to the challenge.

Through situations unrelated to John's PTSD, his adult children have been exposed to some gruesome events and losses. In each case, he has provided a sounding board and encouraged the child to process the trauma and grief. He has confided his ongoing struggles with reexperiencing trauma and pointed to his own life as an example of how to carry on with residual symptoms that remain over time. Reaching out to them has not reduced his own nightmares, but he is comforted to see that his ability to endure suffering has served as a positive model for his children.

The therapist also learned from the model of John and others. Rather than trying to orchestrate leadership roles, the therapist now uses watchful waiting. When the first hint of such leadership emerges naturally, the therapist nurtures it. Therapist-directed leadership assignments are now reserved for narrow tasks (e.g., giving a new patient a tour of the ward). Often, however, a pattern of more spontaneous helping emerges after a few smaller concrete assignments.

The previous examples each arose in the context of ongoing therapy, and the emphasis on life time lines occurred ad hoc. Another alternative is to offer therapies in which the time line is the central focus.

THE BIG PICTURE—LIFE REVIEW

The importance of placing significant events in a coherent context of one's life history has long been a source of psychological interest and study (e.g., Beardslee, 1989, regarding civil rights workers, cancer survivors, and parents of children with affective disorders). Beardslee traced how self-understanding in resilient individuals evolved with age. Over time, participants developed ways to incorporate their experience into their current life phase (e.g., adults teaching their children about their adolescent experiences in the civil rights movement and, later, incorporating the events into an overarching, multigenerational life review).

This process can be particularly difficult when there is self-criticism of decisions made and actions taken. Laufer (1985, pp. 51–52) wrote:

> The veteran of war faces one problem all veterans encounter: catching up on the early adult tasks of career development. However, there is also the added burden of readaptation to the civil society and the incorporation of the war experience into an integrated identity that morally connects the early stages of development to the "warrior" and postwar self. The problem can be seen as the difficulty in answering the question, "Who am I?" after learning more than one wants to know about the question, "What am I capable of?"

Stone (2006, p. 56) concurs,

> A truth that does not receive enough attention is that killing in combat is the beginning of a long journey for most soldiers. At the moment of killing, a soldier may experience relief, excitement, rage, sickness, sadness, exuberance, numbness, or even satisfaction.
>
>   It is in the years that follow that the decision of an instant works itself out within the life of the individual. The vestiges of these intense memories play out in the dreams, marriage, parenting, and work relationships of a former soldier.

The majority of Vietnam veterans in PTSD treatment admit they have "gone over the line"—participating in wartime acts they deemed immoral (Irving, Teifer, & Blake, 1997). Hendin and Haas (1984) suggest that such divergence from their own values may be a risk factor for PTSD. (Existential questioning is not limited to veterans, however. Salter and Stallard, 2004, show that adolescents also revise their philosophy of life and self after civilian traumas.)

FORGIVENESS INTERVENTIONS

Enright and Fitzgibbons (2000, p. 24) provide a definition of forgiveness, derived from the work of North (1987), that has excellent clinical utility. Their definition differs from popular notions of forgiveness and is a much more workable goal for trauma survivors than many popular versions. The definition, explained at length in Enright and Fitzgibbons (2000) and Enright (2001) focuses on the deliberate decision to abandon resentment and adopt an attitude of beneficence (wishing the guilty party well). It provides as helpful a model for self-forgiveness as for forgiveness of others. Their definition is most helpful, perhaps, in what it excludes. Forgiveness does not pardon, condone, justify, or forget the offense. It does not allow for getting even. It does not require reconciliation or even positive feelings for the other person(s).

Across patient populations, the use of forgiveness interventions has been projected to remain steady or increase during this decade (Norcross, Hedges, & Prochaska, 2002). Such interventions can be particularly applicable after trauma. Many individuals with PTSD are rigidly (self-) condemning, often unable to grant themselves or others any credit for how overwhelming the situation was at the time, as in the case of Bill. Alternatively, others rigidly deny any ambivalence about their own behavior during the trauma, even though their functioning and symptoms are inconsistent with such peace of mind. Inability to forgive self and others correlates with the severity of PTSD and depression (Witvliet, Phipps, Feldman, & Beckham, 2004). Forgiveness interventions have been found to increase forgiveness and hope, and reduce anxiety and depression in trauma survivors (Freedman & Enright, 1996).

Compared to survivors without PTSD, those with PTSD are more likely to experience a change (usually a reduction) in their religiosity (Falsetti, Resick, & Davis, 2003). Connor, Davidson, and Lee (2003) found spirituality and anger were associated with poor adjustment. Trauma survivors, because of the events they have endured, often report a spiritual hostility or sense of abandonment by the God they previously trusted. Forgiveness of Man toward God and God toward Man is often an issue.

Case Study: Todd

Todd came back from Iraq with a lot of bitterness about the things he had seen and reluctantly done. Previously active in his faith community, he returned furious at God for allowing the whole situation. His faith was further strained when his prayers for relief from his anger and nightmares seemingly went unanswered. He stopped attending church, refused to pray with his children, and prohibited his children from attending church with neighbors. This bitterness remained long after exposure therapy reduced most of his symptoms and cognitive therapy diminished other negative thoughts.

Focusing discussion on the present (what he had lost in losing his positive relationship with God) rather than on the past (how God had failed him) enabled him to discuss the topic without accentuating his bitterness. First, he decided he was being unfair to deprive his children of the faith he had previously enjoyed, and he allowed them to return to church with others. Gradually, he began to separate his ongoing spiritual questions about the trauma from other aspects of his relationship with God. He began to look at the balance of things for which he is grateful versus the hardships he had and continues to endure. Therapy began to focus on nurturing the positive experiences to increase the grateful side of the ledger. As this was accomplished, he could retain questions about the trauma and his disability, but forgo the bitterness that had previously accompanied these. He has not resolved why certain things occur, but he can now accept that they do occur this way and acknowledges that he wants to resume a relationship with God. The process of fully forgiving God is still ongoing, but the anger is gone, prayer has resumed, and Todd has attended church a few times.

LIFE APPRAISAL GROUP

Although shame, guilt, forgiveness of self and forgiveness of others are common issues in trauma therapy, our clinic has encountered resistance when offering group interventions under these labels. We have had more success packaging these topics under the broader heading of *life appraisal*. The popularity of the topic when it is framed this way is consistent with Fontana and Rosenheck's (2005) report that restoration of meaning is what predicts treatment seeking for trauma-related distress. We have had moderate success covering these topics in a time-limited outpatient group. However, the setting in which the group has been most successful is in our 7-week residential treatment program. It is offered as a three- or four-session series on Friday afternoons during the latter weeks of the cohort admission. Patients have found it helps them shift from the war focus of exposure-based therapy and the problem focus of skills training. It thus sets a positive tone for the weekend at home, bolstering motivation to follow through on individual weekend goals that were developed during other classes earlier in the week.

To set the framework for the group, the therapist begins the first session by giving each participant a handout listing the following questions:

- How do you define a good life/a good person?
- Have you lived a good life? Do you consider yourself a good person?
- What things did you consider in deciding how to rate your life and yourself?
- Is this list different than the list you would have identified when you were younger?
- Do others (family, peers, society) consider these same factors, or do they rate you by different criteria?
- Is there an ultimate standard by which you believe your life will be judged?
- Where do your views come from regarding what is important about how a person lives?
  —From significant individuals in your life? Who influenced you most?
  —From experiences? What were the significant events or turning points?
- If there are negative things that you hope no one ever finds out about you, how do you deal with that fact?
- How do you deal with past or ongoing actions about which you are ashamed, embarrassed, or feel guilty?
- Overall, are you satisfied with how you and/or others rate your life?
- If you are not satisfied, what can you change about the future that will shift the balance of your life toward a more satisfying rating?

(*Note:* It may be necessary to modify this list or use an entirely different set of questions in different cultures; Fernando, 2005.)

Participants are informed that the questions are provided to stimulate discussion. Some group members are eager to list their answers to every point right away. However, the group is encouraged to spend the first hour-long session in a discussion of the first question: How do you define a good life/a good person? Among Iraq and Vietnam veterans, a strong group cohort effect has been observed that spans war eras. If the first respondent mentions values such as treating others kindly, others often emphasize individual values such as trustworthiness. Conversely, if discussion leads off with remarks about family and relationships, others tend to follow with specific family activities (time with children) or family accomplishments (successful children), rather than individual values. The therapist can offset whichever bias a particular group manifests by stating that other groups have suggested additional elements and asking whether participants think those elements play a role in their own conceptualization. Group members are often surprised to discover that, using their own definition, they have been much more successful than they previously felt.

An occasional group member mentions money or acquisitions as central to a good life. Others usually acknowledge that a certain minimum level of possessions facilitates other life goals, but the consensus has consistently been that values or relationships take primacy. In fact, the regret that members most frequently report is having devoted too much time trying to make money, at the cost of not being with their children during formative years and sacrificing intimacy in marriage. Group members are intrigued to learn that such trade-offs are common in normal life span development (e.g., Schultz & Heckhausen, 1996) and not specific to PTSD. The social isolation inherent in PTSD has often prevented group members from discovering this on their own.

Subsequent sessions focus on where group members learned to value the elements they list as important. As they talk about formative life events and relationships, they have the opportunity to examine how they have changed over time. Inevitably, there is discussion of how their trauma experience has led them to a somewhat different view of life than is held by family and peers who have not been exposed to such major trauma. There is also discussion of how young and inexperienced many of the members were at the time of the trauma. These acknowledgments prime the group for a productive discussion of shame, guilt, and forgiveness of self and others. Conducting the group with patients who have already developed strong peer rapport facilitates such discussion (outpatient groups made less progress than the residential groups, and early in the residential admission was less effective than later in the admission).

Many cohorts readily use these discussions as a springboard for attitudinal and behavior change, increasing their commitment to present and future goals. Some cohorts need more direct prodding. In such cohorts, the therapist uses writing assignments between sessions to nudge the group toward action. Patients can be asked to write in more detail about topics on the discussion list. Additional topics can be added as relevant to the presenting case (e.g., What experiences brought you the most joy before your trauma? Since your trauma, what experiences have brought you the most joy? What are your hopes for the future? What can you do to make these come true?).

The group can help patients accept what is immutable history, and begin to separate that from current and future options that remain open and flexible. In this respect, it shares perspective with acceptance and commitment therapy (Hayes, 2005) and other cognitive-behavioral approaches. Individuals come to such acceptance at different paces, and it is important to respect where the patient is in the recovery process. People should not be rushed in addressing these issues (Tedeschi, Calhoun, & Engdahl, 2001). Most veterans have given this group positive reviews, but one participant was particularly critical. Interestingly, when the critical individual returned for a subsequent admission, he reported that this group was the treatment component he had thought about most after his initial discharge, and he rated it as the most valuable part of his second admission.

This life appraisal group bears a strong resemblance to Fava's well-being therapy (e.g., Fava et al., 1998). Their approach is focused on moments of well-being that occurred during the past 1 to 2 weeks, whereas our group takes a wide-angle life review. In Fava et al. (1998), eight 40-minute group sessions address the following topics: examination of the situational context for episodes of subjective well-being (2 sessions), use of techniques of rational-emotive and cognitive restructuring to modify automatic/irrational thoughts and beliefs that short-circuit episodes of well-being (3 sessions); identification of deficits in specific dimensions of well-being, "stimulate awareness of personal growth and recovery" (p. 479) and reinforce behaviors that promote well-being (via mastery/pleasure tasks and exposure to feared situations; final 3 sessions). The therapy includes self-monitoring episodes of well-being between sessions, and assertiveness training and problem solving are often incorporated. Readers interested in more detail may want to consult Fava (1999) or Fava and Ruini (2003). A four-session condensed version of the intervention is presented in Fava et al. (2005). Like our life appraisal group, Fava's well-being therapy is conceptualized as a supplemental technique to be applied in the residual stage of the disorder after more symptom-based therapy has already been conducted.

REFRAMING DEVELOPMENTALLY RELATED RELAPSES

As trauma survivors age, they may experience periods of increased symptoms due to shifting coping strategies and new development tasks. Learning to deal with physical decline, failure experiences and other negative events is part of normative aging (Shultz & Heckhausen, 1996). The challenge can be accentuated in trauma survivors when developmental issues are analogous to elements of the trauma experience (frailty, dependency, loss, isolation, facing death; Shmotkin & Lomranz, 1998). Helping survivors predict or interpret such problems within a normative developmental framework can reduce anxiety and discouragement.

From youth through middle age, many survivors use exertion—exercise, labor, busyness—to cope with trauma. Many work to exhaustion to suppress problems with sleep onset and nightmares. By filling every moment of the day, there is no time left for ruminations. As cardiac conditions, back injuries, or other ailments force a slower pace, such individuals lose a primary coping strategy. Retirement in general can also unleash intrusive thoughts as more idle time becomes available. Many cases of relapse or "delayed onset" PTSD follow this trajectory.

Trauma also can disrupt normative developmental sequences, requiring the individual to deal with stressors that are beyond the norm for their age. The relatively narrow age-band from which military personnel are recruited sharpens the focus on this phenomenon among veterans. Using an Eriksonian model of development, Wilson (1980) observed the disruption in developmental progression created by combat during late adolescence and early adulthood. Under normal conditions, an individual would experience a linear progression in which each developmental task could be mastered before moving to the next task. In contrast, young troops undergo an accelerated but fragmented developmental process as they simultaneously struggle with the developmental tasks of identity, intimacy, generativity, and integrity. Based on this conceptualization, Wilson (in 1980) predicted with keen accuracy many of the phase-related points at which Vietnam veterans' trauma would likely be reactivated by subsequent developmental tasks. When not viewed within a developmental framework, such increases in trauma-related thoughts and images tend to be viewed by veterans, families, and clinicians as a relapse. However, viewed through a developmental lens, such exacerbations demonstrate that these survivors are in the process of integrating their trauma past with their current developmental tasks.

Case Study: Leroy

Currently in his early 60s, Leroy—like his nonmilitary peers—has reached an age where the number of deaths of family members and friends is increasing exponentially. He had not experienced such a frequency of losses since his combat days, and finds himself reflecting back on those days. At that time, the pressures of war demanded that any mourning be truncated and concentration had to be quickly redirected back to personal survival. Now he finds himself out of step with nonmilitary peers who have learned more gradually and at a more mature age how to grieve openly and adaptively. Nonmilitary peers and family view him as hard-hearted due to his "they're gone, get over it" demeanor. As he tries to make sense of and express his own contemporary grief, he fears the floodgates of past grief starting to give way. His efforts at emotional control become all the more rigid as images of the past haunt his dreams and ruminations with increasing frequency and intensity. He fears that he is losing his sanity, and that anxiety further fuels his symptoms.

Dan's current situation parallels Leroy's but is further complicated by the fact that several of the friends he has recently lost have been fellow veterans who died of cancers or complications of diabetes. Dan suspects Agent Orange played a role. This thought reignites old anger at "the system" and elicits worry about his own health status.

Reframing Leroy's fears within a normative developmental context can quickly vent the fears that are fueling such a spiral of distress, paring the issues back to the narrower task of grieving. Often, such a change in cognitive appraisal can help survivors appreciate the skills they learned from the earlier trauma, enabling them to share their strength to endure with others. Leroy was later able to help his son process the trauma and grief of witnessing a family suicide. In contrast, Dan is not only facing normative losses, but has a new combat-related stress to adjust to—the idea that Vietnam may still pose a threat to him. Helping him separate the normative from the trauma-related issues can make both more manageable.

THERAPIST PREPAREDNESS

As professionals interested in psychological trauma, many readers are probably accustomed to addressing confessions of atrocities, spiritual angst, and other complex topics that survivors present in therapy. This can be foreign turf for therapists whose background is with other populations. It can be particularly challenging for students who are not only relocating to a different geographic region but also moving from an academic milieu with one set of political and spiritual views into a community with quite different views.

It is important for therapists to consider their own readiness to deal with the issues that will arise (Fontana & Rosenheck, 2005; Sanderson & Linehan, 1999). Houston's (1999) recommendations for dealing with angry dying patients are applicable to addressing life-evaluation issues with nonterminal trauma survivors. Classic articles by Marin (1981) and Haley (1974) can help therapists think through the challenge of treating patients who have overstepped the moral boundaries that apply in peacetime, but that may be much harder to define under combat fire. It is also helpful to recall that people commit heinous acts for much more mundane reasons, as obedience experiments demonstrate (Blass, 1991). At the same time, the therapist must have antennae tuned to recognize individuals who fabricate dramatic stories of trauma, keeping in mind that nearly one third of people who present for specialized therapy for combat-related PTSD were never actually exposed to combat and some were never even in the military (Frueh et al., 2005).

There will not be unanimity in how the actions of war are interpreted and evaluated among troops and veterans, perhaps even less so among civilian clinicians. Veteran-psychologist Figley (in Johnson & Hampson, 2006) commented on an alleged killing of civilians at Haditha, Iraq, that "the only thing that surprised him about the Haditha reports was 'that anyone was surprised. This is what happens in war.'" Veteran-author Caputo (in Caputo, Solis, Gerecht, & Clark, 2006, p. 42) stated, "Incidents like this [alleged killing of civilians] are not just likely; they're inevitable in insurgencies . . . that kind of war can bring out a psychopathic streak in men of otherwise normal behavior and impulses." High-ranking military contributors to the forum disagreed. Veteran-psychologist Stone (2006, p. 56) writes, "On the home front, most noncombatants . . . rarely make the connection of their own personal involvement in these moments. The soldier is only the tip of the spear. The voters and taxpayers do not see their participation as meaningful, yet without them, young soldiers would not be in deadly positions that require killing." Arguing the other side of the issue, civilian military advisor Wessely (2005) asserts that civilian therapists may be deterred by shame and guilt associated with just such an awareness.

When veterans confide their past to us, "We aren't just counselors; we're almost priests. They come to us for absolution as well as help" (Marin, 1981, quoting Shad Meshad). Cross-sectional research shows that openness to religious change correlates with posttraumatic growth (Calhoun, Cann, Tedeschi, & McMillan, 2000). Faith is a topic veterans often want or need to discuss, particularly since values and beliefs provide the context for cognitive appraisal of the trauma (Taylor, 1999). However, many therapists are poorly equipped for this task. Reports following Hurricane Katrina (Law, 2006) describe disaster responders as ill-prepared to deal with the religious values of evacuees. Perhaps this is not surprising, as Brawer, Handal, Fabricatore, Roberts and Wajda-Johnson (2002) report that psychology graduate programs offer very little training in how to address clients' religious and spiritual issues. Even though two thirds of medical schools offer classes on faith and spirituality (Puchalski, 2001), many physicians are ambivalent about addressing this topic (Krause, 2004). Interfacing with local clergy is encouraged (Eisenman et al., 2006; Krause, 2004; Lyons, 2001; Taylor, 2001). McMinn, Aikins, and Lish (2003) offer a general discussion on how to promote effective collaboration. However, only 52% to 60% of Veterans Affairs medical centers surveyed by Suris, Davis, Kashner, Gillaspy, and Petty (1998) had a chaplain available, and only 28% to 31% of total patients had contact with the chaplain. Thus, trauma therapists need to be open to and prepared for discussion of faith-related issues. It is important that the therapist does not impose personal cultural norms or spiritual beliefs (Taylor, 1999; Tedeschi et al., 2001), yet this separation can be complex (Fontana & Rosenheck, 2005) and even spokespersons on cultural and spiritual sensitivity dismiss certain beliefs as "rigid personality defences [sic]" (Taylor, 2001).

Complex moral, political, and spiritual issues are hard to avoid in trauma therapy. They can be addressed effectively in both group and individual therapies, but doing so can be challenging. If the therapist differs from the patient in cultural perspective (e.g., is a nonveteran or is of another faith or political persuasion), consider whether therapy might benefit from incorporating a broader range of perspectives (through reading, consultation, supervision, cotherapy, group therapy, etc.). Group therapy offers a particularly powerful and efficient tool for survivors to explore multiple perspectives on controversial issues and come to terms with their own choices and actions.

SUMMARY

Getting sufficient resources to traumatized veterans is an international problem, whether in systems such as the United States VA medical centers or in countries such as Britain where veterans are blended into the "universal access" system. Iversen et al. (2005) reported that 72% of help-seeking British veterans received care that was limited to what their primary care team could provide (largely medication management and nondirective counseling). Only 4% received cognitive behavioral therapy. While the separate care systems offered to American and Australian veterans may facilitate more specialized care for PTSD, resources are often stretched. Thus, therapy that aims to promote growth and does not stop at mere recovery may at first glance seem extravagant. However, Fava et al. (1998) cite evidence that quality of life predicts recurrence of depression better than symptom ratings. Furthermore, the framework outlined in this chapter can often be accomplished during routine follow-up visits or in an efficient group format and may promote a productive focus on the more traditional aspects of PTSD treatment. While we have not manualized our implementation of these ideas to a degree that would allow systematic empirical testing, initial patient reports and clinical observation have been favorable.

Summary Points

- Helping trauma survivors place their experiences and reactions within a developmental framework is an important supplement to standard cognitive-behavioral therapies. Although standard interventions such as exposure therapy effectively reduce symptoms, additional interventions may be needed to promote growth.
- A balance is needed between honoring the survivor's history, facilitating a robust life in the present, and promoting positive planning for the future.

- Cross-cultural awareness is crucial. In working with veterans, the culture of the military must be considered along with other cultural groups to which the patient belongs.
- Clinicians (and their administrators) need increased training and increased openness to effectively address the conflicts of faith that survivors often experience.
- Vicarious/secondary traumatization and compassion fatigue are familiar concepts among trauma therapists. We must also embrace the inverse of that, which is "vicarious posttraumatic growth." As we serve our patients, we are also served by them in the life lessons that their endurance and heartrending choices can impart.

REFERENCES

American Psychiatric Association. (2000). *Diagnostic and statistical manual of mental disorders* (4th ed., text rev.). Washington, DC: Author.

Beardslee, W. R. (1989). The role of self-understanding in resilient individuals: The development of a perspective. *American Journal of Orthopsychiatry, 59,* 266–278.

Blass, T. (1991). Understanding behavior in the Milgram Obedience Experiment: The role of personality, situations, and their interactions. *Journal of Personality and Social Psychology, 60,* 398–413.

Bonanno, G. A. (2004). Loss, trauma, and human resilience: Have we underestimated the human capacity to thrive after extremely aversive events? *American Psychologist, 59,* 20–28.

Bradshaw, S. L., Jr., Ohlde, C. D., & Horne, J. B. (1991). The love of war: Vietnam and the traumatized veteran. *Bulletin of the Menninger Clinic, 55,* 96–103.

Bramsen, I., van der Ploeg, H. M., & Boers, M. (2006). Posttraumatic stress in aging World War II survivors after a fireworks disaster: A controlled prospective study. *Journal of Traumatic Stress, 19,* 291–300.

Brawer, P. A., Handal, P. J., Fabricatore, A. N., Roberts, R., & Wajda-Johnson, V. A. (2002). Training and education in religion/spirituality within APA-accredited clinical psychology programs. *Professional Psychology: Research and Practice, 33,* 203–206.

Calhoun, L. G., Cann, A., Tedeschi, R. G., & McMillan, J. (2000). A correlational test of the relationship between posttraumatic growth, religion, and cognitive processing. *Journal of Traumatic Stress, 13,* 521–527.

Caputo, P., Solis, G., Gerecht, R. M., & Clark, W. (2006, June 12). Rules of engagement [Forum]. *Time, 167*(24), 42.

Connor, K. M., Davidson, J. R. T., & Lee, L. (2003). Spirituality, resilience, and anger in survivors of violent trauma: A community survey. *Journal of Traumatic Stress, 16,* 487–494.

Eisenman, D., Weine, S., Green, B., de Jong, J., Rayburn, N., Ventevogel, P., et al. (2006). The ISTSS/Rand guidelines on mental health training of primary healthcare providers for trauma-exposed populations in conflict-affected countries. *Journal of Traumatic Stress, 19,* 5–17.

Enright, R. D. (2001). *Forgiveness is a choice: A step-by-step process for resolving anger and restoring hope.* Washington, DC: American Psychological Association.

Enright, R. D., & Fitzgibbons, R. P. (2000). *Helping clients forgive: An empirical guide for resolving anger and restoring hope.* Washington, DC: American Psychological Association.

Erikson, E. H. (1963). *Childhood and society* (2nd ed.). Toronto, Ontario, Canada: Norton. (Original work published 1950)

Falsetti, S. A., Resick, P. A., & Davis, J. L. (2003). Changes in religious beliefs following trauma. *Journal of Traumatic Stress, 16,* 391–398.

Fava, G. A. (1999). Well-being therapy: Conceptual and technical issues. *Psychotherapy and Psychosomatics, 68,* 171–179.

Fava, G. A., Rafanelli, C., Cazzaro, M., Conti, S., & Grandi, S. (1998). Well-being therapy: A novel psychotherapeutic approach for residual symptoms of affective disorders. *Psychological Medicine, 28,* 475–480.

Fava, G. A., & Ruini, C. (2003). Development and characteristics of a well-being enhancing psychotherapeutic strategy: Well-being therapy. *Journal of Behavior Therapy and Experimental Psychiatry, 34,* 45–63.

Fava, G. A., Ruini, C., Rafanelli, C., Finos, L., Salmaso, L., Mangelli, L., et al. (2005). Well-being therapy of generalized anxiety disorder. *Psychotherapy and Psychosomatics, 74,* 26–30.

Fernando, G. A. (2005). Finding meaning after the Tsunami disaster: Recovery and resilience in Sri Lanka. *Traumatic StressPoints, 19*(1), 1, 12.

Foa, E. B., Keane, T. M., & Friedman, M. J. (2000). *Effective treatments for PTSD: Practice guidelines from the international society for traumatic stress studies.* New York: Guilford Press.

Fontana, A., & Rosenheck, R. (2005). The role of loss of meaning in the pursuit of treatment for posttraumatic stress disorder. *Journal of Traumatic Stress, 18,* 133–136.

Freedman, S. R., & Enright, R. D. (1996). Forgiveness as an intervention goal with incest survivors. *Journal of Consulting and Clinical Psychology, 64,* 983–992.

Frueh, B. C., Elhai, J. D., Grubaugh, A. L., Monnier, J., Kashdan, T. B., Sauvageot, J. A., et al. (2005). Documented combat exposure of U.S. veterans seeking treatment for combat-related post-traumatic stress disorder. *British Journal of Psychiatry, 186,* 467–472.

Haley, S. A. (1974). When the patient reports atrocities: Specific treatment considerations of the Vietnam veteran. *Archives of General Psychiatry, 30,* 191–196.

Hayes, S. (2005). *Acceptance and Commitment Therapy (ACT).* Retrieved December 6, 2006, from www.acceptanceandcommitmenttherapy.com/act/.

Hendin, H., & Haas, A. P. (1984). Combat adaptations of Vietnam veterans without posttraumatic stress disorders. *American Journal of Psychiatry, 141,* 956–960.

Houston, R. E. (1999). The angry dying patient. *Primary Care Companion Journal of Clinical Psychiatry, 1*(1), 5–8. Retrieved June 1, 2006, from www.psychiatrist.com/pcc/pccpdf/v01n01/v01n0102.pdf.

Irving, L. M., Teifer, L., & Blake, D. D. (1997). Hope, coping, and social support in combat-related posttraumatic stress disorder. *Journal of Traumatic Stress, 10,* 465–479.

Iverson, A., Dyson, C., Smith, N., Greenberg, N., Walwyn, R., Unwin, C., et al. (2005). 'Goodbye and good luck': The mental health needs and treatment experiences of British ex-service personnel. *British Journal of Psychiatry, 186,* 480–486.

Johnson, K., & Hampson, R. (2006, June 14). Combat stress takes toll. *USA Today.* Retrieved June 15, 2006, from www.usatoday.com/news/world /2006–06–14-iraq-stress_x.htm.

Kessler, R. C., Sonnega, A., Bromet, E., Hughes, M., & Nelson, C. B. (1995). Posttraumatic stress disorder in the National Comorbidity Study. *Archives of General Psychiatry, 52,* 1048–1060.

Koss, M. P., & Burkhart, B. R. (1989). A conceptual analysis of rape victimization: Long-term effects and implications for treatment. *Psychology of Women Quarterly, 13,* 27–40.

Krause, N. (2004). Religion, aging, and health: Exploring new frontiers in medical care. *Southern Medical Journal, 97,* 1215–1222.

Laufer, R. S. (1985). War trauma and human development: The Viet Nam experience. In S. M. Sonnenberg, A. S. Blank, & J. A. Talbott (Eds.), *The trauma of war: Stress and recovery in Viet Nam veterans* (pp. 31–55). Washington, DC: American Psychiatric Press.

Law, B. M. (2006). Katrina's cultural lessons. *Monitor on Psychology, 37*(9), 40–42.

Lyons, J. A. (1991). Self-mutilation by a man with posttraumatic stress disorder. *Journal of Nervous and Mental Diseases, 179,* 505–507.

Lyons, J. A. (2001). Partnering with clergy in school-based interventions following a rural school shooting. *Texas Journal of Rural Health, 19*(2), 22–29.

Marin, P. (1981, November). Dealing with moral pain. *Psychology Today,* 68–80.

McMinn, M. R., Aikins, D. C., & Lish, R. A. (2003). Basic and advanced competence in collaborating with clergy. *Professional Psychology: Research and Practice, 34,* 197–202.

Nice, D. S., Garland, C. F., Hilton, S. M., Baggett, J. C., & Mitchell, R. E. (1996). Long-term health outcomes and medical effects of torture among U.S. Navy prisoners of war in Vietnam. *Journal of the American Medical Association, 276,* 375–381.

Norcross, J. C., Hedges, M., & Prochaska, J. O. (2002). The face of 2010: A Delphi poll on the future of psychotherapy. *Professional Psychology: Research and Practice, 33,* 316–322.

North, J. (1987). Wrongdoing and forgiveness. *Philosophy, 62,* 499–508.

Puchalaski, C. M. (2001). The role of spirituality in health care. *Proceedings (Baylor University Medical Center), 14*(4), 352–357. Retrieved October 31, 2006, from www.pubmedcentral.nih.gov/articlerender.fcgi?artid=1305900/.

Rafanelli, C., Park, S. K., Ruini, C., Ottolini, F., Cazzaro, M., & Fava, G. A. (2000). Rating well-being and distress. *Stress Medicine, 16,* 55–61.

Ruini, C., Ottolini, F., Rafanelli, C., Tossani, E., Ryff, C. D., & Fava, G. A. (2003). The relationship of psychological well-being to distress and personality. *Psychotherapy and Psychosomatics, 72,* 268–275.

Salter, E., & Stallard, P. (2004). Posttraumatic growth in child survivors of a road traffic accident. *Journal of Traumatic Stress, 17*, 335–340.

Sanderson, C., & Linehan, M. M. (1999). Acceptance and forgiveness. In W. R. Miller (Ed.), *Integrating spirituality into treatment: Resources for practitioners* (pp. 199–216). Washington, DC: American Psychological Association.

Seligman, M. E. P., Rashid, T., & Parks, A. C. (2006). Positive psychotherapy. *American Psychologist, 61*, 774–788.

Shmotkin, D., Blumstein, T., & Modan, B. (2003). Tracing long-term effects of early trauma: A broad-scope view of Holocaust survivors in late life. *Journal of Consulting and Clinical Psychology, 71*, 223–234.

Shmotkin, D., & Lomranz, J. (1998). Subjective well-being among Holocaust survivors: An examination of overlooked differentiations. *Journal of Personality and Social Psychology, 75*, 141–155.

Shultz, R., & Heckhausen, J. (1996). A lifespan model of successful aging. *American Psychologist, 51*, 702–714.

Stone, P. (2006, May). Post-traumatic faith: Understanding the plight of Christians who have killed in combat. *Christianity Today*, p. 56. Retrieved June 2, 2006, from www.christianitytoday.com/ct/2/0/06/21.56.html.

Suris, A. M., Davis, L. L., Kashner, T. M., Gillaspy, J. A., & Petty, F. (1998). A survey of sexual trauma treatment provided by VA medical centers. *Psychiatric Services, 49*, 382–384.

Taylor, A. J. W. (1999). Value conflict arising from disaster. *Australasian Journal of Disaster and Trauma Studies* (2). Retrieved June 1, 2006, from www.massey.ac.nz/~trauma/issues/1999–2/taylor.htm.

Taylor, A. J. W. (2001). Spirituality and personal values: Neglected components of trauma treatment. *Traumatology, 7*(3). Retrieved June 1, 2006, from www.massey.ac.nz/~trauma/issues/1999–2/taylor.htm.

Tedeschi, R. G., Calhoun, L., & Engdahl, B. (2001). Opportunities for growth in survivors of trauma. *National Center for Posttraumatic Stress Disorder Clinical Quarterly, 10*, 23–25.

Wessely, S. (2005). War stories: Invited commentary on. . . . Documented combat exposure of U.S. veterans seeking treatment for combat-related post-traumatic stress disorder. *British Journal of Psychiatry, 186*, 473–475.

Wilson, J. P. (1980). Conflict, stress, and growth: The effects of war on psychosocial development among Vietnam veterans. In C. R. Figley & S. Leventman (Eds.), *Strangers at home: Vietnam veterans since the war* (pp. 123–165). New York: Praeger.

Witvliet, C. V. O., Phipps, K. A., Feldman, M. E., & Beckham, J. C. (2004). Posttraumatic mental and physical health correlates of forgiveness and religious coping in military veterans. *Journal of Traumatic Stress, 17*, 269–273.

CHAPTER 13

Recovery from Brain Injury and Positive Rehabilitation Practice

JOANNA COLLICUTT MCGRATH

I THINK I HAVE always been a positive psychologist. In the summer of 1977, as a rather reluctant and naïve clinical psychology trainee, I began a placement on a rehabilitation unit that served people with severe long-term mental illness. Early on in the placement, I asked my supervisor, Geoff Shepherd, how the gamut of behavior therapy techniques that I was rapidly acquiring could be applied to achieve a cure for these people. He laughed and said something along the lines of, "You've got a long way to go if you can't see that we're not in the business of curing. We're in the business of helping them build some sort of life."

That conversation opened my eyes. I recognized that my previous vague unease with clinical psychology had been about its apparent emphasis on treating pathology rather than building life. The psychological management of acute distress seemed to be informed by a negative "get a grip" philosophy focused on reducing symptoms. I started to see that clinical practice directed at the longer-term management of chronic conditions was informed by a more holistic, socially and physically contextualized positive "get a life" philosophy. I therefore embraced rehabilitation psychology with enthusiasm, finally settling on a career in the rehabilitation of people with acquired brain injury (ABI).

In recent years, the unease with symptom-focused psychological therapy that I struggled with as a new clinician has been eloquently articulated by Martin Seligman (e.g., Seligman, 2002), and is a central tenet of the positive psychology movement. Rehabilitation should be an ideal setting within which to apply positive psychology (Emmons, 1996; Siegert, McPherson, & Taylor, 2004), composed as it is of a number of positive therapies aimed at

259

building skills and strengthening physical and psychological resilience. Nevertheless, brain injury rehabilitation presents particular challenges to patients, families, and professionals that can make a positive attitude almost unsustainable at times (Gans, 1983, p. 178). This chapter considers the question of whether insights from positive psychology, particularly the area of growth and resilience in adversity, can be helpfully applied to the situation of people recovering from ABI.

ACQUIRED BRAIN INJURY

Anyone can acquire a brain injury, and at any age. The most common causes of ABI are closed head injury (due to road traffic accidents, assaults, or falls), stroke, subarachnoid haemorrhage, cerebral hypoxia (secondary to prolonged cardiac arrest, near drowning), hypoglycaemia, carbon monoxide poisoning, and cerebral infections (meningitis, encephalitis). These sorts of events occur suddenly and without warning, often under traumatic conditions. When the brain is involved, almost any combination of cognitive and physical disabilities can result. (For a detailed review from a psychological perspective see Collicutt McGrath, 2007a.) There is often an initial period of rapid recovery followed by a much slower phase. For all but the most minor brain injuries, complete recovery of previous levels of function is never achieved.

Thus, ABI is a life-threatening event that combines initial acute trauma with emerging chronic adversity. This is because primary physical disabilities have a secondary effect on employment status, financial position, and social relationships. These features are also characteristic of some other conditions, for instance, spinal cord injury. What makes ABI distinctive and especially challenging is its psychological attributes; the associated cognitive and emotional processing deficits. A person with ABI is likely to be troubled by major problems in areas such as memory, concentration, language processing, empathic feeling, social skills, and spatial orientation. He will thus have reduced psychological resources with which to make sense of his new situation (much of which is itself psychological in nature). Perhaps the most distressing aspect of ABI is the effect that the combination of losses has on the sense of personal identity (Jackson & Manchester, 2001). A patient with ABI may be experienced by both herself and others as a totally different person. This is one of the things that leads to relationship breakdown in the years following the brain injury (Oddy, 1995). In contrast, in my work with people with spinal cord injury, I have often heard them and their relatives express their gratitude that, despite their disabilities and all the problems these bring, the patient is essentially the same *person* as before. This source of comfort is not available for those with ABI.

EMOTIONAL IMPACT OF ABI

It is not surprising that psychological distress is thought to be common in people with ABI, though estimating prevalence rates is fraught with methodological problems (see, e.g., Burvill et al., 1995a, 1995b; Deb, Lyons, Koutzoutkis, Ali, & McCarthy, 1999; Fann, Katon, Uomoto, & Esselman, 1995; Silver et al., 2001). It has finally been recognized that people with traumatic brain injury can develop posttraumatic stress disorder even if they cannot recall details of the traumatic event (Bryant, Marosszeky, Crooks, & Gurka, 2000; McMillan, Williams, & Bryant, 2003), almost certainly due to the processing of fear by an implicit memory system (LeDoux, 1992). In addition, rates of family distress and breakdown are high (Marsh, Kersel, Havill, & Sleigh, 1998; Webster, Daisley, & King, 1999).

The development of systematic psychotherapeutic approaches to the emotional distress and psychological problems faced by people with ABI is in its infancy.[1] This is for two main reasons. First, it has often been assumed (wrongly) that much of the distress experienced and expressed by people with ABI is a direct result of brain changes, is psychologically meaningless, and is therefore not amenable to a psychotherapeutic approach. Second, it is difficult (though not impossible) to use talking therapies with people who have very poor language skills, forget much of what is said to them, or are unable to sustain concentration for more than a few minutes.

Furthermore, the flavor of many psychotherapeutic approaches has been markedly negative. There has been an enormous—and not fully justified—starting assumption that people with ABI are likely to have very poor insight into their situation and current level of abilities—to be inhabiting something of a "fool's paradise."[2] This has been seen as a cognitive deficit that is at least in part a direct result of organic brain changes—a symptom to be treated before any further psychotherapeutic work can be done. The result is that much of the psychotherapeutic component of many rehabilitation programs has been aimed at instilling realistic insight at all costs, that is, helping the patient to become aware of and acknowledge his *losses.*

There has been relatively less emphasis on validating the experience of the patient and helping him to become aware of his assets and strengths. Such approaches are often dismissed as a type of "collusion" with the

---

[1] For some examples of a cognitive approach, see Khan-Bourne and Browne, 2003; Kinney, 2001; McGrath and King, 2004. For a more humanistic approach; see Prigatano, 1999, 201–227.

[2] In fact, the situation is highly variable and complex—see Giacino and Cicerone, 1998, for a full discussion.

patient's distorted perspective.[3] Going further and acknowledging net *gains* is simply unheard of.

Some years ago, I carried out a study of the emotional impact of ABI (McGrath, 1998). I wanted to explore the nature of the distress experienced by this group of people. At the time, I thought that even those people who did not have full insight into their situation would nevertheless report distress if given an appropriate opportunity to do so. I also thought that this distress might not conform simply to conventional psychiatric descriptions of anxiety and depressive disorders, and was thus under recognized by clinicians. I therefore presented the 82 ABI patients in my study with an open-ended question: "How have you been feeling (emotionally) over the last week?"

The results indicated a high level of psychological distress, with feelings of frustration, confusion, sadness, and fear most commonly reported, a pattern subsequently noted by other investigators (Prigatano, 1999, p. 33). What I was unprepared for, however, was the amount of *positive* emotion that was also reported. Thirty-five of the 101 responses were exclusively positive. Fourteen of the 44 different adjectives that were used to describe feelings were positive (e.g., optimistic, happy, wanted). The sample of patients was of mixed diagnosis but the positive reports occurred irrespective of diagnosis.

In a separate but related study using the same group of participants, I followed up a subgroup who, early in rehabilitation, reported high levels of distress during an interview or in response to the Hospital Anxiety and Depression Scale (Zigmond & Snaith, 1983). I found that reported distress levels fell and remained low for the majority of these people *once a positive goal-focused rehabilitation program had been implemented*, and this pattern was confirmed by observer ratings (McGrath & Adams, 1999). No other intervention was required to manage their distress. They appeared to be remarkably resilient. This confirmed the impression I had gained as a result of many lengthy interviews. What struck me most in these interviews were the patients' courage, stoicism, ability to generate positive coping responses,[4] and reluctance to trouble professionals with their personal pain. (Of course there were some very visible exceptions!) I began to question the common stereotypes of ABI patients as either weak and vulnerable, or ego-

---

[3] ABI practitioners have something to learn here from practice in the area of dementia, where there is a greater emphasis on validating the experience of the patient (e.g., Kitwood, 1997).

[4] Of 127 coping responses generated in response to an open-ended question about upsetting situations 36 involved positive thinking and 11 involved increased physical effort.

centric and demanding. It seemed that they could just as well be described as strong and self-reliant.

The rates of premorbid mental health problems in people with traumatic brain injury are rather higher than the general population (Jorge, Robinson, Starkstein, & Arndt, 1994). Nevertheless, most people who sustain a brain injury do not have preexisting problems in this area. That is, the majority are psychologically robust. Despite their acquired cognitive and emotional processing problems, they seem to maintain a sense of personal stability or coherence. In confirmation of this, a more recent study in which I was involved reported high scores on the Sense of Coherence-13 Scale (Antonovsky, 1993) in a sample of people with severe ABI (Collicutt McGrath & Linley, 2006).

POSTTRAUMATIC GROWTH

Positive change following trauma and adversity has been demonstrated for a wide range of clinical groups (Linley & Joseph, 2004). The areas in which positive change most typically occurs are personal relationships, self-concept, and life philosophy or spirituality. Because of their cognitive and emotional processing problems, which often impact on social and relationship skills (Hornak et al., 2003; Rolls, Hornak, Wade, & McGrath, 1994), it seems unlikely that people with ABI would be in a position to derive any benefits from their particular trauma and adversity. Yet, the participants in my study, all of whom had severe ABI and most of whom had major physical disabilities, were more psychologically resilient than one might expect. And while the literature on the psychosocial sequelae of severe ABI is largely pessimistic, there are some suggestive exceptions (Adams, 1996; Elliott & Kurylo, 2000).

The first systematic study into positive changes following brain injury was carried out by me in collaboration with Alex Linley (Collicutt McGrath & Linley, 2006). This study was in some respects limited. The total sample size of 21 was small and the majority of participants had ABI of cerebrovascular origin. Therefore, generalizing the findings to people with closed head injury would be unwise. Nevertheless some participants did have closed head injury (see Table 13.1), and all had sustained very severe brain injury resulting in significant cognitive and physical deficits, and had required long periods of in-patient rehabilitation.

The main findings of this study were that the sample achieved high scores on one measure of positive change, the Posttraumatic Growth Inventory (Tedeschi & Calhoun, 1996). Ten participants in the early stages of recovery and resident in a rehabilitation unit (mean 7 months after injury) achieved scores comparable to survivors of accidents and assaults. The

Table 13.1

Participants (*N* = 21) in a Study on Positive Changes Following Brain Injury

	Early Sample	Late Sample
Sex ratio	4 females, 6 males	6 females, 5 males
Diagnoses	8 stroke, 1 closed head injury, 1 subarachnoid haemorrhage	6 stroke, 1 closed head injury, 2 subarachnoid haemorrhage, 1 tumor, 1 hypoxia
Mean age (range)	52 (27–66)	46 (27–63)
Median Barthel* score (range)	13.5 (8–20)	18.0 (4–20)
Mean time since injury (range)	7 months (3–16)	118 months (60–209)

*Barthel Activities of Daily Living Index, a measure of functional independence focusing on self-care and mobility (Collin et al., 1988).

Source: "Posttraumatic Growth Following Acquired Brain Injury: A Preliminary Small Scale Study," by J. Collicutt McGrath and P. A. Linley, 2006, *Brain Injury 20*, 767–773.

other 11 participants, matched with the first sample for age, sex, diagnosis, and disability level (see Table 13.1), had long since completed rehabilitation (mean 118 months after injury). This "Late" sample achieved significantly higher scores, which were also higher than most groups previously studied. The areas where most positive change was reported were "Appreciation of life," "Relating to others," and "Personal strength."

The Posttraumatic Growth Inventory requires the participant to make a judgment about herself compared with the past and implicitly to attribute change to the traumatic event itself. So a participant who is in denial (Taylor 1983; McFarland & Alvaro, 2000) or has problems with self-awareness or memory might achieve high scores. As already noted, people with ABI have been thought to be particularly vulnerable to problems with self-awareness, so interpreting the high scores on this inventory requires caution.

Some strong evidence that the participants in this study were not simply unaware or in denial of the negative impact of their brain injuries is provided by the distribution of scores on the Hospital Anxiety and Depression Scale, which ranged from 1 to 13 with a median score of 6. The sample was clearly willing and able to endorse statements describing depressed or anxious mood and symptoms of physiological arousal. Of most interest was the strong association found between the anxiety score from this scale and the scores on the Posttraumatic Growth Inventory ($r = .531$, $p < .02$). That is, more reported growth went along with more reported anxiety. This indicates that perception of positive changes following trauma and adversity does not rule out the experience of unpleasant emotion. Indeed, a stronger conclusion would be that perception of benefits can only emerge if the event and its consequences are fully engaged with emotionally, and this is likely to involve the experience of moderately high levels of distress. It might be expected that very high levels of distress would inhibit engagement, reflecting a curvilinear relationship between unpleasant emotion and growth. (Consistent with this, the single participant who reported *extreme* levels of anxiety in this sample reported only modest growth.)

Further (previously unpublished) evidence about the experience of these participants is provided by their responses to three open-ended questions:

1. How do you see your future?
2. To what extent are you the same person as before?
3. Has anything good come out of this at all?

The Future   Of the 10 Early participants, four used the word "hope" in their response to this question. None of the Late sample mentioned hope. Six of the Early sample used the phrase "back to normal." None of the Late sample used this phrase. While only one of the 10 Early participants expressed significant concerns about the future: "I think it's going to be a hard struggle," 5 of the 11 Late participants expressed such concerns, describing the future as potentially "bleak," "precarious," "not as good as now" or just nonexistent. Thus, there was evidence of a more chastened and realistic attitude in the Late sample who had scored more highly on the Posttraumatic Growth Questionnaire.

Personal Identity   One Early participant asserted that he was 100% the same person as before the brain injury. One Early and three Late participants described themselves as essentially the same but not able to express this fully because of acquired disabilities. The remaining 16 participants described themselves as changed in both positive and negative ways. Two of the Early sample reported positive changes, "I'm special now"; "I take others' views more into account, I realize now what's important." Five of the Late sample reported positive changes, "My sister has a brother now" (referring to reduced alcohol intake); "I feel much better now"; "I have far more compassion and understanding for others. My priorities have changed."; "In some ways, I'm more independent," "There has been an intense development of my spiritual life . . . my priorities are different. . . . I have got through it and it has enabled me to let other people in."

Thus, the vast majority of the sample showed evidence of awareness that they had undergone a significant change in personal identity as a result of the injury. There was a tendency for more positive reports of change in the Late sample, consistent with the higher scores achieved on the Posttraumatic Growth Questionnaire.

Benefits Five of the 10 Early participants were emphatic that nothing good had come from their brain injury: "No—definitely"; "Not at all—it's the worst thing that's ever happened to me"; "No—a resounding no"; "No"; "No." One of the Late participants also responded "No." In addition one of the Early and two of the Late sample said, after a period of reflection, that they couldn't think of anything good.

The verbatim reports of benefits by the remaining 12 participants are summarized in Table 13.2.

It is easy to see from Table 13.2 that there were more reports of benefits by the Late group, consistent with the higher scores achieved on the Posttraumatic Growth Questionnaire. What is also striking is that several of these reports temper benefits with losses—of abilities, relationships, and money. These do not read like the accounts of people who are unaware or in denial, but who recognize their losses and, in the struggle to get on with their lives over several years, find that there have been some benefits. They have found new or improved relationships, become aware of inner strengths, reevaluated their priorities, or feel more compassion for others. Of course, none of this may be evident to those around them through dramatic changes in behavior. But the accounts they give are coherent and plausible, and this is an achievement in itself.

IMPLICATIONS FOR REHABILITATION AND PSYCHOLOGICAL THERAPY

GOAL PLANNING

Brain injury rehabilitation involves many disciplines working together. Its overall aim is to support the person with ABI in establishing a new sense of identity continuous with, but not stuck in, the past (McGrath, 2004), while managing the medical complications, pain, and emotional distress that arise during the process.

Rehabilitation is thus rooted in the past—the place the person is coming from—but it is essentially an activity that looks to the future. It is goal-directed (McGrath & Davis, 1992; Wade, 1999b). Goal-directed

Table 13.2
Positive Responses to the Question: Has Anything Good
Come Out of It at All?

Early Sample	Late Sample
Yes—I'm here—I'm still alive. It could have been the other way round. I could have "gone."	I think I am quite ready to cope with my stroke, but my life before was adventurous—climbing mountains—and so I can't do that any more.
My relationship and access to my daughters have improved. I've become closer to my brothers and sisters.	At least I'm still alive, I have the will to live. But my relationships have gone right down. I'll never have another one.
Hard to say—yes—I'm more compassionate and more thoughtful. When I used to see [disabled] people I didn't realize how difficult it was—gives you an insight.	Not happiness. But I wouldn't have found a new career in writing without it. I'm growing up and learning to accept help.
The kids have grown up a lot. They're more independent.	My priorities have changed—they were out of kilter. My compassion for others is a good thing, and an awareness of good friends.
	It has probably made me stronger. I do things despite my disability—I persevere.
	Some people listen to me. People treat me with a bit more respect (friends and family because of my experiences.)
	It got me away from X who I lived with. I met a lot of new friends.
	I gave up a whole lifestyle. A job with high pay. I am now in a new field and moving toward areas of work that are extremely satisfying but poorly paid. I'm very happy with my lifestyle. The best things that ever happened to me were my divorce from my first husband and my brain injury. When you make sense of it you can put it aside and get on with your life.

therapy is stated in terms of aspiration rather than problems, is therefore likely to be individually tailored rather than programmatic, and should be focused on the patient rather than the clinician. (For instance, a goal of rehabilitation therapy might be for Mr. X to walk 10 meters independently with a symmetrical gait, rather than for Dr. Y to treat leg weakness and eliminate asymmetry.)

There are numerous advantages to this kind of approach. The most obvious of these are that it engenders hope that things can be different and, if the goals that are set relate to cherished values and hopes, it is meaningful and thus motivating to the patient. A less obvious, but as important, agenda in goal-directed rehabilitation is the reconstitution of the person. Many writers have noted that aspiration and approach toward meaningful goals are central to personal identity (Carver & Scheier, 1990; McGrath & Adams, 1999; Siegert et al., 2004; Singer & Salovey, 1993); a dynamic sense of self *emerges* through this activity (Dewey, 1922/2002).

BUILDING ON EXISTING STRENGTHS

If, as the findings discussed in this chapter indicate, people with ABI are relatively resilient and able to generate positive coping strategies, then they should be utilized in any psychological and other rehabilitation therapies undertaken. This is first for practical reasons—it is obviously more effective to make use of well-established ways of coping if these are still available. Second, it connects the patient with the person she used to be—someone who coped. Third, it helps the patient to see herself in a positive light. This extends to therapists and relatives. One way that we have tried to emphasize this at Rivermead Rehabilitation Center in Oxford is by a routine interview shortly after admission. The Rivermead Patient's Expectations and Wishes Interview (Wade, 1999a, p. 20) asks the question: "What do you think your strong points are?" Our clinical impression is that people with ABI are often surprised to be asked this in a hospital setting, most can identify some strong points (such as courage, perseverance, intelligence), but a small minority with depressed mood find it impossible to do so.

FOCUSING ON POSITIVES

Identifying existing character strengths is only one way of focusing on positives. It is also possible to identify positive aspects of the current situation. This may involve processes that range from simple downward comparison—"I walk with a limp, but since I've seen other people who can't walk at all, I've started to realize how lucky I am," through benefit finding—"I've made some really good friends in hospital," to shifts in priority—"I now realize that family comes before work," or worldview—"I have discovered a spiritual perspective that has changed everything."

People with ABI may need permission to express these sorts of ideas, and also help with formulating them. In general, psychotherapeutic approaches to people with ABI need to be more directive than with other groups (though a light touch is still required in order to avoid inappropriate imposition of the therapist's agenda). This is because these people can have difficulty in generating ideas spontaneously due to problems with executive function arising from frontal lobe damage. They benefit from prompts, or forced choice alternative questions, rather than the open-ended approach favored in more conventional psychotherapeutic practice (Patterson & Scott-Findlay, 2002).

Focusing on positives can completely alter the tone of a therapeutic encounter, lightening the mood of both therapist and patient. For instance, my experience of administering the Posttraumatic Growth Inventory directly to patients with ABI is far more positive than that of administering the Beck Depression Inventory. The former tends to leave a feeling of buoyancy, the latter a feeling of sadness. The emotional tone of the encounter is particularly important when working with people with ABI whose memory for factual information is often poor but, as noted earlier in this chapter, whose memory for feelings is usually relatively well preserved (Collicutt McGrath, 2007b).

Engaging with Loss

Table 13.2 shows that participants could both focus on positives and admit losses in their situation. This fits with the clinical experience that some of the positives only emerge when the extent of loss has been acknowledged. For instance, it is only when we empathize with the effort, pain, frustration, and fear involved in learning to walk again that we understand and can acknowledge many people recovering from ABI for their courage and determination.

A therapeutic approach that merely looks on the bright side is crass and insulting to people who are going through an experience of deep suffering, just as the more usual approach of drawing attention to acquired deficits is dispiriting and insensitive to people who are doing their best to cope. A balance between empathizing and encouraging engagement with the losses, and identifying positives and offering hope of a way forward should characterize each therapeutic encounter.

INTEGRATING LOSS AND HOPE INTO A PERSONAL NARRATIVE

The task of anyone faced with trauma or adversity is to process events and incorporate them into their understanding of himself, the world, and his place in it. A very common way of doing this is to build a story. Stories incorporate a number of features; they occur within a time frame, they are organized around intentions and goals, they are about persons, notable and unexpected events occur within them that require some resolution, they develop in the telling and retelling (Bruner, 1991). Participants from the Late group described earlier had clearly developed personal narratives that incorporated both losses and benefits. But the process would have been made additionally challenging, complex, and thus slow for them by the presence of cognitive problems, such as lack of cognitive stamina, difficulties with focusing attention, or retaining information. This sort of process could be supported by psychologically informed techniques. These include:

- Giving the patient sufficient time within a busy rehabilitation schedule to think about and talk through what has happened.
- Prompting the patient with ways of framing the event and connecting it with both the cherished past and hope for the future.
- Using journals, tape recordings, and pictures to support deficient memory or speech and language function.
- Encouraging the integration of affect as well as events into the story, and providing a "safe space" for this activity, so that affect is not overwhelming.
- Keeping the emotional tone positive.
- Acknowledging that this is effortful, tiring psychological work and building in rest periods as appropriate.
- Where appropriate, involving significant others in the construction of the story.

RELIGIOUS AND SPIRITUAL APPROACHES

Narratives often incorporate elements that could be described as religious or spiritual. This will not always be the case, but because religion deals with existential questions and because significant existential questions are raised by brain injury, religious themes are fairly common in the talk of people with ABI (Prigatano, 1989).

Religious ritual is also often concerned with liminal states—the beginning and end of life, new relationships, the move from childhood to adulthood, and so on (Van Gennep, 2004). The person recovering from ABI is in a liminal state, moving between the familiar old and the profoundly un-known new in almost every aspect of her being. This is also true for families and friends, who often express the need to "mourn" the previous person and who seek a way of putting her to rest.

The spiritual and religious needs of people with ABI and their families are sadly neglected in the literature. Yet, religion(s) may have a good deal to offer in providing a framework around which people can carry out the necessary cognitive and emotional processing of losses and identification of benefits. For instance, Christianity, Islam, and Judaism all share the story of Abraham who journeyed into the dangerous unknown desert, leav-ing behind all that was familiar and secure, who suffered both loss and hardship, but also fulfillment.

SUMMARY

Like Abraham, the journey of those recovering from brain injury is into largely uncharted terrain, but a good rehabilitation plan offers a basic map, and positive rehabilitation practice offers an assurance that the journey is worth making.

Summary Points (Practice and Research)

- Common causes of ABI are closed head injury (due to road traffic accidents, assaults, or falls), stroke, subarachnoid haemorrhage, cere-bral hypoxia (secondary to prolonged cardiac arrest, near drowning), hypoglycaemia, carbon monoxide poisoning, and cerebral infections (meningitis, encephalitis).
- Following ABI, there is often an initial period of rapid recovery fol-lowed by a much slower phase. For all but the most minor brain injuries complete recovery of previous levels of function is never achieved.
- ABI is associated with major problems in areas such as memory, con-centration, language processing, empathic feeling, social skills, and spatial orientation, and on the sense of personal identity.
- While the literature on the psychosocial sequelae of severe ABI is largely pessimistic, psychological resilience is common and positive change has also been reported.
- Brain injury rehabilitation is goal-directed and can engender hope that things can be different and help in the reconstitution of the person.
- Rehabilitation can incorporate positive psychological interventions to help build strengths, focus on positive changes, engage with loss and integrate loss into personal narrative.
- However, it is cautioned that a therapeutic approach that merely looks on the bright side is inappropriate, just as the more usual approach of

drawing attention to acquired deficits can be dispiriting and insensitive to people who are doing their best to cope.
- A balance between empathizing and engaging with the losses and identifying the positives and hope of a way forward should characterize each therapeutic encounter.
- ABI rehabilitation could potentially be enhanced for some by the inclusion of religious and spiritual perspectives

REFERENCES

Adams, N. (1996). Positive outcomes in families following traumatic brain injury. *Australian and New Zealand Journal of Family Therapy, 17,* 75–84.

Antonovsky, A. (1993). The structure and properties of the Sense of Coherence Scale. *Social Science and Medicine, 36,* 725–733.

Bruner, J. (1991). The narrative construction of reality. *Critical Inquiry, 18,* 1–21.

Bryant, R., Marosszeky, J., Crooks, J., & Gurka, J. (2000). Posttraumatic stress disorder and severe traumatic brain injury. *American Journal of Psychiatry, 157,* 629–631.

Burvill, P., Johnson, G., Jamrozik, K., Anderson, C., Stewart-Wynne, E., & Chakera, T. (1995a). Anxiety disorders after stroke: Results from the Perth community stroke study. *British Journal of Psychiatry, 166,* 328–332.

Burvill, P., Johnson, G., Jamrozik, K., Anderson, C., Stewart-Wynne, E., & Chakera, T. (1995b). Prevalence of depression after stroke: The Perth community stroke study. *British Journal of Psychiatry, 166,* 320–327.

Carver, C., & Scheier, M. F. (1990). Origins and function of positive and negative affect: A control process view. *Psychological Review, 97,* 19–36.

Collicutt McGrath, J. (2007a). *Ethical practice in brain injury rehabilitation* (Chaps. 2–3, pp. 13–51). Oxford: Oxford University Press.

Collicutt McGrath, J. (2007b). Fear, anxiety, and depression following traumatic brain injury. In A. Tyerman & N. King (Eds.), *Psychological approaches to rehabilitation after traumatic brain injury.* Oxford: Blackwell.

Collicutt McGrath, J., & Linley, P. A. (2006). Posttraumatic growth following acquired brain injury: A preliminary small scale study. *Brain Injury, 20,* 767–773.

Collin, C., Wade, D., Davis, S., & Horne V. (1988). The Barthel, ADL Index: A reliability study. *International Disability Studies, 10,* 61–63.

Deb, S., Lyons, I., Koutzoutkis, C., Ali, I., & McCarthy, G. (1999). Rate of psychiatric illness 1 year after traumatic brain injury. *American Journal of Psychiatry, 156,* 374–378.

Dewey, J. (2002). *Human nature and conduct.* Mineola, NY: Dover. (Original work published 1922)

Elliott, T., & Kurylo, M. (2000). Hope over acquired disability: Lessons of a young woman's triumph. In C. Snyder (Ed.), *Handbook of hope: Theory, measures, and application* (pp. 373–386). San Diego, CA: Academic Press.

Emmons, R. (1996). Striving and feeling: Personal goals and subjective well-being. In P. Gollwitzer & J. Bargh (Eds.), *The psychology of action: Linking cognition and motivation to behavior* (pp. 313–337). New York: Guilford Press.

Fann, J., Katon, W., Uomoto, J., & Esselman, P. (1995). Psychiatric disorders and functional disability in outpatients with traumatic brain injuries. *American Journal of Psychiatry, 152,* 1493–1499.

Gans, J. (1983). Hate in the rehabilitation setting. *Archives of Physical Medicine and Rehabilitation, 64,* 176–179.

Giacino, J., & Cicerone, K. (1998). Varieties of unawareness after brain injury. *Journal of Head Trauma Rehabilitation, 13,* 1–15.

Hornak, J., Bramham, J., Rolls, E., Morris, G., O'Doherty, J., Bullock, P., et al. (2003). Changes in emotion after circumscribed surgical lesions of the orbitofrontal and cingulated cortex. *Brain, 126,* 1691–1712.

Jackson, H., & Manchester, D. (2001). Towards the development of brain injury specialists. *Neurorehabilitation, 16,* 27–40.

Jorge, R., Robinson, R., Starkstein, E., & Arndt, S. (1994). Influence of major depression on one year outcome in patients with traumatic brain injury. *Journal of Neurosurgery, 81,* 726–733.

Khan-Bourne, N., & Brown, R. (2003). Cognitive behavior therapy for the treatment of depression in individuals with brain injury. *Neuropsychological Rehabilitation, 13,* 89–107.

Kinney, A. (2001). Cognitive therapy and brain injury: Theoretical and clinical issues. *Journal of Contemporary Psychotherapy, 31,* 89–102.

Kitwood, T. (1997). *Dementia reconsidered: The person comes first.* Buckingham, England: Open University Press.

LeDoux, J. (1992). Brain mechanisms of emotion and emotional learning. *Current Opinion in Neurolobiology, 2,* 191–197.

Linley, P. A., & Joseph, S. (2004). Positive change following trauma and adversity: A review. *Journal of Traumatic Stress, 17,* 11–21.

Marsh, N., Kersel, D., Havill, J., & Sleigh, J. (1998). Caregiver burden at 6 months following severe traumatic brain injury. *Brain Injury, 12,* 225–238.

McFarland, C., & Alvaro, C. (2000). The impact of motivation on temporal comparisons: Coping with traumatic events by perceiving personal growth. *Journal of Personality and Social Psychology, 79,* 327–343.

McGrath, J. (1998). *Fear following brain injury.* Unpublished doctoral dissertation, Oxford Brookes University.

McGrath, J. (2004). Beyond restoration to transformation: Positive outcomes in the rehabilitation of acquired brain injury. *Clinical Rehabilitation, 18,* 767–775.

McGrath, J., & Adams, L. (1999). Patient-centered goal planning: A systemic psychological therapy? *Topics in Stroke Rehabilitation, 6,* 43–50.

McGrath, J., & Davis, A. (1992). Rehabilitation: Where are we going and how do we get there? *Clinical Rehabilitation, 6,* 255–235.

McGrath, J., & King, N. (2004). Acquired brain injury. In J. Bennett-Levy, J. G. Butler, M. Fennell, A. Hackmann, M. Mueller, & D. Westbrook (Eds.), *The Oxford guide to behavioural experiments in cognitive therapy* (pp. 331–348). Oxford, England: Oxford University Press.

McMillan T., Williams, H., & Bryant, R. (2003). Post-traumatic stress disorder and traumatic brain injury: A review of causal mechanisms, assessment, and treatment. *Neuropsychological Rehabilitation, 13,* 149–164.

Oddy, M. (1995). He's no longer the same person: How families adjust to personality change after head injury. In N. Chamberlain (Ed.), *Traumatic brain injury rehabilitation* (pp. 167–180). London: Chapman and Hall.

Patterson, B., & Scott-Findlay, S. (2002). Critical issues in interviewing people with traumatic brain injury. *Qualitative Health Research, 12,* 399–409.

Prigatano, G. (1989). Work, love, and play after brain injury. *Bulletin of the Menninger Clinic, 53,* 414–431.

Prigatano, G. (1999). *Principles of neuropsychological rehabilitation.* New York: Oxford University Press.

Rolls, E., Hornak, J., Wade, D., & McGrath, J. (1994). Emotion related learning in patients with social and emotional changes associated with frontal lobe damage. *Journal of Neurology, Neurosurgery, and Psychiatry, 57,* 1518–1524.

Seligman, M. (2002). Positive psychology, positive prevention, and positive therapy. In C. Snyder & S. Lopex (Eds.), *Handbook of positive psychology* (pp. 3–9). New York: Oxford University Press.

Siegert, R., McPherson, M., & Taylor, W. (2004). Toward a cognitive-affective model of goal-setting in rehabilitation: Is self-regulation theory a key step? *Disability and Rehabilitation, 26,* 1175–1183.

Silver, J., Kramer, R., Greenwalds, S., & Weissman, M. (2001). The association between head injuries and psychiatric disorders: Findings from the New Haven NIMH Epidemiologic Catchment Area Study. *Brain Injury, 15,* 935–945.

Singer, J., & Salovey, P. (1993). *The remembered self: Emotion and memory in personality.* New York: Free Press.

Taylor, S. (1983). Adjustment to threatening events: A theory of cognitive adaptation. *American Psychologist, 38,* 1161–1173.

Tedeschi, R., & Calhoun, L. (1996). The posttraumatic growth inventory: Measuring the positive legacy of trauma. *Journal of Traumatic Stress, 9,* 455–471.

Van Gennep, A. (2004). *The rites of passage.* London: Routledge.

Wade, D. (1999a). Goal planning in stroke rehabilitation: How? *Topics in Stroke Rehabilitation, 6,* 8–15.

Wade, D. (1999b). Goal planning in stroke rehabilitation: Why? *Topics in Stroke Rehabilitation, 6,* 1–7.

Webster, G., Daisley, A., & King, N. (1999). Relationship and family breakdown following traumatic brain injury: The role of the rehabilitation team. *Brain Injury, 13,* 593–603.

Zigmond, A., & Snaith, P. (1983). The Hospital Anxiety and Depression Scale. *Acta Psychiatrica Scandinavica, 67,* 361–370.

CHAPTER 14

Professional Quality of Life and Trauma Therapists

DEBRA LARSEN and BETH HUDNALL STAMM

THERE IS NOT a single outcome or characteristic that summarizes trauma work for therapists; the issues influencing trauma therapists' effectiveness and well-being are multidimensional. It includes the context of the work (e.g., geographical location, culture, work environment), characteristics of the trauma survivor (e.g., symptom presentation, trauma typology, engagement), and therapist variables (e.g., personal resources, training, personal trauma history). Because of the multidimensional complexity of the issues, it is important to examine the broad scope of *professional quality of life* when discussing trauma work and mental health workers. Professional quality of life, by definition, includes both positive and negative variables at the individual, organizational, and societal levels that influence the well-being and effectiveness of the professional. The dynamic interaction of positive and negative factors creates this overarching construct of professional quality of life. Consequently, both the rewarding and the deleterious aspects alike are critical to understanding the impact of trauma work for mental health professionals.

Perhaps the need for taking a broad professional quality-of-life view can, in part, be illustrated by briefly examining retention, the question of whether a therapist continues the work/job. Difficulties with therapist retention are frequently discussed as an outcome for trauma therapists. Individuals who report good professional quality of life may provide better quality of care and are more likely to stay in their positions (McCammon, 1996; National Rural Health Association [NRHA], 2006), but no single variable accurately predicts these outcomes. It is likely that there are many roads to poor retention with individual, organizational, and community characteristics contributing unique positive and negative influences for each therapist's professional quality of life.

This chapter discusses the positive and negative aspects of professional quality of life identified in trauma work. We also review specific factors identified in the literature as risk or protective factors for trauma therapists. The implications for training and practice are also explored and specific prevention and intervention strategies are identified for these settings.

NEGATIVE EFFECTS OF TRAUMA WORK

Working with trauma has the potential for several types of negative effects including direct and indirect trauma exposure. Reflecting the complexity of the concept, there are multiple terms used in the literature to describe these work-related effects. The most common terms are *burnout, countertransference, compassion fatigue, vicarious trauma,* and *secondary traumatic stress.* Classical burnout theory (Freudenberger, 1974; Maslach, 1982) is not linked to trauma exposure as its aetiology but instead proposes that a person's coping resources are finite and prolonged use leads to depletion of a person's resources, resulting in reduced work capacity and engagement. Similarly, countertransference—the therapist's response to the patient's projection of their experience onto the therapist—is not dependent on the presence of trauma exposure (c.f. Wilson & Lindy, 1994). Compassion fatigue strikes a middle ground, generally leaning toward trauma exposure as a critical element. Figley (1995, 2002) suggests that some forms of stress, although not life-threatening, are so demanding on the helper that they can induce trauma. Vicarious traumatization (McCann & Pearlman, 1990; Pearlman & Saakvitne, 1995) speaks to the work-related indirect trauma conceptualized in terms of the relationship dynamics between trauma survivor and helper. Secondary traumatic stress (Stamm, 1995/1999) differentiates primary exposure—those that are directly in harm's way—from secondary exposure, that is, related to helping the original victim (Stamm, 2002). In the next section, we discuss each of these issues in greater depth.

Direct Trauma Exposure

Direct exposure to traumatic events has long been recognized in the extant literature on Posttraumatic Stress Disorder (PTSD), but less is known about how this relates to mental health providers. Many mental health workers are "in harm's way" and risk direct exposure to potentially traumatizing events by providing trauma care in communities or circumstances embroiled with violence or danger (Stamm, 1995/1999). For example, much nongovernmental organization (NGO) work in disaster and war-torn regions includes "living and working with terror" (Stamm, Higson-Smith, & Hudnall, 2004). These extreme conditions are not the only risk for trauma exposure, however. An APA (2002) task force estimated that 35% to 40% of psychologists have been at risk for assault by a patient at some point during their career. Literature indicates that 60% to 66% of therapists report a personal trauma history (Kassam-Adams, 1999; Pearlman & Mac Ian, 1995), but there is no way to determine what proportion of that trauma history is professional/work-related.

Exposure to a potentially traumatizing event does not guarantee a traumatic stress reaction. The research indicates that only 25% of the individuals exposed to a traumatic event will actually develop diagnosable PTSD following exposure (Foa, Keane, & Friedman, 2000). However, it is also a mistake for providers to believe that their training, professional experience, and role somehow make them immune to traumatic stress following direct exposure (Stamm et al., 2004). We do not currently have accurate data on what proportion of the professional population is experiencing traumatic stress symptoms as a result of direct work trauma exposure. Nonetheless, it is important for trauma workers and their organizations to be aware of potential risks and be proactive in addressing prevention and postexposure concerns.

BURNOUT

There is significant literature on job burnout in the helping professions. Burnout is a frequent consequence when organization/work environment demands exceed the resources of the worker. By definition, burnout includes three components: emotional exhaustion, depersonalization of patients, and decreased personal accomplishment (Adams, Boscarino, & Figley, 2006; Maslach, Schaufeli, & Leiter, 2001; Rupert & Morgan, 2005). The emotional exhaustion related to burnout represents the depletion of the individual's emotional resources. This includes an inability to "care" or emotionally engage in the work or interpersonal relationships in that setting. The depersonalization component refers to a distancing and cynicism toward patients, for example, when professionals refer to patients by labels (e.g., the borderline in room 12, the suicide attempt that came in last night). With depersonalization, there is dehumanization or objectification of the patient in a way that distances the caregiver from the care recipient. The third component of burnout, decreased personal accomplishment, often includes feelings of the futility of personal effort in making any positive difference in the system. The health care worker has an overwhelming sense that the "work is never done" or that it is impossible to accomplish everything necessary for true success.

These three aspects of burnout can be influenced by characteristics of the provider, the clientele, and/or the organization. These characteristics have several themes, including an *imbalance* between the work demands and resources, with the demands always exceeding resources; and the *chronic* nature of work stressors and the demands. An acute crisis, while difficult, is not likely to result in burnout. Finally, *conflict* between individuals (e.g., clients, coworkers, supervisors), role demands, or important values result in a work environment characterized by constant emotional tension and unrealistic expectations (Maslach & Goldberg, 1998), a fertile environment for burnout development.

Several authors have noted that there is some overlap between secondary traumatic stress and burnout given the emotional exhaustion that they have in common (Adams, Mattos, & Harrington, 2001; Figley, 2002; Sabin-Farrell & Turpin, 2003; Stamm, 2002). There is a subtle difference, however. Burnout is not specifically related to exposure to traumatic material but to the overwhelming demands of the work and environment. It is possible for client characteristics common for trauma victims to contribute to the client conflict noted as typical of burnout (Maslach & Goldberg, 1998). For example, high levels of therapeutic support demands may be frequent among complex trauma victims, but this "client conflict" is not exclusive to trauma work even when it does contribute to burnout.

Burnout is more common than secondary traumatic stress among providers. Therapists assisting with trauma issues have the possibility of experiencing both secondary traumatic stress and burnout, but trauma work is not necessary for burnout to take place. Research suggests that therapists, in general, are at high risk for burnout regardless of the level of trauma work they do. One study indicates that a high percentage of licensed psychologists report emotional exhaustion (40%) and depersonalization (34%)—burnout symptoms. Our research with the whole range of mental health providers supports this. In a study of rural professional quality of life ($n = 174$; 120 females and 54 males), 48% of the rural professionals had a "high risk" burnout rating (Larsen, Stamm, & Davis, 2006) on the Professional Quality of Life Measure (ProQOL; Stamm, 2005). The risk of burnout for rural providers actually may be higher than for their metropolitan counterparts due to the shortage of resources and high workload that is more common for rural providers. Although specific prevalence for trauma workers is not currently available in published data, it is clear that mental health workers are exposed to additional stressors beyond those of other health workers due to the nature of their work in assisting individuals with mental health difficulties for extended periods of time (Meldrum, King, & Spooner, 2002).

This is likely to have a direct effect on increased burnout rates for trauma therapists.

INDIRECT EXPOSURE TO TRAUMATIC MATERIAL

Countertransference (CT) originates from psychodynamic theory and describes an emotional reaction to a client by the therapist (Stamm, 1995/1999). As noted in the introduction to this section, countertransference is not dependent on the presence of traumatic material in a therapy relationship. Countertransference has been defined by Corey (1991) as a process of over identifying with the client and seeing oneself in the client. It was the first term applied to trauma work describing therapists' reactions to knowledge of war atrocities (Haley, 1974). There are three unique aspects of countertransference that are relevant to trauma work: (1) it must be assumed that countertransference only happens within the context of therapy, (2) countertransference is the therapist's reaction to client transference actions, and (3) it is a negative consequence of therapy and should be prevented or eliminated whenever possible (Figley, 1999).

McCann and Pearlman (1990) introduced the idea of vicarious traumatization in their paper on the impact of trauma work on therapists. While discussing the countertransference concept, these authors suggested that countertransference does not fully represent the pervasive impact of trauma work. Empathically engaging with trauma survivors transforms the therapist beyond the temporary countertransference impact in the therapy room (Pearlman, 1999). The person's daily life and professional work are significantly altered and the world is never quite the same. Vicarious traumatization transformations include lasting and pervasive schema changes about the self and one's world, a characteristic that would not be included in the countertransference concept (McCann & Pearlman, 1990; Pearlman & Saakvitne, 1995).

The processes of change encompassed in vicarious traumatization parallel survivors' experiences and can alter the person's sense of self, spirituality, worldview, and interpersonal relationships (Pearlman, 1999; Pearlman & Saakvitne, 1995). Pearlman (1999) notes that the "hallmark" of vicarious traumatization is this "disrupted frame of reference" or altered sense of the person's self-identity, worldview, and spirituality. Vicarious traumatization focuses on identity and worldview challenges in the quest of meaning. By definition, this includes the possibility that these changes may represent significant personal growth as well as negative or disruptive processes. While the emphasis of vicarious traumatization is on this internal process, the experiential aspect can include such things as intrusive images and sleep interruption as well as other posttraumatic symptomology. Although these experiences can be distressing or even debilitating, Pearlman proposes that vicarious traumatization is best thought of as an "occupational hazard" for any profession who engages empathically with trauma survivors. Vicarious traumatization is a natural response to identity and worldview disruptions and attempts to view this within the context of the individual as a whole (Pearlman & Saakvitne, 1995).

In the early 1990s, Figley began to discuss *compassion fatigue* as part of the cost of caring. Compassion fatigue consists of the therapists' reduced capacity for empathic engagement as a natural consequence of "bearing the suffering" of clients (Figley, 1995). While it is important for therapists to recognize the limits of their ability to help alleviate suffering, therapy effectiveness research has repeatedly reported that the ability to empathize and understand or have compassion is critical to therapeutic change (Figley, 2002; Kahn, 1999; Zuroff & Blatt, 2006). *Compassion fatigue* represents the emotional exhaustion associated with the degree to which therapists utilize compassion in their work. Compassion fatigue was initially proposed to be interchangeable with the term secondary traumatic stress as a more "user friendly" and less blaming term (Figley 1995, 2002). It also has been proposed that compassion fatigue is the broader concept that encompasses vicarious traumatization, secondary traumatic stress, and burnout as latent "clinical features" (Adams et al., 2006).

However, these terms are frequently used as if they were different as well as interchangeably in the literature, making the nuances of meaning less clear.

The definition of secondary traumatic stress includes the disengagement typical of compassion fatigue and traumatic stress reactions for the therapist that can parallel PTSD symptoms (Figley, 1995; Stamm, 1997). The criterion for PTSD includes the possibility of exposure to trauma by "learning" of another's trauma (American Psychiatric Association, 2000), and this secondary exposure is key to secondary traumatic stress (Figley, 1999). Secondary traumatic stress symptoms can become severe enough, Figley (1999) suggests, to be labeled as secondary traumatic stress disorder (STSD). The symptoms of STSD are usually rapid in onset and associated with a particular event. They may include being afraid, having difficulty sleeping, having images of the upsetting event pop into the therapist's mind, or avoiding things that remind the therapist of the event (Stamm, 2005).

Despite this parallel of STSD to PTSD, it is important to note that secondary traumatic stress is seen as a natural consequence of trauma work and not necessarily pathological in nature (Figley, 1995; Stamm, 1999). This view of secondary traumatic stress as one of many potentially stressful experiences in life with the distinction of being *traumatically* stressful and, therefore, requiring greater reorientation of the self (Stamm, 1999). When encountering primary or secondary stressors, greater demands by the event and fewer resources by the recipient make it more likely for the stress response to be traumatic or pathological. Yet, secondary traumatic stress may also function as a catalyst for positive change and self-reorientation, which is similar to the view of vicarious traumatization.

Although these terms have subtle differences, they are frequently used interchangeably and are difficult to distinguish in much of the literature (Larsen, Stamm, & Davis, 2002). The overarching theme seems to be that caregiving, especially trauma work, can be stressful and is likely to impact the provider on some level. Regardless of the term used (i.e., countertransference, vicarious traumatization, compassion fatigue, or secondary traumatic stress), the process is likely to be distressing to the therapist but not necessarily pathological in nature. For the remainder of this chapter, this domain will be referred to as S/VT for simplicity's sake, recognizing that this may not entirely represent the nuances noted earlier. Given the implications of S/VT, awareness and actively addressing secondary traumatic stress issues is critical for the therapist to remain effective and engaged.

Looking across the literature, the prevalence of S/VT can be argued as a major issue for trauma therapists. Facing human suffering on a regular basis can have a high cost. One study of psychological distress for 100 psychotherapists with an average of 8.7 years work experience indicated that nearly half of the sample reported high levels of intrusive and avoidant symptoms of S/VT (Kassam-Adams, 1999). Another study of 185 clinical social workers indicated that over 46% of these therapists reported that they were bothered somewhat or a great deal by the intrusion of client material during off-work hours (Adams et al., 2001). Results from New York City psychologists following the September 11 terrorist attacks is even more striking. Eidelson, D'Alessio, and Eidelson (2003) reported that 83% of psychologists ($n = 712$) reported that their personal lives had been affected negatively by their work. Our recent research with rural mental health providers (Larsen et al., 2006) indicates that 13% of participants in a web-based measure of professional quality of life reported high risk S/VT ratings. In a recent study of nonrecertifying emergency medical services (EMS) workers, 92% ($n = 143$) reported that responding to children's emergencies was more stressful than responding to adults, older adults, and mixed ages, raising the issue that working with children may be more difficult than working with adults (Stamm et al., 2007).

POSITIVE EFFECTS OF TRAUMA WORK

While the potential for negative effects of caregiving are striking, it is important to remember that even though trauma work may create a situation "ripe" for a traumatic stress response, stress reactions are not necessarily always injurious. We spoke earlier of the negative consequences of caring, yet therapists continue to do this work in a committed and effective way. Many of us who work in trauma have repeatedly been asked, "How can you do that for a living; it would be *so hard?*" Perhaps part of the answer lies in the fact that the challenges to one's sense of self and the world incumbent in trauma work can be catalysts for varied outcomes, some of which are positive (Stamm, 1999). In order to understand the broader picture of professional quality of life, we must understand both the "negative costs of caring" and the "positive payments" that come from helping work (Stamm, 2002). There is very little literature available on the positive results of this work for mental health providers. Much of what is reported in qualitative rather than quantitative. We briefly explore two specific positive aspects of professional trauma work: compassion satisfaction and posttraumatic or adversarial growth.

Compassion satisfaction is a term used to describe the sense of fulfillment or pleasure that therapists derive from doing their work well (Stamm, 2002, 2005). For example, the mental health worker may feel pleasure from helping others or gratified by the ability to contribute to the work setting or the greater good of society (Stamm, 2005). As noted earlier, compassion or emotional engagement is a key component to successful therapeutic work (Figley, 2002; Kahn, 1999; Zuroff & Blatt, 2006). We would argue that compassionate engagement makes this fulfillment unique in comparison to other types of vocational satisfaction. Compassion satisfaction is related to overall professional quality of life of helping professions, not just in regard to working with trauma survivors. The focus of compassionate satisfaction is on the powerful experience of emotional engagement, compassionate helping, and the outcomes of that interaction (on an individual and societal level) despite any inherent risks and costs of caring. The idea the "I am doing something at makes a difference" is frequently an overriding theme in compassion satisfaction.

Initial research in this area confirms the interpersonal nature of work satisfaction for psychotherapists and the importance of its role. In Farber & Heifetz's (1981) study, psychotherapists reported that the most satisfying aspects of their work included promoting growth and change for patients and emotional engagement with patient's lives. The association between professional satisfaction or passion and social connectedness of psychotherapeutic work was also noted in Dlugos & Friedlander's (2001) work. Therapists nominated by peers as especially passionate and enthusiastic about their work repeatedly reported that the sense of the importance of their work in the community and a sense of social responsibility increased their personal satisfaction and enthusiasm for the work.

Our research with the ProQOL (Larsen et al., 2006) confirmed the view that compassion satisfaction is critical to understanding the professional therapists' quality of life. There can be high negative costs of caring as well as strong compassion satisfaction. For example, in the previously discussed sample of rural mental health workers, 48% reported high burnout scores. This same group reported exceptionally strong compassion satisfaction with 75% of scores within the moderate to extremely high range. We believe that this ability to simultaneously embrace the benefits of the work while experiencing the negative costs serves as a buffer or protective force for trauma workers. Compassion satisfaction may be the most potent force in motivating continued work even in the presence of the negative "costs" of caring. Compassion satisfaction is not impervious to these negative costs, however. Burnout can erode compassion satisfaction (Stamm, 2002). In fact, one of the more common configurations found is secondary traumatic stress and burnout. This combination has a real potential for negative outcomes for both the therapist and those receiving help. Fear (secondary traumatic stress) and helplessness (burnout) are not a good combination. Fortunately, compassion satisfaction seems to tap into the altruism of mental health helpers even in the presence of significant secondary traumatic stress symptoms (Stamm, 2005). Truly, this is a dynamic process.

There has been a burgeoning literature about posttraumatic/adversarial growth that originated out of the positive psychology field examining the potential for personal growth following trauma exposure (Linley & Joseph, 2004). The research examining how secondary trauma exposure fosters personal growth is theoretically supported (Pearlman, 1999; Stamm, 1999), but there is very little research in this domain. The majority of the information we have about adversarial growth for therapists is qualitative and anecdotal. Despite the limited research in this area, there is some initial indications that trauma therapists experience personal growth as a function of their work. Linley, Joseph, and Loumidis (2005) used standardized questionnaires to assess therapist growth and found that trauma therapists self-reported growth in the domain of existential changes. This would suggest that therapists can increase their sense of meaningfulness to their work and to their life in general as a result of trauma work. Similarly, Linley and Joseph (2007) examined a range of occupational and psychological factors in relation to positive and negative changes in therapists as a result of their therapy work, finding a range of associations across positive and negative change variables.

These two types of positive growth are quite different. The first type, compassion satisfaction, occurs as a result of positive feelings arising from helping others, particularly those exposed to traumatic stressors.

Posttraumatic growth, on the other hand, occurs as a result of direct or indirect trauma exposure while working with trauma survivors.

PROTECTIVE AND RISK FACTORS
FOR TRAUMA WORKERS

Protective and risk factors can have an inverse relationship to each other. For example, access to professional training through scientific conferences, continuing education, and online resources is a protective factor for positive professional quality of life (Stamm, 1999). The absence of these opportunities acts as a risk factor for negative consequences for professional work. It appears that there is an inverse relationship to many risks and protective factors for professional quality of life. The absence of one (e.g., protective factor) predicts the presence of the other (e.g., risk factor). Given the many similarities between burnout and S/VT and the overlap of these constructs in the literature, it is not surprising that they have several risk and protective factors in common. Therefore, we generally note the protective and risk factors for positive professional quality of life without distinguishing the specific domain of impact unless there is clarity in the literature.

Risks for negative impact on professional quality of life from the organizational or environmental perspective include high caseload demands, limited access to supervision, a nonsupportive work environment, and poor work environment safety (Adams et al., 2001; Meldrum et al., 2002). Caseloads high in the number of trauma victims treated, especially sexual abuse victims, escalate both S/VT and burnout symptoms for professionals (Cunningham, 1999; NRHA, 2006; Pearlman & Mac Ian, 1995; Schauben & Frazier, 1995). Professional isolation and unsupportive or nonexistent social networks are also a major risk factor for the development of S/VT or burnout (Maslach & Goldberg, 1998; Stamm, 1999). This isolation can be the result of a number of factors including geography, climate, low population density, and social barriers such as race, class, or war. For example, rural mental health workers, who more frequently experience professional isolation, report significantly higher rates of S/VT and burnout symptoms than their metropolitan counterparts (Larsen et al., 2006; Meldrum et al., 2002). A personal history of trauma for the therapist increases risk (Ghahramanlou & Brodbeck, 2000; Pearlman & Mac Ian, 1995). Likewise, the years of work experience on both ends of the distribution (low and high) are higher risk periods for negative professional quality of life impact (Ghahramanlou & Brodbeck, 2000; Moulden & Firestone, 2007).

Protective factors for therapists can come in the form of access to work tools, including access through creative uses of telecommunication resources (Larsen et al., 2002; NRHA, 2006). Sufficient income, limited overtime, vacation coverage, and personal leave time are also important protective factors (NRHA, 2006; Stamm, 1999). Balanced caseload demands in the number of sessions and the ratio of trauma cases is protective (Cunningham, 1999; Ghahramanlou & Brodbeck, 2000; Pearlman & Mac Ian, 1995). Quality supervision, peer consultation, and specific training in trauma treatment techniques are helpful as well (Cunningham, 1999; Pearlman, 1999; Pearlman & Mac Ian, 1995). High work satisfaction is also a strong protective factor (Ghahramanlou & Brodbeck, 2000; Stamm, 2002).

One of the most important protective factors for psychotherapists is consistent attention to self-care issues (Figley, 2002; Pearlman, 1999). This includes intentionally engaging in a personally balanced lifestyle with work being only a portion of one's life. Rudolph, Stamm, and Stamm (1997) suggest that "quality time" minimally includes personal time (e.g., family, friends, extended family, alone time) and physical self-care (e.g., exercise, sufficient sleep). Surveyed mental health workers' time allocation self-reported as the following: work (34%), quality/personal time (27%), sleep (36%), and exercise (3%). It is interesting to note that the quality/personal time consists of spending time with extended family (6%), immediate family (32%), friends (28%), and alone (34%). There is no criteria by which to determine if these proportions represent a balanced lifestyle that provides reenergizing or positive personal power. Pearlman (1999) suggests that balance represents specific goals of activities rather than time categories. This view of balance suggests that activities that increase spirituality, improve physical health, and develop connectedness to loved ones are the key to protective factors.

IMPLICATIONS FOR TRAINING AND SUPERVISION

When examining how training might impact professional quality of life for trauma therapists, it is especially important to think about the content of the training itself. Specific training regarding treatment techniques and protocols for trauma treatment is a critical protective factor for trauma therapists (Cunningham, 1999; Pearlman & Mac Ian, 1995; Pearlman & Saakvitne, 1995). Being trained in trauma therapies is generally important, but particularly important in regard to treating sexual abuse trauma because it appears to be the most potent domain in influencing negative outcomes on the therapist. The field is falling short in this aspect; psychotherapists often report that their training programs did not include specific training sufficient to address treatment of trauma (O'Halloran & O'Halloran, 2001).

Training on S/VT is in itself content for training therapists (Cunningham, 1999; Pearlman, 1999; Pearlman & Saakvitne, 2002). Training on S/VT should include information about signs and symptoms, prevention techniques, and intervention strategies (Pearlman, 1999; Pearlman & Saakvitne, 2002). Perhaps the most important component of S/VT education is the normalization of these reactions. It is helpful to endorse the view of S/VT as a natural part of the difficult work that therapists do and that it cannot be avoided but can be mitigated (O'Halloran & O'Halloran, 2001; Pearlman & Saakvitne, 2002). Viewing S/VT as "part of the job" and addressing it in a proactive manner enhances performance and reduces the impact of S/VT at the same time (Figley, 2002; Pearlman, 1999; Pearlman & Saakvitne, 1995; Stamm, 1999). Munroe (1995) even proposes that training should include informed consent, that being a trauma therapist carries the risk of experiencing negative effects from the work.

Supervision is also critical to positive trauma work. It can include models of peer support and consultation (Pearlman & Saakvitne, 2002). The Zero to Three trauma treatment group suggests a specific model called *Reflective Supervision* that can be adapted to address trauma supervision needs (Parlakian, 2001). This model of supervision includes a reflective stance that steps away from the immediately intense experience to ask questions about the meaning of the experience (e.g., What did this experience say about the therapist or about myself?). The supervisor is responsible for providing an environment of safety, support, and calmness in the process of this exploration of S/VT reactions. It focuses on maintaining awareness of one's personal strengths and vulnerabilities, a model that nicely parallels the view of S/VT necessary to maintain positive professional quality of life.

IMPLICATIONS FOR PRACTICE

As noted earlier, it is critical for therapists to be constantly aware of the balance in their personal and professional life. This need does not go away with work experience and may even become more important as time passes and one hears more "stories." Since this is the case, personal awareness and proactive prevention and intervention should be a regular part of any trauma clinician's world. It is reasonable to think about prevention and intervention both on the individual (i.e., how a therapist can help themselves) and organizational (i.e., what the employer and work group can do) levels. Table 14.1 notes options for intervention and prevention on the individual practice level, and Table 14.2 examines organizational considerations.

SUMMARY

The awareness of the potential positive and negative effects of being a trauma therapist has permeated nearly all of the field. This awareness is well supported by the research. Exactly what to call the negative or even the positive

Table 14.1
Individually Based Prevention/Intervention of Negative
Effects on Professional Quality of Life

Self-Assessment

History of traumatic events

If you have a history, welcome to the 50% who do.

What are your triggers?

Can you reduce their potency by therapy or other positive means?

Stressor load outside of work environment

Do you do things that refresh you?

What tasks do you have to do that use your energy?

Is there a way to share the load with friends or family?

What can you "not do" (e.g., should you alter your expectations of what is "necessary")?

Health Behaviors

Sleep: Most people are sleep deprived, which makes you more physically and psychologically vulnerable.

Exercise: Even 20 minutes three times a week makes a difference.

Consider exercising with people who help "refresh" you, multitasking!

Diet: Consider the following:

Do you eat at regular intervals, skip meals?

Do you eat enough fresh foods?

How about your caffeine, nicotine intake?

Interpersonal Relationships: Ask yourself:

Do you have unfinished business with others that uses energy?

Can you tell your friends and colleagues about how your work affects you (not your client's details) and ask for their support?

Can you tell your friends and family not to expect you to solve their problems because you are "so good at it"?

Other Assessment

What would your friends and family tell you about your work?

Can you use friends and family to help monitor your exposure, let you know when you start to seem stressed?

What do you learn from your supervision?

Is your supervision "safe," or do you monitor what you tell your supervisor? If it is not safe, can you change supervisor? Should you add an "outside-of-work" supervisor (e.g., a coach)?

Table 14.2
Organizationally Based Prevention/Intervention of Negative
Effects on Professional Quality of Life

Caseload

Can you vary your caseload?

If you cannot see a variety of patients/clients with differing issues, can you:

Intersperse patients/clients with administrative tasks.

Distribute the level of distress of cases, mix people who are doing well and nearer completion of their therapy or more stable cases for case management with those who are more volatile and struggling.

Try to end the day (if at all possible) with a positive activity so that you don't head home with fresh feelings of distress that you have not had time to dissipate in the work setting where they belong. Otherwise, it is all too easy to carry them with you into your home/personal sphere.

Collegial and Professional-Peer Support

Can you count on your colleagues to:

Help or listen if you are struggling?

Tell you when you are struggling (more than a conversation by the coffeepot); when you need to seek supervision or professional support to deal with your feelings about work?

If you cannot count on your work colleagues:

Find a collegial group you can trust, for example, a professional "lunch" group that meets for support. Alternatively, you can utilize technology, (e.g., tele-health or a virtual community).

Set basic ground rules for confidentiality:

Client confidentiality: you don't have to tell their story; you really need to deal with how working with them made you feel. This is about you, not them.

Provider confidentiality: What you share should be considered confidential unless the person (group) agrees to share particular information. It is a necessary part of feeling safe to share.

---

effects of doing psychotherapy with trauma survivors may not become clear for decades. However, professional hope is important to both. Burnout and trauma can eat away the mental health worker's ability to envision a better life. Those who have professional hope are far better at offering it to others.

Summary Points (Practice)

- Protective factors and risk factors tend to be inversely related: By mitigating the risk factors for trauma therapists, there is the likelihood that simultaneously they are enhancing their protective factors.

- Access to professional training through conferences, continuing education, and online education is a protective factor for positive professional quality of life.
- Attention to self-care, for example, ensuring a balanced lifestyle, time for renewal, and connectedness with key others are important protective factors.
- S/VT is not uncommon nor does it mean that a person's career is in shambles. Addressed proactively through things like workload changes, organizational protections, individual reflective supervision, and as appropriate, individual psychotherapy, positive growth can occur.
- High caseloads, limited supervision, a nonsupportive or unsafe work environment all contribute to risk factors for negative effects.
- Rural mental health workers appear to be at greater risk because of their professional isolation and lack of social and personal networks. As such, they are a priority for intervention and support.
- Mental health workers working with children may be at greater risk due to societal expectations for children's safety as well as the possibility of identifying client-children with your own children.
- Both early career and late career therapists tend to be at higher risk for negative effects, although it is not clear why.
- It is important to think about prevention and intervention on the basis of both the individual practice level and the organizational structure level.

Summary Points (Research)

- There are both positive and negative effects that can ensue from working with trauma survivors; research should focus on understanding both types of effects and the possible interactions between them.
- There is conceptual confusion across many of the terms used for the negative effects (burnout, countertransference, compassion fatigue, vicarious trauma, and secondary traumatic stress). These terms are sometimes used distinctly and sometimes interchangeably. Empirical and theoretical developments should focus on the specificity and utility of each term in relation to trauma therapists and other vicariously exposed populations. It may be that there is not a functional difference between the terms, but at this time it is impossible to tell.
- There is similar conceptual confusion across many of the terms used for the positive effects of trauma work (posttraumatic growth, positive changes, compassion satisfaction). Again, empirical and theoretical developments should focus on the specificity and utility of each term in relation to trauma therapists and other vicariously exposed

populations. As with terms for the negative effects of working with trauma, there may be no functional difference but without research, we do not know.

• The prevalence of both positive and negative effects of trauma work in therapist populations is unknown, and remains a focus for future research.

REFERENCES

Adams, R. E., Boscarino, J. A., & Figley, C. R. (2006). Compassion fatigue and psychological distress among social workers: A validation study. *American Journal of Orthopsychiatry, 76*(1), 103–108.

Adams, K. B., Mattos, H. C., & Harrington, D. (2001). The traumatic stress institute belief scale as a measure of vicarious trauma in a national sample of clinical social workers. *Families in Society: Journal of Contemporary Human Services, 82*(4), 363–371.

American Psychiatric Association. (2000). *Diagnostic and statistical manual of mental disorders* (4th ed., text rev.). Washington, DC: Author.

American Psychological Association. (2002). Ethical principles of psychologist and code of conduct. *American Psychologist, 57*, 1060–1073.

Corey, G. F. (1991). *Theory and practice of counseling psychotherapy.* Belmont, CA: Brooks/Cole.

Cunningham, M. (1999). The impact of sexual abuse treatment on the social work clinician. *Child and Adolescent Social Work Journal, 16*(4), 277–290.

Dlugos, R. F., & Friedlander, M. L. (2001). Passionately committed psychotherapists: A qualitative study of the experiences. *Professional Psychology: Research and Practice, 32*(3), 298–304.

Eidelson, R. J., D'Alessio, G. R., & Eidelson, J. I. (2003). The impact of September 11 on psychologists. *Professional Psychology: Research and Practice, 34*(2), 144–150.

Farber, B. A., & Heifetz, L. J. (1981). The satisfactions and stressors of psychotherapeutic work: A factor analytic study. *Professional Psychology, 12*(5), 621–630.

Figley, C. R. (1995). Compassion fatigue as secondary traumatic stress disorder: An overview. In C. R. Figley (Ed.), *Compassion fatigue: Coping with secondary traumatic stress disorder in those who treat the traumatized* (pp. 1–20). New York: Brunner/Mazel.

Figley, C. R. (1999). Compassion fatigue: Toward a new understanding of the costs of caring. In B. H. Stamm (Ed.), *Secondary traumatic stress: Self-care issues for clinicians, researchers, and educators* (2nd ed., pp. 1–28). Baltimore: Sidran Press.

Figley, C. R. (2002). Introduction. In C. R. Figley (Ed.), *Treating compassion fatigue* (pp. 1–14). New York: Brunner-Routledge.

Foa, E. B., Keane, T. M., & Friedman, M. J. (2000). Guidelines for treatment of PTSD. *Journal of Traumatic Stress, 13*, 539–588.

Freudenberger, H. J. (1974). Staff burn-out. *Journal of Social Issues, 30*(1), 159–165.

Ghahramanlou, M., & Brodbeck, C. (2000). Predictors of secondary trauma in sexual assault trauma counselors. *International Journal of Emergency Mental Health, 2*(4), 229–400.

Haley, S. A. (1974). When the patient reports atrocities: Specific treatment considerations of the Vietnam veteran. *Archives of General Psychiatry, 30,* 191–196.

Kahn, M. (1999). *Between therapist and client: The new relationship.* New York: Freeman.

Kassam-Adams, N. (1999). The risks of treating sexual trauma: Stress and secondary trauma in psychotherapists. In B. H. Stamm (Ed.), *Secondary traumatic stress: Self-care issues for clinicians, researchers, and educators* (2nd ed., pp. 37–50). Baltimore: Sidran Press.

Larsen, D., Stamm, B. H., & Davis, K. (2002). Telehealth for prevention and interventions of the negative effects of caregiving. *Traumatic Stress Points: Newsletter for the International Society for Traumatic Stress Studies, 16*(4).

Larsen, D., Stamm, B. H., & Davis, K. (2006, August). *Rural healthcare providers' row to hoe: The impact on professional quality of life.* Poster presentation at the annual American Psychological Association conference, New Orleans, LA.

Linley, P. A., & Joseph, S. (2004). Positive change following trauma and adversity: A review. *Journal of Traumatic Stress, 17,* 11–21.

Linley, P. A., & Joseph, S. (2007). Therapy work and therapists' positive and negative well-being. *Journal of Social and Clinical Psychology, 26,* 385–403.

Linley, P. A., Joseph, S., & Loumidis, K. (2005). Trauma work, sense of coherence and positive and negative changes in therapists. *Psychotherapy and Psychosomatics, 74,* 185–188.

Maslach, C. (1982). *Burnout: The cost of caring.* Englewood Cliffs, NJ: Prentice Hall.

Maslach, C., & Goldberg, J. (1998). Prevention of burnout: New perspectives. *Applied and Preventive Psychology, 7,* 63–74.

Maslach, C., Schaufeli, W. B., & Leiter, M. P. (2001). Job burnout. *Annual Review of Psychology, 52,* 379–422.

McCammon, S. L. (1996). Emergency medical service workers: Occupational stress and traumatic stress. In D. Paton & J. M. Violanti (Eds.), *Traumatic stress in critical occupations: Recognition, consequences and treatment* (pp. 58–86). Springfield, IL: Charles C Thomas.

McCann, I. L., & Pearlman, L. A. (1990). Vicarious traumatization: A framework for understanding the psychological effects of working with victims. *Journal of Traumatic Stress, 3*(1), 131–149.

Meldrum, L., King, R., & Spooner, D. (2002). Secondary traumatic stress in case managers working in community mental health services. In C. R. Figley (Ed.), *Treating compassion fatigue* (pp. 85–106). New York: Brunner/Mazel.

Moulden, H. M., & Firestone, P. (2007). Vicarious traumatization: The impact on therapist who work with sexual offenders. *Trauma, Violence, and Abuse, 8*(1), 67–83.

Munroe, J. F. (1995). Ethical issues associated with secondary trauma in therapists. In B. H. Stamm (Ed.), *Secondary traumatic stress: Self-care issues for clinicians, researchers, and educators* (pp. 211–229). Lutherville, MD: Sidran Press.

National Rural Health Association. (2006). *Recruitment and retention of a quality health workforce in rural areas.* Retrieved from www.nrharural.org/advocacy/sub/issuepapers/ProfQualityWF-15.pdf.

O'Halloran, M. S., & O'Halloran, T. (2001). Secondary traumatic stress in the classroom: Amelioration stress in graduate students. *Teaching in Psychology, 28*(2), 92–97.

Parlakian, R. (2001). *Look, listen and learn: Reflective supervision and relationship-based work.* Washington, DC: Zero to Three.

Pearlman, L. A. (1999). Self-care for trauma therapists: Ameliorating vicarious traumatization. In B. H. Stamm (Ed.), *Secondary traumatic stress: Self-care issues for clinicians, researchers, and educators* (2nd ed., pp. 65–79). Baltimore: Sidran Press.

Pearlman, L. A., & Mac Ian, P. S. (1995). Vicarious traumatization: An empirical study of the effects of trauma work on trauma therapists. *Professional Psychology: Research and Practice, 26*(6), 558–565.

Pearlman, L. A., & Saakvitne, K. W. (1995). *Trauma and the therapist: Countertransference and vicarious traumatization in psychotherapy with incest survivors.* New York: Norton.

Pearlman, L. A., & Saakvitne, K. W. (2002). Treating therapists with vicarious traumatization and secondary traumatic stress disorders. In C. R. Figley (Ed.), *Treating compassion fatigue* (pp. 1–14). New York: Brunner-Routledge.

Rudolph, J. M., Stamm, B. H., & Stamm, H. E. (1997, November). *Compassion fatigue: A concern for mental health policy, providers and administration.* Poster presentation at International Society for Traumatic Stress Studies conference in Montreal, Canada.

Rupert, P. A., & Morgan, D. J. (2005). Work setting and burnout among professional psychologists. *Professional Psychology: Research and Practice, 36*(5), 544–550.

Sabin-Farrell, R., & Turpin, G. (2003). Vicarious traumatization: Implications for the mental health of health workers? *Clinical Psychology Review, 23,* 449–480.

Schauben, L. J., & Frazier, P. A. (1995). Vicarious trauma: The effects on female counselors of working with sexual violence victims. *Psychology of Women Quarterly, 19,* 49–64.

Stamm, B. H. (1997, Spring). Work-related secondary traumatic stress. *PTSD Research Quarterly, 8.* Available from www.ncptsd.org/research/rq/rqpdf/V8N2.PDF.

Stamm, B. H. (1999). *Secondary traumatic stress: Self-care issues for clinicians, researchers, and educators* (2nd ed.). Lutherville, MD: Sidran Press. (Original work published 1995)

Stamm, B. H. (2002). Measuring compassion satisfaction as well as fatigue: Developmental history of the compassion fatigue and satisfaction test. In C. R. Figley (Ed.), *Treating compassion fatigue* (pp. 107–119). New York: Brunner-Routlege.

Stamm, B. H. (2005). *The ProQOL manual: The professional quality of life scale—Compassion satisfaction, burnout and compassion fatigue/secondary trauma scales.* Lutherville, MD: Sidran Press.

Stamm, B. H., Higson-Smith, C., & Hudnall, A. C. (2004). The complexities of working with terror. In D. Knafo (Ed.), *Living with terror, working with trauma* (pp. 369–400). Lanham, MD: Rowman & Littlefield.

Stamm, B. H., Howard, B., Hudnall, A., Chicoine, K., Wolfley, D., & Gainor, D. (2007). *Draft Report from the Idaho Department of Health and Welfare Emergency Medical Service Bureau Attrition through Non-Recertification Survey.* Boise: Idaho Department of Health and Welfare.

Wilson, J. P., & Lindy, J. D. (Eds.). (1994). *Countertransference in the treatment of PTSD.* New York: Guilford Press.

Zuroff, D. C., & Blatt, S. J. (2006). The therapeutic relationship in the brief treatment of depression: Contributions to clinical improvement and enhanced adaptive capacities. *Journal of Consulting and Clinical Psychology, 74*(1), 130–140.

PART IV

BEYOND THE STRESS–GROWTH DISTINCTION: ISSUES AT THE CUTTING EDGE OF THEORY AND PRACTICE

CHAPTER 15

A Contrarian View of Growth Following Adversity

JULIAN D. FORD, HOWARD TENNEN, and DAVID ALBERT

THE CONCEPT OF posttraumatic growth is a potentially important paradigm shift in the traumatic stress field. Reports of individuals experiencing personal growth in the face of adversity run contrary to the dominant scientific, clinical, and lay views that psychological trauma primarily causes damage to the body, mind, and relationships. Although posttraumatic growth has become an icon in the positive psychology movement, we review evidence that suggests that growth in the aftermath of psychological trauma is better conceptualized as the resumption or continuation of preexisting psychobiological development, or as an artifact of cognitive attribution processes that lead persons who experience psychological trauma to believe that they have experienced growth.

First, we offer a model for understanding the psychobiology of personal growth. Next, we assert that growth following adversity, though important for theory building and planning interventions, actually may be quite rare when alternative explanations for what appears to be "growth" are considered. Third, we explain why a rare phenomenon such as growth following adversity might nevertheless be reported as occurring frequently by research participants, and we question whether posttraumatic growth scales actually or accurately measure "growth." We argue that what is believed to be posttraumatic growth often may be either a self-protective psychological adaptation or a contrast effect resulting from the resumption of pretraumatic development. We conclude by suggesting steps toward greater conceptual and methodological precision in the measurement of the sequelae of exposure to traumatic stressors including adaptive as well as problematic outcomes.

A CONCEPTUAL MODEL OF PSYCHOLOGICAL GROWTH AS ENHANCED SELF-REGULATION

Progressive increase in the ability to self-regulate (i.e., to exert conscious control of otherwise automatic psychobiological processes and states by engaging in self-reflective information processing) is the hallmark of biopsychosocial development from early childhood (Schore, 2001; Siegel, 2001) through adolescence (Spessot, Plessen, & Peterson, 2004; Tobin & Graziano, 2006), and into adulthood (Rawn & Vohs, 2006). A variety of self-regulatory capacities are acquired in the course of psychological development (e.g., the ability to modulate affect, inhibit impulses, explore and balance independence and interdependence). For example, in order to reliably inhibit impulses, it is necessary not only to form and act on an intention to not respond impulsively, but also to be able to modulate affective responses and motivational tendencies. Such modulation of affect and motivation may occur as the result of habitual reflexive response tendencies (e.g., a person who is temperamentally cautious but not excessively inhibited, or naturally easygoing and able to delay gratification). However, effortful modulation of affect and motivational proclivities requires the capacity to self-regulate by consciously observing and reshaping one's own affect states and goals/aversions in order to planfully reevaluate the expected consequences of different courses of action—what Fonagy (2003) describes as "mentalizing," self-reflection on one's own internal states, drives, and ways of thinking about how to manage them.

Self-regulation develops as a result of biological maturation and experience-based alteration in complex neural information processing networks (Berger-Sweeney & Hohman, 1997), including both the central nervous system (CNS) and neural pathways in the body's periphery (the autonomic nervous system, ANS). The ANS maintains bodily arousal (i.e., energy, alertness, readiness to act) at optimum levels by homeostatically adjusting arousal based on input from other body systems and from areas in the CNS that automatically monitor bodily integrity (e.g., cerebellum, brainstem, midbrain, hypothalamic-pituitary-adrenal axis). The ANS has two branches: The sympathetic branch is akin to an accelerator, producing the "fight-flight" stress response (Mayes, 2000; Southwick et al., 1999). The parasympathetic branch serves as a regulator or "brake" that maintains levels of sympathetic ANS arousal at levels high enough to permit effective thought and action but low enough to prevent inefficient action and excessive strain on the body (Mayes, 2000, p. 275).

The CNS can be understood as a "continuous nonlinear network" (Grossberg, 1988, p. 17): new information is processed on an ongoing basis by searching for recognizable patterns from long-term memory that permit the learner to formulate and test new or revised hypotheses—rather than only reacting based on simple stimulus-response (S-R) relationships. In order to sort out and adapt flexibly to the flood of inputs constantly available outside and within the body, the CNS appears to use automatic rapid reactions (Grossberg, 1988) and also to operate as a "computation machine" (Duchaine, Cosmides, & Tooby, 2001, p. 225) that flexibly self-organizes and self-stabilizes so as to avoid "fatal capacity catastrophes" (i.e., breakdown due to overload; Grossberg, 1988, p. 40). Most importantly, the CNS is thought to reshape itself as it constructs, tests, and utilizes "privileged hypotheses" (Duchaine et al., 2001, p. 226) that guide psychobiological self-regulation not only in peak periods of growth in early childhood and adolescence (Giedd et al., 1999; Kanemura, Aihara, Aoki, Araki, & Nakazawa, 2003; Spessot et al., 2004) but in adulthood as well. However, if CNS pathways are altered in early development due to excess or depleted messenger availability or activity (e.g., due to psychological trauma), lifelong impairments may occur in perception, attention, anxiety expression, learning, memory, and behavioral control (Berger-Sweeney & Hohman, 1997).

These findings have two key implications for the conceptualization of posttraumatic growth. First, growth in the capacity to self-regulate occurs across the life span as a result of both innate maturational processes and experience-based learning in the CNS, and takes the form of hypothesis testing that results in a preference for certain "privileged" hypotheses that become guiding beliefs. Second, psychological trauma can profoundly disrupt the development and use of self-regulatory capacities and, in critical periods (e.g., early childhood, adolescence), may fundamentally override the growth of self-regulatory capacities (Ford, 2005). If an individual is likely, as the result of innate biological tendencies or social learning, to believe that adversity can be not only overcome but also a source of growth, this "privileged" hypothesis may lead to the conclusion that psychological trauma has produced growth even when factually the traumatic events have caused a disruption in, or even damage to, the person's ability to self-regulate. As we shall discuss, counterfactual defensive beliefs actually may be strengthened if psychological trauma disrupts or damages self-regulatory capacities, that is, strengthening the belief that growth has occurred as a result of trauma in order to provide a compensatory form of self-protection from the distress associated with dysregulation. In order to understand how posttraumatic growth may be a counterfactual self-protective illusion, we must consider how self-regulation can serve as a factual basis for defining psychobiological growth.

CNS and ANS development provide the biological basis for the emergence and elaboration of three core self-regulatory psychological processes during childhood, and for sustaining and refining them during the adolescent and adult years: (1) monitoring and adjusting bodily states (*somatic self-regulation*); (2) goal-directed behavior guided by appraisals, goals, plans, and evaluations informed by experiences (*cognitive self-regulation*); and (3) integrating somatic and cognitive information into emotion states that motivate and guide further somatic adaptation and cognition (*affect regulation*).

Somatic self-regulation develops earliest, beginning before birth with innate bodily systems (e.g., "sucking, swallowing, breathing, thermoregulating, vocalizing"; Doussard-Roosevelt, Porges, Scanlon, Alemi, & Scanlon, 1997, p. 174). From these innate somatic self-regulation reflexes, the ability to consciously regulate bodily processes develops in infancy, laying a foundation for cognitive self-regulation (e.g., sustained selective attention, social affiliation) and affect regulation (e.g., mood management, frustration tolerance) to develop during childhood (Doussard-Roosevelt et al., 1997).

Cognitive self-regulation emerges as children develop the capacity for narrative knowledge (i.e., "a temporally and spatially unified 'movie-in-the-brain' . . . [when] the brain makes neural patterns in its neural circuits and turns those neural patterns into explicitly mental patterns of the whole range of possible sensory images, which stand for any object, any relationship, concrete or abstract, any word or any sign") and autobiographical self-awareness (i.e., "a sense of self in the act of knowing"; Parvizi & Damasio, 2001, p. 137). Newborns actively categorize perceptions based on the egocentric functions of objects (e.g., providing food when hungry), but in the second half of the first year of life (with the onset of crawling) they shift toward using a more objective approach (e.g., based upon perceptual similarities and differences) that is fully evident as early as 18 months (M. Johnson & Mareschal, 2001). *Affect regulation* emerges as the child increasingly is able to recognize and use somatic and cognitive information as emotions: not merely as a mirror representing perceptual observations, but also as a vehicle for modifying and modulating somatic states in order to achieve a sense of well-being and to articulate and accomplish goals through sequences of action.

The capacity to integrate somatic, cognitive, and affect regulation emerges at the end of the second year of life and continues to develop across the life span (Parvizi & Damasio, 2001). At this time, neural projections from the brainstem and midbrain to the limbic system (e.g., the amygdala for self-protection and, in conjunction with the hippocampus, for memory consolidation) and the cortex (e.g., the prefrontal cortex [PFC] for emotion processing and goal-directed behavior) become fully functional (Berger-Sweeney & Hohman, 1997; Mayes, 2000). Self-regulation further evolves across the life span with the acquisition of capacities such as "pre-emptive" control (i.e., reining in reactive responding; Matsumoto, Suzuki, & Tanaka, 2003), self-awareness of meaningful and adaptive connections between emotions, goals, and behaviors (Rawn & Vohs, 2006), awareness of self and others as separate persons with distinct goals, expectations, and emotions (Adolphs, 2002; Frith & Frith, 1999), and complex emotions (e.g., shame, moral anger, empathy, pride; Kagan, 2001).

IMPACT OF PSYCHOLOGICAL TRAUMA ON SELF-REGULATION

The truism, adapted from Nietzche (1888/1990), that "what does not destroy me makes me stronger," captures the widely held belief that adversity strengthens people if they are able to survive. However, adversity—and psychological trauma in particular—does not appear to strengthen self-regulation, but instead causes a shift from ordinary self-regulation to crisis-based regulation geared to achieve survival (Ford, 2005). Most people exposed to psychological trauma experience transient stress reactions that interfere with (but may also temporarily enhance) biopsychosocial functioning; most posttraumatic stress reactions resolve within several months (Adams & Boscarino, 2006; Charney, 2004). However, a substantial minority of persons who have experienced psychological trauma develop persistent biopsychosocial impairment, most often when preexisting vulnerabilities lead to complicated comorbid disorders (Guthrie & Bryant, 2006; North, Kawasaki, Spitznagel, & Hong, 2004; Schnurr, Lunney, & Sengupta, 2004). A subset of these individuals develops chronic biopsychosocial impairment, for which the primary risk factors are the extent and nature of trauma exposure and the posttrauma environment (Schnurr et al., 2004). These and related neurobiological findings (Charney, 2004) suggest that psychological trauma leads to substantial alterations in the body's fear and stress response systems that may become chronic psychobiological and interpersonal (mal)adaptations. Assertions that psychological trauma may be followed by growth therefore must be considered within the context of evidence of heightened and potentially persistent and maladaptive posttraumatic stress reactivity.

In the extreme, early life stressors such as abuse or neglect may lead not only to insecurity and stress reactivity but to an inability self-regulate without external assistance—so-called "disorganized attachment" (Cassidy & Mohr, 2001). Behaviorally, abused children often show a chaotic mix of excessive help-seeking and dependency, social isolation and disengagement, impulsiveness and inhibition, submissiveness and aggression. Neurobiological studies have reported elevated excitatory brain chemical messenger levels proportionate to the duration of Posttraumatic Stress Disorder (PTSD) in maltreated children, and altered sleep-wake cycles of stress hormones, as well as either hyper- (if abuse is in the past) or hypo- (if abuse is ongoing) re-activity to stressors (Kaufman, Plotsky, Nemeroff, & Charney, 2000; Teicher et al., 2003) and impaired left hemisphere brain development (Teicher et al., 2003). Recent evidence suggests that emotional abuse may be more strongly associated with impairment in self-regulation than physical or sexual abuse *per se* (although they often are intertwined; Teicher, Samson, Polcari, & Mc-Greenery, 2006). Child neglect, particularly when involving very limited physical and emotional nurturance by caregivers, also is associated with profound socioemotional and cognitive impairments consistent with disor-ganized attachment (Maunder & Hunter, 2001).

Maltreatment or other interpersonal violence in childhood is associated with risk of depression, addiction, and conduct problems (May et al., 2004). Physically abused children (compared to age-matched nonabused children) are vigilant in recognizing potential threats (e.g., angry faces), more readily categorizing stimuli as anger-related, searching for and detecting angry (versus other emotion) faces, perceiving angry faces as salient and distinc-tive, and having difficulty disengaging attention from angry faces (Pollak & Tolley-Schell, 2003, p. 324), consistent with generalized expectancies for physical or sexual harm (Gully, 2003) and a hostile/aggressive information processing style that is predictive of subsequent conduct problems (Dodge, Pettit, Bates, & Valente, 1995). Sexually abused children report generalized expectancies for feeling angry and scared and for being sexually/physi-cally harmed (Gully, 2003). Maltreated children with PTSD also may have deficits in selective or sustained attention, hypothesis testing and problem solving, and semantic organization (Beers & DeBellis, 2002), as well as short-term and delayed semantic memory (Cordon, Pipe, Sayfan, Melinder, & Goodman, 2004; Elzinga & Bremner, 2002). However, their memory for traumatic events may be detailed and over-inclusive (Cordon et al., 2004).

As adults, survivors of childhood traumatic stress are at risk for not only PTSD (Kassam-Adams & Winston, 2004; Widom, 1999) but also for other forms of compromised self-regulation (Cicchetti & Toth, 1995), including anxiety, affective, addictive, psychotic, and personality disorders (Heim & Nemeroff, 2001; J. Johnson, Cohen, Brown, Smailes, & Bernstein, 1999; Nel-son et al., 2002), neuropsychological alterations involving attention, vigi-lant visual scanning, short-term, working, episodic, and autobiographical memory, and socioemotional judgment (Bremner, Vythilingham, Vermet-ten, Southwick, McGlashan, Nazeer, et al., 2003; Bremner, Vythilingham, Vermetten, Southwick, McGlashan, Staib, et al., 2003; Nixon, Nishith, & Resick, 2004), medical conditions such as diabetes, heart disease, and im-mune system disorders (Heim & Nemeroff, 2001), and re-victimization (Nelson et al., 2002; Whitfield, Anda, Dube, & Felitti, 2003).

These findings suggest that maltreatment may alter brain structure and function in childhood by requiring survival-adaptive (Teicher et al., 2003) changes (e.g., avoidance of or over-reliance on relationships, vigilant threat detection/expectancies, and impulsive reward-seeking) that decades later can lead to problems with attention, learning, and memory when confronted with cues (or actual recent events, e.g., being raped) that explicitly or implicitly (e.g., success or failure on a cognitively demanding but otherwise neutral task) activate a sense of threat or negative affect. Even when traumatic threats are neither present nor likely, the individual may be so biologically over-prepared to seek, find, and avoid threats that the neural pathways necessary for working memory and autobiographical memory (as well as for somatic and affective self-regulation) may be displaced by less consciously accessible self-protective neural pathways. The dilemma of self-regulation posed by psychological trauma thus may be due not to a neurobiological deficit but instead to *resilience* in the face of threats to survival. Trauma exposure sets in motion a cascade of relatively automatic self-protective responses that compete for scarce neural resources with ways perceiving, feeling, thinking, remembering, and pursuing goals and relationships that do not primarily involve surviving danger and harm. If self-protective survival responses persist following trauma, ordinary adaptive development and functioning are impaired due to a scarcity of psychobiological resources. This view is consistent with findings suggesting that posttraumatic dissociation is not only transient but less of a risk factor for long-term posttraumatic impairment than chronic dissociation (Briere, Scott, & Weathers, 2005) or rumination (Halligan, Herbert, Goodyer, & Murray, 2004). Posttraumatic dysregulation may take the form of compensatory defensive strategies such as thought suppression, which has been shown to partially mediate the relationship between distress and PTSD among women with histories of sexual assault (Rosenthal, Cleavens, Lynch, & Follette, 2006).

Most self-regulation involves reflexive or habitual adjustments that maintain a fairly stable (homeostatic) somatic and cognitive equilibrium. However, when stressors require adaptations that exceed innate somatic and cognitive capacities, the body activates a "neurochemical switch" (Mayes, 2000) that initiates a second set of regulatory reactions which are slower, longer-lasting, and involve encoding (Moghaddam, 2002), re-consolidation and retention (Riedel, Platt, & Micheau, 2003) of fear memories, and disrupted learning and memory of coping behaviors (Reidel et al., 2003). As a result, before purposeful self-regulation can be enacted, a person's somatic, cognitive, and affective resources already may be depleted ("allostatic load," Charney, 2004; McEwen & Stellar, 1993), disorganized (Moghaddam, 2002), or modified by the imprint of indelible fear memories (Riedel et al., 2003). In the extreme, when faced with psychological trauma, automatic defensive modes of biopsychosocial "survival coping" may override controlled information processing during and in the immediate wake of the trauma, and moreover may produce a proclivity to activate these same or similar modes of survival coping in response to many subsequent stressors—with a corresponding chronic attenuation of self-regulation. This dilemma of an over-performing biological survival system is particularly likely when trauma disrupts early psychobiological development and maturation (Ford, 2005) but may also in effect "derail" well-formed adaptive self-regulatory capacities when adults experience psychological trauma for the first time and go on to develop persistent PTSD (Halligan et al., 2004).

POSTTRAUMATIC GROWTH: A SYNOPSIS OF THE EVIDENCE

Thus far, we have argued that psychological trauma elicits automatic psychobiological survival adaptations that, if they persist, may disrupt the self-regulatory processes necessary for ordinary development and functioning. If growth is conceptualized as progressively enhanced self-regulation, such posttraumatic impairment is incompatible with growth. However, most trauma survivors do not develop persistent clinically significant impairment (Charney, 2004), and those who do often report periods of relatively quiescent symptoms on any given day (Frueh, Elhai, & Kaloupek, 2004) and in some cases for periods of weeks, months, or years of remission (Schnurr et al., 2004). Some trauma survivors describe feeling as if they have been given a second chance and as a result have a keener sense of the importance of living life mindfully and finding value in every experience. Others say that they feel a sense of clarity of vision and purpose where they had been stagnating or living reflexively before (Salter & Stallard, 2004). Thus, the fact that survival responses may override ordinary self-regulation does not rule out the possibility that posttraumatic growth (PTG)—new, stronger, or better elaborated self-regulatory capacities—may occur after psychological trauma.

Examples of PTG, or of positive changes resulting from exposure to adverse events, are readily found in popular culture, literature, and religion. Indeed, if there is a common thread that binds nearly every comic-book superhero (think of Batman, Wonder Woman, Superman, or Spiderman, for example) it is the hero's experience of a traumatic event (usually in childhood, and usually involving the traumatic loss of a parent) that precipitates the hero's acquisition of super-powers and serves as a powerful motivator in times of challenge or adversity.

Empirical research on PTG yields a more mixed picture. Such research has typically focused on three domains of improvement following exposure to an adverse event: changes in self-perception, changes in interpersonal relationships, and changes in philosophical approach to life (Tedeschi & Calhoun, 1996). While a substantial number of studies have attempted to measure PTG along these domains (e.g., 39 studies reviewed by Linley & Joseph, 2004), a consistent lack of methodological rigor complicates any attempt to draw conclusions. The most problematic methodological issues include: inconsistency across studies with regard to instrumentation, an over-reliance on self-reported change, and a lack of longitudinal studies that include preevent data.

The vast majority (27/39) of the studies reviewed by Linley and Joseph (2004) failed to use well-validated measures of PTG. Of the seven published instruments that measure PTG only two—the Changes in Outlook Questionnaire (CiOQ; Joseph, Williams, & Yule, 1993) and the Revised Stress-Related Growth Scale (SRGS-R; Armeli, Gunthert, & Cohen, 2001)—inquire about negative as well as positive change (see Table 15.1). Thus, respondents may over-report positive changes simply because the measures establish a response set that is biased toward positive change. Broadening the field of measurement to include positive as well as the more often assessed negative sequelae of traumatic experiences is an important advance in the assessment and conceptualization of psychological trauma. However, measurement tools for PTG should be designed either to include or to be co-presented with other measures of negative sequelae, and to assess threats to validity such as defensive response sets (e.g., the validity scales included in some multimodal posttraumatic symptom assessments; Briere & Spinazzola, 2005).

The specific indicators or items used to operationalize PTG tend to be diverse, infrequently grounded in a systematic theoretical model (for exceptions see Armeli et al., 2001), and of uncertain content and construct validity. Most importantly, PTG instruments do not differentiate between

Table 15.1

Instructions and Sample Posttraumatic Growth Inventory (PTGI) and Changes in Outlook Questionnaire (CiOQ) Items

PTGI	CiOQ
Indicate the degree to which this change occurred in your life as a result of your crisis:	As a result of _____.
A sense of closeness with others.	I value my relationships much more now.
I'm more likely to change things that need changing.	I'm a more understanding and tolerant person now.
Knowing I can handle difficulties.	I value other people more now.

positive states or outcomes that are an extension or continuation of prior psychological growth or development versus sequelae of trauma exposure that represent qualitative discontinuities in the person's development. Similarly, Frazier and Kaler (2006) note that retrospective self-report measures of PTG are vulnerable to error because of the well-documented difficulty that people have in accurately recalling past states or attributes, making it unlikely that they can accurately compare current states or attributes to past ones when estimating the nature or extent of "growth." Nor do the instruments rule out alternative explanations for outcomes that are putatively the product of exposure to psychological trauma (e.g., mobilization of social support, temporary suspension of life routines and responsibilities during trauma recovery, defensive avoidance of trauma reminders). Thus, what is presumed to be caused by trauma may actually be inaccurate, due to being indirectly mediated by more proximal causal agents and therefore spuriously related to traumatic experiences.

These threats to the psychometric internal and external validity of measures of PTG are compounded by wishful thinking, particularly in the wake of stressful events (Frazier & Kaler, 2006). McFarland and Alvaro (2000), for instance, found that trauma survivors' reports of positive changes in personal attributes exceeded those of third-party observers. Specifically, survivors tended to rate their preevent functioning less favorably than did other observers, which Smith and Cook (2004) suggest may exemplify Taylor and Brown's (1988) concept of a "positive illusion." Such an illusion may be understood as an adaptive coping strategy whereby an individual alters his or her self-perceptions in order to increase a sense of control following an adverse event.

Frazier and Kaler (2006) cast further doubt on the validity of self-report measures of stress-related growth based on the results of three studies. In the first, they found that cancer survivors did not differ from matched controls in well-being. In their second study, college students who reported benefiting from their worst life experience did not differ on measures of well-being compared to those who did not report benefiting. Finally, and perhaps most tellingly, they found limited evidence for convergent or discriminant validity with a self-report measure of PTG (Perceived Benefit Scales, PBS; McMillen & Fisher, 1998) in relation to other self-report measures of corresponding aspects of well-being (i.e., family closeness, life priorities, spirituality, self-efficacy, compassion). They also found that the PBS subscales were substantially intercorrelated ($r = .38 - .68$), suggesting that the positive appraisals assessed by the scale do not reflect discrete types of "growth" or even well-being.

Indeed, the distinction between PTG and positive cognitive appraisals or coping strategies is frequently blurred in the literature. For instance, Salter and Stallard (2004) concluded from their study of PTG among child survivors of automobile accidents that 42% of their participants demonstrated PTG, "most notably in terms of their philosophy of life." However, this "growth" was evidenced by statements made by some child survivors that they felt "lucky" to be alive. As one respondent put it, "Anything you want, go for it quicker as you never realize when you are going to go." It is unclear whether this sort of attitude following exposure to a traumatic event represents PTG, or an attempt to cope with the heightened realization of mortality that is a hallmark symptom of PTSD (i.e., sense of foreshortened future). This attitude also may reflect a dispositional trait that Rabe, Zöllner, Maercker, and Karl (2006) describe as "goal-related approach tendencies" (p. 883). In a study with survivors of life-threatening motor vehicle accidents on average 5 years later, Rabe and colleagues (2006) found that subscale scores from the Post-Traumatic Growth Inventory (Tedeschi & Calhoun, 1996) consistent with striving to gain control and find meaning (*New Possibilities, Changed Relationships, Appreciation of Life, Personal Strength*) were associated with greater degrees of frontal cortical activation in the left (versus right) hemisphere. This EEG pattern is related to trait-like tendencies to be goal directed and to cope with adversity by setting goals and seeking personal control and meaning. The Spirituality subscale of the PTGI, by contrast, was unrelated to laterality of cortical neural activity. Although these relationships were independent of a general tendency toward optimism and positive emotions, the study's findings suggest that the "growth" reported by respondents may be a longstanding trait rather than a change.

In order to accurately measure growth resulting from exposure to an adverse event, we need a reliable measure of preevent functioning. The strategy of choice for such a study would be a prospective design. Linley and Joseph (2004) identified three longitudinal studies of PTG, none of which measured preevent functioning. Two other longitudinal studies included pretrauma baseline measures. Davis, Nolen-Hoeksema, and Larson (1998) followed bereaved adults during a hospice program on average 3 months prior to a loved one's death, for 18 months. Controlling for preloss distress levels, they found that making sense of the loss was associated with less distress in the first year postloss, and reporting benefiting from the experience was associated with less distress in the 13- to 18-month period. However, it is not clear that the preloss distress levels were a true baseline because the loss was imminent and the stress of caregiving often already was protracted at the time of the baseline assessment. It also is not clear that the "benefit" was associated with the loss *per se,* as opposed to other factors such as support received or characterological resilience.

Ickovics and colleagues (2006) also obtained a baseline assessment of psychological distress from inner city adolescent girls who were sexually active (half of whom were pregnant), and re-interviewed them every 6 months for 18 months. Trauma history and posttraumatic growth were assessed only at the 12-month assessment, respectively, by open-ended responses to a question asking about the "hardest thing [they] ever had to deal with" and the PTGI. Only the four PTGI subscales reflecting approach tendencies were used, and were sufficiently intercorrelated ($r = .50 - .68$) that the authors used only a total score for primary analyses. Controlling for baseline distress, PTGI at 12-months predicted reduced emotional distress 6 months later. However, the traumatic events occurred at any point in the girls' lives, rarely following the baseline interview, so there actually was no pretrauma baseline. Stability or change in PTGI was not assessed. Therefore, PTGI's putative prospective association with emotional distress in this study is as likely to reflect unmeasured factors such as dispositional coping, cognitive styles, or social support as actual growth.

Longitudinal studies with time series assessments beginning with a pretrauma baseline (or better yet, a pretrauma series of assessments to establish not just a baseline but a pretrauma trajectory) clearly are needed in order to demonstrate that purported "change" or "growth" are qualitative discontinuities rather than merely quantitative changes, or no actual change at all. The few extant longitudinal studies suggest that PTG has varied trajectories, including increases that are followed by reductions (Frazier & Kaler, 2006)—suggesting that reported "growth" may actually be fluctuating states of mind, affect, or motivation that are at best transient and at worst epiphenomenal.

In addition, much of the research on PTG actually involved people facing serious illness and other events that may not fulfill the gold standard criteria for trauma established by the American Psychiatric Association (1994; i.e., life threatening or a violation of bodily integrity, and eliciting reactions of extreme fear, helplessness, or horror). Thus, the specificity of growth to the occurrence of psychological trauma, as opposed to a relationship between growth and a range of subtraumatic and traumatic stressors, has not been demonstrated. It may seem intuitively more plausible that subtraumatic stressors that do not elicit the extreme alterations in self-regulation might more readily be sources of growth than traumatic stressors because of their less intense impact. However, there is no evidence that growth is more likely after subtraumatic than traumatic stressors, and there is much evidence that chronic subtraumatic stressors (e.g., divorce, unemployment, debilitating but not terminal illnesses) can have profoundly debilitating allostatic effects (McEwen & Stellar, 1993).

In sum, despite ample references to PTG in popular culture, and despite numerous studies purporting to measure PTG, methodological weaknesses in many of these studies makes drawing conclusions problematic. Growth may be the result of overcoming adversity, but the jury is out as to whether what has been designated as "growth" in studies of people facing adversity is (a) actual sustained growth; (b) transient changes in mood, expectancies, and lifestyle; (c) adaptive (defensive) reappraisals to compensate for distress (e.g., positive illusions); (d) the restoration of prior capacities following an adaptive shift from ordinary to survival-based self-regulation (i.e., resilience); or (e) measurement artifact. This uncertainty is evident in the relatively guarded conclusion of Linley and Joseph (2004) at the conclusion of their comprehensive review of the literature: "we conclude that greater traumatic experience, dealt with by means of positive reinterpretation and acceptance coping, in people who are optimistic, intrinsically religious, and experience more positive affect, is likely to lead to reports of greater adversarial growth" (p. 17).

POSTTRAUMATIC GROWTH: A CONTRARIAN CHALLENGE AND REDEFINITION

Acute traumatic experiences can seem to provide an epiphany, in which the individual experiences a sense of awakening and powerful motivation and ability to make fundamental changes in lifestyle, priorities, and even personality. However, as we have shown, research on the sequelae of psychological trauma suggests that such PTG either is accompanied by, or actually is an outgrowth of, survival responses that are highly automatic, defensive, self-reinforcing, and resistant to extinction (e.g., the colloquial "adrenaline rush" that may be transiently pleasurable due to the co-activation of dopaminergic reward systems; Moghaddam, 2002). The result may be growth, but tends to be a fairly transient heightened state of alertness, relief, or dissociation that can be sustained (or partially recreated) only at the expense of self-regulation (e.g., by substance use, risk taking, or self-harm).

However, it also is possible that psychological trauma may be a catalyst for sustained growth as a result of the drastic changes it causes in the person's environment or experience, which can elicit self-reflection by punctuating otherwise habitual ways of living and placing in bold relief the value of choices and goals that have been taken for granted. However, to capitalize on this opportunity, it is necessary to first support defensive survival coping, and then (when circumstances no longer involve threat or danger) [re]activate self-reflective controlled information processing. Although there is evidence of a progressive decline in posttraumatic stress symptoms reported by most trauma survivors over the following 4 to 12 months (Mancini & Bonnano, 2006), there is no evidence that growth *per se* progressively increases over time following trauma. If resilience (or "resistance," per Layne, Warren, Shalev, & Watson, 2007) is understood as defined by Mancini and Bonnano

(2006, p. 972)—"the ability of adults . . . who are exposed to an isolated and potentially highly disruptive event such as the death of a close relation or a violent or life-threatening situation to maintain relatively stable, healthy levels of psychological and physical functioning"—then optimal posttraumatic outcomes do not necessarily involve growth. Mancini and Bonnano (2006) add that resilience also may involve "the capacity for generative experiences and positive emotions" (p. 972), but it is not clear from the extant clinical and research literatures that this is caused by psychological trauma as opposed to occurring before, during, and after traumatic experiences as an enduring or potential characteristic of the person.

Thus, instead of being due to experiencing and surviving or recovering from psychological trauma, growth may be a misnomer for heroic survival coping or for the reemergence of prior psychobiological growth that actually was disrupted or blocked during traumatic experiences. Just as resilience differs from recovery (Mancini & Bonnano, 2006), so too growth (i.e., the enhancement of self-regulation) must be differentiated from posttraumatic survival adaptations and from resilience, resistance, or recovery in the aftermath of psychological trauma. Rather than hoping that growth can be a silver lining following psychological trauma, it may be better to focus on how the self-regulatory capacities of persons who have suffered trauma can be regenerated and enhanced.

How then can one reconcile our position—that growth following adversity has not been clearly demonstrated to occur—with the empirical literature showing that posttraumatic growth may be common? Based on converging evidence from personality, social, and cognitive psychology, it appears that common cognitive heuristics, memory distortions, and fundamental flaws in investigators' measurement strategies may frequently lead research participants to report growth even when it has not actually occurred. We now turn our attention to these heuristics, distortions, and flawed measurement strategies, described by Tennen and Affleck (2005).

DO POSTTRAUMATIC GROWTH SCALES MEASURE GROWTH?

The upsurge in research on posttraumatic growth has been hastened in large part by the availability of scales purporting to measure growth in the context of adversity. Two of the most widely used scales, the Posttraumatic Growth Inventory (PTGI; Tedeschi & Calhoun, 1996) and the Changes in Outlook Questionnaire (CiOQ; Joseph et al., 1993, 2005), are easy to administer and they demonstrate good internal consistency. Scores on these scales typically predict outcomes we expect growth to predict such as well-being and low levels of distress, and growth scores, in turn, are predicted by personal characteristics we expect to predict growth following adversity, such as optimism and a sense of mastery (Linley & Joseph, 2004; Tedeschi & Calhoun, 2004). These scales also have excellent face validity and for this reason they are readily accepted by research participants, many of whom find that the scale items map well onto their personal experience. Armed with scales that have the trappings of psychometric excellence, investigators have used these measures to examine posttraumatic growth's nomological network (Cronbach & Meehl, 1955).

WHAT DO GROWTH SCALES REQUIRE OF RESEARCH PARTICIPANTS?

Although research participants readily complete measures of posttraumatic growth, an examination of scale items raises concerns as to whether people can accurately portray growth experiences. Table 15.1 presents sample items from the PTGI and the CiOQ and instructions to participants. Instructions for the PTGI ask participants to rate how much they have changed on each scale item as the result of the crisis they experienced. For example, people are asked to share how much closer they feel to others as a consequence of their crisis. Similarly, the CiOQ requires participants to evaluate how much they experienced each of the personal changes depicted in the scale as a result of the adverse event they experienced. For example, someone completing this scale is asked to rate how much more he or she values other people as an upshot of the selected adverse event.

We find it instructive to consider the mental operations required to provide ratings for PTGI and CiOQ items. A response to each scale item requires the respondent to engage in five assessments. S/he must: (1) evaluate her/his current standing on the dimension described in the item, for example, a sense of closeness to others; (2) recall his or her previous standing on the same dimension; (3) compare the current and previous standings; (4) assess the degree of change; and (5) determine how much of that change can be attributed to the traumatic event or stressful encounter. By engaging in these five steps, the participant can respond to each scale item. It is tempting to argue that our research participants do not actually make such evaluations and calculations, but rather they offer global impressions of personal change. Yet, this line of reasoning easily becomes a slippery slope. If people simply offer their global impressions of change, they are not reporting stress related or trauma related change, which is precisely what we seek to measure. In other words, the *best* we can hope for is that individuals who complete scales measuring growth in the face of adversity are actually engaging in the five appraisals, recollections, comparisons, and determinations we propose.

RECALLING PERSONAL CHANGE

Put simply, we assert that people *cannot* accurately generate or manipulate the information required to faithfully report trauma- or stress-related growth. All published measures of stress- or trauma-related growth require respondents to recollect personal change over time. The implicit assumption is that people can accurately recall personal change. Yet, there is no empirical support for this assumption. Indeed, the psychological literature demonstrates consistently that people are unable to recollect personal change accurately. We now summarize several key studies that demonstrate how recollections of personal change are flawed.

Herbst, McCrae, Costa, Feaganes, and Siegler (2000) assessed the "Big 5" personality traits (neuroticism, extraversion, openness, conscientiousness, and agreeableness) twice over 6 years. After the second assessment participants were asked to report changes in their personalities over the 6 years between the two formal assessments. Costa et al. found that perceived changes in personality were at best weak predictors of residual change scores. Similarly, Henry, Moffitt, Caspi, Langley, and Silva (1994), who had collected 18 years of repeated measures of well-being and behavior from their large and well-characterized cohort, asked participants to recall how much they changed on the measured constructs. Their findings echoed those of Herbst et al. (2000): Retrospective reports of change showed poor agreement with prospective data documenting actual changes. More recently, Robins and colleagues (Robins, Noftle, Trzesniewski, & Roberts, 2005) reported the findings of a study that measured college students' personality 6 times over 4 years. After the Year 4 assessment, they measured perceived personality change. Most of these students believed that their personality had changed substantially in positive ways—from their reports we might be led to infer that they experienced "transition-to-college related growth." However, the correspondence between actual change measured prospectively and perceived change was, once again, quite modest.

Each of these studies that revealed modest concordance between recalled personal change and prospectively assessed change examined changes over 4 to 18 years. Perhaps people are better at recalling personal change over briefer periods of time. Although this is a reasonable speculation, the assertion that recall of personal change is not accurate over long periods of time puts current theorizing about posttraumatic growth in a thorny situation. Current theory asserts that growth is more likely later in the coping process, after prior adjustments. Just how late remains ambiguous. However, if people cannot recall change accurately over long periods of time, it would seem as though the limits of personal recall would make it difficult at best to measure growth later in the coping process. Furthermore, a recent meta-analysis found time since adversity to be unrelated to PTG (Helgeson, Reynolds, & Tomich, 2006). Growth represents progressive change over time (albeit not necessarily a linear or unbroken trajectory), and as such should not be able to occur with equal likelihood or strength at any point following adversity.

This conceptual-methodological quagmire aside, there is also rather clear evidence that people cannot recall personal change accurately even over a few months. In a pivotal study, Wilson and Ross (2001) asked college students to rate their social skills, self-confidence and life satisfaction in September, and then again in November. Their September self-ratings were somewhat more favorable than their November ratings. But when these students were asked in November to describe themselves as they were in September on these same attributes, they rated their September self as inferior to their November self. In other words, they perceived improvement in the face of actual decline. Had Wilson and Ross asked their study participants how much they had changed since September, they would have almost surely found evidence of "growth" when there was actually less than none.

Perceived Positive Change in Relationships

One area of growth following adversity that has been described consistently in the literature is improved close relationships and feeling closer to family and friends. Although the evidence reviewed to this point reveals that people are unable to accurately report personal change, perhaps they are more accurate in reporting positive relationship change. Fortunately, there is a well-developed literature related to this issue. In one of several studies of perceived growth in close relationships, Kirkpatrick and Hazan (1994) asked dating couples to assess the current quality of their relationship once a year for 4 years. In year 4, these couples were asked about the quality of their relationship in each of the previous years that they had participated in the study. As a group, couples recalled that the strength of their love had grown over time, just as participants in studies of posttraumatic growth report that their close relationships have deepened and grown. Yet, the prospective ratings Kirkpatrick and Hazan had collected revealed *no* increases in reported love and attachment. These findings are important for another reason. In the posttraumatic growth literature, even modest agreement regarding change between the participant and a significant other has been interpreted as strong evidence for the validity of the reported change. Such agreement, which is rarely sought in studies of posttraumatic growth, is interpreted frequently as evidence for the accuracy of such reports (e.g., Park, Cohen, & Murch, 1996). Kirkpatrick and

Hazan's findings demonstrate that within-couple agreement about positive relationship change does not mean that such change actually occurred.

Kirkpatrick and Hazan's findings have received conceptual replication. Karney and Coombs (2000) found that wives in couples who had been assessed over a 10-year period recalled their initial assessments of their marriages, made 10 years earlier, as worse than they actually were. Consequently, they reported that their marriages had improved. In fact, these women held *more negative* appraisals of their marriage than they had 10 years earlier. Their reports of relationship growth were misguided not only in magnitude, but also in direction. This and related evidence led Karney and Frye (2002) to conclude that, "marriage partners manufacture improvement out of thin air by rewriting history." Taken together, these studies of couples' recollections of relationship change present a formidable challenge for the assessment of posttraumatic growth. They also provide a clue as to how a sense of growth might emerge when none has occurred: People rather easily come to believe they have grown by deprecating their past selves so as to experience personal progress. This tendency to distance one's current self from a past self through deprecation of the past self (McFarland & Alvaro, 2000), or by temporally distancing the past self in response to motivational concerns (Ross & Wilson, 2002) or by making downward temporal comparisons (Albert, 1977) means that reports of growth in the aftermath of adversity cannot be taken at face value from scores on the PTGI, CiOQ or related measures. Furthermore, the evidence that partners manufacture improvement by rewriting their history as a couple suggests that we cannot rely on a partner's agreement with growth reports as a validity check.

Attributing Growth to a Traumatic Experience   Thus far, we have demonstrated that even if people are able to accurately evaluate their current standing on the dimensions described on posttraumatic growth and stress-related growth inventories, most do not reliably recall their previous (preevent) standing on these dimensions. Whether this inaccurate recall is motivated by a desire to distance the current self (or relationship) from a past self (or relationship), or it simply reflects memory decay, the evidence is clear: Recall of one's previous self or relationship is flawed. Without an accurate recollection of the pretrauma self and relationships, people cannot realistically compare their current and previous standings on the various dimensions assessed in traumatic growth inventories, and they cannot assess the degree of change correctly. But even if people were not burdened by these well-documented recall problems, to complete current measures of posttraumatic growth they would need to accurately engage in the fifth judgment we mentioned previously, that is, they need to determine how much change can be attributed to the traumatic event or stressful encounter.

In other words, people must be able to accurately judge covariation or a contingency between the event and subsequent personal changes.

A good deal of evidence demonstrates how judgments of covariation or contingent relationships are biased through illusory correlation (Chapman, 1967), whereby the individual who expects a relationship between the two variables tends to overestimate the magnitude of any relation that might exist, or even infer a relation when none exists. In other words, people have great difficulty detecting, let alone recalling, covariation. For example, Todd et al. (2005) compared people's *questionnaire* reports that they drank alcohol in response to negative affect—a contingent relationship—with real-time electronic diary data that actually captured negative affect and drinking as they occurred. The retrospective questionnaire-based accounts of "drinking to cope" showed a remarkably modest concordance with the association between negative mood and drinking as they were measured close to their real-time occurrence. Todd et al. conjectured that participants' implicit theories (Ross, 1989) of when people drink may have guided their retrospective reports but not their actual drinking patterns. Several investigators have conjectured that the same sorts of implicit theories are at work when people are asked to describe ways in which they have grown in the face of adversity (Conway & Ross, 1984; Tennen & Affleck, 2002).

Posttraumatic Growth in Popular Culture: Implications for Assessment

Although Wortman (2004) and others have warned about the risks of having the concept of posttraumatic growth embraced by the popular culture, there is ample evidence that the notion of growth following adversity has already infused popular culture (Tennen & Affleck, 2005) and this infusion, in turn, has fortified people's implicit theories regarding this phenomenon. The American Psychological Association (APA) has contributed to the popularization of growth following adversity through its *Road to Resilience* campaign by offering the public inspiring vignettes depicting people who have experienced posttraumatic growth along with encouraging reminders to regularly reassess one's own growth following an adverse experience by using their online version of the PTGI.

Ross (1989) has argued convincingly that people maintain personal theories about how personal change occurs and that these theories "may lead them to overestimate the amount of change that has occurred" (p. 342). He also notes that the more widely a theory of change is embraced in a culture, the more likely it is that most people will accept that theory. Western culture has long held the premise that people gain wisdom and more productive lives in the aftermath of trauma. That premise is echoed and magnified through our daily exposure to popular magazines and newspapers proffering poignant stories about individuals claiming personal growth in response to adversity, and through web sites such as APA's *Road to Resilience* that encourage people who have been victimized to look for signs of posttraumatic growth. These forces of popular culture create a genuine challenge to investigators trying to measure and understand posttraumatic growth.

Are We Measuring Growth?

Our review of the literature documenting the significant limitations in people's capacity to recall personal change leads us to conclude that people cannot generate, manipulate, or reconstruct the information required to faithfully report posttraumatic growth. Recall decay aside, people are motivated to experience personal progress and to avoid or distance themselves from failure. But even among those relatively few people with near perfect recall and no motivational axe to grind, the challenge of detecting and recalling trauma-related change, that is, change that takes into account the impact of shocking, demoralizing, and potentially life-threatening experiences and calibrates change based on complex developmental trajectories, is formidable at best. We must conclude that in the context of the recall and information processes we have discussed, current indicators of posttraumatic growth do not and cannot adequately measure the experience of growth in the aftermath of adversity.

AN ALTERNATIVE PARADIGM: ENHANCED OR RECONSTITUTED SELF-REGULATION AFTER TRAUMA

What is needed is a framework for accurately understanding the aftermath of traumatic life experiences that neither reframes trauma as a growth experience nor tacitly encourages people to devalue their previous self or relationships in order to cultivate the illusion of having transcended trauma through growth. Such defensive adjustments are more consistent with the hallmark features of PTSD (e.g., avoidance of troubling memories or emotions, emotional numbing, deprecation of self and relationships) than with resistance, recovery, or resilience in the aftermath of trauma. We suggest that posttraumatic biopsychosocial impairment should be viewed as a breakdown in self-regulation, and that protective factors (e.g., social support, socioeconomic resources, psychosocial and biological interventions) promote positive outcomes posttrauma by reinstating or enhancing pretraumatic self-regulatory capacities. This perspective is consistent with the reformulation of posttraumatic recovery proposed by Layne and colleagues (2007), who note that "stress resistance and resilience are now largely regarded as the outcome of common developmentally linked regulatory processes (e.g., coping skills, social support, self-concept, self-efficacy, self-regulation) that promote positive adaptation, not only under heightened or extreme adversity, but also under conditions of normal everyday stress and strain . . . (p. 502)." Recovery from psychological trauma thus may involve growth but alternately may be a process of (re)building of the person's "adaptive coping repertoire, including problem-solving and support-seeking skills; improving parenting skills; and buttressing extended social support networks" (Layne et al., 2007). Surviving psychological trauma has not been shown to cause, or to be reliably or even occasionally followed by genuine personal growth. However, trauma may nevertheless *set the occasion for* growth when posttraumatic events or circumstances support the development or enhancement of adaptive self-regulatory capacities.

SUMMARY

What appears to be posttraumatic growth instead may be a combination of the reconstitution or amplification of preexisting development of self-regulatory capacities by posttraumatic experiences that foster recovery, along with methodological artifacts due to limitations in the self-report methods typically used to measure posttraumatic change. In our view, the growth potential of psychological trauma comes from drastic changes that traumatic stressors cause in the person's/community's environment and experience, which interrupts otherwise highly routinized and largely automatic patterns of functioning. Sadly, the resultant survival-based adaptations in self-regulation may persist in the form of symptoms that override adaptations that previously supported healthy functioning and development. However, the opportunity highlighted by the concept of posttraumatic growth is that the shock and adaptive shift caused by trauma can provide a platform for conscious intentional reevaluation of how one regulates oneself somatically, cognitively, affectively, and in relationships. Psychotherapy for PTSD involves the planful reconstruction of memory, self-appraisals, relationship patterns, and core values, beliefs, and commitments—whether this is done with a primary focus on regaining the capacity to face memories without avoidance (e.g., prolonged exposure, EMDR, or cognitive processing therapies) or with a broader focus on reclaiming the ability to think, feel, and act without being driven by terror, grief, shame, or anger (Ford, Courtois, van der Hart, Nijenhuis, & Steele, 2005). The narratives of trauma survivors (e.g., Weinrib, Rothrock, Johnsen, & Lutgendorf, 2006) that have been interpreted as reflecting "growth" may alternatively be construed as ways in which people have used formal processes such as therapy or informal ways of coping and getting help through natural support systems in order to regain (and possibly to enhance) the capacity to be self-regulated in dealing with memory, emotion, health, and familial, social, and vocationally significant relationships. When self-regulation is working, people typically do not notice, let alone pin their hopes on, achieving personal growth except at times when life provides either a breather or a challenge that permits or requires self-appraisal. What the research literature on posttraumatic growth suggests is that at those times it can be helpful (in terms of hope, intimacy, and self-efficacy) to have the hope for, or illusion of, personal growth. Whether posttraumatic growth is real, illusory, or simply a measurement artifact remains to be determined with more rigorous research. For now, we, and our patients and students, may be able to grow by recognizing that we have much yet to learn about, and from, trauma, so long as we do not make the fundamental mistake of prematurely reifying trauma as a source of personal growth.

Summary Points (Practice)

- Assessment of PTG should distinguish between new beliefs/capacities versus the reinstatement or reconstitution of pretrauma beliefs and self-regulatory capacities.
- Client descriptions of PTG should be carefully examined to avoid missing continued or new instances of defensive "flight into health" and to therapeutically assist clients in recognizing the self-regulation skills that may enable them to both recover from traumatic stress, and potentially, to grow psychologically.
- Although growth may occur following exposure to psychological trauma, the source of such growth should be attributed to the client's skills for self-regulation rather than to sources outside the client's control (e.g., "what does not kill us makes us stronger"). The latter attributions are likely to decrease efficacy and responsibility because of their external, unpredictable, unstable nature.

Summary Points (Research)

- Longitudinal studies with pretrauma assessments and prospective rather than retrospective measurement of hypothesized PTG changes are needed to reduce the bias introduced by retrospective studies of PTG.
- Ecologically valid measurement, including close to real-time monitoring of events and cognitive, affective, and behavioral responses, is needed to determine the extent to which hypothesized PTG changes reflect artifacts of retrospective summary reports.

- Nonlinear as well as linear trajectories of change must be modeled, rather than timepoint-to-timepoint difference scores, to identify idiographic as well as nomothetic patterns of posttraumatic change.
- PTG must be distinguished conceptually and in trajectory models from posttraumatic resistance, resilience, and delayed or reinstated impairment (Layne et al., 2007).
- Research is needed to identify the self-regulation capacities that increase the likelihood of posttraumatic resistance, resilience, and growth.

REFERENCES

Adams, R., & Boscarino, J. (2006). Predictors of PTSD and delayed PTSD after disaster: The impact of exposure and psychosocial resources. *Journal of Nervous and Mental Diseases, 194*, 485–493.

Adolphs, R. (2002). Neural systems for recognizing emotion. *Current Opinion in Neurobiology, 12*, 169–177.

Albert, S. (1977). Temporal comparison theory. *Psychological Review, 84*, 485–503.

American Psychiatric Association. (1994). *Diagnostic and statistical manual of mental disorders* (4th ed.). Washington, DC: Author.

Armeli, S., Gunthert, K. C., & Cohen, L. H. (2001). Stressor appraisals, coping, and post-event outcomes: The dimensionality and antecedents of stress-related growth. *Journal of Social and Clinical Psychology, 55*, 29–35.

Beers, S., & DeBellis, M. (2002). Neuropsychological function in children with maltreatment-related posttraumatic stress disorder. *American Journal of Psychiatry, 159*, 483–486.

Berger-Sweeney, J., & Hohman, C. F. (1997). Behavioral consequences of abnormal cortical development: Insights into developmental disabilities. *Behavioural Brain Research, 86*, 121–142.

Bremner, J. D., Vythilingam, M., Vermetten, E., Southwick, S., McGlashan, T., Nazeer, A., et al. (2003). MRI and PET study of deficits in hippocampal structure and function in women with childhood sexual abuse and posttraumatic stress disorder. *American Journal of Psychiatry, 160*, 924–932.

Bremner, J. D., Vythilingam, M., Vermetten, E., Southwick, S., McGlashan, T., Staib, L., et al. (2003). Neural correlates of declarative memory for emotionally valenced words in women with posttraumatic stress disorder related to early childhood sexual abuse. *Biological Psychiatry, 53*, 879–889.

Briere, J., Scott, C., & Weathers, F. (2005). Peritraumatic and persistent dissociation in the presumed etiology of PTSD. *American Journal of Psychiatry, 162*, 2295–2301.

Briere, J., & Spinazzola, J. (2005). Phenomenology and psychological assessment of complex posttraumatic states. *Journal of Traumatic Stress, 18*, 401–412.

Cassidy, J., & Mohr, J. (2001). Unresolvable fear, trauma, and psychopathology. *Clinical Psychology: Science and Practice, 8*, 275–298.

Chapman, L. J. (1967). Illusory correlation in observational report. *Journal of Verbal Learning and Verbal Behavior, 6,* 151–156.

Charney, D. S. (2004). Psychobiological mechanisms of resilience and vulnerability. *American Journal of Psychiatry, 161,* 195–216.

Cicchetti, D., & Toth, S. (1995). A developmental psychopathology perspective on child abuse and neglect. *Journal of the American Academy of Child and Adolescent Psychiatry, 34,* 541–565.

Conway, M., & Ross, M. (1984). Getting what you want by revising what you had. *Journal of Personality and Social Psychology, 47,* 738–748.

Cordon, I., Pipe, M., Sayfan, L., Melinder, A., & Goodman, G. (2004). Memory for traumatic experiences in early childhood. *Developmental Review, 24,* 101–132.

Cronbach, L., & Meehl, P. (1955). Construct validity in psychological tests. *Psychological Bulletin, 52*(4), 281–302.

Davis, C., Nolen-Hoksema, S., & Larson, J. (1998). Making sense of loss and benefiting from the experience. *Journal of Personality and Social Psychology, 75,* 561–574.

Dodge, K., Pettit, G., Bates, J., & Valente, E. (1995). Social information-processing patterns partially mediate the effect of early physical abuse on later conduct problems. *Journal of Abnormal Psychology, 104,* 632–643.

Doussard-Roosevelt, J., Porges, S., Scanlon, J., Alemi, B., & Scanlon, K. (1997). Vagal regulation of heart rate in the prediction of developmental outcome for very low birth weight preterm infants. *Child Development, 68,* 173–186.

Duchaine, B., Cosmides, L., & Tooby, J. (2001). Evolutionary psychology and the brain. *Current Opinion in Neurobiology, 11,* 225–230.

Elzinga, B., & Bremner, J. D. (2002). Are the neural substrates of memory the final common pathway in posttraumatic stress disorder? *Journal of Affective Disorders, 70,* 1–17.

Fonagy, P. (2003). The development of psychopathology from infancy to adulthood: The mysterious unfolding of disturbance in time. *Infant Mental Health Journal, 24,* 212–239.

Ford, J. D. (2005). Treatment implications of altered neurobiology, affect regulation and information processing following child maltreatment. *Psychiatric Annals, 35,* 410–419.

Ford, J. D., Courtois, C., van der Hart, O., Nijenhuis, E., & Steele, K. (2005). Treatment of complex post-traumatic self-dysregulation. *Journal of Traumatic Stress, 18,* 467–477.

Frazier, P., & Kaler, M. (2006). Assessing the validity of self-reported stress-related growth. *Journal of Consulting and Clinical Psychology, 74,* 859–869.

Frith, C., & Frith, U. (1999). Interacting minds—A biological basis. *Science, 286,* 1692–1695.

Frueh, B. C., Elhai, J., & Kaloupek, D. (2004). Unresolved issues in the assessment of trauma exposure and posttraumatic reactions. In G. Rosen (Ed.), *Posttraumatic stress disorder: Issues and controversies* (pp. 63–84). Chichester, West Sussex, England: Wiley.

Giedd, J., Blumenthal, J., Jeffries, N., Castellanos, F., Liu, H., Zijdenbos, A., et al. (1999). Brain development during childhood and adolescence: A longitudinal MRI study. *Nature Neuroscience, 2,* 861–863.

Grossberg, S. (1988). Nonlinear neural networks. *Neural Networks, 1*, 17–61.

Gully, K. (2003). Expectations Test. *Child Maltreatment, 8*, 218–229.

Guthrie, R., & Bryant, R. (2006). Extinction learning before trauma and subsequent posttraumatic stress. *Psychosomatic Medicine, 68*, 307–311.

Halligan, S., Herbert, J., Goodyer, I., & Murray, L. (2004). Exposure to postnatal depression predicts elevated cortisol in adolescent offspring. *Biological Psychiatry, 55*, 376–381.

Heim, C., & Nemeroff, C. (2001). The role of childhood trauma in the neurobiology of mood and anxiety disorders. *Biological Psychiatry, 49*, 1023–1039.

Helgeson, V., Reynolds, K., & Tomich, P. (2006). A meta-analytic review of benefit finding and growth. *Journal of Consulting and Clinical Psychology, 74*, 797–816.

Henry, B., Moffitt, T. E., Caspi, A., Langley, J., & Silva, P. A. (1994). On the "remembrance of things past": A longitudinal evaluation of the retrospective method. *Psychological Assessment, 6*, 92–101.

Herbst, J. H., McCrae, R. R., Costa, P. T., Jr., Feaganes, J. R., & Siegler, I. C. (2000). Self-perceptions of stability and change in personality at midlife: The UNC alumni heart study. *Assessment, 7*, 379–388.

Ickovics, J., Meade, C., Kershaw, T., Milan, S., Lewis, J., & Ethier, K. (2006). Urban teens: Trauma, posttraumatic growth, and emotional distress among female adolescents. *Journal of Consulting and Clinical Psychology, 74*, 541–550.

Johnson, J., Cohen, P., Brown, J., Smailes, E., & Bernstein, D. (1999). Childhood maltreatment increases risk of personality disorders during early adulthood. *Archives of General Psychiatry, 56*, 600–606.

Johnson, M., & Mareschal, D. (2001). Cognitive and perceptual development during infancy. *Current Opinion in Neurobiology, 11*, 213–218.

Joseph, S., Linley, P. A., Andrews, L., Harris, G., Howle, B., Woodward, C., et al. (2005). Assessing positive and negative changes in the aftermath of adversity: Psychometric evaluation of the Changes in Outlook Questionnaire. *Psychological Assessment, 17*, 70–80.

Joseph, S., Williams, R., & Yule, W. (1993). Changes in outlook following disaster: The preliminary development of a measure to assess positive and negative responses. *Journal of Traumatic Stress, 6*, 271–279.

Kagan, J. (2001). Emotional development and psychiatry. *Biological Psychiatry, 49*, 973–979.

Kanemura, H., Aihara, M., Aoki, S., Araki, T., & Nakazawa, S. (2003). Development of the prefrontal lobe in infants and children. *Brain and Development, 25*, 195–199.

Karney, B. R., & Coombs, R. H. (2000). Memory bias in long-term close relationships: Consistency or improvement? *Personality and Social Psychology Bulletin, 26*, 959–970.

Karney, B. R., & Frye, N. E. (2002). "But we've been getting better lately": Comparing prospective and retrospective views of relationship development. *Journal of Personality and Social Psychology, 82*, 222–238.

Kassam-Adams, N., & Winston, F. (2004). Predicting child PTSD: The relationship between acute stress disorder and PTSD in injured children. *Journal of the American Academy of Child and Adolescent Psychiatry, 43*, 403–411.

Kaufman, J., Plotsky, P., Nemeroff, C., & Charney, D. (2000). Effects of early adverse experiences on brain structure and function. *Biological Psychiatry, 48,* 778–790.

Kirkpatrick, L. A., & Hazan, C. (1994). Attachment styles and close relationships: A four-year prospective study. *Personal Relationships, 1,* 123–142.

Layne, C. M., Warren, J., Shalev, A., & Watson, P. (2007). Risk, vulnerability, resistance, and resilience: Towards an integrative conceptualization of posttraumatic adaptation. In M. J. Friedman, T. M. Keane, & P. A. Resick (Eds.), *Handbook of PTSD: Science and practice* (pp. 497–520). New York: Guilford Press.

Linley, P. A., & Joseph, S. (2004). Positive change following trauma and adversity: A review. *Journal of Traumatic Stress, 17*(1), 11–21.

Mancini, A., & Bonnano, G. (2006). Resilience in the face of potential trauma. *Journal of Clinical Psychology in Session, 62,* 971–985.

Matsumoto, K., Suzuki, W., & Tanaka, K. (2003). Neuronal correlates of goal-based motor selection in the prefrontal cortex. *Science, 301,* 229–232.

Maunder, R., & Hunter, J. (2001). Attachment and psychosomatic medicine: Developmental contributions to stress and disease. *Psychosomatic Medicine, 63,* 556–567.

May, J. C., Delgado, M., Dahl, R., Stenger, A., Ryan, N., Fiez, J., et al. (2004). Event-related magnetic resonance imaging of reward-related brain circuitry in children and adolescents. *Biological Psychiatry, 55,* 359–366.

Mayes, L. C. (2000). A developmental perspective on the regulation of arousal states. *Seminars in Perinatology, 24,* 267–279.

McEwen, B. S., & Stellar, E. (1993). Stress and the individual: Mechanisms leading to disease. *Archives of Internal Medicine, 153,* 2093–2101.

McFarland, C., & Alvaro, C. (2000). The impact of motivation on temporal comparisons: Coping with traumatic events by perceiving personal growth. *Journal of Personality and Social Psychology, 79,* 327–343.

McMillen, J., & Fisher, R. (1998). The Perceived Benefits Scales. *Social Work Research, 22,* 173–187.

Moghaddam, B. (2002). Stress activation of glutamate neurotransmission in the prefrontal cortex: Implications for dopamine-associated psychiatric disorders. *Biological Psychiatry, 57,* 775–787.

Nelson, E., Heath, A., Madden, P., Cooper, L., Dinwiddie, S., Bucholz, K., et al. (2002). Association between self-reported childhood sexual abuse and adverse psychosocial outcomes. *Archives of General Psychiatry, 59,* 139–145.

Nietzche, F. W. (1990). *Twilight of the idols.* New York: Penguin Books. (Original work published 1988)

Nixon, R., Nishith, P., & Resick, P. (2004). The accumulative effect of trauma exposure on short-term and delayed verbal memory in a treatment-seeking sample of female rape victims. *Journal of Traumatic Stress, 17,* 31–35.

North, C., Kawasaki, A., Spitznagel, E., & Hong, B. (2004). The course of PTSD, major depression, substance abuse, and somatization after a natural disaster. *Journal of Nervous and Mental Diseases, 192,* 823–829.

Park, C. L., Cohen, L. H., & Murch, R. L. (1996). Assessment and prediction of stress-related growth. *Journal of Personality, 64,* 71–105.

Parvizi, J., & Damasio, A. (2001). Consciousness and the brainstem. *Cognition, 79,* 135–159.

Pollak, S., & Toley-Schell, S. (2003). Selective attention to facial emotion in physically abused children. *Journal of Abnormal Psychology, 112,* 323–338.

Rabe, S., Zöllner, T., Maercker, A., & Karl, A. (2006). Neural correlates of posttraumatic growth after severe motor vehicle accidents. *Journal of Consulting and Clinical Psychology, 74,* 880–886.

Rawn, C., & Vohs, K. (2006). The importance of self-regulation for interpersonal functioning. In K. Vohs & E. Finkel (Eds.), *Self and relationships: Connecting intrapersonal and interpersonal processes* (pp. 15–31). New York: Guilford Press.

Riedel, G., Platt, B., & Micheau, J. (2003). Glutamate receptor function in learning and memory. *Behavioural Brain Research, 140,* 1–47.

Robins, R. W., Noftle, E. E., Trzesniewski, K. H., & Roberts, B. W. (2005). Do people know how their personality has changed? Correlates of perceived and actual personality change in young adulthood. *Journal of Personality, 73,* 489–521.

Rosenthal, Z., Cleavens, J., Lynch, T., & Follette, V. (2006). Thought suppression mediates the relationship between negative mood and PTSD in sexually assaulted women. *Journal of Traumatic Stress, 19,* 741–745.

Ross, M. (1989). The relation of implicit theories to the construction of personal histories. *Psychological Review, 96,* 341–357.

Ross, M., & Wilson, A. E. (2002). It feels like yesterday: Self-esteem, valence of personal past experiences, and judgments of subjective distance. *Journal of Personality and Social Psychology, 82,* 792–803.

Salter, E., & Stallard, P. (2004). Posttraumatic growth in child survivors of a road traffic accident. *Journal of Traumatic Stress, 17*(4), 335–340.

Schnurr, P. P., Lunney, C., & Sengupta, A. (2004). Risk factors for the development versus maintenance of posttraumatic stress disorder. *Journal of Traumatic Stress, 17,* 85–95.

Schore, A. (2001). The effects of early relational trauma on right brain development, affect regulation, and infant mental health. *Infant Mental Health Journal, 22,* 201–269.

Siegel, D. (2001). Toward an interpersonal neurobiology of the developing mind. *Infant Mental Health Journal, 22,* 67–94.

Smith, S. G., & Cook, S. L. (2004). Are reports of posttraumatic growth positively biased? *Journal of Traumatic Stress, 17*(4), 353–358.

Southwick, S., Bremner, J. D., Rasmusson, A., Morgan, C. A., Arnsten, A., & Charney, D. (1999). Role of norepinephrine in the pathophysiology of PTSD. *Biological Psychiatry, 46,* 1192–1204.

Spessot, A., Plessen, K., & Peterson, B. (2004). Neuroimaging of developmental psychopathologies: The importance of self-regulatory and neuroplastic processes in adolescence. In R. Dahl & L. Spear (Eds.), *Adolescent brain development: Vulnerabilities and opportunities* (pp. 86–104). New York: New York Academy of Sciences.

Taylor, S. E., & Brown, J. D. (1988). Illusion and well-being: A social psychological perspective on mental health. *Psychological Bulletin, 103,* 193–210.

Tedeschi, R. G., & Calhoun, L. G. (1996). The Posttraumatic Growth Inventory: Measuring the positive legacy of trauma. *Journal of Traumatic Stress, 9,* 455–471.

Tedeschi, R. G., & Calhoun, L. G. (2004). Posttraumatic growth: Conceptual foundations and empirical evidence. *Psychological Inquiry, 15,* 1–18.

Teicher, M., Andersen, S., Polcari, A., Anderson, C., Navalta, C., & Kim, D. (2003). Neurobiological consequences of early stress and childhood maltreatment. *Neuroscience and Biobehavioral Reviews, 27,* 33–44.

Teicher, M., Samson, J., Polcari, A., & McGreenery, S. (2006). Sticks and stones and hurtful words: Relative effects of various forms of childhood maltreatment. *American Journal of Psychiatry, 163,* 993–1000.

Tennen, H., & Affleck, G. (2002). Benefit-finding and benefit-reminding. In C. R. Snyder & S. J. Lopez (Eds.), *Handbook of positive psychology* (pp. 584–597). New York: Oxford University Press.

Tennen, H., & Affleck, G. (2005, May). *Positive change following adversity: In search of novel theories, meticulous methods and precise analytic strategies.* Presented at the APA conference on Perspectives on Positive Life Changes, Benefit-Finding and Growth Following Illness, Storrs, CT.

Tobin, R., & Graziano, W. (2006). Development of regulatory processes through adolescence. In D. Mroczek & T. Little (Eds.), *Handbook of personality development* (pp. 263–283). Mahwah, NJ: Erlbaum.

Todd, M., Armeli, S., Tennen, H., Carney, M. A., Ball, S. A., Kranzler, H. R., et al. (2005). Drinking to cope: A comparison of questionnaire and electronic diary reports. *Journal of Studies on Alcohol, 66,* 1121–1129.

Weinrib, A., Rothrock, N., Johnsen, E., & Lutgendorf, S. (2006). The assessment and validity of stress-related growth in a community-based sample. *Journal of Consulting and Clinical Psychology, 74,* 851–858.

Whitfield, C. L., Anda, R., Dube, S., & Felitti, V. (2003). Violent childhood experiences and the risk of intimate partner violence in adults. *Journal of Interpersonal Violence, 18,* 166–185.

Widom, C. S. (1999). Posttraumatic stress disorder in abused and neglected children grown up. *American Journal of Psychiatry, 156,* 1223–1229.

Wilson, A. E., & Ross, M. (2001). From chump to champ: People's appraisals of their earlier and present selves. *Journal of Personality and Social Psychology, 80,* 572–584.

Wortman, C. B. (2004). Posttraumatic growth: Progress and problems. *Psychological Inquiry, 15,* 81–90.

CHAPTER 16

The Paradox of Struggling with Trauma: Guidelines for Practice and Directions for Research

LAWRENCE G. CALHOUN and RICHARD G. TEDESCHI

WE COINED THE term *posttraumatic growth* to describe the experience of positive change resulting from the struggle with a major life crisis (Calhoun & Tedeschi, 1999; Tedeschi & Calhoun, 1996) and we have been looking at this phenomenon, in the dual roles of scientists and practitioners, for more than 25 years. Our original scholarly efforts in this area emerged from some quite basic qualitative work with persons who had become physically handicapped as adults and a group of older adults, mostly women, who had experienced the death of their spouses. We were struck by the degree to which much of what these people told us reflected ways in which they had been, without having the choice, changed in positive ways, and sometimes in ways they considered of major importance (Calhoun & Tedeschi, 1989–1990; Tedeschi & Calhoun, 1988; Tedeschi, Calhoun, Morrell, & Johnson, 1984).

We began an extensive search of the available literature in the social and behavioral sciences on people experiencing positive change from what were clearly highly negative events (from their perspective and from ours). Identifying potential sources was difficult, since none of the key words that searches required in those days reflected the phenomena in which we were interested. We usually found references to growth or perceived benefits buried in methods sections. We also looked more broadly and, as we already knew, we had discovered "nothing new under the sun."

The idea that something positive can be intermingled with, or can come out of, the struggle with something very difficult and distressing is an ancient point of view. This view is a theme in literature, religion, and philosophy and it has been present for a very, very long time. And, although we would like to have been the first to suggest this possibility in the more academic domains of inquiry, there has been a quite long tradition in the social and behavioral sciences that points to the possibility of growth from the struggle with crisis (Tedeschi & Calhoun, 1995).

The idea that the human experience contains within it the broad intermingling of positive and negative aspects has also been reflected in the work of a variety of scholars in the twentieth century. Humanistic psychologists, such as Abraham Maslow (1954), called on psychologists and others to focus their scholarly efforts on the positive aspects of human being and behavior. Similarly, Viktor Frankl (1963) was publishing his ideas on the search for meaning as the central human motivation, influenced by his experiences and observations as a prisoner in one of the infamous concentration camps of World War II. Gerald Caplan (1964) argued that life crises, if handled in particular ways and with the provision of appropriate supports, could lead to personal changes that would lead the individual to be better able to cope with subsequent life difficulties. Although not exactly describing the phenomenon with the same focus that we have taken, Caplan's view is very, very similar to the current interest in posttraumatic and stress-related growth. Yalom (1980) suggested that honest acknowledgment of, and wrestling with, existential dilemmas might be uncomfortable, but these would ultimately produce positive changes in individuals. The observation that the struggle with major life tragedy can lead to positive change, then, is clearly ancient, and several scholars of the modern era have already discussed the phenomenon.

However, it was not until the 1990s that social and behavioral scientists began to focus their research attention on the phenomenon of posttraumatic growth as a distinct area of inquiry. Important research and theory were published by Martin Seligman and Mihaly Csikszentmihályi (2000), Jeanne Schaefer and Rudolph Moos (1992), Virginia O'Leary and Jeanette Ickovics (1995), Crystal Park, Lawrence Cohen, and Renee Murch (1996), and we published the first book on this topic, from the point of view of scientist-practitioner psychologists, in 1995 (Tedeschi & Calhoun, 1995). Since then, interest in the area of posttraumatic growth, stress-related growth, perceived benefits, and similar areas has increased dramatically. From the vantage point of a relatively new area of focus for research and theory in psychology, but with the recognition that the idea that growth can arise from the struggle with very difficult life circumstances is not new, we offer a few suggestions for clinical work and some directions for future work in this area. Our goal here is to be succinct, simple, and practical, recognizing that such a focus has some inherent risks. To use a gastronomical metaphor, here we offer a few tastings. Full servings of the complete dishes are available elsewhere.

WORKING WITH REAL PEOPLE FACING REAL CRISES: RECOMMENDATIONS FOR CLINICAL WORK

The published work on posttraumatic growth has come primarily from the perspective of scientific research on the phenomenon. More recently, however, some attention has been given to the ways in which posttraumatic growth may be included in interventions for persons who have faced significant traumatic events.[1] For an extensive discussion of the possible ways of including posttraumatic growth in clinical work, we provide a comprehensive discussion elsewhere (Calhoun & Tedeschi, 1999). Here we offer a few simple recommendations for how to work with persons exposed to highly challenging sets of life circumstances.

CLINICIAN'S PERSPECTIVE: A GENERAL ORIENTATION

One way to think about the clinician's role when trying to be of assistance to persons facing traumatic events is to assume the stance of an *expert companion* (see Tedeschi & Calhoun, 2004b, 2006 for broader discussions of this clinical stance). Trained clinicians clearly are, or should be, experts in the provision of psychological services. We have extensive training, we are required to have extensive experience as part of our training and certification process, and most of us, whether required to or not, do our best to keep up with the field, particularly the identification of the kinds of clinical approaches that are supported by clinical research. Good clinicians know a great deal about the typical impact of traumatic events and the good ways to go about helping persons exposed to those kinds of circumstances.

However, we are not experts on what it is like to be exposed to different kinds of crisis events, particularly if we consider not only the kinds of events clients have faced, but also the influence of varying sociocultural contexts and preexisting personality differences. Although we are experts as clinicians, we do not know about the experience of individual persons in individual contexts—and so *we must learn from the client*. Here they are the experts and not we; we can be their companions on a journey to work to adapt and survive psychologically. Our suggestion is that clinicians

---

[1] As we have elsewhere (e.g., Calhoun & Tedeschi, 1999; Tedeschi & Calhoun, 2004a), we use the terms *trauma, crisis, major stressor,* and related terms as essentially synonymous expressions to describe circumstances that significantly challenge or invalidate important components of the individual's assumptive world.

working with persons exposed to traumatic events adopt this stance of *expert companion*. Sometimes the clinician's role is, in a metaphorical sense, to teach and sometimes the role is simply to listen and learn.

POSTTRAUMATIC GROWTH IN CLINICAL WORK: SPECIFIC SUGGESTIONS

It is an empirical question, and sufficient data are not yet available: What are the consequences of engaging in clinical interventions directly designed to "give" or directly encourage posttraumatic growth? We are somewhat ambivalent about the wisdom of trying to "produce" growth in trauma survivors. Some persons, and in some contexts perhaps many, will not experience posttraumatic growth. And it seems reasonable to assume that some persons, when exposed to the assumption that they can or should experience growth from their struggle with trauma, may be adversely affected by that implied message (Wortman, 2004). The received message could be: "People grow from exposure to trauma and if you do not then somehow you are deficient." At least until the data suggest otherwise, we prefer to refrain from attempts to "give" clients growth. The assumption that trying to induce posttraumatic growth is always "good" may be, at least in some cases, erroneous. Experiencing growth and experiencing lower levels of general distress, we believe, are not only conceptually distinct, but appear also to be empirically independent (Helgeson, Reynolds, & Tomich, 2006; Zoellner & Maercker, 2006). In addition, the process employed to set the stage for growth, for example, highlighting human mortality, might enhance the likelihood of the client's active engagement with important questions, and perhaps lead to a greater degree of existential awakening (Martin, Campbell, & Henry, 2004; McQuellon & Cowan, 2000), but it might also lead to somewhat greater levels of anxious distress. So, for now, until data lead us to change our minds, we recommend that clinicians *not engage in direct attempts to induce posttraumatic growth*, but to be companions in a process that is essentially guided by the client.

If you are going to work with any clients who will be coming to you for difficulties connected to the adaptation to highly stressful events, then a necessary qualification is *to have accurate knowledge of what the general themes of posttraumatic growth tend to be*. There are some general categories of posttraumatic growth that tend to be experienced in a variety of contexts, but there may also be themes that may be more likely, perhaps unique, to persons facing specific sets of circumstances (see Calhoun & Tedeschi, 2006, for summaries of both kinds of themes).

Although we are somewhat resistant to direct attempts to induce or "give" growth, we strongly urge all clinicians assisting persons coping with major life crises to *listen for themes of growth* because the available data suggest that for most clients at least some themes of posttraumatic growth are likely to emerge in what clients experience and say.

Another suggestion for clinicians is, if the client articulates themes of growth, *acknowledge them.* Perhaps the simplest and most effective way of doing this is to engage in empirically supported therapy relationships generally, and to focus on empathy in particular (Norcross & Hill, 2004). When clients' communications suggest the presence of growth, the clinician simply engages in the constellation of clinical responses that indicate a full understanding of the individual's phenomenological world. Although the word *growth* may sometimes be appropriately used by clinicians to describe what they view as the client's experience, it is probably better to *use the same general vocabulary that the client employs.* Our clinical experience suggests that people rarely use the word growth itself. Rather, they describe changes that they have experienced and their descriptions indicate they view those changes as positive. *Acknowledge the changes the client reports, but labeling them explicitly as posttraumatic growth seems unnecessary.*

It is also desirable to attend carefully to the general way in which you acknowledge and talk about growth with clients. We strongly encourage clinicians to talk about growth as having come about *as a result of the struggle with* difficult circumstances and not the circumstances themselves. Although this may seem minor and inconsequential, minor alterations in the words clinicians use to engage clients, when they refer to themes that may reflect growth, can greatly affect the way clients respond. It is an entirely different matter to speak of a bereaved parent's having experienced positive change as a result of having to *struggle with the grief* produced by that loss, than to speak of positive change produced by the child's death. The first may reflect an accurately empathic response, while the second may connote a cold and insensitive misunderstanding of parental grief. The following is a transcript of a conversation between a clinician (T) and a client (C) whose husband died, that illustrates the stance of expert companionship and how to facilitate a process of posttraumatic growth:

C: This is forcing me to do a lot of things I don't like. I just hate this.
T: What kinds of things do you hate?
C: Dealing with the legal and financial stuff.
T: You never had to handle those things before. Carl always did that.
C: Yeah. But you know, it is also the emotional side. The looks from people.
T: Looks?
C: Some kind of pitying look—"you poor thing." I hate that, too.
T: You'd rather have people treat you like they did before?
C: Well, I don't think that exactly. I mean, if they act like nothing has happened, that bothers me, too. I guess I can't win.

T: Relationships are confusing, I guess.

C: It's a mess. But I think maybe I don't give people enough credit. I mean, they are trying.

T: Trying to figure out how to be supportive.

C: Yes. Some people have been better at it than others. Some have been wonderful.

T: Like your neighbor Ellen.

C: Exactly. I love being with her. She's an amazing woman.

T: It seems you weren't that close before.

C: No, not like this. It's funny, I can just talk to her. She seems strong and sure. I really trust her.

T: It is funny that it has happened that way with her.

C: You know, I think I am more open with her. She always was there, I just need to talk more now. And cry, of course.

T: You are more open.

C: Absolutely.

T: Compared to when Carl was alive.

C: Yeah, we relied on each other a lot. I don't think I had to reach out to others.

T: Now you do.

C: Absolutely. Or I'd go nuts. This has made me freer with that, I guess. You know, I think I am more like myself if that makes sense.

T: How do you mean?

C: Well, I just act more like me, or say what I think and feel. At least to someone like Ellen, I don't mean with everybody.

T: Although you did kind of educate that lady at church a few weeks ago, when she said that you had to get over this and not be so sad.

C: Oh, yes, that one. Yes, I guess I am a bit outspoken at times now. You know, you've shown me how what I am doing is okay, and other people implying that I am messed up or grieving wrong really rubs me the wrong way now.

T: So, there is a strength or confidence in the midst of all this sadness.

C: True. That's true. And people like Ellen who I feel I can trust, I go ahead and say what's on my mind and how I feel.

T: That's different.

C: Sure is. I guess without Carl, I am on my own, my own person more. We got married so young, maybe I didn't really ever see myself as separate.

T: This may sound like a cliché, but you are finding out who you are.

C: Yeah—you hear that—but that is how it is for me. I am being more myself. It actually feels pretty good while being lonely too. God, do I miss him.

T: You can feel strong and like you are really more yourself, while also missing Carl so much.
C: Right, it is really mixed up like that.

Notice that *the clinician stays close to what the client says, but also picks up on the hints of growth in the story.* Of course, it is important to have your clinical ear attuned to what growth may be happening, and this clinician does. Themes of personal strength, and deeper relationships are gently uncovered. At the same time, the distress is not denied. This mixture of distress and growth that we often hear clients reflect on is a convincing indication that the growth that is described is not merely an illusion, and that clients can be trusted with their interpretations of these changes. This is in the spirit of expert companionship, staying close to clients' experiences and understandings of them.

However, one of the general findings of social psychologists in the past 25 or so years has been the identification of a variety of ways in which people tend to process information to maintain or enhance their perception of self. A related, but different theme has emerged in some areas of psychological counseling and treatment, with the popularization of the concept of, or at least the word, *denial*. A concern that some have raised is the degree to which posttraumatic growth may reflect, at least in part, some form of self-enhancing interpretational bias, or some form of denial. The importance of separating illusion from reality is much more important from the scientific and theoretical point of view (we address this later) than it is for work in the clinical setting.

Unless the clinician has clear evidence of delusional thinking, or that indeed the client is psychologically incapable of accepting what is an incontrovertible truth (e.g., the loved one is indeed dead but the survivor still persists in the belief that the person is alive), *we suggest that clinicians work within the client's general framework for understanding the world, and their interpretations of posttraumatic growth in particular.* As others have already suggested (Taylor & Brown, 1994), positive illusions may indeed serve adaptive purposes, and even if the perception of growth is illusory, it may serve as a means for providing some meaning for the person's suffering. More importantly, however, except in the most extraordinary circumstances, we think that intemperate "myth busting" of possible illusions of growth may have the potential to be psychologically harmful, and under some circumstance might be unethical. And, the data available indicate that the experience of growth is typically not simply the result of a cognitive distortion (Calhoun & Tedeschi, 2006).

Clinicians need to be sure to remind themselves that *posttraumatic growth is not a universal experience,* and that the persons with whom they are working may never experience it. In addition, although clients may experience it, they may never articulate it in the context of psychological treatment, and *the experience of growth may not be a necessary component of a successful intervention for some*, perhaps many, clients who come for assistance in coping with significant posttraumatic distress. But for many clients, the experience and acknowledgment of posttraumatic growth can be a helpful and meaningful component of professional intervention.

FUTURE RESEARCH

Although there are some data suggesting that some reports of posttraumatic growth may be influenced by cognitive biases or distortions (McFarland & Alvaro, 2000; Widows, Jacobsen, Booth-Jones, & Fields, 2005), *there are still no operational means for identifying such distortions at the specific moment they are expressed*. Although some promising steps have been taken on a broad scale (Zoellner & Maercker, 2006), we know of no study or process by which clinicians or researchers can reliably identify illusory growth in individual persons at a particular time. From the scientific perspective, this would seem to be a desirable domain for investigation, but the methodology has still not been developed to do so. Although when drawing on the strategies and models of social psychology the data suggest that, in aggregated form, quantitative assessments of growth may reflect some cognitive biases, particularly involving the active nature of human memory, at least two questions remain: (1) Even if there is a general tendency toward self-enhancement in personal cognitions, does their presence necessarily mean that the report of growth must therefore be erroneous? (2) If some reports of growth are erroneous, how do you tell if an *individual person's* description of growth is erroneous?

For example, what if a client reports to me that 8 months ago she was experiencing a lot of discomfort with chemotherapy and had significant depression, but today she is much better, compared to that horrible time. But I have her ratings from distress and depression from that time and I can tell, empirically, that she misremembers her reactions as being worse than they were—does that mean she is really not feeling as good as she says? The available data, which are very sparse indeed in this area, do suggest that perceptions of posttraumatic growth may have elements of self-enhancement. This is not a surprise.

But, on the other hand, quantitative reports of growth are not related to social desirability measures (Tedeschi & Calhoun, 1996), they tend to be corroborated by others (Park et al., 1996; Weiss, 2002), they co-occur with reports of high levels of distress, they are correlated with measures of severity of exposure (Calhoun & Tedeschi, 2004; Tedeschi & Calhoun,

2004a), and these kinds of distortions tend to occur in only a small minority of cases (Dohrenwend et al., 2004). Furthermore, clients themselves report that their views on life in the aftermath of trauma seem to them to be less naïve, wiser, and allow for clearer recognition of the tragedies of life compared to how they saw things prior to their traumatic experiences.

Most reports of growth, then, would seem to be "real" most of the time, but there do appear to be instances where growth is "illusory." What we still need to try to discover is—when and how can those specific, individual instances of "illusion" be identified?

MEASURING POSTTRAUMATIC GROWTH

There are several quantitative measures of growth already developed and well established (Frazier, Oishi, & Steger, 2003; Park & Lechner, 2006) and refinements are also being developed. Quantitative measures can always be refined, but there are some directions that seem more desirable than others.

An occasional criticism of the scales currently in wide use is that they do not allow respondents to report "negative growth." Curiously, we have not seen similar criticism of the multitude of psychological inventories that measure negative psychological states, such as depression and anxiety, arguing that such inventories should also include items measuring positive psychological states. And, to the best of our knowledge, there are no empirical data that suggest that the content of the items do indeed produce the assumed positivity bias. But, it is not unreasonable to suggest that assessments be expanded to include negative experiences in the same domains that characterize posttraumatic growth. To the extent that new measures are developed to achieve the goal of allowing respondents to report negative experiences, *we would argue against the use of bipolar items.* Bipolar items force the individual to categorize an experience in a specific area as *either or,* not allowing for the expression of the very complexity of posttraumatic reactions such scales might be designed to reflect.

If there is an interest in developing measures of "negative growth," then the preferred alternative would seem to be scales that contain separate positive and negative items, tapping the same specific areas of growth (Tomich & Helgeson, 2004). Preliminary data suggest two general patterns of response on such scales: (1) respondents report both positive and negative changes in the typical domains of posttraumatic growth; and (2) they report significantly more growth than "negative growth" (Baker, Kelly, Calhoun, Cann, & Tedeschi, in press). If you are going to measure both positive and negative aspects of the posttrauma experience, with a focus on growth (we already know a great deal about the negative experiences trauma can produce), then we would urge you to develop ways of assessing negative experiences *in the same areas that you are assessing growth,* and that you do so with pairs of items and not bipolar items.

Broaden the Scope of Inquiry

It is also highly desirable to broaden the use of *qualitative* methodologies in the study of posttraumatic growth. There is a growing tide of interest in this broad and amorphously defined approach to inquiry and this general trend is welcome. However, we would urge researchers whose interests take them in this direction to be aware of the general philosophical assumptions on which much of qualitative research rests, and also to be judicious in their choice of methodologies.

The general area called qualitative is not nearly as well delimited and there is a much greater heterogeneity of methods than is the case with the traditional, quantitative, approach that is commonly taught to university students in the "harder" social and behavioral sciences. Qualitative approaches do tend to have, however, a common perspective that reflects a *postmodern* view of knowledge, whereas the general focus of, for example, contemporary scientific psychology, appears to be still firmly planted in *modern* science with its emphasis on a priori statements of hypotheses, experimentation, control of variables, and reliance on statistical analysis.

As clinical psychologists who consider themselves scientist-practitioners, we tend to recommend qualitative methods that at least have some of the characteristics of scientific inquiry, particularly the use of methodology that is repeatable by others. Certainly, this is possible only in part, since a key element of the qualitative approach is to view the investigator's experience as a crucial element in the process. We find the approach developed by Egon Guba and Yvonna Lincoln (e.g., 1985) to be particularly appealing along with similar approaches (Carverhill, 2002).

Read Some of the "Old Stuff"

We are often called on to serve as reviewers for journals and we have noticed what seems to be, to us at least, something of a trend. Sometimes research is done in areas that have already been investigated in the "distant" past (for some researchers "distant" seems to be more than 20 years ago) and sometimes authors cite "old" sources, but contemporary citations in manuscripts submitted for review sometimes suggest a clear lack of familiarity with some of the very works cited. Given the explosion of information and new findings in the social and behavioral sciences, it is becoming increasingly difficult for scholars to keep up even with their own specific areas of interest and expertise (e.g., PsychInfo lists about 50 more sources on posttraumatic growth than a year ago). In the area of posttraumatic growth, there are indeed sources that have previously dealt with this phenomenon, at least in some ways, from the points of view of psychiatry and psychology and we listed some of these at the beginning of the chapter. We would urge particularly younger clinicians and scholars to examine some of those sources because they may provide some new ideas about what you are investigating, and they may also indicate that some of the ideas that some consider to be new, are indeed not.

REFERENCES

Baker, J. M., Kelly, C., Calhoun, L. G., Cann, A., & Tedeschi, R. G. (in press). An examination of posttraumatic growth and posttraumatic depreciation: Two exploratory studies. *Journal of Loss and Trauma.*

Calhoun, L. G., & Tedeschi, R. G. (1989–1990). Positive aspects of critical life problems: Recollections of grief. *Omega, 20,* 265–272.

Calhoun, L. G., & Tedeschi, R. G. (1999). *Facilitating posttraumatic growth: A clinician's guide.* Mahwah, NJ: Erlbaum.

Calhoun, L. G., & Tedeschi, R. G. (2004). The foundations of posttraumatic growth: New considerations. *Psychological Inquiry, 15,* 93–102.

Calhoun, L. G., & Tedeschi, R. G. (Eds.). (2006). The foundations of posttraumatic growth: An expanded framework. In L. G. Calhoun & R. G. Tedeschi (Eds.), *Handbook of posttraumatic growth: Research and practice* (pp. 1–23). Mahwah, NJ: Erlbaum.

Caplan, G. (1964). *Principles of preventive psychiatry.* New York: Basic Books.

Carverhill, P. A. (2002). Qualitative research in thanatology. *Death Studies, 26,* 195–207.

Csikszentmihályi, M. (1990). The domain of creativity. In M. A. Runco & R. S. Albert (Eds.), *Theories of creativity* (pp. 190–212). Thousand Oaks, CA: Sage.

Dohrenwend, B. P., Neria, Y., Turner, J. B., Turse, N., Marshall, R., Lewis-Fernandez, R., et al. (2004). Positive tertiary appraisals and posttraumatic stress disorder in U.S. male veterans of the war in Vietnam: The roles of positive affirmation, positive reformulation, and defensive denial. *Journal of Consulting and Clinical Psychology, 72,* 417–433.

Frankl, V. E. (1963). *Man's search for meaning.* New York: Pocket Books.

Frazier, P., Oishi, S., & Steger, M. (2003). Assessing optimal human functioning. In W. B. Walsh (Ed.), *Counseling psychology and optimal human functioning* (pp. 251–278). Mahwah, NJ: Erlbaum.

Helgeson, V. S., Reynolds, K. A., & Tomich, P. L. (2006). A meta-analytic review of benefit findings and growth. *Journal of Consulting and Clinical Psychology, 74,* 794–816.

Kelly, C. M. (2006). *Assessing growth and loss using a revised PTGI: An investigation of the use of a paired format to assess responses to traumatic events.* Unpublished master's thesis, University of North Carolina, Charlotte.

Lincoln, Y. S., & Guba, E. G. (1985). *Naturalistic inquiry.* Beverly Hill, CA: Sage.

Martin, L. L., Campbell, W. K., & Henry, C. D. (2004). The roar of awakening—Mortality acknowledgment as a call to authentic living. In J. Greenburg, S. L. Koole, & T. Pysxczynski (Eds.), *Handbook of experimental existential psychology* (pp. 431–448). New York: Guilford Press.

Maslow, A. H. (1954). *Motivation and personality.* New York: Harper.

McFarland, C., & Alvaro, C. (2000). The impact of motivation on temporal comparisons: Coping with traumatic events by perceiving personal growth. *Journal of Personality and Social Psychology, 79,* 327–343.

McQuellon, R. P., & Cowan, M. A. (2000). Turning toward death together: Conversation in mortal time. *American Journal of Hospice and Palliative Care, 17,* 311–318.

Norcross, J. C., & Hill, C. E. (2004). Empirically supported therapy relationships. *Clinical Psychologist, 57*(3), 19–24.

O'Leary, V. E., & Ickovics, J. R. (1995). Resilience and thriving in response to challenge: An opportunity for a paradigm shift in women's health. *Women's Health: Research on Gender, Behavior, and Policy, 1,* 121–142.

Park, C. L., Cohen, L., & Murch, R. (1996). Assessment and prediction of stress-related growth. *Journal of Personality, 64,* 645–658.

Park, C. L., & Lechner, S. C. (2006). Measurement issues in assessing growth following stressful experiences. In L. G. Calhoun & R. G. Tedeschi (Eds.), *Handbook of posttraumatic growth: Research and practice* (pp. 47–67). Mahwah, NJ: Erlbaum.

Schaefer, J. A., & Moos, R. H. (1992). Life crisis and personal growth. In B. N. Carpenter (Ed.), *Personal coping: Theory, research, and application* (pp. 149–170). Westport, CT: Praeger.

Seligman, M. E. P., & Csikszentmihályi, M. (2000). Positive psychology: An introduction. *American Psychologist, 55,* 5–14.

Taylor, S. E., & Brown, J. D. (1994). Positive illusions and well-being revisited: Separating fact from fiction. *Psychological Bulletin, 116,* 21–27.

Tedeschi, R. G., & Calhoun, L. G. (1988, August). *Perceived benefits in coping with physical handicaps.* Paper presented at the annual meeting of the American Psychological Association, Atlanta, GA.

Tedeschi, R. G., & Calhoun, L. G. (1995). *Trauma and transformation: Growing in the aftermath of suffering.* Thousand Oaks, CA: Sage.

Tedeschi, R. G., & Calhoun, L. G. (1996). The posttraumatic growth inventory: Measuring the positive legacy of trauma. *Journal of Traumatic Stress, 9,* 455–471.

Tedeschi, R. G., & Calhoun, L. G. (2004a). The foundations of posttraumatic growth: New considerations. *Psychological Inquiry, 15,* 1–18.

Tedeschi, R. G., & Calhoun, L. G. (2004b). *Helping bereaved parents.* New York: Brunner-Routledge.

Tedeschi, R. G., & Calhoun, L. G. (2006). Expert companions: Posttraumatic growth in clinical practice. In L. G. Calhoun & R. G. Tedeschi (Eds.), *Handbook of posttraumatic growth: Research and practice* (pp. 291–310). Mahwah, NJ: Erlbaum.

Tedeschi, R. G., Calhoun, L. G., Morrell, R. W., & Johnson, K. A. (1984, August). *Bereavement: From grief to psychological development.* Paper presented at the annual meeting of the American Psychological Association, Toronto, Ontario, Canada.

Tomich, P. L., & Helgeson, V. S. (2004). Is finding something good in the bad always good? Benefit finding among women with breast cancer. *Health Psychology, 23,* 16–23.

Weiss, T. (2002). Posttraumatic growth in women with breast cancer and their husbands: An intersubjective validation study. *Journal of Psychosocial Oncology, 20,* 65–80.

Widows, M. R., Jacobsen, P. B., Booth-Jones, M., & Fields, K. K. (2005). Predictors of posttraumatic growth following bone marrow transplantation for cancer. *Health Psychology, 24,* 266–273.

Wortman, C. B. (2004). Posttraumatic growth: Progress and problems. *Psychological Inquiry, 15,* 81–89.

Yalom, I. (1980). *Existential therapy.* New York: Basic Books.

Zoellner, T., & Maercker, A. (2006). Posttraumatic growth in clinical psychology—A critical review and introduction of a two component model. *Clinical Psychology Review, 26,* 626–653.

CHAPTER 17

Reflections on Theory and Practice in Trauma, Recovery, and Growth: A Paradigm Shift for the Field of Traumatic Stress

STEPHEN JOSEPH and P. ALEX LINLEY

V ARIOUS TERMS HAVE been used to describe the phenomenon of growth following adversity. But as is clear from the present volume, no single term is used consistently and systematically, and a variety of other terms have also been used to describe the phenomena of growth following adversity, such as perceived benefits, benefit finding, positive changes, and thriving. Terminology is not trivial. Each of the terms has been developed to reflect particular historical lineages in the research literature, or has been developed from different theoretical perspectives, and which term we use inevitably reflects our own conceptions of what growth following adversity is about.

For example, the most popular term is that of posttraumatic growth, the term coined by Tedeschi and Calhoun (1995). This has proved a hugely successful term in drawing interest to the area and stimulating new research activity, and the fact that the field has now become so widely known and well established must surely be attributable, at least in part, to the popularization of the term posttraumatic growth. However, when we start to unpack the term *posttraumatic growth,* we can see how even just this simple label for a construct has important, but often unspoken, implications. The obvious counterpart with which many clinicians and researchers—as well as laypeople—will be familiar, is posttraumatic stress disorder (PTSD). Implicitly, these similarities set up a series of associations.

First, posttraumatic infers something that arises following trauma. In *DSM-IV*, Criterion A for the diagnosis of PTSD specifies what the nature of an event must be for it to qualify as traumatic:

> The person has been exposed to a traumatic event in which both the following were present: (1) The person experienced, witnessed, or was confronted with an event or events that involved actual or threatened death or serious injury, or a threat to the physical integrity of self or others; (2) the person's response to the event must involve intense fear, helplessness, or horror. (American Psychiatric Association, 1994, p. 424)

However, although Tedeschi & Calhoun's (1996) conceptualization did not specify these criteria as necessary for an event to be a precipitator of posttraumatic growth, the use of the term posttraumatic growth has led to some misunderstanding that people must either have experienced a traumatic event as defined by *DSM*, or that they must have received a diagnosis of PTSD.

Second, posttraumatic specifies something that occurs following the trauma, and so is implicitly understood to have been influenced, if not caused by, the traumatic event. Understood in this way, posttraumatic growth is nonnormative, being a distinct outcome from a distinct event, rather than a more normative developmental process, a point also made by Ford, Tennen, and Albert (this volume).

Third, growth refers to some positive shift in a person's physical, psychological, social, or metaphysical standing, when assessed preevent and postevent (interestingly, posttraumatic growth in medical terminology refers to bones that are stronger at the places where they have healed following a break; e.g., Karrholm, Hansson, & Selvik, 1982). Thus, growth again indicates a step-change in development over time, also as noted by Ford and colleagues (this volume).

When these implicit associations are understood in this way, we can begin to see how a particular conception of posttraumatic growth has developed through its association with the diagnostic category of PTSD; that is, assumptions that posttraumatic growth is qualitatively different to more normative growth experiences, arises only following traumatic events as defined by *DSM* Criterion A for PTSD, and occurs only in people who received a diagnosis of PTSD.

The implicit associations of the term with posttraumatic stress disorder has perhaps unwittingly imbued posttraumatic growth with the connotation that it is somehow an extension or positive parallel of the construct of PTSD, that is, as something which, when it is understood from the perspective of the illness ideology, is viewed as being distinct from normal human experience, or "outside the range of normal human experience" as traumatic events were originally defined within the *DSM*. However, it is clear both from empirical research (Linley & Joseph, 2004a) and from sociological, philosophical, religious, and literary inquiry (Linley, 2003) that the experience of growth or positive change following trauma and adversity is not a qualitatively different experience that is distinctly different from normal human development, but rather is a natural, albeit infrequent, life span developmental event.

Simply put, trauma is inescapable, and as Valent (1999) has argued, the life-trauma dialectic is more appropriate as a metaphor than is the life-death dialectic. That is to say, the essential tension is not between life and death, since, by definition, life ends when death begins, but between life and trauma, which co-exist. Similarly, we do not see posttraumatic stress and growth as an either-or dichotomy, but rather as a more integrative way of understanding the variety of processes and outcomes that may ensue following trauma, and which may, to a greater or lesser extent, be continuations or amplifications of more normative life span developmental trajectories (cf. Wink & Dillon, 2002). Implicit within this understanding is that posttraumatic stress and posttraumatic growth are not separate ends of a continuum, nor indeed separate, unrelated phenomena, but are rather two aspects of human experience following stress and trauma that can be associated with each other in a variety of ways (Linley & Joseph, 2004a). It is for these reasons that we have often used the term growth following adversity in an attempt to avoid these associations and parallels with PTSD. As we shall go on to argue, it is our view that the topic of growth offers a new paradigm for the study of traumatic stress, and not simply a parallel avenue of investigation.

INTEGRATIVE PERSPECTIVE ON POSTTRAUMATIC STRESS AND GROWTH FOLLOWING ADVERSITY

As indicated earlier, it is possible that the term posttraumatic growth has served, inadvertently, to conceptually divide the field into those people who are interested in posttraumatic stress and those people who are interested in posttraumatic growth; whereas what we need is an integrative perspective on adaptation following adversity that is able to synthesize what we know about posttraumatic stress and growth following adversity.

Taking a broader lens on psychology as a whole, positive psychology grew out of the idea that for too long researchers and clinicians had been overly focused on the negative side of human experience, and there was a need for equal attention to be paid to the positive side. Just as early empirical work focused on PTSD as an outcome following trauma, psychology more generally was predisposed to focus on psychopathology and distress. Just as the literature on posttraumatic growth suggested that there was much to be learned from the study of the positive consequences of traumatic events, so positive psychology argued that there was much to be learned from the positive sides of human experience: for example, success, excellence, and optimal human functioning (Seligman & Csikszentmihalyi, 2000).

Shifting the focus of our attention solely to the positive side, however, is as unbalanced as was the focus on the negative: it falls into the same abyss through seeing the human condition through only one lens, from only one perspective. What is needed is a perspective that encompasses both the positive and the negative, integrating our knowledge into a more complete and holistic understanding of what it means to be human. As we have argued elsewhere in relation to positive psychology generally (Linley & Joseph, 2004b), what is needed now are theoretical frameworks that are able to encompass both sets of literature, on stress and on growth. What we are interested in is ultimately about both positive and negative sides of human experience, and how they relate to each other, and this volume is an attempt to begin to integrate these two often distinct literatures.

In looking to the future and the development of the field, we think it is important to recognize that we cannot fully understand growth without taking into account the distress that precedes it, and we cannot fully understand recovery from posttraumatic stress without taking into account the possibility of growth. The way forward is to develop theoretical frameworks that are able to integrate what we know about posttraumatic stress and growth following adversity. As noted in Chapter 1, at a broad level, it is already possible to understand how people react to stressful and traumatic events, and the social and cognitive processes underpinning change—both positive and negative—using the psychosocial framework (Joseph & Williams, 2005) and the organismic valuing theory of adjustment to threatening events (Joseph & Linley, 2005). We would argue that growth following adversity is not a new field of enquiry; rather it is a paradigm shift in the traumatic stress field.

The most pertinent question in our view, therefore, is whether the growth literature simply promises to offer new add-on techniques to existing treatments for trauma, or whether, as we expect it does, it offers a paradigm shift in our ways of thinking about trauma. If the concept of growth following adversity does ultimately offer this paradigm shift, then it has the potential eventually to supersede and replace existing ways of thinking about, and working with people following trauma.

Most existing approaches to the alleviation of traumatic stress are grounded in the medical model and an illness ideology, and the growth paradigm presents alternative conceptualizations of trauma. As Lyons (Chapter 12, this volume) points out, the label of PTSD can serve to disempower people. More widely, the negative effects of labeling have been well documented (Maddux, Snyder, & Lopez, 2004; Reznek, 1987), and yet the medical model and illness ideology have become the dominant cultural perspective on the ways in which we understand reactions to trauma. The paradigm of growth following adversity has the potential to change this through enabling a deeper and more integrated understanding of how posttraumatic reactions are not some categorically distinct construct of human experience, but are rather indicative of more normative subjective emotional processing and possible subsequent personality and schema change.

Without being explicit about how the perspective of growth following adversity can serve to shape and redefine our understanding of adaptations following traumatic events, however, we run the risk that the growth paradigm becomes subsumed within the dominant medical model and illness ideology (cf. Joseph & Linley, 2006). For example, if the growth literature is seen as something that provides an "add on" to what is already known about posttraumatic stress, then the point is missed that in contrast, the growth literature provides a fundamentally different way of understanding human experience following trauma. That is, a way of understanding the life-trauma dialectic as an inescapable element of human experience, and one that can serve to trigger or amplify existing normative developmental trajectories. Without this explicit recognition of the challenge of the growth paradigm to the medical model way of understanding posttraumatic stress, the risk is that the field of growth following adversity becomes subsumed within the dominant medical model discourse on traumatic stress.

This issue of a positive psychological perspective offering a more integrative way of understanding human experience—that is distinct from the traditional medical model view—is one what we have also highlighted in relation to positive psychology more broadly (Linley & Joseph, 2004b) and in relation to psychotherapy specifically (Joseph & Linley, 2006). In the next section, we offer some of our perspectives on how work within the positive psychology field might specifically inform future theoretical and empirical developments within our understanding of adaptation following trauma and adversity.

PERSPECTIVES FROM POSITIVE PSYCHOLOGY

First and foremost, positive psychology has challenged researchers and practitioners to examine what can be learned and gained from the study and facilitation of the positive side of human experience. We would concur that the advent of the growth-following-adversity literature has done much to raise this perspective on the agenda of posttraumatic stress and more traditional views of negative reactions and outcomes following trauma, so much so that the potential for positive change following trauma and adversity is now firmly recognized in traumatic stress, clinical psychology, and psychiatry journals.

Second, positive psychology has lent impetus to the study and understanding of well-being, leading to greater clarity and empirical attention to what well-being is and how it may be variously conceptualized. Central to this is the distinction between subjective well-being (affect and life satisfaction) and psychological well-being (existential engagement with the challenges of life) that we have found very helpful in thinking about the relationship between traumatic stress and growth (Joseph & Linley, 2005).

Third, and following from this greater attention to well-being, has been the emerging but hugely influential literature on positive emotions, especially Fredrickson's (1998) broaden-and-build theory of positive emotions. Traditionally, emotions research had focused largely on negative emotions such as anger, fear, sadness, and anxiety, with positive emotions often being dismissed as irrelevant epiphenomena of no substantial merit. Fredrickson turned this faulty assumption on its head, positing that positive emotions had an evolutionarily adaptive role through broadening thought-action repertoires and building physical, psychological, and social resources. In our review of the growth research literature published to that time (Linley & Joseph, 2004a), we found that positive affect had the strongest associations with growth of all variables: a finding which we, initially, dismissed as synonymous, thinking that positive affect was simply a representation of growth. However, from the perspective of the broaden-and-build theory of positive emotions, it is clear that positive affect (positive emotion) may have a much more central role to play.

POSITIVE EMOTIONS

In research unrelated to trauma, it has been shown that the experience of positive emotions speeds cardiovascular recovery from stressful events through undoing the effects of negative emotion (Fredrickson & Levenson, 1998), and that positive emotions broaden attentional focus and expand behavioral repertoires (Fredrickson & Branigan, 2005). Applied more specifically to traumatic events, Fredrickson, Tugade, Waugh, and Larkin (2003) showed in a prospective longitudinal study that higher levels of positive emotion before the September 11, 2001, terrorist attacks predicted greater levels of resilience and growth in the month following.

What might be the mechanisms through which positive emotions influence growth following adversity? It seems likely that there are several, with some of the most pertinent candidates being the undoing effect on negative emotions, the broadening of thought-action repertoires, and the building of physical (physiological), psychological, and social resources. We shall consider each in turn, within the context of the psychosocial framework (Joseph & Williams, 2005), which posits the interaction of appraisals, emotional states, coping styles, and the cycles, either upward (toward well-being) or downward (toward distress) that ensue. Thus, we can contextualize the role of positive emotions as discussed by Fredrickson within the psychosocial framework, allowing an contextualized understanding of how positive emotions can start an upward spiral of appraisal, emotional states, and coping styles in trauma survivors.

Following traumatic events, it is well-established that people are likely to experience cycles of reexperiencing and avoidance, together with hyperarousal, all indicative of negative subjective emotional states. These negative emotional states, experienced over time, have the effect of creating more negative event appraisals, reducing effective coping strategies, and isolating potential sources of social support, the result of which can become a downward negative spiral. In contrast, the experience of positive emotions (e.g., humor, gratitude, appreciation, interest, love, curiosity) in the aftermath of the traumatic event may serve to undo the effects of these negative emotions, and prevent the development of the longer-term negative emotional sequelae that are characteristic of posttraumatic stress.

From where might these positive emotions arise? Experiencing valued social support following the traumatic event, people may feel increased gratitude, love, and kindness toward others, all of which were documented in a national U.S. sample following the September 11, 2001, terrorist attacks (Peterson & Seligman, 2003). Appreciation, a factor that has been identified within the construct of posttraumatic growth, can arise when people value the things that they have following the trauma, such as being grateful for being alive, for small mercies, or for the support of friends and family.

Within the Posttraumatic Growth Inventory specifically, appreciation of life and gratitude for others have been established as important dimensions of posttraumatic growth (Tedeschi & Calhoun, 1996). More broadly, gratitude has been shown to be related to higher levels of well-being (Park, Peterson, & Seligman, 2004) as well as contributing to well-being independently of traditional coping styles (Wood, Joseph, & Linley, in press). As such, the experience of gratitude and appreciation (which are both positive emotions, as well as aspects of posttraumatic growth) may serve to undo the effects of negative emotion following trauma. In a study of gratitude in combat veterans, Kashdan, Uswatte, and Julian (2006) found that dispositional gratitude was associated with daily well-being, pleasant days, intrinsically motivating activity and self-esteem in combat veterans with a diagnosis of posttraumatic stress disorder.

In essence, the broadening of thought-action repertoires refers to increased creativity and greater behavioral flexibility in people experiencing higher levels of positive emotion. Applied to the construct of posttraumatic growth, there are again interesting parallels. One factor of the Posttraumatic Growth Inventory (Tedeschi & Calhoun, 1996) deals with new possibilities or opportunities that arose as a result of the traumatic event. The experience of positive emotions, and the attendant broadening of thought-action repertoires, is one possible pathway through which this may have come about: people experiencing positive emotions following trauma are likely to be more creative in their perceptions of the options that are open to them, as well as being more flexible and open to the possibilities of what things may work out.

In terms of building physical (physiological) resources, one study has already shown that posttraumatic growth is associated with quicker cortisol habituation in relation to other stressors (Epel, McEwen, & Ickovics, 1998), and within the medical community, posttraumatic growth refers to a broken bone that has healed and that is stronger at the broken places (e.g., Karrholm et al., 1982). It is entirely conceivable that positive emotions could serve to undo the negative physiological sequelae of traumatic events (e.g., Fredrickson, Mancuso, Branigan, & Tugade, 2000) and further to build future physiological resilience against subsequent stressors (Epel et al., 1998). In relation to psychological resources, positive emotions have been shown to create upward spirals of well-being (Fredrickson & Joiner, 2002), and again there are parallels with aspects of posttraumatic growth, specifically, the Personal Strength dimension of the PTGI that is concerned with an enhanced perception of one's strengths and abilities.

In relation to social resources, positive emotions have been shown to enhance social relationships through bonds of sharing and reciprocation (Oatley & Jenkins, 1996), just as a major element of posttraumatic growth is the improvements reported in interpersonal relationships as people learn to trust and depend on each other more, together with an increased sense of valuing and appreciation. These positive changes in relationships have even been shown on a community-wide scale, with Americans demonstrating greater gratitude, kindness, love, and teamwork following the September 11, 2001, terrorist attacks (Peterson & Seligman, 2003).

Taking the lens on positive emotions (and by extension, happiness and well-being) more widely, it is clear that there are further instructive parallels. Positive affect, traditionally regarded as a largely irrelevant epiphenomenon, has now been shown to be related to, and longitudinally predictive of a range of behavioral, psychological, social, and health variables (see Lyubomirsky, King, & Diener, 2005; Pressman & Cohen, 2005, for extensive reviews). Similarly, evidence is beginning to emerge that growth is predictive of lower levels of subsequent depression (Helgeson, Reynolds, & Tomich, 2006). Frazier, Conlon, and Glaser (2001) found that positive changes that were reported after 2 weeks and were retained over time predicted significantly lower levels of negative change 1 year later (see also Frazier, Tashiro, Berman, Steger, & Long, 2004). Linley, Joseph, and Goodfellow (2007), in a 6-month longitudinal study of people at varying times since a traumatic event, found that people who reported positive changes at the first time point reported significantly lower levels of posttraumatic stress, depression, and anxiety at the 6-month follow-up.

From this emerging evidence, we might legitimately conclude that a consensus is now beginning to build around the value of earlier positive emotional experiences in facilitating and predicting later positive psychological outcomes, irrespective of intervening negative events or otherwise. The psychosocial framework (Joseph & Williams, 2005) posits that people adapt following trauma through processes of appraisal, leading to positive or negative emotional states, with different coping styles then being used to deal with any negative emotional states.

The traditional focus has been on the downward spirals into negative emotion and distress that can come about through this process. Introducing and exploring the role of positive emotions reveals that the experience of positive emotions—and growth may be an important factor in creating and enhancing positive emotions—by contrast leads to upward spirals toward well-being (Fredrickson & Joiner, 2002; Sheldon & Houser-Marko, 2001). In this way, the psychosocial framework (Joseph & Williams, 2005) provides the context for understanding both positive and negative emotional reactions following trauma and adversity. These findings suggest a number of pertinent future research directions, as we now go on to discuss.

FUTURE RESEARCH

On this basis, we urge a reconceptualization of research and practice of the processes of adjustment to traumatic and stressful events that is equally concerned with the phenomena of posttraumatic stress and growth. It is now becoming clear that we cannot treat posttraumatic stress and growth following adversity as separate constructs in isolation from one another, but rather that we should consider them as two elements of a more integrative conceptualization of both positive and negative change following trauma and adversity. Like Frazier and Berman, we also call for more sophisticated research testing the relation between measures of growth and distress, which also includes mediator and moderator variables. While there exist encouraging early indications that earlier growth may be predictive of later positive adjustment and reduced symptomatology, we still know far too little about the factors that may inhibit or enhance these processes. It is clear that positive emotions may have an important role to play, and that appropriate social support and a facilitative social environment can be integral to growthful development, but we do not know this with any certainty or specificity, and hence these remain foci for future research.

There is also a need for theoretical development to drive the research process. In particular, we agree with Ford et al.'s analysis that we need to investigate the possibility that growth may represent the possibility of an amplification of preexisting development of self-regulatory capacities. Growth following adversity may not be a phenomenon that is specific to the outcome of traumatic events, but may be a natural developmental tendency (cf. Sheldon & Kasser, 2001; Wink & Dillon, 2002) that is kick-started or amplified by the trauma and the emotional churning that it ensues. We welcome this analysis, and concur with its importance in setting the scene for future theoretical development. In our own work, we have, as discussed in Chapter 1, begun to develop an organismic valuing theory of growth following adversity that is based on the humanistic writings of Rogers (1959) in which we propose that individuals are intrinsically motivated toward optimal functioning, and through adversity this intrinsic motivation toward optimal functioning can be released (Joseph, 2004; Joseph & Linley, 2005).

We would also urge more qualitative research alongside quantitative research. We need both, as Cordova notes, if we are to improve our sensitivity to and understanding of growth. Calhoun and Tedeschi also note the value of qualitative research, and we extend their observations by noting that an undue reliance on quantitative methods for the assessment and understanding of growth prejudges the parameters and domains of growth to be those of the researchers labeling the construct, rather than the phenomenological fields identified by survivors of trauma themselves.

A theme that resonates across several chapters (Collicutt McGrath, Chapter 13, this volume; Cordova, Chapter 10, this volume; Frazier & Berman, Chapter 9, this volume; Mahoney, Krumrei, & Pargament, Chapter 6, this volume; Weiss & Berger, Chapter 5, this volume), and that we think is especially worth drawing attention to, is that of religious change and the question of the relationship of spirituality to growth (see Shaw, Joseph, & Linley, 2005, for a review). As Lyons notes, spiritual issues are hard to avoid in trauma therapy, and yet we know very little about the role of religion and spirituality in growth. As Mahoney, Krumrei, and Pargament (Chapter 6, this volume) explore, the relation between spirituality, stress, and growth is not a simple one, with the potential for spiritual beliefs to be either strengthened or shattered following trauma. Thus, further qualitative research in this area that seeks to understand the different factors that drive the strengthening or shattering of spiritual beliefs following trauma would be fruitful.

Toward the Second Generation of Measurement Tools

But the most immediate research direction must be the question of growth itself, what it is, and how it can be measured (see also Helgeson et al., 2006). Some caution over the validity of self-reports of growth is a theme running throughout several chapters. Frazier and Berman point to several concerns and emphasize the need for prospective longitudinal research. But in particular, Ford et al. (Chapter 15, this volume) raise serious questions about the use of retrospective measures. Although we concur with Calhoun and Tedeschi (Chapter 16, this volume) that growth is real, we welcome Ford et al.'s detailed analysis of the extant measurement literature and agree fully that the criticisms raised by Ford et al. must be addressed. We do need to be alert to the possibility that retrospective self-report measures are limited, and we must now look toward the second generation of measurement in the field.

Growth is, by definition, a process that unfolds over time, so relying unduly on retrospective self-report, with all the cognitive operations and potential biases that it introduces, is problematic. Yet, it is equally the case that with the evolution of any research field, measurement and methodology improves over time as journal standards and reader expectations become more rigorous. We believe that we are now at that watershed for research in growth following adversity, and Ford et al. make a compelling case for understanding the reasons why our methodologies and measurement approaches need to be improved.

We should also recognize, however, that to some extent the criticisms made by Ford et al. are criticisms of researchers' choices of methodology, rather than criticisms of the measures themselves. There will be occasions where the only possibility is to assess growth retrospectively and cross-sectionally: for example, when people have not been assessed prospectively or longitudinally (a critique that applies to much clinical and social psychological research), yet we are still interested in how they perceive that they have grown. To be clear, this methodological approach is still liable to the critique made by Ford et al., and in such circumstances it is important to be mindful of the limitations of the research methodology, and the extent to which one can legitimately and accurately draw conclusions from. Yet in these contexts, the use of retrospective measures is appropriate because it is perhaps the only methodology available.

When we turn our attention to understanding the temporal course of growth, and to establishing the validity of growth more rigorously, then it is clear that prospective longitudinal designs are much more warranted. One cannot truly claim to understand the process of growth, which is by definition about positive change over time, without assessing that change over time. And when we begin to focus specifically on posttraumatic growth, then as Ford et al. put forward, we need to establish further that the growth identified is above and beyond more normative developmental growth trajectories. These are thorny issues indeed, and they raise yet another issue for consideration.

As researchers, when we are using self-report assessments of growth following adversity, we are asking people to respond to question sets that ask them about their perceptions of how they have changed. This is entirely appropriate for post hoc retrospective analyses of growth, but they simply do not work when applied to prospective longitudinal studies, where we are much more interested in the temporal comparison of a given person's standing in relation to a particular construct or behavior.

As we identified in Chapter 2 of this volume, growth following adversity is about psychological well-being and changes in assumptions about the self and the world. Hence, in research contexts where there are multiple time points in which change can be temporally documented, there is not the need to employ retrospective measures. For example, extant measures of psychological well-being taken at several time points both previous to and subsequent to an event would provide evidence for the development of what might be termed growth. If those changes can be related statistically to event and event appraisal variables, then this provides supporting evidence for the hypothesis that growth arises out of the struggle with an event.

Fundamentally, then, the issue of the choice of measure is intrinsically related to the temporal framework in which one is operating. For postevent analyses where preevent baselines are simply not available, there is little option but to rely on retrospective self-assessments as change, while recognizing that these are subject to the potential errors and biases identified by Ford et al. In contrast, where designs permit prospective longitudinal data collection, there exists the opportunity to use markers of functioning that are assessed at multiple time points pre- and postevent, with analysis of pre- and postevent positive differences then being attributable to growth. On this basis, although as researchers we are constrained by the limitations of the samples and methodologies available to us, it is equally incumbent on us to be mindful of making claims about the veracity and validity of growth that are based on retrospective self-reports, when more rigorous prospective longitudinal designs allow surer understanding of the temporal processes and psychological mechanisms that may be involved.

A second issue that arises when considering measurement is the assessment of both positive and negative schematic changes. There is undoubtedly a need to develop measures that are able to assess both positive and negative changes, and to understand better the relation between positive and negative changes. We would urge caution, however, in the assumption that positive and negative changes are bipolar dimensions that can be assessed by including both a positive pole and a negative pole to any response items. Our own work suggests that positive changes and negative schematic changes may be best understood as independent dimensions of experience that may have a range of associations (Joseph et al., 2005), but the development of items and the question of bipolarity is both a theoretical and empirical question. We cannot simply assume that positive and negative changes are mirror opposites that should be assessed as separate dimensions. It is important that we do not impose our conception of growth over and above the empirical evidence, or equally to ignore meaningful theory in favor of limited empirical data.

From the evidence available so far, it is clear that a more integrated and holistic understanding of positive and negative aspects of functioning following traumatic experiences is required. If we are to understand fully the nature of posttraumatic reactions, and specifically the way in which positive and negative changes may influence one another, we need to be mindful of understanding and assessing both dimensions.

Going forward, it is our view that much work remains to be done in understanding what exactly is meant by negative change and positive change, which then provides a basis from which to begin to construct assessment tools to tap these dimensions of experience. For example, the Changes in Outlook Questionnaire (Joseph, Williams, & Yule, 1993) was originally developed from verbatim statements made by trauma survivors, and the positive and negative change subscales were established on the basis of simple content analysis of the statements made, before being supported by subsequent psychometric work (Joseph et al., 2005). Yet, it is unlikely that these scales capture all the possible elements of positive and negative change following trauma and adversity, so a starting point may usefully be more initial exploratory qualitative work to understand the core themes, both positive and negative, that are reported by trauma survivors. This may appear to some as if we are taking a step back in relation to what is known about growth following adversity, but if we really are to establish a strong foundation on which to build our understanding of the process of positive and negative change following trauma, and then to create therapeutic approaches that harness this knowledge, we must establish the right basis from which to begin.

CLINICAL IMPLICATIONS

Clinically, the current retrospective measures of growth, despite their research limitations, will continue to be useful in assessing people's perceptions of how an event has impacted them and in developing avenues for therapeutic discussion. While we acknowledge and accept their limitations in relation to establishing categorically the temporal course and process of growth, we also note that, these limitations notwithstanding, retrospective self-report measures of growth can be a useful means by which to open a conversation with a client about how the experience of the traumatic event has impacted them. Whether we debate the validity of these self-report measures, at the very least the *perception* that people have changed in positive directions can be powerful to them (cf. Zoellner & Maercker, 2006). In walking with someone through the aftermath of trauma, first and foremost we should be fellow human beings who conavigate the way forward using the client's own compass and frame of reference.

In this vein, we asked contributors to provide us with case illustrations wherever possible to illustrate their theoretical points, and to show the application of growth in real-world contexts. We are pleased with how much the volume conveys the sense of practice. The amount of clinically relevant research that has been generated by researchers in the past few years is hugely impressive, and the chapters in this volume testify to the potential application of the growth paradigm in a number of areas. There is yet a need to be cautious about the recommendation of large-scale interventions, as noted in several places throughout the volume, but new areas are fast opening up and we are encouraged to see the increasing influence of the growth paradigm in those areas traditionally associated with the study of trauma, such as veterans (Lyons) and women following sexual assault (Frazier & Berman). We are especially encouraged to see new areas of application opening up, such as those illustrated by Collicutt McGrath in her discussion on brain injury, and in health psychology such as with cancer patients as discussed by Cordova, and Lechner, Stoelb, and Antoni. Most discussions of clinical interventions are concerned with one-to-one settings, but one of the most exciting avenues for future clinical work is likely to be the development of group-based therapeutic approaches, such as those discussed by Lechner and her colleagues. Lyons also notes that group therapy can be particularly powerful and efficient. What is clear it that research support is urgently needed to establish firmly the role of group therapy in effective recovery and growth following trauma, so that large-scale interventions can become more widely used, even extending so far as community-based initiatives (cf. Vázquez et al., Chapter 4, this volume).

In our own work, we have found the work of early pioneers in humanistic psychology, such as Abraham Maslow and Carl Rogers, particularly useful in developing our understanding of change following adversity, as well as in our positive psychology perspective more generally (Joseph & Linley, 2004; Linley & Joseph, 2004b). As such, we welcome Calhoun and Tedeschi's discussion on clinical implications, which have much resonance with the writings in humanistic and existential psychology: for example, that we must learn from the client, strive to be companions in a process that is guided by the client, and to stay close to the client's world and frame of reference. Calhoun and Tedeschi have not only been pioneers in the new field of growth, but they have been important bridge builders back to the principles of humanistic psychology, and in pioneering therapeutic ways of working which have a depth of humanity to them, in a clinical psychology culture that is often—wrongly, in our view, captivated by manualised treatments and approaches to therapy.

As well as these general therapeutic principles, many potentially useful techniques and strategies are discussed throughout this volume. Lyons offers a life span model, which we find particularly intriguing from the perspective of our organismic valuing theory of growth (Joseph & Linley, 2005), and we have begun to speculate on how these approaches can be integrated into a more sophisticated developmental model. The need not to impose growth on the client is a fundamental point made in several of the chapters, for example by Cordova in his chapter on working with cancer patients, and by Weiss and Berger in their chapter on immigration. These more humanistically derived clinical perspectives seem to us to be so fundamentally central to the emerging growth paradigm that they cannot be overemphasized. Of central importance is for the therapeutic setting to provide a forum where people are able to express their thoughts and emotions freely, without concern of judgment or inappropriate direction. From this viewpoint, the account-making perspective provided by Harvey, and illustrated so richly with case examples, demonstrates poignantly that often the role of the confidante or therapist is simply to listen and to be fully present for the person in his or her darkest moment. If this volume helps those working with people following trauma to do just this, to be fully present for the person in their darkest moment, then we will feel that we have achieved our goal.

REFERENCES

American Psychiatric Association. (1994). *Diagnostic and statistical manual of mental disorders* (4th ed.). Washington, DC: Author.

Epel, E. S., McEwen, B. S., & Ickovics, J. R. (1998). Embodying psychological thriving: Physical thriving in response to stress. *Journal of Social Issues, 54*, 301–322.

Frazier, P., Conlon, A., & Glaser, T. (2001). Positive and negative life changes following sexual assault. *Journal of Consulting and Clinical Psychology, 69,* 1048–1055.

Frazier, P., Tashiro, T., Berman, M., Steger, M., & Long, J. (2004). Correlates of levels and patterns of positive life changes following sexual assault. *Journal of Consulting and Clinical Psychology, 72,* 19–30.

Fredrickson, B. L. (1998). What good are positive emotions? *Review of General Psychology, 2,* 300–319.

Fredrickson, B. L., & Branigan, C. A. (2005). Positive emotions broaden the scope of attention and thought-action repertoires. *Cognition and Emotion, 19,* 313–322.

Fredrickson, B. L., & Joiner, T. (2002). Positive emotions trigger upward spirals toward emotional well-being. *Psychological Science, 13,* 172–175.

Fredrickson, B. L., & Levenson, R. W. (1998). Positive emotions speed recovery from the cardiovascular sequelae of negative emotions. *Cognition and Emotion, 12,* 191–220.

Fredrickson, B. L., Mancuso, R. A., Branigan, C., & Tugade, M. M. (2000). The undoing effect of positive emotions. *Motivation and Emotion, 24,* 237–258.

Fredrickson, B. L., Tugade, M. M., Waugh, C. E., & Larkin, G. R. (2003). What good are positive emotions in crises? A prospective study of resilience and emotions following the terrorist attacks on the United States on September 11th, 2001. *Journal of Personality and Social Psychology, 84,* 365–376.

Helgeson, V. S., Reynolds, K. A., & Tomich, P. L. (2006). A meta-analytic review of benefit finding and growth. *Journal of Consulting and Clinical Psychology, 74,* 797–816.

Joseph, S. (2004). Client-centered therapy, posttraumatic stress disorder and posttraumatic growth: Theory and practice. *Psychology and Psychotherapy: Theory, Research, and Practice, 77,* 101–120.

Joseph, S., & Linley, P. A. (2004). Positive therapy: A positive psychological theory of therapeutic practice. In P. A. Linley & S. Joseph (Eds.), *Positive psychology in practice* (pp. 354–368). Hoboken, NJ: Wiley.

Joseph, S., & Linley, P. A. (2005). Positive adjustment to threatening events: An organismic valuing theory of growth through adversity. *Review of General Psychology, 9,* 262–280.

Joseph, S., & Linley, P. A. (2006). Positive psychology versus the medical model? *American Psychologist, 61,* 332–333.

Joseph, S., Linley, P. A., Andrews, L., Harris, G., Howle, B., Woodward, C., et al. (2005). Assessing positive and negative changes in the aftermath of adversity: Psychometric evaluation of the Changes in Outlook Questionnaire. *Psychological Assessment, 17,* 70–80.

Joseph, S., & Williams, R. (2005). Understanding posttraumatic stress: Theory, reflections, context, and future. *Behavioral and Cognitive Psychotherapy, 33,* 423–441.

Joseph, S., Williams, R., & Yule, W. (1993). Changes in outlook following disaster: Preliminary development of a measure to assess positive and negative responses. *Journal of Traumatic Stress, 6,* 271–279.

Karrholm, J., Hansson, L. I., & Selvik, J. (1982). Roentgen stereophotogrammetric analysis of growth pattern after pronation ankle injuries in children. *Acta Orthopaedica Scandinavica, 53,* 1001–1011.

Kashdan, T. B., Uswatte, G., & Julian, T. (2006). Gratitude and hedonic and eudaimonic well-being in Vietnam war veterans. *Behavior Research and Therapy, 44,* 177–199.

Linley, P. A. (2003). Positive adaptation to rauma: Wisdom as both process and outcome. *Journal of Traumatic Stress, 16,* 601–610.

Linley, P. A., & Joseph, S. (2004a). Positive change following trauma and adversity: A review. *Journal of Traumatic Stress, 17,* 11–21.

Linley, P. A., & Joseph, S. (2004b). Toward a theoretical foundation for positive psychology in practice. In P. A. Linley & S. Joseph (Eds.), *Positive psychology in practice* (pp. 713–731). Hoboken, NJ: Wiley.

Linley, P. A., Joseph, S., & Goodfellow, B. (2007). *Positive changes in outlook following trauma and their relation to subsequent posttraumatic stress, depression, and anxiety.* Manuscript submitted for publication.

Lyubomirsky, S., King, L., & Diener, E. (2005). The benefits of frequent positive affect: Does happiness lead to success? *Psychological Bulletin, 131,* 803–855.

Maddux, J. E., Snyder, C. R., & Lopez, S. J. (2004). Toward a positive clinical psychology: Deconstructing the illness ideology and constructing an ideology of human strengths and potential. In P. A. Linley & S. Joseph (Eds.), *Positive psychology in practice* (pp. 320–334). Hoboken, NJ: Wiley.

Oatley, K., & Jenkins, J. M. (1996). *Understanding emotions.* Cambridge, MA: Blackwell.

Park, N., Peterson, C., & Seligman, M. E. P. (2004). Strengths of character and well-being. *Journal of Social and Clinical Psychology, 23,* 603–619.

Peterson, C., & Seligman, M. E. P. (2003). Character strengths before and after September 11. *Psychological Science, 14,* 381–384.

Pressman, S. D., & Cohen, S. (2005). Does positive affect influence health? *Psychological Bulletin, 131,* 925–971.

Reznek, L. (1987). *The nature of disease.* London: Routledge & Kegan Paul.

Rogers, C. R. (1959). A theory of therapy, personality and interpersonal relationships, as developed in the client-centered framework. In S. Koch (Ed.), *Psychology: A study of a science: Vol. 3. Formulations of the person and the social context* (pp. 184–256). New York: McGraw-Hill.

Seligman, M. E. P., & Csikszentmihalyi, M. (2000). Positive psychology: An introduction. *American Psychologist, 55,* 5–14.

Shaw, A., Joseph, S., & Linley, P. A. (2005). Religion, spirituality, and posttraumatic growth: A systematic review. *Mental Health, Religion, and Culture, 8,* 1–11.

Sheldon, K. M., & Houser-Marko, L. (2001). Self-concordance, goal attainment, and the pursuit of happiness: Can there be an upward spiral? *Journal of Personality and Social Psychology, 80,* 152–165.

Sheldon, K. M., & Kasser, T. (2001). Getting older, getting better: Personal strivings and psychological maturity across the life span. *Developmental Psychology, 37,* 491–501.

Tedeschi, R. G., & Calhoun, L. G. (1995). *Trauma and transformation: Growing in the aftermath of suffering.* Thousand Oaks, CA: Sage.

Tedeschi, R. G., & Calhoun, L. G. (1996). The Posttraumatic Growth Inventory: Measuring the positive legacy of trauma. *Journal of Traumatic Stress, 9,* 455–471.

Valent, P. (1999). *Trauma and fulfillment therapy: A wholist framework.* Philadelphia: Brunner/Mazel.

Wink, P., & Dillon, M. (2002). Spiritual development across the adult life course: Findings from a longitudinal study. *Journal of Adult Development, 9,* 79–94.

Wood, A. M., Joseph, S., & Linley, P. A. (in press). Coping style as a psychological resource of grateful people. *Journal of Social and Clinical Psychology.*

Zoellner, T., & Maercker, A. (2006). Posttraumatic growth in clinical psychology—A critical review and introduction of a two-component model. *Clinical Psychology Review, 26,* 626–653.

Author Index

Subject Index